Resurgent Adventures with Britannia

RESURGENT ADVENTURES WITH

*B*RITANNIA

Personalities, Politics and Culture in Britain

Edited by Wm. Roger Louis

I.B.Tauris

London · New York

Harry Ransom Center

Austin

Published in 2011 by I.B.Tauris & Co Ltd
6 Salem Road, London W2 4BU
In the United States of America and Canada, distributed by
Palgrave Macmillan, a division of St. Martin's Press
175 Fifth Avenue, New York NY 10010
www.ibtauris.com

Harry Ransom Center
University of Texas at Austin
P.O. Drawer 7219
Austin, Texas 78713-7219

The paper used in this publication meets the minimum requirements of
American National Standard for Information Sciences—
Permanence of Paper for Printed Library Materials

ISBN 978-1-78076-057-5 hardcover
ISBN 978-1-78076-058-2 paperback

Library of Congress Control Number: 2011936954

Print production by Studio Azul, Inc., Austin, Texas

Table of Contents

List of Authors

Neal Ascherson was born in Edinburgh and educated at Eton and King's College, Cambridge, where he studied history. He has written for the *Manchester Guardian*, the *Observer*, the *Scotsman*, and the *New York Review of Books*. His books include *The Struggles for Poland* (1987), *Black Sea* (1995), and *Stone Voices: The Search for Scotland* (2002). He was editor of the journal *Public Archaeology* (1999–2009) and is an Honorary Fellow of University College London.

John Berry is a geologist, educated at Pennsylvania and Columbia Universities. He began his career in Zambia with Anglo American Corporation. Since settling permanently in the United States, he has worked for the Earth Satellite Corporation and Shell Oil Company, where he established the Remote Sensing group in 1986 and developed techniques for prioritizing offshore basins for exploration.

Glen Bowersock is Professor of Ancient History at the Institute for Advanced Study in Princeton. After five years as a Rhodes Scholar at Balliol, where he is now an Honorary Fellow, he taught at Harvard University (1962–80) in the History and Classics Departments. He came to the Institute in 1980. His books include *Greek Sophists in the Roman Empire* (1969), *Roman Arabia* (1983), *Hellenism in Late Antiquity* (1990), and *Mosaics as History* (2006).

Archie Brown has held professorships in political science at Oxford, Yale, Columbia, and the University of Texas at Austin. His most recent book is *The Rise and Fall of Communism* (2009). He is a Fellow of the British Academy and a Foreign Honorary Member of the American Academy of Arts and Sciences. In 2005 he was awarded a CMG for "services to UK-Russian relations and the study of political science and international affairs."

Selina Hastings is a journalist and biographer. She graduated from St Hugh's College, Oxford, and then worked for nearly twenty years on the book page of the *Daily Telegraph* before becoming literary editor of *Harpers & Queen*. She is the author of four biographies: *Nancy Mitford*, *Evelyn Waugh* (winner of the Marsh Biography Prize), *Rosamond Lehmann*, and *The Secret Lives of Somerset Maugham*. She has also written a number of books for children.

Steven Isenberg is Executive Director of the PEN American Center in New York. He has served as publisher of New York *Newsday,* executive vice president of the *Los Angeles Times,* and chief of staff for New York mayor John V. Lindsay. An Honorary Fellow of Worcester College, he was educated at Berkeley, Yale Law School, and Oxford. He has taught literature at the University of Texas at Austin, Yale, and the University of California, Berkeley.

Dan Jacobson is a novelist and critic. Born and brought up in South Africa, he holds an Honorary D.Litt. from Witwatersrand University. His autobiography, *Time and Time* (1985), won the J. R. Ackerley Prize. His other works include the memoir *Heshel's Kingdom* (1998), the criticism collection *Adult Pleasures* (1988), and the novels *The Confessions of Josef Baisz* (1977) and *All for Love* (2005). He has taught English for many years at University College London.

Donna Kornhaber is a Lecturer in the English Department at the University of Texas at Austin. She received her PhD from Columbia University, her MFA in Dramatic Writing from the Tisch School of the Arts at New York University, and her BFA from NYU Film School. In addition to her academic work, she has worked professionally in film and has served as a contributor to the Arts & Leisure section of the *New York Times.*

Phyllis Lassner is Professor at Northwestern University and the author of two books on the Anglo-Irish writer Elizabeth Bowen, *British Women Writers of World War II* (1998), *Colonial Strangers: Women Writing the End of the British Empire* (2004), and *Anglo-Jewish Women Writing the Holocaust* (2008). She is also the creator and editor of the Northwestern University Press book series Cultural Expressions of World War II and the Holocaust: Preludes, Responses, and Memory.

Joanna Lewis is a Lecturer in Africa and Empires at the London School of Economics. Her doctoral research at Cambridge became the book *Empire State-Building: War and Welfare in Kenya, 1925–52* (2000). She has since published on popular imperialism, the press, the end of empire, and white settlers in Northern Rhodesia. She is currently conducting research for a book on the death and memorialization of Dr. David Livingstone in central Africa.

Kenneth O. Morgan was Fellow and Tutor, The Queen's College, Oxford, 1966–89 and Vice-Chancellor, University of Wales, 1989–95. His thirty books on British history include *The Oxford Illustrated*

History of Britain (more than 750,000 copies sold), histories of modern Wales and Britain since 1945, and biographies of Keir Hardie, Lloyd George, James Callaghan, and Michael Foot. He became a Fellow of the British Academy in 1983 and a Labour Peer in 2000.

Thomas Pinney is Professor of English at Pomona College, Claremont, California. He has worked on Kipling for thirty years, publishing *The Letters of Rudyard Kipling* (6 vols., 1990–2004). He has recently completed an edition of Kipling's poems, the first genuinely complete edition. He has also published a two-volume history of wine in America and has edited George Saintsbury's classic *Notes on a Cellar-Book,* a work dedicated to Kipling.

Bernard Porter is Professor of History at Newcastle University. He has also taught at Hull, Cambridge, Yale, and the University of Sydney. His books include *The Lion's Share* (1975, now in its fifth edition), *The Absent Minded Imperialists: Empire, Society, and Culture in Britain* (2004), and *The Battle of the Styles* (2011). He contributes regularly to the *London Review of Books* and occasionally to the *Guardian.* He lives mainly in Sweden.

Priscilla Roberts is an Associate Professor of History at the University of Hong Kong. She has published extensively in international history, especially Anglo-American and Sino-American relations. She has edited *Window on the Forbidden City: The Beijing Diaries of David Bruce* (2001) and *Lord Lothian and Anglo-American Relations, 1900–1940* (2010). She is completing a biography of the banker Frank Altschul and a study of Anglo-American think tanks and China policy.

Roberta Rubenstein is Professor of Literature at American University in Washington, D.C. Her scholarly books include *The Novelistic Vision of Doris Lessing: Breaking the Forms of Consciousness* (1979), *Boundaries of the Self: Gender, Culture, Fiction* (1987), *Home Matters: Longing and Belonging, Nostalgia and Mourning in Women's Fiction* (2001), and, most recently, *Virginia Woolf and the Russian Point of View* (2009), as well as more than thirty essays on contemporary writers.

Berny Sèbe (FRGS, D.Phil. *Oxon.*) is a Lecturer in Colonial and Postcolonial Studies at the University of Birmingham, with research interests in the cultural history of the British and French empires, Saharan history, the decolonization of Africa, and Franco-African relations. He has published many articles and book chapters, is currently revising his doctoral thesis for publication as *Heroic Imperialists*, and is co-editing a volume titled *Echoes of Empire*.

Peter Stansky is the Field Professor of History at Stanford University. He has written extensively on modern Britain, particularly William Gladstone, William Morris, George Orwell, and the Bloomsbury Group. His most recent book, with William Abrahams, is *Julian Bell: From Bloomsbury to the Spanish Civil War* (2011). In January 2011 he received an Award for Scholarly Distinction from the American Historical Association.

Geoffrey Wheatcroft is an English journalist, a former literary editor of the *Spectator* and the "Londoner's Diary" editor of the *Evening Standard*, who now writes for the *International Herald Tribune, New York Times, New York Review of Books*, and *New Republic*, among others. His books include *The Randlords* (1985), *The Controversy of Zion* (1996), which won a National Jewish Book Award, *The Strange Death of Tory England* (2005), and *Yo Blair!* (2007).

Samuel Williamson is an historian and former President of the University of the South. He has taught at the U.S. Military Academy, Harvard, the University of North Carolina at Chapel Hill, and Sewanee. He has published extensively on the crisis of July 1914, most recently on the role of Austria-Hungary. His *The Politics of Grand Strategy: Britain and France Prepare for War, 1904–1914* (1969) won the George Louis Beer Prize of the American Historical Association.

Crawford Young is Emeritus Professor of Political Science at the University of Wisconsin–Madison, where he taught from 1963 to 2001. He also served as visiting professor in Congo-Kinshasa, Uganda, and Senegal. His major books include *The Politics of Cultural Pluralism* (1976), *The Rise and Decline of the Zairian State* (1985, coauthor), and *The African Colonial State in Comparative Perspective* (1997). He is a past President of the African Studies Association.

The editor, Wm. Roger Louis, is Kerr Professor of English History and Culture and Distinguished Teaching Professor at the University of Texas at Austin. He is an Honorary Fellow of St Antony's College, Oxford. His books include *Imperialism at Bay* (1976), *The British Empire in the Middle East* (1984), and *Ends of British Imperialism* (2006). He is the Editor-in-Chief of the *Oxford History of the British Empire*. In 2001, he was President of the American Historical Association.

Introduction

WM. ROGER LOUIS

I happen to think almost daily of Arthur Conan Doyle. The reason is not necessarily connected with Sherlock Holmes, though he often comes to mind as well. It is because Doyle's desk—the one on which he wrote most of the Holmes stories—is in the British Studies office at the University of Texas. When the Humanities Research Center purchased the Doyle papers, the desk accompanied them. When the Britannia series appeared to have reached its concluding volume with *Ultimate Adventures,* it seemed natural that I should think of Reichenbach Falls. I have yielded to those who think the Britannia volumes serve a useful purpose. I was influenced by a telephone call from Karl Meyer, then one of the editors at the *New York Times,* saying that he kept a set of *Adventures with Britannia* in the editorial offices of the *Times* as a reminder that scholars and the public can actually communicate with each other. The present volume re-launches the series with *Resurgent Adventures.*

This volume begins, as have its predecessors, with an endorsement of G. H. Hardy's affirmation that the agony of having to repeat oneself is so excruciating that it is best to end the agony by offering no apology for doing so. In the spirit of the adventurous refrain—more, still more, yet more, ultimate, and resurgent—I again follow his example. This book consists of a representative selection of lectures given to the British Studies seminar at the University of Texas at Austin. Most of the present lectures were delivered in the years 2010–11.

Lectures are different from essays or scholarly articles. A lecture presumes an audience rather than a reader and usually has a more conversational tone. It allows greater freedom in the expression of personal or subjective views. It permits and invites greater candor. It is sometimes informally entertaining as well as anecdotally instructive. In this volume, the lecture sometimes takes the form of intellectual autobiography—an account of how the speaker has come to grips with a significant topic in the field of British Studies, which, broadly defined, means things British throughout the world as well as things that happen to be English, Irish, Scottish, or Welsh. The scope of British Studies includes all disciplines in the social sciences and humanities as well as music, architecture, and the visual arts. Most of the lectures in this collection fall within the fields of history, politics, and literature, though the dominant theme, here as previously, is historical. Occasionally, though rarely, the lectures have to be given in absentia—in this case, the ones by Glen Bowersock and Neil Ascherson. In such cases, the lectures or at least substantial parts of them are read and then critically discussed. The full sweep of the lectures will be apparent from the list at the end of the book, which is reproduced in its entirety to give a comprehensive idea of the seminar's evolution and substance.

In 2011, the British Studies seminar celebrated its thirty-sixth year. The circumstances for its creation were favorable because of the existence of the Humanities Research Center, now known as the Harry Ransom Center, at the University of Texas. Harry Ransom was the founder of the HRC, a Professor of English and later Chancellor of the University, a collector of rare books, and a man of humane vision. Through the administrative and financial genius of both Ransom and the present Director, Thomas F. Staley, the HRC has developed into a great literary archive with substantial collections, especially in English literature. Ransom thought a weekly seminar might provide the opportunity to learn of the original research being conducted at the HRC as well as to create common bonds of intellectual interest in a congenial setting of overstuffed armchairs, Persian carpets, and generous libations of sherry. This was an ingenious idea. The seminar was launched in the fall semester of 1975. It had the dual purpose of providing a forum for visiting scholars engaged in research at the HRC and of enabling the members of the seminar to discuss their own work.

The sherry at the Friday seminar sessions symbolizes the attitude. The seminar meets to discuss whatever happens to be on the agenda, Scottish or Indian, Canadian or Jamaican, English or Australian. George Bernard Shaw once said that England and America were two great countries divided by a common language, but he understated the case by several countries. The interaction of British and other societies is an endlessly fascinating subject on which points of view do not often converge. Diverse preconceptions, which are tempered by different disciplines, help initiate and then sustain controversy, not end it. The ongoing discussions in British Studies are engaging because of the clash of different perspectives as well as the nuance of cultural interpretation. Though the printed page cannot capture the atmosphere of engaged discussion, the lectures do offer the opportunity to savor the result of wide-ranging research and reflection.

The British Studies seminar has two University sponsors, the College of Liberal Arts and the Harry Ransom Center. We are grateful to the Dean of Liberal Arts, Randy Diehl, for his support and especially for allocating resources to sustain the program of Junior Fellows—a half dozen or so assistant professors appointed each year to bring fresh blood, brash ideas, and new commitment to the program. We are equally grateful to the Director of the HRC for providing a home for the seminar. I wish also to thank Frances Terry, who has handled the week-by-week administrative details from early on in the seminar's history. Above all, I am indebted to Kip Keller for his assistance with the publications program of the seminar.

The seminar has been the beneficiary of generous gifts by many friends, both living and dead. Those who have died include Creekmore and Adele Fath, Baine Kerr, Edwin Gale, Charles Wright, and Lowell Lebermann. And for their continuing support, I offer my gratitude to Mildred Kerr of Houston, John and Susan Kerr of San Antonio, Becky Gale of Beaumont, Custis Wright of Austin, Tex Moncrief of Fort Worth, and the two dozen stouthearted members of the seminar who have generously contributed to its endowment. We are indebted to Dean Robert D. King for his help over many years. I again extend special thanks to Sam Jamot Brown and Sherry Brown of Durango, Colorado, for enabling the seminar to offer undergraduate and graduate scholarships and generally to advance the cause of the liberal arts. The students appointed to scholarships are known as Churchill Scholars. The Churchill Scholars, like the Junior Fellows, not only contribute to the vitality of the seminar but also extend its age range from those in their late teens to the late eighties.

THE CHAPTERS—MORE PRECISELY, THE LECTURES—are clustered together more or less chronologically. The first deals with mid-Victorian Gothic architecture, which seemed to many at the time and later to be an oddity or aberration, a return to medieval inspiration in an age of unprecedented industrial and technological development. **Bernard Porter** explains the coherence of the neo-Gothic movement as well as the controversy among the elite who took an interest in architecture. Its champion was Gilbert Scott, who, according to his critics, wanted to Gothicize all of London and indeed the entire country. Scott was the leading architect of the era, with some 800 buildings and works to his credit, including the St. Pancras hotel and the Albert Memorial. His influence could be seen in all parts of the Empire, perhaps most obviously in the neo-Gothic Bombay railway station. Gothic style was never dominant, but it was conspicuous. To its enthusiasts, it was a matter of pride because it was indigenous and represented the eternal values of England in the face of industrialization and capitalism. Mid-Victorian architecture had a distinction of its own quite different from that of the concrete and steel of a later age. Neo-Gothic structures with ribbed vaults, flying buttresses, and crocheted spires seemed to reflect nostalgia for the pre-industrial past. But Gothic style also stood for mid-Victorian scientific rationality, embodying, as its enthusiasts saw it, the virtues of truth, honesty, and, above all, progress.

The assessment of Rudyard Kipling by **Thomas Pinney** focuses on his American years in the 1890s, though Kipling had earlier traveled in what was still called the Wild West. His reaction to American life was ambivalent. He witnessed lawlessness, violence, jingoism, and vulgarity. He believed the American habit of spitting to be something like a national plague. But he loved American literature, married an American woman, marveled at American ingenuity, and thought the British could learn from American patriotism. He began writing "The White Man's Burden" before the conquest of the Philippines. What he meant by the phrase "lesser breeds without the law" probably applied to a large part of the American population as well as the Boers of South Africa and, anticipating a violent theme in his later writings, the Germans. In America, the anti-British sentiment of the late 1890s as well as his domestic difficulties caused him to return to England rather than settle permanently in Vermont. At the time, the circumstances of his marriage led him to reflect on the virtues of restraint and humility. America on the whole proved to be a disappointment. It can also be seen as an era in his life that led him to take an increasingly cynical view of life. Nevertheless, his experience seemed to reinforce his belief in the supremacy of law.

Berny Sèbe reflects on the legacy of colonial heroes in the nineteenth century whose prestige has long fallen. Certain missionaries, explorers, and military figures remain famous. Cardinal Charles Lavigerie continues to hold a prominent place in French history because of his struggle against the slave trade and the founding of the missionary society known as White Fathers. David Livingstone's fame endures because of his mythic status not only as a Scottish missionary martyr but also as an explorer in central Africa. Pierre Savorgnan de Brazza and Henry Morton Stanley attracted public interest because of their additions to scientific knowledge, especially regarding Africa's geography. Stanley's books on the exploration of the continent became unrivalled commercial successes. Brazza is remembered as a charismatic and humane figure who, alone of the great explorers, has a capital city in Africa that still bears his name. Of those involved in the epic struggle for the Sudan, General Gordon has some seventy streets still named for him in London. The two military commanders who clashed at Fashoda, Jean-Baptiste Marchand and Horatio Herbert Kitchener, played a part in forging the colonial ideologies of the two countries. Marchand represented the betrayal by the civilian government in Paris that prevented him from realizing the full glory of France in tropical Africa. Kitchener came to embody Britain's national prestige and stature in the famous First World War poster "Your Country Needs You!" In the interwar period, the fierce but now slightly subdued pride in empire was perhaps most apparent at the time of the 1924 Wembley exhibition, which was represented by fifty-eight countries of the Empire and Commonwealth and attracted twenty-seven million visitors. Sir Edward Elgar composed the "Empire March," which reflected the pomp and power of the British Empire in the interwar years. In France, Marshal Hubert Lyautey presided over the Exposition coloniale internationale in 1931. The habits of empire endured. At the time of the Suez crisis of 1956, a remarkable cartoon appeared, depicting camels continuing to deliver Pernod to the French residents of Cairo.

As **Priscilla Roberts** makes clear, Henry James had a delicate political as well as literary sensitivity. He moved in the same social circles as Theodore Roosevelt and Henry Cabot Lodge. He was acquainted with the works of the naval theorist Alfred Thayer Mahan. Above all, James corresponded extensively with his brother, the psychologist and philosopher at Harvard, William James. Though in the later part of his life Henry James lived mainly as an expatriate in England, he was intimately aware not only of upper-class society in both countries but also of the growth of American wealth and power. From his writings in the 1870s onward can be found the theme of relative British decline. He did not necessarily welcome

American ascendancy, and indeed he wrote of the Americans as comparable to the barbarians beyond the Roman Empire. His political views can be detected in his novels not only in his portrayal of American innocence and European corruption but also in themes applicable to both the Americans and the British, such as greed, lust, hypocrisy, betrayal, and manipulation, attributes that certainly applied to what he called the "grabbed up" British Empire. On the other hand, he admired Kipling and believed in close Anglo-American relations. But in the 1880s, he increasingly wrote of British decadence. He regarded Gladstone as "an incurable shirker and dodger." In the 1890s, James approved of the conquest of the Sudan and regarded the dervishes as "bloody demons." At the turn of the century, he viewed the impact of the Boer War on Britain as nothing less than sinister and the Spanish-American War as an unparalleled disaster in American history. To James, Queen Victoria's death marked "the growing weakness of the British Empire" while the Americans had grown wealthier and tougher. All these themes play out in James's major and minor works. He did not like British decline but realistically recognized that the Americans had come to hold the economic and psychological advantage.

Roberta Rubenstein traces the influence of Russian writers on Virginia Woolf in her formative years and virtually to the end of her life. Woolf read *War and Peace* before her marriage, while she was still Virginia Stephen, in 1910. Tolstoy, along with Dostoevsky and Chekhov, were critical in her break with Victorian and Edwardian literary traditions. She reviewed Russian fiction in translation for the *Times Literary Supplement;* she and her husband, Leonard, studied Russian together; and their Hogarth Press published at least seven translations from Russian in the 1920s. Woolf found inspiration in the psychological complexity and intensity of Dostoevsky. She was fascinated with his representations of consciousness and the emotional activity and thought of his characters. The "giddy rapture" and "seething whirlpools" of Dostoevsky's novels were a catalyst for shaping her own aesthetic and metaphysical vision. Eventually, she found her own sensibility to resemble that of the radically modern Chekhov. His honest and unsentimental focus on personalities and mood, and the abrupt endings and apparent lack of resolution, appealed to her and became a vital strand in her own writing. But Tolstoy she viewed as being in a class of his own. Perhaps her attraction to him can be found in the very tradition she was rebelling against. Tolstoy had read the Victorian novelists, especially Dickens. A year before her death in 1941, she reflected on the "psychological realism" of Tolstoy and how her discovery of his novels was "like touching an exposed electric wire." Tolstoy, Chekhov, Dostoevsky, and, later, Turgenev were models for her renderings of turmoil and the inner life. As she explained it herself, the Russian writers left an emotional residue, inspiring her experiments with narrative form and representations of consciousness.

Samuel Williamson describes General Sir Henry Wilson as one of the remarkable British military personalities before the First World War. Politically committed as an Ulsterman, he was also militarily dedicated to British intervention in the event of a European war. The dual theme of Irish politics and military planning played itself out in the summer of 1914. Since 1910, Wilson had been director of military operations. He cycled the Belgian border and probably had a better knowledge of the terrain than anyone else in the British army. He prepared the British Expeditionary Force of 150,000 men in seven divisions—a relatively small force, but one that made a significant impact in the initial phase of the war. In July 1914, however, no one knew whether the British Cabinet would decide in favor of intervention. The dominant issue was, instead, Home Rule and whether its enactment might provoke civil war. Wilson conspired to make certain that there would be an army mutiny to prevent the imposition of Home Rule in the six counties of Northern Ireland. Civil war was averted, it seemed to Wilson and others at the time, only because of the outbreak of the European war. Wilson pressed for the dispatch of the expeditionary force that played a key role in disrupting German strategy against France in September. Wilson continued to rise in rank, becoming Chief of the Imperial General Staff in 1918 and Field Marshal in 1919. In 1922, he was murdered on his doorstep in London by Irish nationalists. But he had succeeded in getting his six counties excluded from an independent Ireland, as well as British intervention in the war. There was an even larger significance to the story of his life. The fate of Ireland seemed to some to portend the future of the British Empire, and the British Empire itself seemed to be represented by the British Army in Europe. One of the great proconsuls, Lord Milner, summed up the connection between commitment to Ulster and intervention in the European war by saying that "the man who saved the Empire is Henry Wilson."

Selina Hastings points out that Somerset Maugham lived to be more than ninety and at the end of his life was very much aware of his lack of recognition by critics and fellow writers. In his own description of himself, he was among the first of the second rate. Though trained in medicine, he was extraordinarily successful as a playwright and novelist. But it is as a short-story writer that he will probably have enduring popularity. The story of his own life is significant, among other reasons, because of the way it reveals an example of the steady perfecting of the writer's craft but also because of the double life he led as a homosexual. Another sort of doubling occurred when British intelligence recruited him as a spy. He spent much of his life traveling and living abroad, but while in England, he conducted himself with decorum. Maugham was shy and suffered a lifelong stammer. He moved in high circles and counted as friends Henry James and Winston Churchill, but he preferred listening to talking, and observing English social life rather than participating in it. The turning point in Maugham's life occurred during the First World War when he met Gerald Haxton in Flanders. Haxton became the love of his life and his companion on many ships plying their way to the South Seas and other romantic places depicted in Maugham's fiction. The extroverted Haxton was able easily to strike up conversations with fellow travelers and to tell Maugham of their experiences in life and love, accounts that became incorporated into his short stories. Especially by using Malayan rubber plantations and up-country clubs as background, Maugham was able to relate stories of adultery and gambling as well as friendship and betrayal among judges, civil servants, and planters. During the last part of his life, Maugham lived mainly at Cap Ferrat on the French Riviera. He had many visitors who observed his dual character of warmth and graciousness, on the one hand, and austerity and self-discipline on the other.

Women writers who have dealt with the decline of the British Empire do not fit into a clear feminist category and have often been misunderstood for representing ideologies that they opposed. **Phyllis Lassner** deals especially with Olivia Manning. Lassner argues that Manning herself may not have regarded herself as a feminist writer, and a more comprehensive view of her place in modern British literary history emerges if she is seen along with other British women writers of her time. A substantial part of her writing is about the British Empire in the Middle East. She exposed the hypocrisy of British officials and the irony of fighting the Second World War for freedom while continuing to exploit colonial subjects. One of her foremost works was the collection of novels called *The Levant Trilogy*. Perhaps as much as any other writer at the time, she was aware of the probable racial consequences if German forces had emerged victorious at the battle of El Alamein in 1942 and had occupied Egypt, perhaps even Palestine. But even as Manning identified the major differences between the Nazi and British colonial regimes, she did not spare the British. El Alamein, though a crucial victory, paradoxically destabilized the British, offering them the way to find coherent war aims based on the principle of equality but leaving in place a colonial regime in the Middle East that was complaisant, self-serving, and corrupt. Though she retained her ultimate faith in the British Empire as a bastion of freedom and opportunity, she stood as a relentless critic of British racial arrogance and almost farcical incompetence.

The lecture by **Peter Stansky** is an autobiographical account of how he came to write on Julian Bell, a poet killed in the Spanish Civil War in 1937. There are four interlocking themes: the place of the Spanish Civil War in the intellectual currents of the 1930s; the significance of Julian Bell himself, the son of Vanessa Bell and a nephew of Virginia Woolf, as a life cut short of its full potential; the influence of William Abrahams, or "Billy," Stansky's partner of almost four decades, in helping crystallize the meaning of Bell's life in the context of the war; and finally, Stansky's own development as an historian of Britain. The story begins with Stansky as an undergraduate at Yale, writing his senior thesis on the Spanish Civil War. The autobiography then progresses to a critical time in his life, two years in Cambridge at King's College. He eventually comes full circle to his original work from the 1950s on the Spanish Civil War by writing *Julian Bell* in 2010.

Steven Isenberg is a self-described lifetime English major. It took a lot of nerve for a young man to set up meetings with W. H. Auden, E. M. Forster, Philip Larkin, and William Empson. To do anything more than relate a little of the background would spoil his story, but a few details about Isenberg himself perhaps will be of interest. After graduating with an English degree from the University of California at Berkeley in 1962, he worked as assistant editor at *Newsday,* later becoming its editor. In his incarnation as a journalist, he eventually became Vice President of the *Los Angeles Times.* Previously, he had earned a Yale law degree in the 1970s while serving as assistant to the mayor of New York City, John Lindsay. Throughout this remarkable career, he continued to devote himself to English literature and became a lifelong friend of Christopher Ricks (Professor of Poetry at Oxford, 2004–9). The account of the meetings with Auden, Forster, Larkin, and Empson conveys certain surprising aspects of their lives and interests, but the reader becomes aware of Isenberg's own personality and the reason he was a welcome companion.

Maurice Bowra was an Oxford classicist renowned for wit and conversation. As **Glen Bowersock** makes clear, his reputation as a classicist has faded, and indeed his work is held in scorn by scholars of Greek literature. Bowra was controversial in his own time, and not merely for academic reasons. His famous Oxford reputation has been revived in a recent biography by Leslie Mitchell, an eminent historian of the eighteenth century but not a classicist. In Bowersock's view, the biography fails to point out the deficiencies of Bowra's scholarship and thus the reason why he did not succeed Gilbert Murray as Regius Professor of Greek in 1936. Quite apart from any concerns about Mitchell's biography, Bowra's life is worth reassessment. He found his calling as Warden of Wadham College, a position he held for more than three decades (1938–70). He continued to write, but his books on modern literature as well as the classics were more distinctive as evoking a way of life than as reaching a standard of scholarly excellence. Long before the word "charismatic" became fashionable, his circle of friends recognized him as a unique personality. His quick wit moved from memorable paradox to scurrilous and obscene verse. He loved college companionship, mainly of younger men, though he counted among his lifelong friends Isaiah Berlin, John Sparrow, and Noel Annan. Above all, by challenging conventional views, he inspired subversive intellectual and moral liberation. Bowra is now largely forgotten, but to his contemporaries he represented the legendary Oxford of his time—in Bowersock's phrase, "The Oxford of Brideshead."

Hugh Trevor-Roper makes a curious contrast to Bowra. Trevor-Roper came close to destroying his own reputation in 1983 when he authenticated as genuine a set of Hitler diaries that quickly proved to be fake. **Neil Ascherson** assesses his personality and his inability to complete his major work on the English Civil War as well as more than a half dozen other unfinished manuscripts. In some ways, Trevor-Roper personified Bowra's vision of the good life of a privileged Oxford don nonchalantly yet arrogantly at war against the philistines of narrow academic culture. Yet Bowra regarded him as a cold fish, not an uncommon view even though Trevor-Roper's prose was witty and humane. In fact, Trevor-Roper at Christ Church in the years before the Second World War excelled at dissolute living, drinking and smashing glasses, again in a certain Brideshead tradition. He published his sole full-length book of history, *Archbishop Laud,* in 1940. Under an intelligence assignment at the end of the war, he wrote *The Last Days of Hitler,* which remains an unsurpassed masterpiece. As Regius Professor in Oxford (1957–80), he found his métier in long critical essays that ranged from revisionist accounts of the Elizabethan gentry to attacks on Arnold Toynbee and A. J. P. Taylor as well as essays dismissing the legitimacy of Scottish and African history. He had a driving intellectual curiosity, a superbly limpid style, and a gift for malicious gossip (his description of Nuffield College as a kind of Oxford Tibet is a mild example). With the benefit of distance in time and having perhaps a more tolerant view than many of his critics during the Hitler diary debacle, we can now see that Trevor-Roper remains one of our great historical essayists.

In the lecture on Aneurin ("Nye") Bevan, **Kenneth O. Morgan** reflects on the paradoxical reputation of a politician believed to be among the most fiery and irreconcilable of the Far Left of the Labour Party. Bevan was the scourge of the capitalist class. Yet the key to his success as a politician was his willingness to compromise. His greatest achievement was the creation of the National Health Service in 1948 while Minister of Health in the Attlee government. As a young Labour politician, Bevan had risen in the ranks of the Labour movement from the time he was a teenage miner in South Wales. He gained the reputation of a Celtic firebrand. During the Second World War, he attracted Attlee's attention as a dynamic personality with a coherent outlook. Bevan was a reformer as well as a patriot. He saw the period of the Second World War as an opportunity for social progress—unlike Churchill, who once denounced him as a "squalid nuisance." Bevan replied in kind to such taunts. In 1948, he referred to the Tories as "lower than vermin." He made that comment at about the time he managed to bring the plan for a comprehensive national health service to fruition. Bevan's signal achievement was to persuade the members of the medical profession to include hospitals in the scheme. The National Health Service represents his legacy to the British people.

With the zither's fraught and engaging chords in the opening scenes of *The Third Man* (1949), it may strike the present-day viewer that the film seemed destined for classic status from the outset. **Donna Kornhaber** demonstrates that nothing could be further from the truth. The film was pieced together step by step, and each step could have led to disaster. From the beginning, the film narrative departed from Graham Greene's script, mainly for commercial reasons. Originally set in London, the location changed when Alexander Korda, one of the producers, saw the need for a European market. The film eventually found a home in Vienna, but can one imagine it in Rome? The director, Carol Reed—one of the innovative figures in modern British film—by chance came across the zither as a way to convey the mood of Vienna, using accompanying images of a city with an imperial past and a criminal presence. The choice of the cast was just as accidental and pragmatic. The American producer, David Selznick, needed a film that would appeal to Americans. One of the central figures is Holly Martens (played by Joseph Cotten). In Greene's script, he was an Englishman, but in the film is transformed into an American. Martens comes to Vienna to see his old school pal, Harry Lime (Orson Welles). With Martens as a guileless American, the racketeer Lime had also to be an American because otherwise the school link would make no sense. Selznick was able to bring in as well the young Italian actress Alida Valli (Anna) because he had her under contract and thus, as with Cotten, could lend her to the production at no cost. This was one of the ingenious strokes of the film. Selznick was influenced by his production of *Gone with the Wind*. Anna's toughness resembles Scarlett O'Hara's. She remains loyal to Lime, or, in other words, she stays faithful to a rat. In the ultimate scene, Anna returns from Lime's grave and snubs the naïve American without so much as a glance—much as Scarlett O'Hara might have done.

In February 1960, Harold Macmillan spoke to the South African Parliament about the "wind of change" blowing through the African continent. It is one of the great orations in British historical memory. **Joanna Lewis** assesses the reasons for its success at the time, making clear that the circumstances of Macmillan's African journey were sometimes tense, chaotic, and even absurd (appropriately enough, since Macmillan had an eye for the preposterous). The trip included Ghana, Nigeria, and Northern Rhodesia (present-day Zambia) before South Africa, as if in a crescendo building up to confrontation with apartheid. In Northern Rhodesia, Macmillan faced two sets of adversaries, British expatriates dominating the Copperbelt, and African nationalists, including Kenneth Kaunda, who had been only recently released from prison. Some of Macmillan's critics, in Britain as well as in Africa, believed that British rule embraced apartheid in all but name. The "color bar," as it was known throughout the British colonial world, meant not only racial discrimination and vastly unequal opportunity for education but also a wage differential of seven to one, for example, for a white worker on the Rhodesian railways doing essentially the same job as an African. Africans anticipated continued economic domination, while whites feared a sellout of their privileges. In Northern Rhodesia, as in Britain, Macmillan had to balance the sentiment of kith and kin with African demands for universal suffrage. If his trip had ended in Northern Rhodesia, it would hardly have been regarded as a success. In the view of at least one British journalist, his performance revealed hypocrisy because of the reality of the color bar. His achievement in Cape Town rested on his direct and clear statement on the issue of inequality. It took considerable political courage on Macmillan's part to affirm the ideals of the British Empire and Commonwealth in the South African Parliament. It was perhaps his finest hour.

Crawford Young poses the question why the colonial empires of the Netherlands, Belgium, and Portugal, all at different times, came to such an abrupt end that it seemed to contemporaries—above all to the Dutch, Belgians, and Portuguese themselves—to be catastrophic. The larger empires of Britain and France on the whole fared better, in part because of sheer size and diversity of experience. The British drew from constitutional precedent that allowed colonial subjects the prospect of self-rule, while the French offered a degree of assimilation and substantial subsidies. Both the British and French fought bitter wars of counterinsurgency, and both managed to withstand the pressure of settlers, the British in Kenya, the French (or to be more specific, de Gaulle) in Algeria. The three cases of the Netherlands, Belgium, and Portugal are perhaps more striking for their differences than similarities, though the ending of the colonial empires had certain things in common. The Dutch faced the almost wholly unusual circumstances of a nationalist movement ultimately supported by the United States. In the case of the Belgian Congo, security forces proved incapable of containing massive nationalist demonstrations that broke out in 1959. The Belgians were in a weak position to maintain control, but they gambled that the Congolese would continue to depend on Belgian assistance to maintain a unitary state after independence. The Portuguese fought prolonged anti-insurgency campaigns in Mozambique and Angola, and they committed a far greater percentage of their manpower and resources than any of the other colonial powers. The end came with the revolution in Portugal itself. The similarities of the three colonial regimes included self-deception. The Dutch, Belgian, and Portuguese all believed in a paternalistic colonial ideology that assumed an enduring and beneficial relationship. For the Dutch, decolonization meant the loss of a vital part of their economy, while for the Belgians and Portuguese it involved substantial transfers of settler populations. The long-term effect has probably been greatest for Belgium. The loss of the Congo contributed to the shattering of the fragile bond between Walloons and Flamands and called into question the continued existence of the Belgian state.

John Berry is a geologist. In this lecture, he is also something of an archeological sociologist, rescuing from oblivion the way of life and work in the Zambian Copperbelt in the six years after Zambia's independence (1966–72). Berry and his wife arrived in Zambia in the mining city of Kitwe. Surrounded by a cluster of mining areas,

Kitwe had a population of 100,000, 85 percent African and 15 percent expatriate, including a significant number of Indians and, in the British component, a large cohort of Scots (the annual Burns Dinner would seat three hundred). He worked for a subsidiary of the Zambian Anglo American Corporation, which offered lifetime employment, retirement at fifty-nine and a half, free medical care, and houses far better than expatriates could afford in Britain, Europe, or the United States. Berry's job was to explore for copper by means of pits and trenches, and to determine the quality of the copper ore. A typical exploration pit might be sixty feet in depth but only shoulder wide. Descending could be dangerous because of snakes and other creatures. The workforce under Berry's supervision might include 60 workers, but with wives, children, and others could make up a "family" of about 150. Exploration camps in the Copperbelt region were always situated on a stream, where bathing and laundering took place. Cooking was done on a charcoal stove or clay fire pit. But sometimes the water was polluted with fecal and typhoid bacteria, and cooking from time to time was impossible because of flies. The town of Kitwe itself resembled a multiracial community dominated by the expatriates. Indians ran the clothing shops, the Greeks the grocery stores and restaurants, and the Italians the garages. Madame Fufu from the former Belgian Congo operated a brothel. For expatriates, the social life was extraordinary. There were theater and sports clubs, even a flying club. There were musicals, drama productions, and poetry readings. Kitwe had comfortable hotels, two hospitals, good schools, parks, a library, a theater, and a golf course. Perhaps the word "paternalistic" best describes the mining-town society of the time, but Berry remembers with some astonishment its vivacity, color, and diversity: "an idyllic spot" where the mystique of the white man survived from the colonial period.

Archie Brown argues that Margaret Thatcher played a surprising and significant part in the end of the Cold War by identifying Mikhail Gorbachev as a radical reformer. "We can do business together," she exclaimed in December 1984. But her awareness of Gorbachev's true potential developed between 1984 and 1987, and it occurred almost in spite of some of the guidance she received from her advisers at the Foreign Office. The question in the early 1980s was whether change might be even remotely possible within the Soviet Union. The Prime Minister reached beyond the official establishment to secure the views of academic authorities on Russia, in her words, "people who have really studied Russia—the Russian mind." Archie Brown was among those who took part in a seminar held at Chequers, the Prime Minister's country residence, in September 1983, and a comparable gathering in February 1987. Through the Freedom of Information Act, he managed to secure the official records of the seminars, including the copies of papers written by him and others and annotated by Thatcher. At the 1983 seminar, she heard for the first time the view that Gorbachev was a likely future Soviet leader of reformist disposition. That seminar saw the germination of the idea of inviting Gorbachev to visit Britain, which he did before becoming the Soviet top leader. When Thatcher herself made a high-profile visit to the Soviet Union in March 1987, she again prepared herself well, having held another major seminar at Chequers in the previous month. Her views increasingly diverged from those of some senior members of the American government, although Ronald Reagan shared her desire for dialogue with the new Soviet leader. Within the U.S. government, such officials as Caspar Weinberger and William Casey were reluctant to believe that change might be possible within the Soviet Union. They were also highly skeptical of Gorbachev. The history of Thatcher's championing of Gorbachev provides fresh perspective on the end of the Cold War and explodes the simplistic interpretation of American military and economic pressure bringing about the collapse of the Soviet Union.

During his imprisonment of over two decades on Robben Island, Nelson Mandela drew inspiration from the poem "Invictus." **Dan Jacobson** connects W. F. Henley, the Victorian author of the poem, with Mandela and the film of 2009 directed by Clint Eastwood, with Mandela played by Morgan Freeman. The film successfully captures Mandela's personality and achievement, but the lecture itself is about much more than Mandela and the theme of the movie, rugby. As if telling the parable of his native country, Jacobson explains that by the mid-1990s, some shrewd Afrikaner leaders saw that Mandela would be more useful to them out of prison than in. Mandela had no interest in revenge. This was a successful gamble on the part of the Afrikaner Prime Minister F. W. de Klerk, but it has to be understood against the background of the collapse of the Soviet Union. An isolated South Africa was now a pariah among nations. The end of both communism in Europe and apartheid in South Africa came much more rapidly than anyone at the time anticipated. Mandela united the country. In a symbolic moment dramatically portrayed in the film, he handed over the rugby world championship trophy to the captain of the Afrikaner team. At the time, it seemed like a happy end to the tale of a country on the verge of revolution and civil war. But happy endings, alas, do not endure. Nor does the message of a single poem, which Jacobson realistically assesses. "Invictus" was hardly a mantra, but it did give heart to Mandela during his imprisonment.

Geoffrey Wheatcroft traces the origins of the Anglo-American "special relationship" to Churchill and the early years of the Second World War. Subsequent Prime Ministers, especially Harold Macmillan, paid tribute to the idea of a common heritage and political alignment, but it was Churchill who consciously shaped the policy. His aims were laced with tenacious realpolitik—the necessary reliance on the United States in order to win the war—but were also intertwined with calculated yet genuine sentimentality. Churchill's views led to an historical distortion. Following the romantic thread of his interpretation, American and British public figures have sometimes portrayed a harmonious relationship from the time of the American Revolution. On the contrary: British as well as American attitudes, on balance, were hostile. Neville Chamberlain and Edward Heath, for example, had similar views of expecting nothing from the Americans unless it was based on pure self-interest. Yet on the whole, Prime Ministers from Lord Salisbury to Mrs. Thatcher tempered their skepticism, espoused Anglo-American friendship, and tried realistically to use American power or resources to their own advantage. The conspicuous exception is Tony Blair. To his critics, he grotesquely embraced the mystical union without attempting to secure British benefits. Virtually without qualification, he committed Britain to the American invasion of Iraq. According to prominent critics, including Sir Rodric Braithwaite (former Ambassador to Russia and later Chairman of the Joint Intelligence Committee), Blair bent intelligence assessments for political purposes and ignored the Foreign Office. The conclusion is damning: Blair did more damage to Britain's position in the Middle East than any other Prime Minister since Anthony Eden.

1

Victorian Gothic Architecture

BERNARD PORTER

The Gothic Revival is a puzzle. In early Victorian times, Britain was widely thought to be—and certainly regarded itself as—the most progressive and modern country in the world: economically powerful, politically liberal, and technologically advanced. Signs of this abounded: Reform Acts, free trade, the growth of its cities, those newfangled steam engines rushing around the country at a frightening thirty miles an hour (those especially), and so on. Most Victorians truly believed they were witnessing the advent of a bright new age, their emergence from the last vestiges of what they called "feudalism." Yet when they came to build for that new age—as they obviously needed to, with the huge increase in their population (England's and Wales's almost tripled during the Victorian years)—what did they do? They went back to feudal times. The most characteristic architectural style of nineteenth-century Britain is "neo-Gothic," based on, even if not directly copying, the architecture of the European Middle Ages, four hundred to seven hundred years before. This puzzled contemporaries too. As one of them put it in 1860: was it not really quite deplorable that in that great age of progress, "while other classes advance," the architects' "eyes and minds are constantly turned back"?[1] It remains a conundrum.

Before trying to explain it, three important caveats should be made. The first is this: although neo-Gothic can fairly be said to be characteristic of nineteenth-century Britain (or, at least, England),

it never completely took over and, indeed, was never even the com-
monest style of architecture of the time. Most buildings erected during the nineteenth century were "classical"; some were what would be
recognized today as "modern"; a few were in other historical styles.
Gothic seems dominant—and seemed so at the time—only because
it tended to stand out more. People were used to dull classical (and
classical had become very dull by the early nineteenth century), and
so were unlikely to be greatly struck by new buildings put up in that
style, as nor are we. Who, for example, ever particularly notices the
huge neoclassical government offices in Whitehall built by George
Gilbert Scott in the 1860s, against his own instincts and principles
(he had originally designed them in Gothic, but Lord Palmerston
forced him to classicize them), by the side of the nearby Perpendicular Gothic Palace of Westminster; or by comparison with Scott's
St. Pancras Station Hotel a couple of miles away (figure 1.1), which
is supposed to be Scott's original design for the government offices?
(It isn't, but it is close.) Gothic buildings were more dramatic, spik-
ier, more colorful (literally), and so disproportionately more visible
than their classical contemporaries. Zealots for the style, like Scott,
did not think it had gone half enough. It was this that lay behind
Palmerston's resistance to Scott's original design for the government
offices, to stop him from "Gothicis[ing] the whole of London," as he
put it, and then the country.[2] Palmerston's victory in that "Battle
of the Styles"—the name given to it at the time—may have turned
the tide and helped ensure that Gothic never did become Victorian
Britain's majority way of building. In the main, it was confined to
churches, colleges, a few villas, and (in its neo-"Jacobethan" variant)
country houses, plus a few public buildings in the provinces. Otherwise, classical still ruled.

The second caveat is that Gothic was never a particularly popular
style, in the sense of people generally liking it much; not necessarily
because they disliked it, but because they did not know or care much
about matters of architectural style at all. This comes out clearly in
that battle over the government offices, which, however fiercely it
was waged, involved only a very small, elite group of people; it was
either ignored or mocked, as a storm in a teacup, by most other
people. The newspapers of the day reveal what must have been a
very general ignorance: their published comments about the competing designs for the Foreign Office often confused the styles quite
ludicrously. This also needs to be borne in mind when considering
the reasons behind the nineteenth-century revival of Gothic, which
may not have had very deep or widespread roots in the society of
the time.

The third preliminary point that needs to be made is that neo-Gothic was not an exclusively English or British style. It originated in England, certainly; indeed, it is probably the only original contribution—together with Arts and Crafts, which grew out of it—that England has ever made to the history of architecture world-wide. It caught on widely in the British colonies—Sydney and Melbourne Universities, and Victoria Station in Mumbai (figure 1.2), for example—but also in Continental Europe (where Scott was active) and in the United States, as all those Gothic churches and Ivy League universities testify (Mitchell Tower at the University of Chicago was copied from the fifteenth-century Magdalen Great Tower at Oxford, for example, and the Collegiate Gothic Harkness Tower at Yale was inspired by the Boston Stump, that is, the tower of St. Botolph's, Boston, Lincolnshire). Henry Hobson Richardson, who designed Trinity Church (1872–7) in Boston, Massachusetts, was a Romanesque-Gothic architect, and the Woolworth Building (1913) in New York is Perpendicular Gothic essentially. All of which suggests that a search for motives for this strange nineteenth-century regression to the Middle Ages cannot be confined to merely "English" ones. Either American motives were different from Britain's (which is possible), or there were causes common to both—and to France, Germany, and all the other countries where Gothic obviously touched a sympathetic nerve.

THIS INTERNATIONAL POPULARITY may be thought to undermine slightly one of the motives often given for the revival of Gothic in England in the nineteenth century, namely, the patriotic one. The idea is this: Gothic appealed to Britons because it was a native style and thus very different from the previously dominant classical, which had originated in faraway and long-ago Greece and Rome, and had then been imposed on the English, first of all by the Roman Empire (and so, as one proponent of Gothic put it, was ever associated with "ancient humiliation"), and then, 1,500 years later, at the time of the Renaissance, by the equally tyrannical Stuart kings.[3] And there is something in this. The early aficionados of neo-Gothic—in the later eighteenth century—often used this kind of argument. Many of them pointed out how late in the day Renaissance architecture had come to England—about 150–200 years after it arrived in Italy—and how Gothic had still clung on in certain areas right through the classical period (Sir Christopher Wren occasionally built in it, for example); both of which factors suggested to them that there was something about the Gothic style peculiarly suited to England. One or two claimed it had been originally invented by the English; or, when that myth was knocked on the head by the discovery of earlier pointed arches in both northern French and "Saracenic" (Islamic) architecture, that the style had reached its "highest point of perfection" in England. In the 1830s, "Gothic or Tudor" was stipulated in the competition to find a design for the new Palace of Westminster because the medieval period was seen as the one in which the freedoms the English were most proud of, including Parliament itself, were born. During the Battle of the Styles, the same point was sometimes made: Gothic was Britons' "National Style"; "something which [we] feel to belong to [our] own race and country";[4] a style that had "sprouted forth of itself from the souls of our forefathers";[5] and so on. It was a powerful enough argument for the patriotic Palmerston to feel the need to answer, which he did by claiming, first, that in fact "the real aboriginal architecture of this country was mud huts and wicker wigwams," not Gothic; and second, that the latter was not so much an English as a dark, medieval, and (worst of all) Roman Catholic style.[6]

But in that particular battle, he probably needn't have bothered. For by that time (the later 1850s), nationalistic pride seems to have receded as a motive for building in Gothic. Very few of the Gothic designs entered in the competition for the new government offices in 1857, for example, were recognizably English Gothic at all, including Scott's winning entry, which was highly international, or cosmopolitan, in line with another common British ideal at that particular time: it was based on a French château, with Flemish and Lombardic features also prominent. So, as the *Building News* put it in 1860, if the main argument for Gothic was that it was the "national style," why did Scott not choose a more "national" form of it? Surely, the paper concluded, by not doing so "the plea of 'nationality' falls to the ground."[7]

One other quite remarkable feature of the competition was that none of the entries (so far as can be determined; not all have survived) was in the Perpendicular style, which is the only exclusively English form of Gothic—it is found nowhere else—and the one that the Palace of Westminster was built in. But there were reasons for this. One was the current unpopularity of the new Houses of Parliament building, which was still under construction. Because its air-cooling system didn't work, its windows had to be opened on hot summer days, letting in the dreadful stench that came up from the Thames from the "ordure, dead cats, dead dogs, and occasionally . . . a dead human being" floating there.[8] MPs tended to blame this malodorousness—unreasonably, perhaps, but this is how architec-

tural ignoramuses think—on the building's style. (It may be significant that the crucial Commons vote in favor of classically designed
government offices came on the hottest July day of 1861.) For the
cognoscenti, however, there was another reason for disapproving of
Perpendicular: it was felt to be a degraded form of Gothic in comparison with earlier and also foreign forms, which were now regarded
as aesthetically superior—hence, Scott's French-Flemish-Venetian
design. Nationality may have been one consideration behind the revival of Gothic, but it was not half so important as certain others, of
which more later.

The second common explanation for this tension between the
modernity of nineteenth-century Britain generally and the frank
antiquarianism of so much of its architecture is that the latter was
an expression of the Victorians' unease about the former, a way of
escaping from some of the more fearful aspects of contemporary
progress: capitalism, industrialism, democracy, the decline of traditional social relationships generally, and, of course, those great
steam locomotives snorting around the country, killing and maim-
ing so many people in their paths. This indeed might seem to be
the obvious reason for as reactionary a movement as the Gothic
Revival; and, again, there is something to be said for the idea. Many
of the early Gothic Revivalists were political and social reactionaries, including the upper-class builders of some of the earliest (eighteenth-century) fake medieval castles—Fonthill Abbey, Strawberry
Hill, and so on—as was the most famous and influential ideologue
of the revival, Augustus Welby Northmore Pugin, who designed the
most Gothicky bit of the Palace of Westminster—the clock tower—
and decorated the rest; he was an antimodernist of the first order. A
Roman Catholic, he believed that English society had been far better in the Catholic Middle Ages, and so championed Gothic architecture partly as a means of returning England to that happy time
and faith. His best-known book, *Contrasts* (1837), illustrated this
graphically; one contrast was drawn (literally) between the treatment of the poor in his own era and in medieval times (figure 1.3).
The comparison is tendentious, to say the least: the poor were never
housed in Benthamite Panopticons in the nineteenth century, nor
in Oxford colleges in the fourteenth; but Pugin was a propagandist,
not an honest scholar. His particular form of propaganda may have
soured more people on his favored style than won them over to it;
Catholicism was an unpopular faith in Protestant Britain for most of
the nineteenth century and in the 1850s in particular, when there
were demonstrations and even riots against it. And only a minority

of Britons then were "reactionary" in any other sense. Which makes
it all the more remarkable that the Gothic Revival should have survived the reactionaries' advocacy.

IT MANAGED TO DO THIS, IN FACT, because it had other things going for it, some of which ran directly counter to the factors so far
mentioned: patriotism and reaction. Two in particular may help us
better understand neo-Gothic's appeal in the nineteenth century
and also its spread to other countries: morality and progress. Gothic
was supposed to have the advantage over all other available styles in
both these respects—in the eyes of its champions, at least.

The superior morality of the Gothic style was felt to lie not mainly
in its religious associations, as one might expect—which in fact were
problematical, depending on whether one regarded it as essentially
"Christian" or "Catholic"—but on the much more basic and denom-
inationally neutral moral qualities it was supposed to embody in-
trinsically: truth, honesty, and seriousness. This was in contrast to
classical, the dominant style of the eighteenth century, and can best
be illustrated by reference to that. Most early Victorians, whether
they were persuaded by the arguments for Gothic or not, looked
down on the classical architecture of their time and the previous
century, for a number of reasons. As mentioned, it was deadly dull.
The years 1750–1820 really were a low period in English architecture: with few talented architects appearing after the deaths of
Wren, John Vanbrugh, and Nicholas Hawksmoor in the 1720s and
1730s. In this vacuum, aristocratic taste faltered; most great buildings were shaped like boxes with rows of pointless columns in front
(Palmerston's own Palladian house, Broadlands, in Hampshire is
an example); and contractors threw up hastily built terraces made
of blackened bricks with square holes punched in them (like the
house Palmerston lived in as Prime Minister, 10 Downing Street).
In addition, the classical style was seen as unprincipled. Even the
best of it was all for show, simply theatrical, merely a style chosen
because it was thought to look good or impressive, rather than for
any more serious reason; and to give this cheap effect, it was often
disguised as something it wasn't. The work of the leading and probably best architect of the period, Thomas Nash, exemplified this,
with great sweeping terraces built of inferior materials but plastered
and painted over to make them look more solid than they were.

The sterility of the classical style showed up in numerous details. Façades had to be symmetrical, whatever the arrangement of
the rooms behind them; they had to have porticos, even though
porticos were useless and artificial in a northern climate; and of-

ten their exteriors were deliberately designed to deceive the on-
looker. A good example of this is St. Paul's Cathedral in London,
with its false curtain walls along the outside of the aisles, hiding
the buttresses behind them, and its double dome: the dome seen
from the outside does not reflect the one seen from the inside,
but in fact is separated from it by several meters and a great brick
cone, which can't be seen from anywhere. All this was superficial
at best, dishonest at worst. Further, most of the details and deco-
rations of classical buildings were highly formalistic and artificial:
simple pediments, conventional Ionic or Corinthian capitals, urns,
and bunches of very unappetizing-looking grapes, usually merely
copied from pattern books. This conformity allowed no creative
choice to the craftsmen working on such buildings, but instead rel-
egated them to the position of simple wage laborers—a condition
that Marx at around this time was describing as "capitalist alienation." It was this that gave the early nineteenth-century critique
of classical architecture a radical political edge, which came to be
attached to the Gothic alternative too. That, and classical having
been so closely associated with the (immoral) British upper classes
since they imposed it on the ordinary and decent people of Britain
in Jacobean times.

It is easy to see why middle-class Victorians, if they were at all interested in architecture, did not want to be represented by this style
of it in their bright, new nineteenth century. It may be less easy to
see why they could regard Gothic as a more acceptable substitute.
What was so serious, after all, about a style that until recently had
been admired—if at all—mainly for its "picturesqueness," even for
the horrible images it stirred up (in Gothic novels, for example),
and mainly used to prettify the mansions of silly romantic men and
women with more money than sense? Was not its employment for
so long by the medieval Catholic Church, the fount of all errors,
bound to cast doubt, among Protestants, on its "truthfulness"? (The
great Evangelical preacher Charles Spurgeon certainly thought
so; he claimed Gothic was an invention of "the Devil," by which he
meant the Pope.)[9] What could be honest about building nineteenth-
century houses to look like medieval castles? Or, indeed, about any
attempt to resuscitate a style that had been born and sustained in
an entirely different, and now long-dead, social environment? "The
great drama of history does not admit of encores," wrote one of Pugin's critics in 1843. "Streams do not flow back to their sources."[10]
Face it, commented the *Building News* in June 1857: "The Planta-
genets have vanished—Victoria reigns."[11] At first glance, therefore,
Gothic did not appear to be much more promising than the classical

as a carrier of the moral values—seriousness, truth, and honesty—
that the Victorian middle classes believed they represented. In the
end, this was probably a major reason why the Gothic Revival fizzled
out.

But there was a case to be made for it in these "moral" terms. For
example: most medieval buildings do not rely on "deceit" as much
as classical ones. What you see is what you get. If it looks like stone,
it is stone; wood is wood, not plastered over; if there have to be external buttresses holding up a building, they are clearly on view,
not hidden behind curtain walls (indeed, flying buttresses, suitably
decorated, are one of the glories of the great French cathedrals);
external form usually expresses internal function "honestly"; roofs
are adapted to the northern European rather than to a Mediterranean climate (that is why they are steeper); the invisible backs of
statues are famously carved with as much detail and verisimilitude
as the fronts (on the grounds that God can see them); carvings are
modeled on nature—leaves, flowers, even animals—rather than on
repetitive patterns, and don't include grapes, because grapes don't
grow in England; and statues and other carvings are sculpted, lov-
ingly, by craftsmen who take pride in their work and therefore accrue more dignity to themselves than mere wage slaves. It is possible
to see more truth and honesty in all this than in most classical architecture, which is bound to have appealed to the moralistic Victorian
middle classes. Most contemporary classicists, incidentally, denied
none of this, but simply thought it was irrelevant to architecture,
which should be guided simply by what they called artistic taste. Unfortunately, taste was something that came only with good breeding
and a classical public school education, which meant that the middle classes were unlikely to have it. Several snobbish architectural
historians in the twentieth century have shared this view, which in
their opinion explains why Victorian Gothic is as tasteless as it is.
But that is another question.

It is also possible to see something quite modern about all of this,
which brings us to the second advantage that Gothic was supposed
to have: it represented progress. On the surface, this may look coun-
terintuitive. What could be less progressive than the Middle Ages?
Well, neoclassical building, for a start. However "backward" the Middle Ages may have been in other areas, and however less enlightened
in some regards than the ancient civilizations whose cultures were
"reborn" in the fifteenth and sixteenth centuries, its architecture
was enormously advanced, at any rate in its structural engineering,
in comparison with what had gone before (in classical times) and
was to come afterward (during and after the Renaissance). And this

skill, which accounts for all those wonderful cathedrals raised all over Europe, was one the medievals' successors could not hope to emulate, even if they had wanted to. Over a period of about three hundred years, the medievals arrived at an incredibly advanced understanding of weights and forces and thrusts, perfecting a way of building that enabled them to build higher than ever before, or after, until the invention of the iron frame; to develop a system of roofing (called vaulting) with a weight of stone resting on pillars that seem, even to modern eyes, far too slender to bear it; and to erect great towers and spires that were not surpassed in height for hundreds of years. These structures, still standing, many of them for five to seven centuries, decorated with the most exquisite carvings and pierced by the most delicate traceries, are arguably the greatest marvels of the Middle Ages, rising above every other cultural achievement of the period—music, painting, literature, and philosophy—like poppies in a field of dandelions.

The fundamental basis of this architectural achievement was the characteristic Gothic pointed arch and vault, which, by doing away with the weakest point in the round arch—the center, or keystone—could carry much greater weights than its predecessors. The architect G. E. Street claimed that despite its antiquity, this was "the greatest invention in construction which ha[d] ever been made." [12] Another contemporary agreed: it "*rendered all previous styles for ever obsolete.*" [13] How much more "modern" could a style get? Just because the trick had been forgotten in the Renaissance—in the eighteenth century, all kinds of explanations were suggested for the use of the pointed arch, such as its resemblance to the shape of praying hands; it was only in the early nineteenth century that its key structural rationale was rediscovered—did not mean that it was not still the most advanced way of bridging gaps; better than the semicircular and trabeated (or straight-headed) solutions that the classicists had returned to. To go back to such expertise, therefore, could not really be regarded as reactionary, any more than unraveling a piece of knitting to get back to the dropped stitch that had made it all go wrong.

The appeal here was to the Victorians' sense of scientific rationality, which was a very nineteenth-century characteristic, one lying at the root of all that century's many technological achievements, including those awful steam locomotives. There was another aspect to it too. Architecture in the Middle Ages had evolved. It had not been static, unlike classical architecture in so many of its manifestations. Driven mainly by structural discoveries and improvements, it had developed: from the heavy, round-arched Romanesque (called

Norman in England); through Early English, when the pointed
arch came in; to various forms of Decorated, when new refinements
in tracery enabled windows to be larger; and, last, to the Perpendicular in England ("Flamboyant" in France), which most mid-
nineteenth-century architectural theorists agreed represented a
falling off, because it had lost sight of the fundamental structural
principles informing the style. (Perpendicular arches, for example,
had become flatter than before; sculpture, more formal and heral-
dic.) Evolution: does not that also ring some modern, nineteenth-
century bells? And what could be more progressive? Which is why
most of the leading Victorian Gothic architects—starting with
Pugin—always insisted that in taking up Gothic, they were not aim-
ing merely to copy the medievals, but also to develop the style further from its highest point, in the early fourteenth century (just
before Perpendicular). This pinnacle was always regarded not as a
pattern or model—those were what the classicists used—but as a
point de départ, as the Gothicists called it, for the new style, fit for
their own times and adaptable, in the way classical wasn't, to any
future demands. Most architectural historians single out a church
by William Butterfield, All Saints, Margaret Street, London (figure 1.4), as marking the moment when Victorian Gothic departed
from its medieval *point* and started developing further, and wonderfully, on its own. (Others think it is merely ugly. But it is well worth
a visit; certainly ahead of George Gilbert Scott's government offices,
or even his St. Pancras Station Hotel.)

Considerations like these help explain the conundrum of a
500-year-old style of architecture being revived for a self-consciously
modern age. The nationalistic and antimodern factors that neo-
Gothic is often attributed to played a part also; but it is highly
doubtful whether neo-Gothic could have been as successful as it was
(and remember, it wasn't all that successful) if it had had to rely
exclusively on reactionary old patriots for its support. Nor would
most Gothic architects and theorists, apart perhaps from Pugin,
have been happy with that kind of advocacy. Most of them were fully
aware of the progressive spirit of their age and were desperate to
be seen to conform to it. Indeed, for both sides in the Battle of the
Styles over the new Foreign Office in the 1850s, this was their major
concern: not to show how English their favored styles were, but how
modern—how they reflected their age rather than their nation. The
classicists did it by claiming that their style was the ideal one, and so
was incapable of being modernized further. The Gothic case, however, seems more convincing for that day and age, and for the middle classes in particular. They rejected both the classical ideal, for

mainly moral reasons, and the idea that they should be governed by past ideals instead of visions of future ones. The latter required change, movement, progress, reform, energy, instability, dynamism, and asymmetry, which were intrinsic to Gothic in a way they were not to classical architecture. It was this that made Gothic the more genuinely contemporary style of the two.

BUT WERE THERE NOT ALTERNATIVES: other styles whose contemporary credentials were as good as or better than Gothic's? Of course there were. One of these was what today would be recognized as modernism: the simple, functional, and universal style usually associated with twentieth-century architects like Walter Gropius and Frank Lloyd Wright, but that also had some very striking nineteenth-century precedents, such as the famous Crystal Palace (1851) in London and King's Cross station, standing right next to Scott's St. Pancras, built twenty years before that great Gothic pile and looking—to our eyes—far more modern. As early as the 1840s, there were also advocates of completely new styles of architecture based on the properties of iron: William Vose Pickett, for example, wrote books about it and even tried to enlist Prince Albert to his cause; and concrete building were pioneered in the 1860s. These could have offered a way "forward," harnessing Victorian science and technology directly to art. But they were false starts, none of them really catching on until the following century. Why not earlier? There are a number of quite good reasons. Pickett could not draw, apparently, so no one could see what his iron-framed buildings might have looked like. Neither iron nor concrete was perfected as a building material until the 1890s—iron buildings proved highly vulnerable to fire, surprisingly—when the materials were combined in the breakthrough form of ferroconcrete (for skyscrapers). So far as "simplicity" is concerned—one of the distinguishing features of modern architecture—it is difficult to see why that should have been taken up before it was. There is no immutable rule that equates modernity to simplicity. Most other modern artifacts are far from simple: computers, space rockets, or even steam locomotives, for example.

Besides, it could be argued—and has been argued by a number of architectural historians, including Nikolaus Pevsner—that most of the really important features of modernism did in fact appear in the later nineteenth century: partly in the great engineering works of the time, especially bridges; partly in buildings like the Crystal Palace and King's Cross station; but also in the guise of Gothic. Gothic, remember, introduced functionalism into architecture: the idea that the form of a building should reflect the uses it is put to. And also structuralism: form should grow out of, and express, a building's material structure. These were seen as universal principles, not narrowly national ones, and so universally applicable: the implication of which can be seen to be today's International Style. As early as the 1860s, several of the more flexible Gothic architects and theorists were musing that development along these lines, starting from that fourteenth-century *point de départ,* might ultimately land them anywhere: to an architecture, for example, that bore no trace of a pointed arch or a ribbed vault or a crocketed spire or a flying buttress, but because it still conformed to the spirit that lay behind those features—functionalism and constructionism, or truth and honesty, as the Victorians preferred to call them—was still Gothic in essence. In this sense, though Victorian Gothic's body now definitely lies a-moldering in the grave, and has done for ninety or a hundred years now (less on some American university campuses), its soul might be said to be still marching on.

Finally, note should be taken of the problems the Victorians faced in their project to devise a new architecture to reflect the glory of their age. It was the "devising" that was the problem. That was not how new architectural styles had generally arisen, historically. Most of them had evolved, like Gothic, over decades or centuries, modified by external influences; or, alternatively, had been imposed on a people by an elite, as in the Renaissance. In neither of these two scenarios had people been given, or even been aware of, a choice of styles they could pick from. In the nineteenth century, this changed, in a quite fundamental way, which Scott picked up on during the Battle of the Styles. "The peculiar characteristic of the present day, as compared with all former periods," he wrote in one of his pro-Gothic manifestos, "is that we are acquainted with the history of art. . . . It is reserved for us alone, of all the generations of the human race, to know perfectly our own standing point, and to look back upon a perfect history of what has gone before us." That, he concluded, was "amazingly interesting to us as a matter of amusement and erudition, but I fear it is a hindrance, rather than a help, to us as artists."[14] It was true. They had eaten of the tree of knowledge—knowledge, that is, of all the world's and history's myriad styles. With all these choices now before them, how could they expect to settle, as Scott passionately wished, on a single, distinctive nineteenth-century style?

Scott saw this as a problem. Others, however, regarded it as a reason for viewing architectural style in a totally different way. In an age of free trade, as the Scottish architect Robert Anderson put it rhetorically to an Edinburgh audience in April 1860, was it so very unreasonable to expect "free trade in the arts of the past"?[15] Their very liberties, wrote J. Henry Stevens, meant that patrons and architects were bound to have very different ideas and tastes; uniformity of style was possible only in either autocratic societies, like the Catholic Middle Ages, where it could be imposed, or in insulated ones, in which people knew no others.[16] Modern architecture, argued Samuel Huggins of the Liverpool Architectural Society in 1858, was bound to take "a variety of shapes analogous to our present complex civilisation, and reflect the hues of different orders, professions, pursuits, and interests."[17]

This, then, was the true solution to the perceived problem of a nineteenth-century architectural style. It is generally called eclecticism, and was justified best (though awkwardly) by the architect Robert Kerr in 1865.

> We live in the era of *Omnium-Gatherum;* all the world is a museum
> . . . And while critics demand, not without contempt, why is it that
> our age has not a *Style of its own,* like all other ages!—How could
> it have a style of its own in such circumstances? Or otherwise, let
> us answer, if it has no style of its own in one sense, it has in an-
> other a very notable style of its own, and a very novel one,—the
> style of this miscellaneous connoisseurship,—the style of instinct
> superseded by knowledge,—a state of things characteristic of our
> age—and not in architecture alone—as no other state of things
> can be characteristic of it.[18]

The eclectics may have been right. A free, democratic, and individualistic society, culture, and polity, which was the direction Britain was heading in Victorian times, could not be represented by any single architectural style without doing enormous violence to Britons' real nature and deepest aspirations. A mixture of styles, therefore, which is what came about in the nineteenth century, did that better. Neo-Gothic was part of this, representing many contemporary trends and discourses—more, probably, than any other style, including, as it did, morality and progress as well as nationalism and nostalgia—but not all of them. Which is why it needed other styles to exist side by side with it in order truly to express the spirit of the age.

Spring Semester 2010

1. *Building News*, 16 Nov. 1860, p. 876.

2. Palmerston, speech in the House of Commons, 11 Feb. 1859, *Hansard*, 3rd ser., vol. 152, cols. 271–2.

3. *The Gothic Renaissance: Its Origin, Progress, and Principles* (London, 1860), p. 4.

4. Ibid., p. 7.

5. "A Cambridge Man," *The New Palaces of Administration* (Cambridge, 1857), p. 22.

6. Palmerston, speech in the House of Commons, 8 July 1861, *Hansard*, 3rd ser., vol. 164, col. 537.

7. *Building News*, 27 July 1860, p. 593.

8. See, for example, the speeches of Earl Granville in the Lords and Sir Benjamin Hall in the Commons, 15 May and 2 July 1857, in *Hansard*, 3rd ser., vol. 145, col. 292, and vol. 146, col. 803.

9. Quoted in Ernest W. Bacon, *Spurgeon: Heir of the Puritans* (London, 1967), pp. 64–5.

10. "Architectural Revivalism and Puginism," *Fraser's Magazine*, Nov. 1843, pp. 600–1.

11. *Building News*, 26 June 1857, p. 652.

12. G. E. Street, "The True Principles of Architecture and the Possibility of Development," paper read to the Oxford Architectural Society, 18 Feb. 1852, and printed in the *Ecclesiologist*, June 1852, pp. 249–50.

13. [Coventry Patmore], review of *Remarks on Secular and Domestic Architecture*, by George Gilbert Scott, *North British Review*, 28 (May 1858), p. 350 (italics in the original).

14. George Gilbert Scott, *Remarks on Secular and Domestic Architecture* (London, 1857), pp. 259–60.

15. Quoted in the *Caledonian Mercury*, 3 Apr. 1860.

16. J. Henry Stevens, "The Revivalists and the Vernacular Architecture," *Builder*, 7 Nov. 1857, p. 639.

17. Samuel Huggins, lecture titled "The Question of Styles," reported in the *Builder*, 15 May 1858, pp. 332–3.

18. Robert Kerr, *The Gentleman's House* (London, 1865), p. 342.

Figure 1.1
George Gilbert Scott's Midland Railway Hotel, St. Pancras, designed
to show the adaptability of the Gothic style to the secular purposes
of the Victorian age. Formerly regarded as a joke, it has been restored to its former glory.

Figure 1.2
Victoria Terminus, Bombay, c.1900. Now known as the Chhatrapati Shivaji Terminus, Mumbai, the station, designed by Frederick William Stevens for the Great Indian Peninsula Railway, opened on 20 June 1887, the date of Queen Victoria's Golden Jubilee.

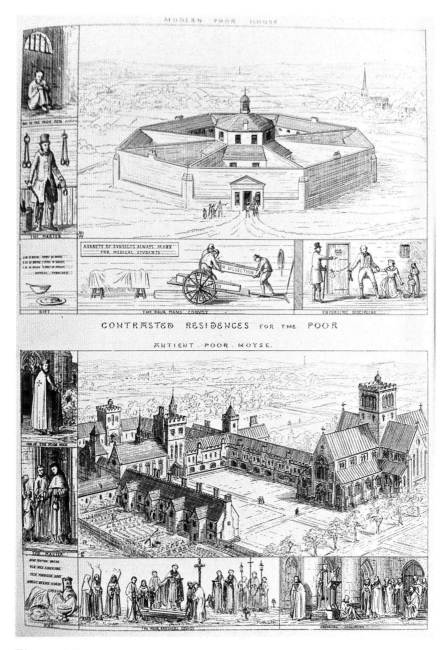

Figure 1.3

A. W. N. Pugin, "Contrasted Residences for the Poor," from *Contrasts* (1837). The outrageously exaggerated contrast was meant to illustrate the social and ethical superiority of medieval "Catholic" architecture over that of his day.

Figure 1.4
William Butterfield's All Saints Church, Margaret Street, London:
the point at which Victorian Gothic architecture broke free from its
medieval models and struck out for itself. The interior is decorated
in rich, and very "Victorian," polychromy. Photo by Steven Zucker.

2

Rudyard Kipling and America

THOMAS PINNEY

When they hear the name "Kipling," many people think at once of India. That is not wrong, and it may well be the permanent association with his name. But it is not the only place that might be thought of. There are good materials for constructing a story about Kipling and South Africa, or Kipling and Canada, or Kipling and France. I have myself perpetrated a little book about Kipling and Australia (*Kipling Down Under*, 2000). But there is also Kipling and America, which is a big subject in itself.

What did Kipling know about America? To begin with, even as a schoolboy he was at home in American literature. He greatly admired Emerson—he kept a picture of Emerson on his desk to the end of his life; he loved Mark Twain, who repaid the compliment. Twain had the highest opinion of Kipling's work, rereading *Kim* every year; together, the two men formed a sort of mutual admiration society. He was on friendly and admiring terms with Henry James and had a shrewdly critical appreciation of James's achievement. But besides the standard authors—James Russell Lowell, Henry Wadsworth Longfellow, William Dean Howells, and so on—he read all the lesser lights—Sarah Orne Jewett, Will Carleton, Joel Chandler Harris, James Whitcomb Riley, Bret Harte, Stephen Crane: it would be hard to find an American writer from the late nineteenth or early twentieth century whose works Kipling did not know. He was the sort of reader who devoured books and who remembered

and learned from what he read. American literature always formed
a large part of his diet.

When Kipling left school at the age of sixteen to work as a journalist in India, the American connection was not broken. He scanned
the reports from American newspapers, and in British India there
was, evidently, a reliable supply of American books and magazines.
It was in India that Kipling's deepest-lying idea about the United
States began to take form. As a journalist serving the British community in India, Kipling had to make up his mind about the imperial enterprise. He decided to support it. Many of the poems and
stories that he wrote in India make fun of the officials who ran the
country and lightly satirize the vanities and foibles of English social
life in a strange land; but beneath that surface there is a steady admiration for the work being done to create material prosperity and,
far more importantly, admiration for the rule of law established under the empire.

At the same time that Kipling was learning to appreciate the benefits of law and order in India, he was forming an idea of American
lawlessness. The British in India were particularly sensitive on this
point: Americans loved to twist the tail of the British lion, and a lot
of that twisting was done in the name of anti-imperial feeling. The
British, so they were told, were oppressing the natives: they stifled
the spark of liberty, they exploited the helpless Hindus, and so on.
These were, to Kipling, false accusations: British power had brought
order and justice to India. And the Americans, while they accused
the British of oppression, were creating a riot of disorder in their
own country. That, or something like that, was Kipling's firm conviction by the time that he came to the end of his seven years' work
in India.

Kipling left India at the beginning of 1889 to seek his literary fortune in London. But he made a point of going the long way around:
crossing the Pacific and then traveling from coast to coast across the
United States before sailing across the Atlantic for England. This
was his American baptism, a four-month immersion in American
places among American people. In the long series of reports of this
trip that he wrote for his paper back in India, it appears that he
tried very hard to like what he found. Of course, he found all those
things to dislike that generations of English travelers had already
found: the hustle and bustle of daily life, the universal spitting, the
jerry-built character of American cities, the ignorant patriotic boast-
ing, and so on. But he was impressed by American resourcefulness,
openness, and directness. Washington, D.C., he found, was "a thoroughly beautiful city."[1] He was greatly moved by a visit to Concord,

where he felt the "'might, majesty, dominion and power' of the Great American Nation."[2] Even the patriotism was not always offensive:

> The men and the women set us an example in patriotism. . . . They believe in their land and its future and its honour and its glory, and they are not ashamed to say so. From the largest to the least runs this same proud, passionate conviction to which I take off my hat and for which I love them.[3]

When he reached the small town of Beaver, Pennsylvania, where he was a guest for some weeks, he found a charmingly peaceful and orderly life. Here, he wrote, were "Americans and no aliens—men ruling themselves by themselves and for themselves, and their wives and their children—in peace, order and decency."[4] There is a hint here of American isolationist behavior—"men ruling themselves by themselves and for themselves"—that Kipling was later to number among the sins of America, but the main feeling was one of approval.

But underneath it all, Kipling felt lawlessness and the violence that went with it always threatening to break out. In San Francisco, as he was making his way to his hotel from the harbor, he came across "a light commotion in the street—a gathering together of three or four and something that glittered as it moved very swiftly."[5] The small group disappeared, and Kipling saw a policeman "supporting a Chinaman who had been stabbed in the eye and was bleeding like a pig." There was no explanation, no consequence. The bystanders went their way, and Kipling went on to his hotel, wondering at what he had seen.

Later in his stay in San Francisco, Kipling visited Chinatown alone, at night. In his account, he found his way to a cellar where a poker game was in progress. The players were all Chinese except for a single Mexican. When a dispute broke out, the Mexican pulled a pistol and shot one of the Chinese dead. Kipling, in a panic of fear, groped his way out of the cellar, reached the street, and, unable to walk because his legs would not support him—and not daring to run—half skipped and half danced his way through the night to the safety of his hotel (the Palace). Did the events of this story really happen? Or was it made up? Although likely made up, it is a true expression of what Kipling was thinking and feeling about being in America. If he didn't actually see a murder, he ought to have.

On his eastward journey across America, Kipling encountered many forms of the lawless and violent, some of them of natural rather than human origin. Seattle, for example, when he arrived, had just burned to the ground—as the insurance companies say, an act of God. But the other sort of violence was human. On the train taking him to Yellowstone Park, Kipling wrote:

> We were a merry crew. One gentleman announced his intention of paying no fare and grappled the conductor who neatly cross-buttocked him through a double window of plate-glass. His head was cut open in four or five places. A doctor on the train hastily stitched up the biggest gash and he was dropped at a wayside station, spurting blood at every hair—a scarlet-headed and ghastly sight. The conductor guessed that he would die and volunteered the information that there was no profit in monkeying with the North Pacific Railway.[6]

In Livingston, Montana, at the gateway to Yellowstone, Kipling encountered cowboys for the first time. In town for the Fourth of July, they were all drunk and shooting off fireworks among the wooden buildings, and one of them, armed with a Winchester, was "kicking about the streets . . . looking for someone."[7] In Chicago, he visited the stockyards, where the wholesale slaughtering of pigs and cattle was carried out in a nightmarish scene reeking of blood. At the end of his stockyard tour, he had a special vision:

> Women come sometimes to see the slaughter, as they would come to see the slaughter of men. And there entered that vermillion hall a young woman of large mould, with brilliantly scarlet lips, and heavy eyebrows and dark hair that came in a "widow's peak" on the forehead. She was well and healthy and alive exceedingly, and she was dressed in flaming red and black and her feet . . . were cased in red leather shoes. She stood in a patch of sunlight, the red blood under her shoes, the vivid carcases stacked round her, a bullock bleeding its life away not six feet away from her and the death factory roaring all round her. She looked curiously, with hard bold eyes, and was not ashamed.[8]

That was not Kipling's final image of America, but it was one that he never forgot.

When he reached England at the end of 1889, he found he had been transformed, almost overnight, into a famous writer. But Kipling was suspicious of his fame—he knew that for fashionable London, at least, he was merely the comet of a season. Nor did he feel comfortable with English life: he had known a different style of things in India, and he had just come from a different style of things in America, some of which seem to have gotten under his skin. In London, he soon made friends with a young American publisher named Wolcott Balestier; two years later, he married Balestier's sister.

The Balestiers, brother and sister, grew up in Rochester, New York, but the family had recently moved to Brattleboro, Vermont. Kipling and his bride at once set off for Vermont, and after a wedding trip that took them to Japan, returned to Vermont to set up housekeeping. It was clearly Kipling's intention to settle permanently. He built a house outside Brattleboro on a hillside looking out over the Connecticut River toward Mt. Monadnock (the house still stands, intact, the property of the Landmark Trust; it can be rented for ski weekends). His first two children were born there, and he himself entered into a period of remarkable creativity. There he wrote the *Jungle Books* when, as he put it, the snow lay level with the windowsill of his workroom. There, too, he wrote most of the poems collected in *The Seven Seas;* he wrote the stories that make up *The Day's Work;* and he wrote his one sustained effort at representing American life, *Captains Courageous.*

Kipling treasured the protected isolation that his life in remote Vermont gave him, but he was at the same time in touch with some of the most cultivated and distinguished Americans of the day: he knew and admired Henry Adams, John Hay, Theodore Roosevelt, and others of their Washington circle; he knew the writers and publishers concentrated in New York City; he especially admired the highly refined Charles Eliot Norton of Harvard, who became a special friend, who showed him all that was interesting and valuable in Boston and Cambridge, who introduced him to William James, and who took Kipling to the football game between Harvard and Brown in 1895. Kipling was privileged to know some of the best elements in American life.

He also knew and liked some of the homely elements too. Consider this lyric evocation, written in a letter of 1894, when Kipling was visiting England. There had finally, in that wet English summer, come some real warmth, and that warmth, he wrote,

> waked in me a lively desire to be back in Main Street Brattleboro Vt. U.S.A. and hear the sody water fizzing in the drug-store and discuss the outlook for the Episcopalian Church with the clerk; and get a bottle of lager in the basement of the Brooks House and hear the doctor tell fish yarns and have the iron-headed old farmers loaf up and jerk out:—"Bin in Yurope haint yer?" and then go home, an easy gait, through the deep white dust with the locust trees just stinking to heaven and the fire flies playing up and down the swamp road and the Katydids giving oratorios free-gratis and for nothing to the whip-poor-will and everybody sitting out on the verandah after dinner smoking Durham tobacco in a cob pipe

with our feet on the verandah railings and the moon coming up behind Wantastiquet.[9]

This sounds as though Kipling was fully and happily assimilated into American life. But other evidence suggests that he still kept a guarded and cautious view of the country where he then lived and worked. It is remarkable that in the four years that he lived in Vermont, he never went west of the Hudson River: he traveled into Canada and through much of New England, frequently to New York City and once at least to Washington. But not west: his cross-country journey in 1899 had evidently been enough, or more than enough, to satisfy his curiosity about that part of the country.

Kipling's fears of American violence were soon realized. Two events toward the end of 1895 greatly troubled him. President Cleveland declared that Britain was violating the Monroe Doctrine in a border dispute with Venezuela over British Guiana; and Doctor Jameson's abortive raid in South Africa stirred up world opinion against Britain. Anti-British feeling ran high even in rural Vermont, and Kipling began making uneasy noises about leaving the country. The determining moment came in May 1896, when Kipling and his wife's younger brother, who was also a neighbor of theirs in Vermont, had a violent quarrel. Beatty Balestier was everything Kipling was not: big, loud, hard drinking, volatile, ne'er-do-well—in short, an American.

When they quarreled, Beatty, in his usual loud extravagance, threatened to kill Kipling; Kipling took that noisy threat literally and had Beatty arrested. A hearing followed, at which Kipling was sorely humiliated—the whole episode was a joke to his American neighbors and to the reporters who had swarmed into Brattleboro to cover the event. Shortly thereafter, Kipling packed up his family and quietly stole away to England, leaving a fully furnished house behind him.

More than two years later, at the beginning of 1899, Kipling apparently had some idea of seeking to re-establish friendly relations with America. He and his family crossed the winter Atlantic and arrived in New York, all with colds. Kipling then developed pneumonia, as did his first child, his American-born daughter Josephine. Kipling barely survived the illness; Josephine died. After some weeks of recovery, Kipling and his remaining family sailed back to England. He would never set foot in the United States again. In later years, he toured Canada from coast to coast, he traveled around the Caribbean, he had many opportunities and many invitations to enter the country, but he would not cross that fatal line again. When Sir

Percy Bates, the head of the Cunard Line, offered to take Kipling to America as the honored guest of the company, Kipling replied: "I would rather die than go to America." "And," Bates added in telling this story, "I think he meant it."

Since Kipling would not go there, there is nothing more to say about his experiences in the country. But the country would not go away. America was a major market for his books; he liked and listened to his American publisher, Frank Doubleday; he stayed in touch with such friends as Theodore Roosevelt; he continued to keep up with American literature; and he had a lot to say about the country in one form or another. But as with so many of Kipling's thoughts and opinions, it is not easy to pin him down.

JUST A FEW DAYS BEFORE WRITING that lyric evocation of sitting on the porch and listening to a chorus of katydids, he wrote, and published in an English paper, a poem called "An American." It is perhaps the best statement of Kipling's idea of America. The poem, in form, is a parody of Emerson's "Brahma." In Emerson's poem, "Brahma" is a mysterious force that unites all the opposites of thought and action, a figure of unimaginable power:

> Far or forgot to me is near;
>> Shadow and sunlight are the same;
> The vanish'd gods to me appear;
>> And one to me are shame and fame.

In Kipling's poem, in contrast, the American is a loose cluster of unreconciled contradictions, an untidy mass of confusion rather than an all-encompassing power:

> Calm-eyed he scoffs at Sword and Crown,
> Or, panic-blinded, stabs and slays;
> Blatant he bids the world bow down,
> Or cringing begs a crust of praise.

How is that? How can such an extravagantly unstable compound ever survive and prosper? Yet the speaker of the poem, the "American Spirit," affirms, "I—I shall save him at the last!" How, one wonders? The answers that the poem gives, if they are answers, are not at all clear. The American, we are told, is an "avatar" of the American Spirit: "They know not much what I am like, / Nor what he is, my Avatar." Presumably, all the excellent qualities belong to the American Spirit that inhabits the avatar, and all the defects belong to the temporary incarnation. That would furnish a reason for believing the conclusion of the poem, that the American Spirit will at last save the avatar. But it is by no means clear how that will come about.

Kipling never got beyond this confusion in his ideas about America, though "confusion" may well be the wrong word; the contradictions are in American life itself and not in the mind of the observer.

Kipling's view of the lawlessness of American life remained a steady theme, and one that had a special force for Kipling. Recall the concluding lines from the poem "The Law of the Jungle":

> *Now these are the Laws of the Jungle, and many and mighty are they;*
> *But the head and the hoof of the Law and the haunch and the hump*
> *is—Obey!*

When Kipling published *The Second Jungle Book* in the year after the first one had come out, he took these two lines as the epigraph to the new book, as though to say that that was what it was all about. No idea was of more importance to Kipling: authority is gained only through discipline and obedience, in recognition of the supremacy of the Law—a word always in capitals for him. The idea is not a doctrine of passivity, but a theory of civilization itself, almost a religious conviction: if one is to do good things, or great things, one can do them only through obedience to the law, through discipline, through self-sacrifice. So that notorious, and usually misunderstood line in "Recessional," the one about "lesser breeds without the law," did not, as is commonly supposed, refer to primitive communities, but to such people as the Germans and, probably, the Americans too, if they remained in selfish isolation and did not take up their international responsibilities.

The forms of lawlessness were many. Political corruption was one of them. Among Kipling's first impressions of America was a visit to a San Francisco saloon where, as he put it,

> gentlemen interested in ward politics nightly congregate. They were not pretty persons. Some of them were bloated and they all swore cheerfully till the heavy gold watch chains on their fat stomachs rose and fell again; but they talked over their liquor as men who had power and unquestioned access to places of trust and profit.[10]

The description is clearly cartoonish, but whether Kipling actually saw such characters or not, the dislike is clear enough. When, in 1895, Kipling visited Washington, D.C., he saw the equivalent scene at a much loftier level of politics. He visited with President Cleveland and members of the Cabinet. When he returned to his hotel, he wrote in his wife's journal this brief third-person report:

Sees the cabinet and talks with the President. He is <u>not</u> impressed but very sorrowful. It is a colossal agglomeration of reeking bounders—awful; inexpressible; incredible. (5 April 1895)

Whatever he saw, or thought he saw, in these men was not the service of the Law but a mere lawless self-seeking, very much after the fashion of what he saw in San Francisco at the beginning of his American experience.

Democracy itself Kipling thought a lawless system, and he made a number of direct and indirect attacks upon it. The absurd monkeys in *The Jungle Book*—the "Bandar Log"—were, Kipling said, his last word on the subject, embodying his views on "the Great God 'Democracy'" or "Government by popular opinion."[11] The monkeys talk big, fritter about, make messes, and do nothing—hardly a flattering image of democracy in action. Earlier, he had called it "that contagious cutaneous disorder which calls itself Democracy."[12] He never changed his opinion on this subject.

Commercial dishonesty was another form of American lawlessness. Here Kipling thought that he had special knowledge. His early work, the stories and poems that he had written in his Indian years and in the first years of his return to England—work that, once it was known outside of India made him instantly famous—was unprotected by copyright in America. Not until 1891 did the United States pass an international copyright act, which gave protection to Kipling's work from that date—but not to anything before that date. Kipling undertook a series of suits in American courts against the pirates, at great expense and trouble, but always in vain. His early work continued to be printed and reprinted free of cost. Indeed, one may say that this situation has greatly helped form Americans' notion of Kipling's work: because the early Indian work was freely available, it has overwhelmed everything else that he wrote during a long and steadily maturing career. He got better as he went on. Indeed, many good critics think that Kipling's highest achievement is in his later work, but much of that remains effectively unknown to his popular audience in America simply because the market has long been inundated with the unprotected early work.

The experience of being plundered by American pirates left Kipling a very angry man. In one of his poems from this time, called "The Rhyme of the Three Captains," he presents himself as a simple law-abiding skipper who has been robbed by an American pirate ship. And this is how he imagines that he might take his revenge if he ever catches the pirate:

> I had nailed his ears to my capstan-head, and ripped them
>   off with a saw,
> And soused them in the bilgewater, and served them to him
>   raw;
> I had flung him blind in a rudderless boat to rot in the
>   rocking dark,
> I had towed him aft of his own craft, a bait for his brother
>   shark;
> I had lapped him round with cocoa-husk, and drenched him
>   with the oil,
> And lashed him fast to his own mast to blaze above my spoil;

And so on through many more lines.

Then there was the wastefulness of American life and, at the same time, Americans' failure to take advantage of their abundance. The wastefulness he had seen on his first encounter with the country, in the west, which was in the process of being skinned and scraped by logging and mining; its cities, thrown up overnight, went up in flames just as quickly, as Portland, as Tacoma, as Seattle, as Vancouver had all recently done at the time of his first visit. Yet in the midst of an abundance that seemed limitless, people had no idea how to use it. Many years after he had left the United States, Kipling suggested to his publisher Frank Doubleday that he commission a book about American food, a subject, Kipling thought, that had been wholly neglected. The subject was enormous, and the book should begin with a "gastronomical map":

> For example, it would not be enough to mark Philadelphia "Scrapple" and no more. There must be several sorts of the stuff in existence, probably among the Pennsylvania Dutch, which should be mapped; and when you get south of Baltimore (which city alone will take a good deal of space) the number of local specialties, white and coloured, are in all likelihood very large. Think for a moment of the cakes, sweets and breads, and the local receipts for them! Again, Pork, its varieties, and preparation, the various ways of dealing with different parts of a swine's interior, is a vast subject in itself. And the whole matter of the coastal fish of the Eastern Seaboard, verges towards infinity.[13]

But given all this variety and abundance, what was the usual result when the American wife prepared her husband's food? "She buys canned goods," Kipling wrote, "and [they die] of dyspepsia." The main chapter of this imagined book, Kipling added, should be called "Wasted Bounty," and the title of the whole should be *Our Great Good Fortune and How We Waste It*. Doubleday never did commission the book, but in the current landscape of fast-food franchises, there might still be some point to it.

Prohibition showed Americans in another ugly light. The scheme itself was, in Kipling's eyes, a foolish measure. As he put it in a poem written at the time, the result was "public strife and naked crime" and, worse, "a people schooled to mock, in time, / All law—not one." In 1930, Kipling was marooned for many weeks in Bermuda, where his wife had fallen ill and was hospitalized. Bermuda is a small place, and there was no way to avoid the shiploads of Americans who, clamoring after the liquor they could not legally buy at home, arrived drunk and stayed that way while they were on the island. Kipling was appalled by their behavior: they hounded him for autographs; they made loud noises when his wife was trying to sleep; and they drank. "I never in all my life," he wrote to his daughter, "realized that such swine could exist as the American. They <u>all</u> drink—men and women. They smell of liquor in the morning and by night they are fairly set . . . They come out of the big ocean, booze-hounds from New York which carry about 800 of 'em, having drunk for 48 hours. Then they start drinking ashore and have what they call 'whoopee-parties.'"[14] They were, he said, "thrice-damned"— damned for their voices, damned for their manners, and damned for their drinking.[15]

But this was not the end of the indictments. The last and worst crime charged against the Americans in Kipling's court was their behavior in the Great War. He did not, he said, expect the Americans to join in the war, but he did expect them to condemn the Germans; strict neutrality was hardly an honorable response, and besides, it put the Americans in the way of making a lot of money while Europe wasted its blood and treasure. As the war dragged on, Kipling grew impatient. At the end of 1916, he published a poem called "The Neutral" (later called "The Question"), in which he likens the United States to St. Peter denying Christ:

> Brethren, how must it fare with me,
>   Or how am I justified,
> If it be proven that I am he
>   For whom mankind has died;
> If it be proven that I am he
>   Who being questioned denied?

When, at last, the United States entered the war, Kipling made the necessary welcoming noises. He wrote a new poem, called "The Choice," congratulating the Americans on at last redeeming themselves. In this poem, he reinvokes the "American Spirit" that he used as the speaker of "An American" back in 1894; but the poem is a frigid effort, one that evidently gave him a great deal of trouble. An early version was printed but then suppressed, suggesting how difficult he found it to launch into praise after so much criticism. Privately, he could never forgive the Americans for their dishonorable behavior, as he held it to be. A poem from 1926 called "The Vineyard" uses Christ's parable of the vineyard as an analogy for the Americans' behavior: they came late to the work; they did not bear the burden and the heat of the day; and yet they undertook to tell the Allies what they should have done. Here Kipling probably has President Wilson in mind; he despised Wilson as a pedant, calling him an "arid schoolmaster" and "an immensely ignorant intellectual," and he was grimly pleased to learn from Theodore Roosevelt that Wilson came from a Virginia family, "none of whose members fought on either side in the Civil War."[16]

There is more, much more, that might be said in illustration of Kipling's hostility to American manners, American politics, and American pretensions. But it is time to look at the other side. Against so heavy a list of indictments, what defense can be offered? What signs, if any, did Kipling show of affection for or admiration for the United States? In 1912, he responded to some verses that accused him of hating the United States. If, Kipling said, the writer "had considered for half a minute he would have seen that my chiefest joys and sorrow came out of that land."[17] One sees something of what Kipling means: his wife was an American, and presumably among his chiefest joys; and his daughter Josephine died in America, certainly one of his chiefest sorrows. But what else can he mean? And how would one discover that meaning by considering "for half a minute"?

His love of American literature is part of the answer. He admired the vision of Emerson; he loved the humor of Mark Twain; Whitman, he said, "shook and distraught me" when, as a boy, he first encountered that poet's work.[18] The sanity of William Dean Howells, the artistry of Longfellow, the homely charm of Sarah Orne Jewett—when Kipling invokes what he calls the "American Spirit," he must have this great literary tradition in mind, not the democratic politics and not the manners of the vulgar American. In the poem, the American Spirit possesses an "ancient humor" that Kipling would have found only in American literature.

More concretely, his idea of American possibilities comes out in one of his American characters, Laughton O. Ziegler, from Ohio, who figures in two of Kipling's stories, "The Captive" (1902) and

"The Edge of the Evening" (1913). Ziegler is a diamond in the rough, but immensely likeable; his fortunes vary wildly—sometimes he is broke, sometimes he is flush—but he is always irrepressible; he is ingenious, fertile in invention; and perhaps most importantly, he likes the English. He seems to be Kipling's ideal, mythic American.

In one of the very last letters that Kipling wrote, only a few days before his death at the beginning of 1936, he replied to an American woman who had evidently asked him about the puzzling contradictions in the poem called "An American." He answered her with a question posed in the language of the minstrel show: "If Ah didn't like de woman, how cum I'd take de trouble to hit her on de haid?"[19] Since he hit the woman on the head a whole lot, he must have really liked her! Or perhaps he was still uncertain. That may be the most interesting thing about Kipling's idea of America—his inability to make up his mind finally. And after all, are the contradictions in the mind of the beholder, or in the thing beheld?

Fall Semester 2010

1. Kipling to Edmonia Hill, 5 Sept. 1889, *The Letters of Rudyard Kipling: Volume 1, 1872–89*, ed. Thomas Pinney (Basingstoke, 1990), p. 337.
2. Kipling to Edmonia Hill, 17 Sept. 1889, in ibid., p. 345.
3. Rudyard Kipling, *From Sea to Sea*, letter no. 36.
4. Ibid.
5. Ibid., letter no. 23.
6. Ibid., letter no. 28.
7. Kipling to Edmonia Hill, 17 Sept. 1889, in *Letters: Vol. 1*, p. 337.
8. Kipling, *From Sea to Sea*, letter no. 35.
9. Kipling to Robert Barr, 28 July 1894, *The Letters of Rudyard Kipling: Volume 2, 1890–99*, ed. Thomas Pinney (Basingstoke, 1990), pp. 143–4.
10. Kipling, *From Sea to Sea*, letter no. 25.
11. Kipling to André Chevrillon, 6 Oct. 1919, in *The Letters of Rudyard Kipling: Volume 4, 1911–19*, ed. Thomas Pinney (Basingstoke, 1999), p. 576.
12. Kipling to Charles Eliot Norton, 18 Feb. 1908, in *The Letters of Rudyard Kipling: Volume 3, 1900–10*, ed. Thomas Pinney (Basingstoke, 1996), p. 308.
13. Kipling to Doubleday, 7 Feb. 1921, in *The Letters of Rudyard Kipling: Volume 5, 1920–30*, ed. Thomas Pinney (Basingstoke, 2003), p. 45.
14. Kipling to Elsie Kipling Bambridge, 14–17 Apr. 1930, in ibid., pp. 537–8.
15. Kipling to Elsie Kipling Bambridge, 18–19 Mar. 1930, in ibid., p. 530.
16. Kipling to C. R. L. Fletcher, 10 Apr. 1915, in *Letters: Vol. 4*, p. 297 note.
17. Kipling to Brander Matthews, 7 May 1912, in ibid., p. 110.
18. Kipling to Andrew Macphail, 25 Oct. 1907, in *Letters: Vol. 3*, p. 277.
19. Kipling to Mrs. Jackson Stoddard, [9–12?] January 1936, in *The Letters of Rudyard Kipling: Volume 6, 1931–36*, ed. Thomas Pinney (Basingstoke, 2004), p. 431.

3

French and British Colonial Heroes

BERNY SÈBE

Outstanding men conquering remote African lands for the glory of their homeland represent the last installment of the enduring tradition of nineteenth-century national heroes in Europe, which started with the Napoleonic wars and ended with the wave of "New Imperialism." In between, the Indian Mutiny provided groundsfor new heroic accounts in mid-Victorian Britain, with the military figures of Sir John Nicholson, John and Henry Lawrence, and, above all, Sir Henry Havelock elevated to mythic status.[1] Then Africa, by far the most mysterious continent (at least in European eyes) in the late nineteenth century, provided the appropriate mixture of remoteness, danger, and "savagery" to enhance the popular appeal of bold, daring, and dashing military heroes, or simple, altruistic, and exemplary religious figures. The scene was set for a new generation of national heroes involved in the exploration, conquest, or administration of Africa on behalf of the European powers.

In their attempt to carve out large shares of the African continent for their empires, advocates of British and French imperial expansion sought moral reasons to justify their endeavors. Ideas derived from Darwinian theories (especially Social Darwinism) were a convenient rationale, and European heroes who shone in Africa could be seen as embodying the racial superiority of their countrymen. Those who brought the Union Jack to remote places were cheered in Britain. In France, those few Frenchmen who unfolded the tricolor in the heart of swampy rain forests or inhospitable deserts became increasingly popular and contributed to an imperial mindset among a population that was initially reticent to indulge in overseas expansion. This was a time when red and pink surfaces, representing British and French colonies respectively, expanded quickly on European maps of Africa. Once back to their home countries (or after they had been killed in service overseas), these standard-bearers of the "civilizing mission" were widely celebrated. They gave rise to a series of cultural constructions that helped shape, but were also influenced by, the dominant beliefs and worldviews of the societies that engendered them. Their exemplarity was a potent justification for imperial development, further embodied their country's supposed genius, and set powerful precedents for self-sacrifice. They opened previously unknown horizons, paving the way for colonial expansion and making it more palatable to the metropolitan public.

Because they were used to promote a variety of ideals and causes—including the imperial one—in their motherlands, imperial heroes show how the colonial mission was perceived and projected as well as the sociocultural background against which it took shape in nineteenth-century Europe. The ways in which colonial heroes who acted in Africa were packaged for cultural consumption in Britain and in France reveal how those two countries conceptualized their imperial roles and the conditions in which they projected the "civilizing mission" that morally supported colonial expansion in Africa, at least in the eyes of the colonizers. The historical context and the social, cultural, technical, and commercial reasons that led to the successful development of legends attached to colonial heroes provide an insight into the *logistics of imperial heroism,* which goes a long way toward explaining the appearance of a new type of heroism in the mid to late nineteenth century, linked to the Scramble for Africa. Looking at the political use of imperial heroes explains why they could swiftly become household names at times of crisis, and what type of cause their fame tended to support. Other potential uses of heroic legends included the promotion of geographic knowledge, religious proselytism, and patriotic and nationalist feelings. Taken together, these uses exemplify the *politics of imperial heroism.* In spite of the multiple purposes that the fame of colonial heroes could serve, their commercial appeal remained perhaps their most important asset, since it enticed a variety of hero makers to promote the heroes' reputations in the hope of securing financial benefit: this was the *economics of imperial heroism.*

IN 1870, THE EUROPEAN PUBLIC barely knew about the interior of Africa, apart from explorers' accounts of limited availability. European control over most of the African landmass was either the result of a handful of "men on the spot" or the consequence of ministerial decisions: the public was rarely inquisitive about African questions and generally showed limited enthusiasm for the "Dark Continent"—apart from a few exceptional cases. Yet colonial expansion in Africa was about to go through a new phase as part of the New Imperialism, which took place a few decades after antislavery campaigns had led to the abolition of slavery in European colonies. As a result of this new wave of conquest, the situation was considerably different in the 1930s. African colonies had become popular, and immensely successful colonial exhibitions were organized or patronized by high-ranking colonial servants. Lord Lugard was involved in the organization of the Wembley show of 1924, while Marshal Lyautey presided over the Exposition coloniale internationale, held in the Bois de Vincennes in 1931. African colonies enhanced the metropolises' self-esteem, especially in France, where the African empire overtook Indochina in importance after the First World War. This change in perception was accompanied, and partly generated, by two generations of daring imperial heroes: David Livingstone (1813–73), General Charles George Gordon (1833–85), Henry Morton Stanley (1841–1904), Lord Horatio Herbert Kitchener (1850–1916), Cecil Rhodes (1853–1902), and Thomas Edward Lawrence (1888–1935) in Britain, and their French counterparts Cardinal Lavigerie (1825–92), Pierre Savorgnan de Brazza (1852–1905), Marshal Hubert Lyautey (1854–1934), Charles de Foucauld (1858–1916), General Henry Laperrine (1860–1920), and Captain Jean-Baptiste Marchand (1863–1934). Together, they changed how Britain and France envisaged their relationship with the African continent and its inhabitants.

The figure of the colonial hero did not appear from nowhere: it took shape against the changing cultural, political, and economic context of the Industrial Revolution. International politics help explain why this type of hero assumed primarily a military form. The century of peace on the European continent between the Treaty of Vienna and the First World War (with the notable exception of the Franco-Prussian War) meant that opportunities for military advancement or official rewards arose primarily overseas, and this at a time when the land available for conquest by European powers was shrinking. In the British case, this new role improved the standing of the army at home, where its image had badly suffered from its use to suppress domestic unrest throughout the first half of the nineteenth century. In France, the defeat by Prussia in 1870 meant that campaigns on the Continent remained out of the question until the French army could hope to resist the shock of a new confrontation east of the Vosges; colonial campaigns seemed, therefore, an attractive alternative for ambitious military commanders longing for better professional prospects than the routine of garrison life. Confronted with the absence of any major opportunity to lead European military campaigns, British and French officers found in overseas operations an opportunity to rise through the ranks and to secure official rewards. Elaborate systems of honors in Britain and France made colonial warfare the most promising prospect for ambitious officers, especially those who came from humble backgrounds. Although the Sirdar Kitchener did not come from the aristocracy, he died Earl Kitchener of Khartoum. Jean-Baptiste Marchand, the son of a carpenter in a remote village of Rhône-Alpes, joined the "elite of the living" (as General de Gaulle later called it) as a Chevalier de la Légion d'honneur at age twenty-six, and he was promoted to the rank of Commandeur only ten years later. There were good reasons to claim that imperial heroes quickly became "veritable walking Christmas trees of stars and collars, medals and sashes, ermine robes and coronets."[2]

This quick rise in official recognition was matched by a longer-term process of celebration, set in stone in the changing urban landscapes of both Europe and new overseas settlements. Steady population growth and urban expansion in Britain and France provided opportunities for christening new streets, squares, or official buildings after imperial heroes. There are still countless streets named after French imperial heroes in the capital and other French cities: no fewer than fifteen Rue Commandant Marchand, eleven Rue Lyautey and thirteen Avenue Lyautey, sixteen Rue Brazza and five Avenue Brazza, twenty-eight Rue Charles de Foucauld and two Avenue Charles de Foucauld. In Britain, in 1991, there were still seventy-one Gordon Roads in Greater London, twenty Gordon Streets in Greater Manchester, and Aldershot also celebrates its former military student with a Gordon Road. Other common celebrations in the public space included the naming of official buildings (see the Gordon Boys School in Woking and numerous French primary and secondary schools named after Brazza, Marchand, Lyautey, and Foucauld, among others) and the erection of statues in squares and parks. Overseas, opportunities to celebrate founding European heroes were even more numerous, since new colonial towns and cities were built either from scratch or alongside existing indigenous settlements, which were frequently stripped of their local toponyms. Some of these cities were named after imperial heroes: Brazzaville in the French Congo, Lyauteyville in Morocco, the Free Church of Scotland mission station of Livingstonia in what would become Nyasaland, and the Northern Rhodesian capital (until 1930), Livingstone. These names often appeared on maps shown to schoolchildren to teach them about the Empire and the world, ensuring the heroes an enduring fame among the population.

Colonial campaigns and the victories that often came with them, flattering public opinion and fueling feelings of superiority, created a celebratory mood that could prove politically useful. Successive reform bills in Britain between 1832 and 1884, and the establishment of universal male suffrage in France, first in 1848 and then as a cornerstone principle of the Third Republic, meant that public opinion became a more important factor than before: it deeply changed the political landscape of the two countries. Used adroitly, imperial heroes could help pro-imperial politicians win public support, which was a particularly difficult task in France, where Germanophobia could lead to a desire to appease England and, hence, a reluctance to expand the empire. Victorious imperial heroes offered a clear rebuttal to the arguments of Little Englanders or the opponents of Greater France.

The gradually increasing involvement of the population in the running of the country coincided with a significant improvement in literacy rates, which augmented the size of the educated population and amplified the impact of printed and written material. Successive governmental initiatives in France and England ensured that the overwhelming majority of the countries' populations were literate by 1900. Better-educated masses, higher wages (which increased spare income), and the appearance of clear patterns of division of labor (which increased workers' leisure time) created new markets for a variety of printed materials. Accounts cloaked in sensationalism, exoticism (or at least geographic discoveries), and the occasional bloodletting (which some imperial campaigns indulged in) attracted high levels of public interest. The legends surrounding imperial heroes reached wide audiences via unprecedented means of promotion driven by speed, efficiency, and cost-effectiveness. Particularly effective was the popular press—the penny press in Britain and the *presse à un sou* in France—which exploited lower costs associated with rotating presses, better distribution networks, and the gradual disappearance of stamp taxes. News agencies such as Havas or Reuters—or in the British case, the innovation of the war correspondent, which the telegraph had made more efficient— created new channels for disseminating information about imperial heroes. The frequent use of books as school prizes in a system of universal education had a similar effect. Last but not least, the widespread adoption of legal protections for copyright meant that biographers and journalists increasingly looked for topics that would sell well and generate royalties—and imperial heroes proved to be among them.

BECAUSE THE LEGENDS AROUND the figures of imperial heroes became in themselves themes of public interest, they could be used as a means of promoting a political vision, of advocating a policy in the ruling of state affairs, and even of enhancing the popularity of a party. Once they had reached the status of public figures, imperial heroes could play multiple roles on the political scene, depending on the place, time, and period. Over the years, four major types of political use can be distinguished.

The first type, the indirect promoter of expansion, slightly predates the period under consideration here. These were heroic figures like David Livingstone or Cardinal Lavigerie, who did not have a clear expansionist agenda and did not openly advocate European expansion, but whose actions (especially in relation to the fight against slavery or to proselytizing efforts) had the net effect of making European imperialism in Africa seem both desirable and humanitarian.

The second type is the direct promoter of expansion, whose action and popular fame directly fostered the conquest or annexation of African territory: this was the typical hero of the era of the New Imperialism. The Italian-born Pierre Savorgnan de Brazza offers a clear example. His expeditions to the Congo awakened public interest in this African region, and his charismatic figure, which appeared as a French competitor to that of his "Anglo-Saxon" rival, Henry Morton Stanley (which culminated in a confrontation between the two at the Paris Stanley Club on 20 October 1882), ensured that the French Parliament swiftly recognized the treaties of protectorate he had signed with the African king Makoko. Although he went far beyond his official remit when he concluded them, the hero's welcome he received each time he returned from Africa, and the press campaign that lionized him in France (in a consolatory effort after the French failure to act with the British in Egypt), made it impossible for the French government to disavow him: Brazza literally gave the colony of the Congo to his adoptive country. In Britain, the embodiment of the direct promoter of expansion was the magnate Cecil Rhodes, the great architect of British expansion in southern Africa and an active promoter of the idea of a British axis from the Cape to Cairo (which collided frontally with the dream of French imperialists, from Dakar to Djibouti).

Third is the imperial hero used as political argument, in which the reputation of a colonial figure was used to whip up public opinion to support or undermine a government. The New Imperialism took off at the same time as the New Journalism acquired its key features, notably under the impulse of W. T. Stead at the *Pall Mall Gazette*. By stressing the distinctive personal qualities of a person (especially through the unprecedented practice of the interview), Stead and the advocates of the New Journalism shifted the emphasis of the press toward the (preferably exceptional) individual, potentially increasing his or her value as a political argument. It is significant that the New Journalism advocated the advent of "government by journalism." A classic case in point was that of General Charles Gordon in the mid-1880s. Stead's influence was key in reshaping the already famous figure of "Chinese Gordon" into "Gordon of Khartoum": his 10 January 1884 interview, entitled "Chinese Gordon on the Soudan," had such a popular resonance that it forced a reluctant Gladstone to dispatch Gordon to Khartoum, bowing to public opinion in spite of his own reservations, which were not unfounded, as the following months showed. Gordon's tragic end in Khartoum was subsequently used by the Tory opposition, and especially Lord Salisbury, to attack the Gladstone government and heap discredit on the Prime Minister: for many, the "G.O.M." ("Grand Old Man") had become "M.O.G." ("Murderer of Gordon") in a matter of months, and Gladstone paid a high political price for it.[3] The popularity of Captain Jean-Baptiste Marchand upon his return to France in May 1899, when he was celebrated as a national hero who had been betrayed by politicians of the Third Republic (an appraisal that tended to ignore the actual balance of power between Britain and France), stirred considerable interest among anti-Dreyfusards and had the potential to turn him into a major political figure, had he wished to be one. He was seen among nationalist and monarchist circles as the next Paul Déroulède, someone whose exploits in the tropics could be used to overthrow the Republic, and his reluctance to be involved in such a scheme explains in large part why that plan never materialized.

The fourth type of political influence that imperial heroes could exert reflected how the colonial project had become a core expression of national interests. In stark contrast with the early years of imperial heroism, when celebrated figures tended to appear as mavericks who stood on the margins of society and seemed to overstretch the boundaries of the national project, the proconsul turned hero embodied the shift from conquest to administration. In the case of the British Empire, Horatio Herbert Kitchener epitomized this type: the "Sudan Machine" (as George Warrington Steevens called him in *With Kitchener to Khartum* [1898]) became a national hero as the architect of the "reconquest" of the Sudan and the founder of modern Anglo-Egyptian Sudan. In France, Marshal Hubert Lyautey reflected upon the position of the military in articles and books such as "On the Social Role of the Officer" (1891) and *The Colonial Role of the Army* (1900) and above all contributed to the French conquest of Madagascar (under Gallieni's orders) and engineered the French protectorate over Morocco in his capacity as resident general between 1912 and 1925.

Imperial heroes were at the heart of the action, and in most cases, they had a direct or indirect political impact on their homelands. Far from being removed from the realities that their countries were facing, they were deeply connected with them, and their direct action, exemplarity, or symbolic value made them public figures with a clear political meaning that, at times, they invested themselves with or that, at other times, was invested upon them.

IN THE SECOND HALF OF THE nineteenth century, the heroes of the exploration of Africa fueled a widespread interest in scientific knowledge, and trust in its beneficial impact on human society, that geographically minded circles tried to promote throughout Europe. These figures became household names because they enjoyed the support of a wide range of national and regional geographic societies that did their best to turn them into living proof of the relevance of the new way of understanding the world that they represented. Yet at the same time, it can be argued that their success reflected the fascination of geography-related topics in European societies hungry for new scientific knowledge. Relations of causality were reciprocal: growing popular interest in geography made imperial heroes attractive public figures, while the heroes' widely publicized successes contributed to the success of geography. Britain and France presented a similar outlook in this respect, each with an early initiative based in the capital (the Société de Géographie in 1821 in Paris and the Royal Geographical Society in 1830 in London), followed by a steady development of regional branches. If the most prestigious incentives came from the national society (expedition support, guest conferences, medals, etc.), conferences at regional societies ensured that the legends of imperial exploration had nationwide resonance.

The exemplarity of imperial heroes went far beyond demonstrating the relevance of science: their tales of courage, endurance, and dexterity in the face of adversity could serve many more purposes in societies with contradictory aspirations, believing on the one hand in European technical superiority and the universality of Western principles, but facing on the other hand, at times, religious uncertainty (resulting from rapid industrialization in Britain and the secularization of the Third Republic in France) and, in the French case, the fear of national decline. Resorting to history and referring to outstanding shapers of the national historical narrative are common reactions for societies faced with an uncertain future, and it is not surprising that Frenchmen who worried about their nation recalled Cicero's concept of *historia est magistra vitae* (history is life's teacher): the edifying power of history and the exemplarity of great men in history could serve as powerful examples and stimuli for a population fearful of decline. Léon Poirier claimed that through his film on Charles de Foucauld, he wanted to "redress the country through the redressing of minds."[4] In the British case, Thomas Carlyle's highly influential lectures collected as *On Heroes, Hero-Worship, and the Heroic in History* (1841), as well as the Victorian fascination with great men past and present, made imperial legends a distinctive feature of a society prone to hero worship. For the Whig interpretation of history, which emphasized the British fight for the triumph of liberal ideas, imperial heroes offered a vivid demonstration of the expansion of Western values and standards through application of the universal rule of law.

Imperial heroes could appeal to a variety of constituencies, depending on which aspect of their lives was being celebrated. In the 1870s, stories about heroes of the British and French empires tended to justify the desirability of overseas territorial expansion, but after the First World War, the same heroes were transformed into trailblazers who had shored up the foundations of glorious empires, which were now needed to support reconstruction efforts. Until the Entente Cordiale, imperial heroes were often featured in Anglophobic and nationalistic French material, but once the two countries reached a rapprochement, the same heroes became models of civilized relations governed by the rules of fair play, men who knew how to avoid full-fledged conflict between their countries in spite of their rivalries. Throughout the period, they epitomized the triumph of the white man over the indigenous population. Militarily or morally superior to the Africans whom he met, the imperial hero displayed qualities that the colonized could only aspire to: leadership, probity, knowledge, organizational skill, and moral or physical strength (which oftentimes meant sexual restraint when faced with the temptations of the Dark Continent). In a word, he embodied the benefits of civilization, which its European promoters used as a heartfelt reason, or a convenient excuse, for the cause of empire.

Religious exemplarity could be a potent rationale for promoting the memory of some imperial heroes. The consensual figure of David Livingstone emerged in an Anglican country whose Protestant missions had been a feature of national imperial activity for centuries. Because of his relentless struggle against the slave trade, but also thanks to the numerous boosters who promoted his image in Britain and abroad (including the famous publicity coup staged by Henry Morton Stanley and the *New York Herald* in the early 1870s), Livingstone epitomized the selfless religious figure who struggled for the salvation of African souls (a narrative that tended to overlook the fact that his only convert was an African chief). General Gordon, whose death in Khartoum at the hands of the Mahdi's warriors was presented as a personal, religious, and national sacrifice, was often described as the prototype of a modern Christian knight, and his death was portrayed in almost mystical terms as "a victory of the soul," with a clear religious meaning.[5] In France, the gradual secularization of the Third Republic fragmented the potential public for religious colonial heroes and made them more complex and controversial. The figure of Charles de Foucauld, dubbed "the hermit of the Sahara" or "the apostle of the Tuaregs," appealed primarily to devout Catholics.[6] Cardinal Lavigerie was celebrated as a dedicated participant in the antislavery struggle (a crusade that crossed party lines), while his efforts to spread Catholicism in Africa (especially through the Missionary Brothers and Sisters of Our Lady of Africa, which he founded) made him also a respected Christian leader. His call to French Catholics to rally to the Republic (the toast of Algiers, 1890) made him a unifying figure who demonstrated the multifaceted uses that could be made of heroic reputations.

The age of the New Imperialism was also the age of nationalisms, and the patriotic value of imperial heroes was a universal feature on both sides of the Channel. Regardless of when they were celebrated, their assimilation into a pantheon of national heroes was inevitable. In the eyes of those who promoted them, they embodied the best the nation had to offer, not only for its own domestic consumption and projection to competing countries, but also as a legacy to the next generations. Their deeds were always interpreted within the framework of a national narrative to which their actions were meant to contribute openly or indirectly. Regardless of whether their exploits consisted of exploring new lands, adding new colonies to the empire, defending "civilization" against "barbarity," or spreading Christianity, the benefit for national self-esteem was never questioned. Jules Ferry once confided that Brazza (although not French by birth) had been "entrusted with something of the national honor,"[7] and Cecil Rhodes's hagiographers argued that the architect of British colonialism in southern Africa had been "selfless, driven by a sense of duty and service towards Britain."[8]

LIKELY TO BE GRANTED SUCH versatile meanings, and enjoying the appeal associated with the unknown, which had been carefully cultivated among the public throughout the nineteenth century, imperial heroes had the potential to be used commercially, especially if they displayed the panache necessary to captivate audiences. The economics of imperial heroes helps explain the resilience of the legends attached to heroic figures of the British and French empires. The sustained level of promotion lavished on imperial heroes throughout the period, whether through engravings prominently featured in newspapers or their Sunday supplements, biographies or other forms of memorabilia, or popular exhibitions (which all came in addition to more traditional ways of celebrating heroes, such as war paintings), was made possible only because there were markets to absorb such goods.

Commercial interest in national heroes was not a new phenomenon: Captain Cook's voyages in the eighteenth century have been described as "a literary eldorado."[9] Once interest in the Pacific subsided, Africa became the new El Dorado, which ambitious journalists like Stanley used to promote their skills and make money. From the perspective of an author in search of a commercially interesting subject, the figure of the imperial hero provided an ideal intermediary between European readers and the exotic African context: someone who would reflect well on the racial assumptions of the time and who would also provide a clear narrative thread. This approach was perfectly compatible with that of pro-colonial propagandists, for whom imperial heroes were an easy way of captivating the public's attention and attracting it to their cause. Print-run figures of major French publishing houses show a clear difference in the commercial reception of books dealing with African territories from a descriptive angle and those telling stories of imperial heroes: the former reached sales figures in the hundreds, but the latter could easily sell in the thousands.[10] Opportunistic serialized publications could also be snapped up by the public: distribution figures show that French bookshops received in total 75,700 booklets of the twenty-eight-volume biographical series on the Marchand mission produced by the nationalist writer Michel Morphy between February 1900 and June 1901. In Britain, a similar phenomenon occurred, but on a far larger scale, a discrepancy that can be explained by the earlier development of a mass market for written products and better coordination between the popular press and publishing markets. The Edinburgh-based publisher Blackwood sold many more copies of G. W. Steevens's *With Kitchener to Khartum* (1898; 236,762 copies within a year and a half of its publication) than it did of John Speke's *Journal of the Discovery of the Source of the Nile* (1863; 10,379 copies sold in the first two years) or James Augustus Grant's *Khartoom as I Saw It* (1885, 1,790 copies sold in total).[11] But Steevens had the same sort of dismal sales when he wrote geographically based books: a few months before *With Kitchener to Khartum,* he had managed to sell only around 900 copies of his book *Egypt in 1898,* in spite of his being a war correspondent for the *Daily Mail.* Books about imperial heroes could genuinely enhance the financial prospects of those who were involved in their production: for instance, *With Kitchener to Khartum* generated for its publisher an overall profit of £6,785 (the equivalent of £550,000 in 2002), and Steevens's royalties proved to be in excess of £2,000 (£165,000 in 2002).

Rich in media inventions, the period under consideration witnessed the extension of the commercial appeal of imperial heroes to new products. Advertising strategies occasionally relied on a heroic figure who had shone in Africa. The Société Continentale du Cosmydor, based in the outskirts of Paris, produced a soap called "Savon des explorateurs," explicitly referring to Brazza, while in the First World War, the pointing finger of the "hero of Omdurman" was used to recruit the volunteers who formed the "Kitchener armies."[12] By making full use of the evocative power of photography, the lectures of the American journalist Lowell Thomas (illustrated with material produced by his photographer, Harry Chase) launched the legend of the "Uncrowned King of Arabia" around the figure of T. E. Lawrence.[13] While making "art and money with films, books and lectures," Thomas popularized a new hero, who would be remembered as "Lawrence of Arabia."[14] Commercial interest also led to the dramatization of heroic legends in films. The gradual evolution of the cinema toward sophisticated forms of storytelling offered new commercial opportunities for imperial heroes as well as the prospect of a high financial return for this money-hungry industry. The cinema was a powerful means of transmitting vivid depictions of heroic legends to new generations. Hero-actors were seen "in action," exploring exotic lands, leading their men, or conquering souls; despite the obvious artifice, the events shown in films appeared real to the audience and provided gripping tales of what was considered a recent but already extinct heroic period. Filmmakers were quick to use the powerful resources of this new medium to launch highly successful productions: Marmaduke A. Wetherell's *Livingstone* was released in 1925, Berthold Vierthel's *Rhodes of Africa* (starring Walter Huston as Rhodes) in 1936, and Henry King's *Stanley and Livingstone* in 1939. In France, Léon Poirier, the filmmaker behind one of the most famous celebrations of the Verdun battlefields in the interwar period (*Verdun, Visions d'histoire*, 1928), embarked on a mission to promote the empire to the French public, an effort that proved remarkably successful: first as the director of the filmic account of André Citroën's *croisière noire* ("black journey," a motorized expedition across Africa in 1924–5), and then as the producer and director of *Charles de Foucauld ou l'Appel du Silence* (1936) and *Savorgnan de Brazza ou l'épopée du Congo* (1939), films that presented highly emotional evocations of two major colonial heroes. Although the making of *L'Appel du Silence* had been difficult to fund, its subject and pro-imperial stance were particularly popular. Awarded the Grand Prix du Cinéma français for 1936, the film (one of the first to be shot on location rather than in studios) was one of the blockbusters of the year, with ten million viewers in eight months.[15] A book with photographs of the film was widely bought, with at least 110,000 copies sold in its first three years.[16] The combination of new hero-making techniques (such as Thomas's slide shows or Poirier's films) and old ones (books, articles in the press) often reinforced sensationalistic treatments of deeds undertaken in exotic contexts, thereby giving a new lease on life to the reputations of imperial heroes in the interwar years. A favorable market reception seems to be the best insurance against oblivion.

LOOKING AT THE GENESIS, DEVELOPMENT, and afterlife of several heroic reputations linked to the expansion of Britain and France in Africa, and at the conditions that made their popular success possible, reveals complex hero-making processes that were facilitated by the sociocultural developments of the Industrial Revolution but also relied heavily on political circumstances and commercial interest. The legends attached to imperial heroes did not arise spontaneously, but were mediated by a variety of promotional materials that obeyed the laws of the market and conveyed messages of political or symbolic relevance to society. Authors, biographers, journalists, war artists, and filmmakers consciously contributed to the manufacturing of these reputations, acting as hero makers for their own professional and financial benefit. Yet they were not the only ones involved in these promotional processes. Because these legends had an exemplary value and could be used to further a variety of causes, such as imperial aggrandizement or religious penetration in Africa, they were also of interest to indirect hero makers: politicians, lobbyists, and the leaders of professional or charitable organizations could find in them an attractive way of furthering their causes.

Although imperial heroes were products of their epoch, the long-lasting fascination they have provoked explains why they do not seem to have entirely lost their relevance in the post-colonial world. Most of them still inspire sustained public interest in the former metropoles (as subjects of popular biographies or documentaries), and a few of those whose views were liberal enough to allow them to be included in the post-independence national pantheons are remembered to this day in Africa. The Congolese state, which has no national museum, has chosen to erect a modern mausoleum to Brazza's memory, designed to celebrate the explorer as the founder of the modern nation of the Republic of the Congo (revealingly, the capital city has retained its colonial name when so many others elsewhere on the continent have changed theirs). Livingstone has remained to this date an important Zambian city, and Malawi's commercial center (and second-largest city), Blantyre, is still named after the birthplace of the nineteenth-century Scottish explorer. Some would argue that such continuations represent the conversion of the New Imperialism into neo-colonialism, while others are inclined to see in this enduring celebration a proof of certain imperial heroes' persisting appeal across cultural and historical boundaries. Beyond any ideological judgment, the numerous websites that refer to these heroes testify that they have successfully passed the test of a new technological revolution. Given their precedents in this domain, it hardly comes as a surprise.

Spring Semester 2010

1. J. M. MacKenzie, "Heroic Myths of Empire," in J. M. MacKenzie (ed.), *Popular Imperialism and the Military* (Manchester, 1992), pp. 109–38.

2. D. Cannadine, *Ornamentalism: How the British Saw Their Empire* (London, 2001), p. 95.

3. "Anecdotes about the Sudan," Baily Papers, Sudan Archive, Durham University, 533/4/29–30.

4. L. Poirier, *Pourquoi et comment je vais réaliser "L'Appel du silence"* (Paris, 1935), opening citation.

5. C. M. Yonge, *Westminster Reading Books* (London, 1890), Vol. VI, p. 255.

6. C. de Foucauld, *Ecrits spirituels de Charles de Foucauld, Ermite au Sahara, Apôtre des Touaregs* (Paris, 1930), with a foreword by R. Bazin.

7. Quoted in I. Dion, *Pierre Savorgnan de Brazza, au cœur du Congo* (Marseille, 2007), p. 130.

8. P. Maylam, *The Cult of Rhodes* (Claremont, South Africa, 2005), pp. 4–6.

9. P. Langford, *A Polite and Commercial People: England, 1727–1783* (Oxford, 1989), p. 512.

10. Sales figures for French publications are taken from the Hachette Papers, Institut mémoires de l'édition contemporaine, Paris.

11. Sales figures for British publications are taken from the Blackwood Papers, National Library of Scotland, Edinburgh.

12. K. Surridge, "More than a Great Poster: Lord Kitchener and the Image of the Military Hero," *Historical Research*, 74, 185 (August 2001), pp. 298–313.

13. L. Thomas, *With Lawrence in Arabia* (London, 1921).

14. H. Reeves, "This is Cinerama," *Film History*, 11, 1 (1999), pp. 85–97.

15. P. Boulanger, *Le Cinéma colonial de "L'Atlantide" à "Lawrence d'Arabie"* (Paris, 1975), p. 123.

16. L. Poirier, *Charles de Foucauld et l'Appel du Silence* (Paris, 1936 [1939]). A copy of this volume (in the private collection of the author) states on the title page "110e mille" (110th thousand).

4

Henry James and British Power

PRISCILLA ROBERTS

The transatlantic novelist Henry James, who settled in Britain from the late 1870s onward, returning to the United States only for visits from then until his death, was both the most prominent transplanted American writer of the late nineteenth and early twentieth centuries and the foremost exponent of what he termed the "international theme." He first made his name during the late 1870s and early 1880s with novels and stories dealing with the relationship between Europe and the United States, returning to this subject twenty years later in his final completed novels. The comparison, implicit or explicit, of the inhabitants of the two continents, especially their elites, was—along with the egotistic demands that art makes of its practitioners and that they, in turn, are willing to impose upon others—a defining theme in James's work.

James is often interpreted, somewhat simplistically, as a writer who juxtaposed innocent and vulnerable Americans with scheming, predatory Europeans who come out victorious in material terms, leaving the Americans morally superior. This is undoubtedly too straightforward an interpretation of a complex writer who, according to his niece, once said: "I hate American simplicity. I glory in the piling up of complications of every sort."[1] Arguably, however, several, though far from all, of his earlier novels and stories can be viewed as accounts of untutored Americans dealing—or failing to cope—with the wiles of far more sophisticated Europeans or Europeanized Americans and frequently coming off worse. Over time,

James's treatment of the international theme changed dramatically, apparently mirroring contemporaneous alterations in the balance of power between the United States and Europe. In his final novels, the Americans largely emerge victorious over less powerful Europeans.

James is usually perceived as a nonpolitical writer, one who focused exclusively upon intricate personal relationships among rarefied American and European elites while offering little broader social or diplomatic commentary. In reality, he possessed very keen political antennae. His correspondence and other writings reveal how attentively he scrutinized British and European imperial affairs and the impact of rising U.S. power internationally. James came from one of those well-to-do, patrician American families that spent extended periods of time in Europe—those of Edith Wharton and Theodore Roosevelt furnish other examples—often feeling more comfortable there than in their native land. As an expatriate, James became a European landmark for those elite Americans who crossed the Atlantic in increasing numbers for pleasure, to pursue literature or art, on business, or as diplomats. In London, he moved in top British circles, dining out with leading political, social, and cultural figures and spending weekends in their country houses. From this ringside seat, James observed almost obsessively both the gradual intermingling through marriage of American and British high society and the slow erosion of Britain's imperial dominance.

The latter was not something James necessarily welcomed. Like many patrician northeastern Americans, James consistently supported close Anglo-American ties, in something approximating an international alliance. In 1888, he told his brother William: "I can't look at the English & American worlds, or feel about them, any more, save as a big AngloSaxon total, destined to such an amount of melting together that an insistence on their differences becomes more & more idle & pedantic."[2] William, who had previously stated that "England is the only *really* civilized country in Europe," replied: "Of course I say amen to all you write about the needlessness of [a chasm] between us and the English."[3] Yet as early as 1876, British reluctance to support the Bulgarian revolt for independence from Ottoman rule caused Henry to fear that if England did "not fight, before long, for some one or something, I am afraid we can order our mourning for English glory." His consolation was that "this will make it a very interesting time to be in London; & if the 'Decadence of England' has really set in, the breaking-up will be a big spectacle—may I be there to see!"[4] Discussing Britain's disinclination for war, in early 1878 Henry presciently predicted:

She will push further & further her non-fighting & keeping-out-of-scrapes-policy, until contemptuous Europe, growing audacious with impunity, shall put upon her some supreme & unendurable affront. Then—too late—she will rise ferociously & plunge clumsily & unpreparedly into war. She will be worsted & laid on her back—& when she is laid on her back will exhibit—in her colossal wealth & pluck—an unprecedented power of resistance. But she will never really recover, as a European power.[5]

Even as he followed the intricacies of international politics, James used the contrast between the United States and Europe as the theme for several of his earliest literary successes, including *Roderick Hudson, The American, Daisy Miller, The Europeans,* and *The Portrait of a Lady.* All explored the relations between Europeans and Americans as played out in the social, sexual, and financial bargains they struck with each other. The hero of *Roderick Hudson* (1875) is a young sculptor from upstate New York whom the patronage of a wealthy older American man enables to study art in Italy. There he becomes besotted with a beautiful young expatriate American woman, Christina Light, whom the reader eventually learns is illegitimate and half-Italian. When she rejects Hudson to marry a wealthy Italian nobleman, the young artist flees to the mountains, where he either kills himself or suffers a fatal accident. The novel, written before James moved to Europe, could be read as a cautionary tale of the dangers an American artist might encounter in abandoning his own country.

James's next novel, *The American* (1877), juxtaposed even more starkly New World innocence and European wiles. Christopher Newman, a Civil War veteran who has made a fortune in business, comes to Europe seeking a wife who will represent some kind of paragon. Through mutual friends, he meets the widowed Comtesse Claire de Cintré, a charming, cultivated, and devout French noblewoman whose family, the Bellegardes, endorse his suit despite his being "only" an American. When a more appropriate British candidate for her hand appears, her mother and elder brother change their minds and pressure her to end the engagement. She does so, but only to enter a Carmelite convent. Through an old servant, Newman learns that in the past, the mother and elder brother murdered the mother's husband, Claire de Cintré's father, information he might be able to use to pressure them to withdraw their opposition to his marriage or, alternatively, to wreak social disgrace upon them. Eventually, he chooses not to do so and burns his evidence of their crime. The somewhat melodramatic plot was not entirely credible. In this novel's preface, James later admitted that, should a "rich and easy American" suitor for one of their daughters materialize, far from driving him away, most French noble families of the time would "positively have jumped" at him. But in James's novel, Newman went away alone and disappointed.

James's first great success, which made him something of a household name, was the novella *Daisy Miller* (1878), its heroine a young, beautiful, and unsophisticated American girl of nouveau riche antecedents, untutored in polite social behavior. Her overly familiar association with Italian admirers in Rome scandalizes expatriate American society there. On an imprudent, unchaperoned nocturnal visit with an Italian male friend to the ruined Colosseum, she catches malaria, of which she dies. This short tale provoked intense journalistic discussion of the accuracy of James's portrayal of young American women and whether these self-confident, wealthy, and outgoing girls with so little respect for established social conventions and mores were a credit or disgrace to their country. At the novella's end, the reader learns that Daisy, who "did what she liked," was nonetheless "the most innocent" young lady her Italian would-be suitor had ever encountered. The chilling, implicit message was that the reward of innocence could be not just unkind gossip but death.

Another relatively short novel James published almost simultaneously, *The Europeans* (1878), took a more lighthearted approach. A half-American brother and sister, Felix Young and the Baroness Eugenia Münster, born and raised in Europe, have fallen on hard times, and so decide to visit their prosperous New England relatives. Felix, a competent artist and born survivor, justifies his name, adapting happily to his new family and marrying Gertrude, a previously discontented female cousin. The baroness, morganatically espoused to the younger brother of a minor German princeling, wishes her to divorce her husband but is less successful in making a new life. One wealthy, cultivated, and reasonably sophisticated neighbor is attracted by her but has second thoughts when he detects her in a social lie. Eventually, Eugenia decides to continue her existing marital arrangements, however problematic, and returns to the petty European court where she belongs. In two other benignly comic stories James published, *An International Episode* (1878) and *Pandora* (1884), wealthy American girls reject the attentions of a British duke and a German diplomat, preferring their own countrymen.

James's most extensive early exploration of American-European relationships was *The Portrait of a Lady* (1881), featuring many of his most vivid characters to date. One trigger for this novel was the illness and death of his youthful cousin Minny Temple, a girl whose great appetite for life was never fulfilled; James imaginatively recreated her as the orphaned Isabel Archer. Taken up by a long-estranged aunt, the wife of an American banker long resident in Britain, Isabel travels to England, eager to make the most of the new experiences open to her. The opposite sex apparently finds her irresistible. For many years, the American businessman Caspar Goodwood, the wealthy and enlightened British peer and politician Lord Warburton, and her ailing cousin Ralph Touchett remain in her thrall, revolving in her orbit. She rejects all three to choose disaster. At her cousin's urging, Isabel's uncle leaves her a fortune, which makes her the target of a pair of ruthless but impoverished former lovers, Gilbert Osmond, whom Isabel marries, and Madame Merle, the secret mother of Pansy, supposedly Osmond's daughter by his dead wife. The marriage quickly becomes most unhappy, and eventually Isabel discovers that it was engineered by Madame Merle, who wished to give Pansy a wealthy and kind stepmother and the ensuing social advantages. The end of the novel leaves Isabel's next move uncertain. Her story is one of enormous charm, vitality, and naïve overconfidence bringing catastrophe in their wake. An inherent theme is just how dangerous wealth can be to the possessor. The money inherited from her uncle, because her cousin wished to see what she would make of life given the means to explore its opportunities fully, proves her greatest curse of all, attracting two unscrupulous fortune hunters whose only real interest in Isabel is for financial and personal exploitation.

In James's early novels, "European" can be a rather elastic term, embracing not just half-European individuals such as Christina, Felix, and Eugenia, but even American expatriates long resident in Europe. For villainy, Osmond and Madame Merle are the foremost examples, two confederates who care only for appearances and social and financial advantage, who have internalized the worst of European norms and cold-bloodedly exploit all around them. Even their love for Pansy, their daughter, demands that she obey them and make a socially prominent marriage, whatever her own wishes. Ironically, among the book's more pleasant characters is an authentic European, the genial, conscientious Lord Warburton. Implicitly, several of James's early novels suggest that while Europeans may be corrupt and evil, transplanted Americans who have spent many years in Europe can be just as bad, even worse. When portraying such characters, the younger James, who probably socialized with American expatriates as much as with genuine Europeans during his early European travels, conceivably had few authentic models to draw upon, so stuck to what he knew. Equally, however, they may have illustrated his own private fears over the potential long-term impact on himself of moving permanently across the Atlantic. His novels portray at least one devastating, hybrid, deracinated figure, Christina Light, half–expatriate American, half-European, who re-appears in a later incarnation as the Princess Casamassima. In the eponymous novel, she leaves a trail of destruction and wrecked lives behind her, taking up and dropping causes and men alike, includ-ing her besotted husband and the hypnotized bookbinder Hyacinth Robinson, who commits suicide at the story's end. Only the commit-ted revolutionary Paul Muniment, who bluntly tells the princess that it is her money, not herself, he and other revolutionaries find useful, is immune to the havoc surrounding her.

More than any other of his novels, *The Princess Casamassima* (1886) reflects contemporary events. James was again contemplating the possibility of British decline, telling an American friend, "the country is gloomy, anxious, and London reflects its gloom." Terrorism was on the rise—"Westminster Hall and the Tower were half blown up two days ago by Irish Dynamiters"—and there were fears for the safety of a British force in the Sudan, "and a general sense of rocks ahead" internationally. Again, James somewhat voyeuristically confessed:

> I can imagine no spectacle more touching, more thrilling and even dramatic, than to see this great precarious, artificial empire, on behalf of which, nevertheless, so much of the strongest and finest stuff of the greatest race (for such they are) has been ex-pended, struggling with forces which, perhaps, in the long run will prove too many for it. If she only will struggle, and not collapse and surrender, and give up a part, which, looking at Europe as it is to-day, still may be great, the drama will be well worth watching from such a good, near standpoint as I have here.[6]

As trouble with Russia intensified, James warned Grace Norton in Boston: "England is distinctly breaking down, and her loss of room in the world will be proportionate. . . . The truth is the British Em-pire isn't what it was, and will be still less so."[7] James was also uncom-fortably conscious of the rising power and ambitions of Germany and its "bull-necked military," telling a British friend in 1890 that "the Germans . . . are somehow not in my line. . . . They are ugly and mighty—they have (I think) lots of future, but a most intolerable present."[8]

FOR TWENTY YEARS AFTER 1883, although absent from his native land, James was, as he told his brother, "by no means cut off from getting American impressions here" in Britain.[9] He followed Ameri-can domestic and international policies closely, not least through his extensive correspondence with William. In imagination, James saw: "The Americans looming up—dim, vast, portentous—in their millions—like gathering waves—the barbarians of the Roman Empire."[10] These were prescient words. James was highly conscious of America's growing international power. In July 1895, during a boundary dispute between Venezuela and the colony of British Guiana, U.S. Secretary of State Richard Olney issued a strongly worded public message urging Britain to submit the dispute to arbitration by a boundary commission. In December of that year, President Cleveland unilaterally created a boundary commission to investigate the dispute. American nationalists praised their government's stance, which caused both James brothers great consternation, since this seemed to threaten war between Britain and the United States. Henry lamented to William that "one must hope that sanity and civilization, in both countries, will prevail."[11] He was much alarmed, however, by "the quantity of resident Anglophobia in the U.S.—the absolute war hunger as against this country."[12] Meanwhile, he told an American friend, the crisis had "darkened all my sky—and made me feel, among many things, how long I have lived away from my native land, how long I *shall* (D.V.) [*Deo volente*, that is, God willing] live away from it and how little I understand it today."[13]

Soon afterward, the two former antagonists were largely reconciled, with Britain tacitly supporting the United States as the latter went to war with Spain over Cuba in the spring of 1898, in the process acquiring the Philippine Islands, another Spanish colony. Henry and William James both initially deplored American intervention against Spain, and William became an ardent public opponent of the war and the subsequent American annexation of the Philippines. Publicly, Henry remained silent, but privately he told his friend Henrietta Reubell: "The misrule, the cruelty of Spain *is* hideous; but it's none of our business. . . . Cuba will be an immeasurable curse to us."[14] He did, however, find "a certain comfort" in Britain's pro-American stance.[15] Once Spain was defeated, it became increasingly clear that the United States government intended to retain the Philippines and suppress native Filipino resistance, developments both brothers deplored. At Christmas 1898, when British public opinion was generally urging the United States to be far more active in world affairs, Henry told a Bostonian friend: "It's strange the consciousness possible to an American here today, of being in a country in which the drift of desire—so far as it concerns itself with the matter—is that we *shall* swell and swell, and acquire and *require*, to the top of our opportunity." This prospect aroused mixed emotions in James, who felt "that we have not been good enough

for our opportunity—vulgar, in a manner, as that was and is, but
that it may be the real message of the whole business to make us
as much better as the great grabbed-up British Empire has, unmis-
takeably, made the English."[16] He applauded William's "admirable
eloquence" in opposing American annexation of the Philippines.[17]
In June 1899, he told William that "we have ceased to be, among the
big nations, the one great thing that made up for our so many cru-
dities, & made us above all superior & unique—the only one with
clean hands & no record of across-the-seas murder & theft."[18]

Henry remained broadly supportive of British imperialism, in
October 1898 hailing British successes in the Sudan, where "the
Dervishes are, I believe, bloody demons."[19] Even so, the outbreak of
the Boer War depressed him, and he thought it "a nightmare."[20] To
his brother, Henry stated: "There is something sinister in this S.A.
[South African] disaster—so *big* a surrender. . . . But such things
make me very British, & I cultivate the British faith."[21] Henry identified so strongly with his adopted country that he felt he had no alternative but to support the British cause. As 1900 began, he nonetheless found "nothing cheerful to talk of," since "South Africa darkens
all our sky here, and I gloom and brood and have craven questions
of 'Finis Britanniae?' in solitude."[22] However gloomy the news, he
nonetheless believed that Britain was resolved to win, and "the nation has taken up the job only to *do* it & *will* do it (won't be deterred
by anything of the like of what has *yet* happened,) before they'll give
up. In fact giving-up has now got to seem quite like chucking up the
very sponge of the B.E. [British Empire]—& that feeling will, *can*,
grow, only, & will be the thing that will see the country through."[23]

A year later, James perceived the death of Queen Victoria as
marking the end of an epoch, perhaps symbolizing the British
Empire's growing weakness. He feared "consequences in and for
this country that no man can foresee." Grimly, James opined that
"the Queen's magnificent duration has held things magnificently—
beneficently—together and prevented all sorts of accidents. Her
death, in short, will let loose incalculable forces for possible ill. I am
very pessimistic."[24] After watching "the dear old Queen's funeral"
procession, James was slightly more optimistic. With relief, he noted
that British views of Kaiser Wilhelm II of Germany had improved
dramatically after his devoted attendance at the Queen's deathbed,
where "she died in his arms."[25] James hoped that this marked an
end to mounting Anglo-German antagonism.

AGAINST THIS BACKGROUND of international turbulence, with ever-
more assertive U.S. overseas policies, sharpening Great Power rival-

ries, and vastly enhanced American wealth, James returned once more in the new century to his international theme, producing his last three major novels, *The Ambassadors* (1903), *The Wings of the Dove* (1902), and *The Golden Bowl* (1904), the first in fact written, though not published, before the second. Taken together, they were an effort to reprise the theme James had made his own a quarter century earlier. The story they told, however, was very different, with wealthy and powerful Americans capably holding their own against and even exploiting those Europeans who once had the upper hand. At a relatively comic level, this was a subplot in his short 1897 novel *What Maisie Knew,* an otherwise rather grim account of a small girl's travails following the divorce of her spectacularly handsome, totally self-absorbed, aristocratic British parents. As his finances and second marriage deteriorate, a flamboyantly showy "brown lady"—a wealthy American "countess" of, James strongly hints, predominantly Native American or African American ancestry—effectively appropriates Maisie's father. Reversing older patterns of colonization, this variation on Pocahontas, a "short fat wheedling whiskered person" who strikes Maisie "more as an animal than as a 'real' lady," with "a nose that was far too big and eyes that were far too small and a moustache," triumphantly bears off her masculine trophy.[26]

Not until 1904 would James revisit the United States, on a lengthy sojourn during which he traveled extensively through his native land, producing a nonfictional account of his experiences. By then, James had already completed all three final major novels. Despite earlier misgivings that he had lost touch with the United States, in the early 1900s he gained the confidence to reassess imaginatively and at length his international theme. For each novel, the germ of the story was an idea he had incubated for several years, but in the final version, James added an American-European dimension missing from his original scenario. Given James's strong interest in international developments, which intensified during the crises of the previous decade, one is driven to believe that the tough American protagonists to some degree reflected not just James's personal observations of those Americans he encountered on their visits to Europe, but also their country's new assertiveness on the world stage.

The plot of *The Ambassadors* centers upon a classic situation, the inexperienced American young man who journeys abroad and falls victim to a foreign adventuress. The male protagonist is Chad Newsome, only son of a domineering New England widow, who expects him to take over the family business in due course. As the novel opens Chad, now twenty-eight, has been absent in France for three years. His mother, anxious that he return to exploit an urgent and potentially lucrative business development, dispatches her own fiancé, Lambert Strether, to persuade her son to come home. Strether initially accepts at face value his assignment to separate Chad from a woman he describes as "base, venal—out of the streets." Europe changes him. When he meets Madame de Vionnet, a cultivated, well-connected Frenchwoman ten years older than Chad, Strether is charmed, especially when mutual friends assure him their relationship is a "virtuous attachment." He feels that Chad has benefited greatly from a friendship that has made him a sophisticated, cultured man of the world. At least by implication, Strether believes that his own life in a small New England town has been limited and unfulfilling. Later in the novel, a chance encounter reveals to him that Madame de Vionnet and Chad have all along been lovers, a situation that is known and accepted by their friends and that Strether is seemingly now prepared to tolerate, but that he recognizes with distress is a relationship without a future. Chad's protestations of devotion to his French mistress notwithstanding, he obviously finds intriguing both the alluring business opportunities awaiting him and the possibility of marrying Maisie Pocock, the attractive sister of his own sister's husband, an alliance his entire family approves of. Chad's sentimental education accomplished, Madame de Vionnet will before long be lamenting her youthful American lover, who will desert her for a younger, more suitable bride.

The Wings of the Dove is in some ways a retelling of *The Portrait of a Lady,* with another heroine based upon James's long-dead cousin Minny Temple. In this reworking, Milly Theale, the only survivor of a wealthy American family, is stupendously rich, "the heiress to all the ages." Strikingly pale with brilliant red hair, emphasized by the mourning black she normally wears, Milly is seriously ill with an unspecified disease, probably leukemia. Traveling to Europe in a desperate effort to live life to the full, she is befriended by Kate Croy, the penniless but beautiful and talented niece of a rich, childless English widow. Striking, intelligent, and vital, Kate is well suited to shine in the worldly milieu in which, courtesy of her aunt, she moves. Kate wishes to marry Merton Densher, a struggling journalist, to whom Milly is also attracted, but her aunt will settle a fortune on Kate only if she marries a candidate her aunt approves of, someone such as Lord Mark, an aspiring though cash-strapped aristocratic politician expected to have a great career. When she learns of Milly's illness, Kate urges Densher to pay court to and perhaps even marry the dying heiress, in the hope of inheriting some of her riches, which would eventually allow him and Kate to marry. There is even some prospect that happiness will restore Milly's health.

Milly realizes that Lord Mark, who proposes to her, does so in part because he covets the wealth that would accrue to him on her death, but—assured by Kate that she herself has spurned Densher's advances—takes the journalist's interest in her at face value. When the rejected Lord Mark eventually reveals to her that Densher and Kate are accomplices who seek to benefit from her wealth after her death, within weeks the devastated Milly finally succumbs to her illness.

So far, it might seem that all the advantages lie with the three British protagonists. Yet her own qualities, not just her millions, make Milly an equally strong character, whom both Kate and Densher genuinely like and respect. Although personally modest, Milly can never really escape the way her vast financial resources set her apart, giving her freedom few can contemplate, but she nonetheless transcends her wealth. Milly is well able to signal that she is interested in Densher, should he be available, and even to use her position as an "American girl," with the freedom to be more frank and outspoken, to do so. However badly hurt by Densher's treachery, she remains generous, bequeathing him a substantial fortune that will enable him to marry Kate. It is Densher himself, still at least half in love with Milly, who refuses the bequest, telling Kate that he will gladly give her the money, but will not use it to finance their marriage, and she must choose between him and Milly's money. The dead American woman has proved the stronger, triumphing over her living rival. The last words of the novel are Kate's: "We shall never be again as we were!"

The Golden Bowl is another, more complex reworking of the same theme, the tale of two talented, attractive lovers without any real money: Amerigo, an impoverished Italian prince, and Charlotte Stant, a cultured, beautiful, orphaned young woman of American parentage, raised in Europe.[27] Since the prince and Charlotte cannot afford to marry each other, they espouse a massively rich American father and daughter, and then rekindle their affair. Put thus starkly, the Americans may seem the victims. The story is far more complicated, however. Adam Verver, the father—a figure for whom James may conceivably have drawn on his brother William's Harvard encounters with John D. Rockefeller, Sr.—has made a vast fortune in business before turning to art collecting on an imperial scale. He values both the prince and his own wife partly as superlative specimens of the best of European civilization, perfect counterparts and complements to the outstanding art works he has amassed. Although Charlotte and the prince eventually resume their relationship, each begins his or her respective marriage in good faith.

What Charlotte has not quite reckoned with is that rather than seeking to shine in high society, her husband and his daughter prefer to spend most of their time together, along with the principino, the small son of Maggie and the prince. Surplus to requirements, the neglected and excluded spouses resemble extremely expensive toys, habitually left on a shelf, and are even encouraged to attend social events together. Maggie, whose passionate love for the prince perhaps sharpens her antennae, eventually realizes that her husband and stepmother are suspiciously close, and—without ever openly telling Adam what has transpired—persuades him to return to the United States with Charlotte, to establish a spectacular art museum in American City, which has been the long-term objective of his voracious collecting.

The end of the novel is extremely ambiguous. The story is largely told from first the prince's perspective and then his wife's, with commentary—not necessarily always dependable—from Fanny Assingham and her husband, Bob, friends and hangers-on of the Ververs. Many critics and readers have queried the reliability of the governess who narrates James's renowned ghost story, *The Turn of the Screw*, suggesting that she creates much of the evil she perceives. Could this be equally true of Maggie's version of events, and does her decidedly oppressive emphasis on goodness, unselfishness, and caring for everyone else mask a less savory story of emotional blackmail and constant demands upon others? Charlotte herself tells Maggie that she wants her own husband back and that the only way she can detach him from his daughter is for them to move to America. Maggie seemingly plays along with this scenario, deliberately appearing devastated by news she welcomes. Yet is this simply an excuse and pretext on Charlotte's part? When Charlotte and Adam visit Maggie and the prince a few hours before embarking for the United States, they are "somehow conjoined . . . as Maggie had absolutely never yet seen them." The senior Ververs have become a unit, intent on a common purpose.

How long have they been so? Is Maggie's perception of the drama, as one in which she determines to remove the threat her father's adulterous wife poses to her own marriage, accurate? Or is Charlotte's liaison with Maggie's husband a ploy, deliberate or unconscious, to precipitate a crisis and propel Adam into putting an ocean between the two of them and his suffocatingly possessive daughter? Adam clearly shrinks from hurting his only child, but are he and his wife perhaps even collaborating to escape Maggie's hold, leaving them free to devote themselves to each other and to establishing their museum? Adam's fabulous wealth, as all the characters recognize, means that all decisions ultimately rest with him.

Yet is Charlotte as "unhappy," bereft, and ignorant of her husband's intentions, and of how much he and Maggie "know" about her intrigue with the prince, as Maggie believes? Or is Maggie the one being manipulated into choosing between husband and father? The possibility that the book ends in a triumph for Charlotte, maybe in partnership with Adam, is intriguing, not just as a reassessment of its plot, but also as perhaps representing James's final resolution in a full-length novel of the issue with which he had wrestled for three decades, the balance of power and virtue between the United States and Europe.

HENRY JAMES WAS A COMPLICATED writer whose novels and stories are never simply about one issue alone. He rarely dealt directly with political themes, and is often perceived as a writer who focused primarily on extremely rarefied emotional interactions among the affluent. Yet close inspection suggests that he possessed an extremely sensitive seismometer, alerting him to shifts in the tectonic plates underlying the conduct of international relations in the late nineteenth and early twentieth centuries, especially the changing balance of power between Europe and his own country. In James's thirty years' worth of tales of greed, lust, hypocrisy, manipulation, and betrayal in transatlantic high society, one can trace with barometric and beautifully calibrated precision contemporary shifts in the distribution of influence from one side of the ocean to the other. Numerous Americans and Europeans alike felt strongly on this subject—one reason why James's apparently trivial and inconsequential portrayals of the American-European relationship often provoked seemingly disproportionate controversy. James initially made his reputation with stories and novels that often, though not invariably, portrayed dealings between Americans and Europeans in a grim, harshly unflattering light, leaving little room for happy illusions. After spending more than twenty years based in London, watching at close quarters what he undoubtedly though unhappily perceived as Britain's imperial decline and the rising power of his distant native land, James returned to this theme with a vengeance, in three massive novels that neatly, even brutally illustrate how the advantage, both economic and psychological, now rested with the United States. Reworking situations and sometimes characters he had used before, James demonstrated just how different and how infinitely more formidable Americans in 1900—and, by extension, the United States—were from their counterparts of the 1870s.

Spring Semester 2011

1. Leon Edel, ed., *Henry James: Letters*, Vol. IV: *1895–1916* (Cambridge, Mass., 1984), p. xxxi.

2. Henry James to William James, 2 Oct. 1988, in Ignas K. Skrupskelis and Elizabeth M. Berkeley, eds., *The Correspondence of William James*, Vol. 2: *William and Henry, 1885–1896* (Charlottesville, Va., 1993), pp. 96–7.

3. William James to Henry James, 26 Apr. 1885, 18 Nov. 1888, in ibid., pp. 17, 99.

4. Henry James to William James, 23 Oct. 1876, in Skrupskelis and Berkeley, eds., *The Correspondence of William James*, Vol. 1: *William and Henry, 1861–1884* (Charlottesville, Va., 1992), p. 274.

5. Henry James to William James, 28 Jan. 1878, in ibid., pp. 297–8.

6. James to Grace Norton, 24 Jan. 1885, in Leon Edel, ed., *Henry James: Letters*, Vol. III: *1883–1895* (Cambridge, Mass., 1980), pp. 66–7.

7. James to Grace Norton, 9 May 1885, in ibid., p. 83.

8. James to Sir John Clark, 13 Dec. 1891, in ibid., p. 367.

9. Henry James to William James, 1 May 1878, in Skrupskelis and Berkeley, *Correspondence of William James*, Vol. 1, p. 301.

10. James, notebook entry, 15 July 1895, in Leon Edel and Lyall H. Powers, eds., *The Complete Notebooks of Henry James* (New York, 1987), p. 126.

11. Henry James to William James, 23 Dec. 1895, in Skrupskelis and Berkeley, *Correspondence of William James*, Vol. 2, p. 384.

12. Henry James to William James, 9 Jan. 1896, in ibid., p. 383.

13. James to W. E. Norris, 4 Feb. 1896, in Leon Edel, ed., *Henry James: Letters*, Vol. IV: *1895–1916* (Cambridge, Mass., 1984), p. 27.

14. James to Henrietta Reubell, 17 Apr. 1898, Henry James Papers, Houghton Library, Harvard University, Cambridge, Massachusetts.

15. Henry James to William James, 22 Apr. 1898, in Skrupskelis and Berkeley, eds., *The Correspondence of William James*, Vol. 3: *William and Henry, 1897–1910* (Charlottesville, Va., 1994), p. 32.

16. James to Norton, 26 Dec. 1898, in Edel, *Henry James: Letters*, Vol. IV, p. 98.

17. Henry James to William James, 2 Apr. 1899, in Skrupskelis and Berkeley, *Correspondence of William James*, Vol. 3, p. 59.

18. Henry James to William James, 3 June 1899, in ibid., pp. 62–3.

19. Henry James to William James, 11 Oct. 1898, in ibid., p. 47.

20. James to Edmund Gosse, 12 Nov. 1899, in Rayburn S. Moore, *Selected Letters of Henry James to Edmund Gosse, 1882–1915: A Literary Friendship* (Baton Rouge, La., 1988), p. 172; also James to Gosse, 28 Oct. 1899, in ibid., 170.

21. Henry James to William James, 18 Nov. 1899, in Skrupskelis and Berkeley, *Correspondence of William James*, Vol. 3, p. 92.

22. James to Mrs. Everard Cotes, 26 Jan. 1900, in Edel, *Henry James: Letters*, Vol. IV, p. 132.

23. Henry James to William James, 10 Feb. 1900, in Skrupskelis and Berkeley, *Correspondence of William James*, Vol. 3, p. 101.

24. James to Clara and Clare Benedict, 22 Jan. 1901, in Edel, *Henry James: Letters*, Vol. IV, pp. 180–1.

25. James to Ariana Curtis, 3 Feb. 1901, in Leon Edel, *Henry James: Selected Letters* (Cambridge, Mass., 1987), pp. 328–9.

26. Quotations from the Penguin Classics edition, Henry James, *What Maisie Knew* (London, 1985), pp. 156–7.

27. Page numbers cited are to the Toby Press edition (2004).

5

Virginia Woolf and Russian Literature

ROBERTA RUBENSTEIN

D uring the decade between 1912 and 1922, Russia was very much "the rage" in England. The stirrings of revolution against the repressive czarist regime prompted British curiosity about its neighbor far to the east, including fascination with its cultural products. Spectators thronged to performances of Sergei Diaghilev's Ballets Russes and Igor Stravinsky's music as well as to exhibitions that featured works by contemporary Russian artists such as Natalia Goncharova, Mikhail Larionov, and Boris Anrep. During the same period, the works of the now-canonical Russian writers of the nineteenth century—Leo Tolstoy, Fyodor Dostoevsky, Anton Chekhov, and Ivan Turgenev—appeared in English translation, many for the first time. The self-taught British translator Constance Garnett rendered nearly the entire oeuvres of Dostoevsky, Chekhov, Tolstoy, Turgenev, Maxim Gorky, Aleksandr Ostrovsky, and several other writers into English during her lifetime. Most of her translations appeared between 1895 and 1922, a period that coincided exactly with Virginia Woolf's formative years as a writer and critic.

During the peak years of British "Russophilia," the works of Russian writers decisively influenced and supported Woolf's early dissatisfaction with the traditional novel form. She was enthralled with Russian writers' apparent disregard of well-constructed plots and with what she and others saw as the daring "formlessness" of their stories, novels, and plays. She admired their depth of psychological

insight and metaphysical inquiry along with their skill in rendering the layered complexity of experience and the elasticity of time.
Their concern with the inner lives of their characters and with what
Woolf termed the "chief character in Russian fiction"—the "soul"—
reinforced her contention that her British contemporaries were far
too preoccupied with social manners and superficial details, to the
neglect of the vital substance of experience, which she hoped to
capture in her own fiction.[1]

It was not simply that Woolf read and absorbed the Russians'
works, beginning with her indelible experience of reading Tolstoy's
War and Peace in 1910, but that she engaged with their fiction in a
number of crucial ways that ultimately influenced her own aspirations and style. Even before she developed her own signature techniques, she cut her teeth as a journalist by reviewing books, including new (typically first) translations into English of works by the
major Russian writers. Between 1917 and 1927, she published fifteen reviews and two essays on Russian literary works, or on writers
and books of Russian interest, in such venues as the *Times Literary
Supplement,* the *New Statesman,* and the *Nation and Athenaeum.* Most
of these reviews and essays appeared between 1917 and 1922, formative years during which she published her earliest experimental
stories—"The Mark on the Wall," "Kew Gardens," and "An Unwrit-
ten Novel"—and her first experimental novel, *Jacob's Room.* Woolf
also conveyed her absorption in Russian literature through the
thoughts and conversations of her characters: most of her novels
contain direct references or allusions to one or another of the major Russian writers. In addition, between 1911 and 1933, she jotted
more than forty-eight pages of notes on her reading of Russian literature for her personal use.

Hence, Woolf's interest in the Russian writers spanned more
than two decades, from her apprentice years through her mature
achievements as a novelist and essayist. She published her first
novel, *The Voyage Out,* in 1915. By the time she published the second
one—*Night and Day,* in 1919—she had begun to express in her book
reviews and literary essays her dissatisfaction with her contemporaries' reliance on inherited literary conventions and her admiration for the Russian models. As a frequent reviewer and an uncom-
monly incisive "common reader," Woolf played a role in shaping her
contemporaries' tastes and understanding of a literature that was
initially quite foreign to British tastes. The Russians undoubtedly
influenced her, and she influenced British views of the Russian writers. Offering her discerning judgments of literary methods, styles,
and ideas, she assisted in the process of assimilating Russian litera-

ture into British understanding as she refined her own critical understanding of what the Russian writers offered.

She and her husband, Leonard, even attempted to learn to read Russian, taking language lessons from their émigré friend Samuel Koteliansky. Though Virginia did not develop as much proficiency as Leonard, she was at one point able to read some Russian. The Woolfs took up the language study in connection with their Hogarth Press, which began as a small printing press in their parlor and later became a major press, publishing such important works as T. S. Eliot's *The Waste Land,* stories by Katherine Mansfield, and Freud's complete works in translation. Koteliansky encouraged the Woolfs to publish belles lettres by Russian writers, directly assisting them by identifying pertinent texts and collaborating with them on translations. Between 1920 and 1923, the Hogarth Press published seven translations from Russian, of which Virginia Woolf was the co-translator for three: *Stavrogin's Confession* (a suppressed chapter of Dostoevsky's *The Possessed*), *The Love Letters of Tolstoi,* and *Talks with Tolstoi.*

The process of rendering words from one language into another convinced Woolf that much was lost in translation. She cautioned readers that the extravagant adulation (including her own) with which Russian writers' works were greeted in England needed to be tempered with awareness that it was impossible to fully understand a literature originally written in another language. Based on her experiences as a translator, she recognized both her own linguistic deficiencies and the obstacles introduced by translation itself:

> When you have changed every word in a sentence from Russian to English, have thereby altered the sense a little, the sound, weight, and accent of the words in relation to each other completely, nothing remains except a crude and coarsened version of the sense.... What remains is, as the English have proved by the fanaticism of their admiration, something very powerful and very impressive, but it is difficult to feel sure, in view of these mutilations, how far we can trust ourselves not to impute, to distort, to read into them an emphasis which is false.[2]

Despite these disclaimers, the Russian writers were the most important catalyst for Woolf's decisive break from Victorian and Edwardian literary conventions and for the experiments in style and form that shaped her as a modernist writer. In 1919, during the peak of her infatuation with the Russian writers, she observed—perhaps a bit hyperbolically but no less emphatically—that "the most elementary remarks upon modern English fiction can hardly avoid some mention of the Russian influence, and if the Russians are mentioned one runs the risk of feeling that to write of any fiction save theirs is a waste of time."[3] In different ways, the Russians liberated and inspired her to experiment with style, narrative form, subject matter, and representations of character and time.

Woolf credited the Russians with introducing readers to the "unknown and uncircumscribed spirit" that she sought to capture in her own fiction.[4] Although they shared that spirit, the great Russian writers are obviously not all cut from a single mold—one would never mistake Tolstoy's writing for Chekhov's, or Dostoevsky's for Turgenev's—nor were their virtues identical for Woolf. Admiring all of them, she responded to their works differently and identified distinct qualities in their writing.

WOOLF'S INFATUATION WITH DOSTOEVSKY, whose fiction she first read in French on her honeymoon in 1912, must be understood in the context of the mystique surrounding the writer during the early years of the British reading experience of his fiction. During the period of Russophilia that bracketed the First World War, a veritable cult of Dostoevsky developed. Of the major Russian writers, Dostoevsky prompted Woolf's most intense and ambivalent responses, ranging from her fascination with his representations of consciousness and the depth of his psychological insights to her mixed feelings about his indifference to form. In view of the many possible approaches that Woolf might have taken to his writing, it is noteworthy that from her earliest published comments on his fiction—reviews of three of Garnett's newly translated volumes of his stories, published in the *Times Literary Supplement* between 1917 and 1919—she repeatedly singled out for comment his representations of his characters' emotional activity and mental processes. Of particular interest for students of modernism is Woolf's attention to what might be called Dostoevsky's proto-stream-of-consciousness technique: his method of representing characters' thought processes as they appear to occur. For example, in her first review, Woolf quotes an illustrative passage from "The Eternal Husband" in which the narrator describes a character's thought processes. Digressing to express her own understanding of the train of thought, she observes,

> From the crowd of objects pressing upon our attention we select now this one, now that one, weaving them inconsequent[ial]ly into our thought; the associations of a word perhaps make another loop in the line, from which we spring back again to a different section of our main thought and the whole process seems both in-

evitable and perfectly lucid. But if we try to construct our mental processes later, we find that the links between one thought and another are submerged. The chain is sunk out of sight and only the leading points emerge to mark the course.[5]

Her remarks describe a mental process that, very soon afterward, Woolf attempted to represent in her own writing. In "The Mark on the Wall," her first experimental story—composed only a few months after her first review of Dostoevsky's fiction in 1917—she endeavored to create a narrative form for the flow of impressions and associations streaming through the mind of a narrator who observes an unidentified mark on the wall above her mantel.

In another review of stories by Dostoevsky published two years later, Woolf once again focused specifically on the writer's depiction of the stream of thought. The narrator of Dostoevsky's "An Unpleasant Predicament" provides multiple glimpses into the apparently rambling thought processes of a civil servant who privately feels superior to a junior clerk in his department. When he finds himself near the house where the clerk is celebrating his wedding, he recalls his earlier insensitive teasing of the young man. In a passage that frames a challenge for later writers aspiring to give verbal form to nonverbal experiences, Dostoevsky's narrator explains:

> It is well known that whole trains of thought sometimes pass through our brains instantaneously as though they were sensations without being translated into human speech, still less into literary language. But we will try to translate these sensations of our hero's, and present to the reader at least the kernel of them. . . . For many of our sensations when translated into ordinary language seem absolutely unreal. That is why they never find expression, though everyone has them.[6]

Dostoevsky's approach to the interior mental processes of his characters supported Woolf's then-developing view that her Edwardian contemporaries—the "materialists" Arnold Bennett, John Galsworthy, and H. G. Wells—were preoccupied with manners at the expense of their characters' psychological complexity.

Searching for her own voice and form, Woolf was struck not only by Dostoevsky's representations of mental processes but also by his concentration on intense emotional experiences, his compression and manipulation of time, and his technique of "doubling" as a method of characterization. A number of his inwardly divided protagonists are narratively represented through one or more other characters who express elements of their personality, including opposing qualities. One of his early novels, *The Double* (1846), pivots directly on this psychological dynamic, tracing the inner turmoil of an emotionally disturbed civil servant who is overwhelmed and psychically destroyed by his own double.

The technical possibilities of the double clearly intrigued Woolf, particularly while she was composing *The Hours,* the novel draft that evolved into *Mrs. Dalloway* (1925). Her diary notes indicate that Dostoevsky was on her mind during the early part of the composition phase of the novel, perhaps because she was also thinking about the essay "The Russian Point of View," which she composed during the same period. As many readers of *Mrs. Dalloway* discover, Clarissa Dalloway and Septimus Warren Smith—a shell-shocked soldier who has recently returned from war—share a number of features and attitudes, including their concern about the integrity of the individual self or soul in a society that demands compromise. The correspondences build to the final connection during the party at the end of the novel, when Clarissa hears of Septimus's suicide and, despite the fact that they never meet, feels "very like him."[7] Septimus's suicide is the catalyst for Clarissa's recovery of her own zest for life. In the preface Woolf wrote for the 1925 American edition of the novel—which, surprisingly, is rarely reprinted with the novel—she explained that "in the first version Septimus, who later is intended to be [Clarissa's] double, had no existence; and . . . Mrs. Dalloway was originally to kill herself, or perhaps merely to die at the end of the party."[8] She seems to have used the introduction as an opportunity to explain, after the fact, the design that had in fact occurred to her quite early in her conception of the novel.

Woolf's intellect, sensibility, and style were fundamentally different from Dostoevsky's. Nonetheless, his unconventional (by British standards) narrative strategies stimulated her experiments with interior monologue, stream of consciousness, and doubled characters. Her complex attitude toward his fiction might be described as a kind of fascinated dissatisfaction. While she admired his psychological depth and intensity and his path-breaking articulation of mental processes, she had her reservations about his apparent aesthetic slackness and the exaggerated emotional pitch of many of his characters and scenes. Her responses must be understood within the context of her own then-evolving artistic method. The heady experience she describes of being overwhelmed by Dostoevsky's "seething whirlpools"—the emotional maelstrom that pulled readers in "against our wills . . . blinded, suffocated, and at the same time filled with a giddy rapture"[9]—was an important catalyst for her aesthetic liberation at a crucial moment in her own development, introducing her to a range of new narrative possibilities. One might say that during the important early stages of her writing career and for some time afterward, Virginia Woolf was indeed creatively possessed by Dostoevsky.

IN BOTH SUBJECT MATTER AND narrative method, Anton Chekhov contributed to the seismic shifts of British modernism in ways that were absorbed more readily than the fiction of Dostoevsky or Tolstoy. Virginia Woolf discerned that Chekhov offered an antidote for readers who at times found Dostoevsky's intense emotional pitch and Tolstoy's encyclopedic narratives daunting and difficult to assimilate. Along with Katherine Mansfield and other contemporaries, Woolf recognized that Chekhov's focus on unremarkable characters engaged in inconsequential actions in stories without plots paradoxically enlarged the possibilities of the art of fiction.

Chekhov is now so canonical that it may be impossible to understand how "difficult" he was when his work first appeared in English. In many ways, he was the most modern of the Russian writers in the unconventional techniques that distinguish both his stories and his plays. From her earliest responses to his fiction, Virginia Woolf grasped the radical modernity of his methods. In her view, he was especially skilled at suggesting, often in very brief narratives, a complex spectrum of human emotions. In expressing the randomness and flux of quotidian experience, he was much closer than Dostoevsky or Tolstoy to Woolf's own sensibility. In turn, Woolf helped shape British appreciation of Chekhov's work by making his apparently formless, plotless stories and plays intelligible to her contemporaries through her literary reviews and a review of a London performance of *The Cherry Orchard*.

What she regarded as the "unfinished" quality of Chekhov's stories—notably their abrupt endings and apparent absence of resolution—especially appealed to her. The writer offered models for telling a different kind of story, one in which vignettes of character or evocations of mood entirely replace plot. She was particularly attentive to his skill at composing narratives out of seemingly prosaic details that accumulate but rarely resolve in the manner of a "well-made story": "What is the point of it, and why does he make a story out of this? we ask as we read story after story."[10] Her own early experimental sketches reveal her interest in Chekhov's method. In "Kew Gardens," for example, there is virtually nothing that one would call a plot; rather, the sketch proceeds by way of vivid sensory impressions, brief sketches of characters, and evocations of mood. Alternating human and snail's-eye views of light and shadow, color and shape, fracture the landscape in an almost cubist manner. The point of view, though literally omniscient, is figuratively that of the garden itself.

Chekhov's stories and plays also supported Woolf's growing conviction that the strategies through which writers had traditionally attempted to sum up their characters were inadequate. His radically different techniques both inspired and reinforced her sense that an irreducible subjectivity defined the limits of character representation. In her first experimental novel, *Jacob's Room* (1922), she attempted to apply that conviction: no matter how much the reader might grasp about Jacob Flanders's "room"—understood not only literally but figuratively, as the environment the central character occupies—the character himself is never entirely knowable. The collage of qualities and "characteristics" that constitute him exceeds the knowledge that others in his life—whether his mother, his college friends, or his several girlfriends—have of him. Nor can the reader fully know him, since the narrator refuses to provide consistent information about Jacob's identity. Rather, through her impressionistic method, Woolf permits the narrative form itself to convey the elusiveness and complexity of personality. A complete portrait of Jacob Flanders—or of any human being—is impossible because, as the narrator observes, "we start transparent, and then the cloud thickens."[11]

In the same novel, Woolf acknowledged her Chekhovian influences not only indirectly but with a bit of intertextual name-dropping. While traveling in Greece, Jacob becomes enamored of a married woman who shares his romantic melancholy. The segment of the narrative that describes their brief encounter almost parodies several of Chekhov's stories, such as "The Lady with the Dog," that focus on romantic infatuation, love, and the disillusionment that occurs when people find themselves involved with unavailable—usually married—partners. Providing Mrs. Sandra Wentworth Williams with a volume of Chekhov—"a little book convenient for traveling"[12]—Woolf uses the book as a vehicle for satire, exposing the woman's banal or sentimental thoughts on profound matters. Mrs. Wentworth Williams, inspired by her reading of Chekhov, feels

> full of love for every one . . . for the poor most of all—for the peasants coming back in the evening with their burdens. And everything is soft and vague and very sad. It is sad, it is sad. But everything has meaning.[13]

The volume of Chekhov's stories is more a prop for Mrs. Wentworth Williams's amour-propre than an occasion for a genuine emotional response to the condition of the Russian underclass. Woolf apparently aimed for a Chekhovian blend of humor and pathos not in each character by herself or himself but through a composite of the novel's characters. Her gentle satire of Mrs. Wentworth Williams provides the comic dimension; Jacob Flanders's own imponderable questions about life, underscored for the reader by the shock of his arbitrary and premature death in the Great War, create its pathos.

Like his stories, Chekhov's plays were also radically unconventional by the standards of the British drama of the day. Woolf was one of the few early reviewers or spectators to appreciate and articulate for others the playwright's unorthodox dramatic treatment of character, plot, and dialogue at a time when many theatergoers simply didn't "get" Chekhov. In her 1920 review of a performance of *The Cherry Orchard,* she identified and explained some of the elements that British audiences found incomprehensible: the plot was difficult to follow, the tone seemed to vacillate between comedy and tragedy, and—particularly difficult for British spectators to grasp—the characters seemed to talk as much to themselves as to other characters on stage. Perhaps to explore these differences in audience expectations, Woolf wrote a short satirical sketch of her own, titled "Uncle Vanya," in which the central character, a British theatergoer, attends a performance of Chekhov's play by that name and entirely misses its point. The sketch is one of three of Woolf's stories whose titles are directly borrowed from Chekhov, an index of her homage to him. The other two are "Happiness" and "The Shooting Party."

The most curious expression of Virginia Woolf's absorption in Chekhov for nearly a decade appears in the draft of an untraced and apparently unpublished review written in 1925, the same year in which she published revised versions of several of her most memorable observations on Russian writers in "Modern Fiction" and "The Russian Point of View" for *The Common Reader.* The occasion for the review was the release of a limited edition of Alexander Pope's *The Rape of the Lock.* Though logic fails to supply a connection between the British Augustan poet and the Russian storyteller—separated by a century and a half, to say nothing of distinctly different literary and moral universes—Woolf's immersion in Russian literature at the time provided the peculiar circumstance in which she read Pope "by the light of Tchekhov" [*sic*].[14]

The initial effect of what Woolf termed the "Russian mist" on her rereading of *The Rape of the Lock* was a peculiar sense of mental expansion, an invigorating stimulus that she emphasized elsewhere in her remarks on Chekhov and on Russian literature. The romantic conception of the soul, combined with the conception of the enormous physical space of Russia in which it apparently flourished, appears in Woolf's responses to works as diverse as Chekhov's "The Steppe," Tolstoy's *War and Peace,* and Dostoevsky's *The Possessed.* Indeed, a recurrent trope in her review of Pope's mock epic is a preoccupation with different magnitudes of scale, perhaps suggested by the perceived geographic immensity of the Russian steppes. Measured against matters of interest to the Russian writers, the universe of Belinda's cosmetic table seems inconsequential. Woolf, peering through a figurative lens that both reduced and distorted the object of her analysis, never resolved her struggle to achieve an appropriate critical perspective or an appreciative reading of Pope's poem. The contrasting perspectives, registered as vast differences not only of scale but also of consequence, recall Alice in Wonderland, who experiences extreme alterations in the size and scale of objects in her environment as her own body shrinks and expands.

In Chekhov's narratives that lack traditional climax or resolution, dramas that seem to lack drama, and dialogues that upset the usual expectations of conversational exchange between people, Woolf found models and inspiration for both formal and thematic innovations. From his palette of tonal colorings, she adapted ideas for her own purposes, ranging from impressionistic renderings of mood and feeling to the important functions of silence and omission: what is not stated but only hinted at or implied. In addition, Chekhov's honest and unsentimental focus on the loneliness at the heart of human experience appealed to Woolf's own metaphysics. Even after the distorting Russian mist dissipated and her vision cleared, Chekhov remained a vital strand in the pattern of her evolution as a writer.

ALTHOUGH TOLSTOY AND TURGENEV influenced Virginia Woolf less noticeably than did Dostoevsky and Chekhov, they are nonetheless significant for understanding the influence of the Russian giants on her writing. Of the four major Russian writers, it is Tolstoy whose name appears most often in her literary and critical observations. His encyclopedic vision and narrative authenticity became standards by which she measured other writers. Her first published commentary on any work of Russian literature was her 1917 review of a volume of Tolstoy's stories, *The Cossacks.* She read *Anna Karenina* two and possibly three times, recording her impressions during two of those readings. Late in her life, she noted in her diary her intention to reread *Anna Karenina* and *War and Peace* once again, though she died before doing so.

Tolstoy's psychological realism was indelibly stamped on her imagination from her earliest encounter with his work—well before her own career as a novelist began, while she was still Virginia Stephen—and lasted to the final year of her life. In 1940, a year before her death, she still vividly recalled the galvanizing effect of her first experience of reading Tolstoy:

> Always the same reality—like touching an exposed electric wire. Even so imperfectly conveyed—his rugged short cut mind—to me the most, not sympathetic, but inspiring, rousing; genius in the raw. Thus more disturbing, more 'shocking'[,] more of a thunderclap, even on art, even on lit.[eratu]re, than any other writer. I remember that was my feeling about W. & Peace, read in bed at Twickenham. . . . [It was] a revelation to me. Its directness, its reality.[15]

Woolf read and reread most of Tolstoy's other major works, including (in addition to *Anna Karenina*) *The Cossacks, Family Happiness, The Kreutzer Sonata,* and several of his treatises on art and religion. In addition, of the major Russian writers who interested her, Tolstoy received the most sustained attention from the Hogarth Press. It published five works in translation by or about him, of which Woolf collaborated on the translation of two: Maxim Gorky's *Reminiscences of Tolstoy* and A. B. Goldenveiser's *Talks with Tolstoi.*

In contrast to Dostoevsky, whose appeal to Woolf and other English readers was the sheer emotional intensity and drive of his narratives, Tolstoy endowed his characters more subtly with psychological depth and metaphysical profundity while situating them in a quotidian reality that was more familiar to British readers, perhaps because Tolstoy learned his craft in part by reading such Victorian writers as Charles Dickens, Laurence Sterne, and George Eliot. From the beginning, Woolf admired his infallible eye for detail and his skill at rendering in depth every element of a scene or character, even when the subjects seem commonplace. As she phrased it in her first review of his stories, "Nothing seems to escape him. . . . We feel that we know his characters both by the way they choke and sneeze and by the way they feel about love and immortality and the most subtle questions of conduct. . . . Tolstoy seems able to read the minds of different people as certainly as we count the buttons on their coats."[16]

As a key figure in Woolf's critical practice, Tolstoy appears frequently by name among a select group of writers—Shakespeare, Sterne, Austen, Stendhal, Dostoevsky, Flaubert, and Proust—who represented her indisputable and indispensable critical benchmarks and to whom she variously refers for comparative purposes throughout her literary essays. He functions in her critical writing as a model for the full scope of possibilities of the novelist's art; he possessed, in her estimation, a range and depth of psychological insight that few other novelists ever reached or sustained. In her much-cited argument with the Edwardian materialists concerning the elements of fiction, Woolf contended that great novels such as *War and Peace, Vanity Fair, Tristram Shandy, Madame Bovary, Pride and Prejudice, The Mayor of Casterbridge,* and *Villette* have in common the "power to make you think" of the full range of human experience, from love and family life and war and peace to "the immortality of the soul." Indeed, there is "hardly any subject of human experiences that is left out of *War and Peace.*"[17] In her sole essay on cinema, she refers to a cinematic version of *Anna Karenina* to argue that the novelist's medium, particularly in the hands of a master like Tolstoy, is far superior to the filmmaker's. While physical images could be richly conveyed through the moving camera's lens—we can directly perceive "the very quivers of [Vronsky's] lips" and experience him and Anna "in the flesh"—what was less successfully translated to celluloid at a time that preceded the introduction of the "talkies" in 1926 was the depth of interiority that Tolstoy so masterfully rendered in language.[18]

As with Dostoevsky and Chekhov, both of whom are discussed in her characters' conversations, Woolf also nodded in Tolstoy's direction in her fiction. In *To the Lighthouse,* Mrs. Ramsay and her dinner guests discuss *Anna Karenina* over *boeuf en daube.* One of the guests, Paul Rayley, thinking about the "books one had read as a boy," recalls the name of Vronsky because "he always thought it such a good name for a villain."[19] Tolstoy's masterpiece lingers in Mrs. Ramsay's mind as she considers the differences between the two young men at her dinner table, the considerate Paul Rayley and the egocentric Charles Tansley.

Among the Russian writers Woolf admired, Tolstoy was in a class by himself. In "The Russian Point of View," she identified him as "the greatest of all novelists—for what else can we call the author of *War and Peace?*"[20] From the very earliest to the final years of her writing life, he remained a fixed star in her literary imagination.

ALTHOUGH TURGENEV WAS THE FIRST Russian writer to be translated into English (in the late 1800s), he earned Virginia Woolf's appreciation only late in her career, after her infatuation for the other Russians, particularly Dostoevsky, had somewhat dissipated. While she was drawn to the liberating opportunities offered by Dostoevsky's and Chekhov's "formlessness" during the apprentice years of her writing career, in her artistic maturity she came to admire

Turgenev precisely for his mastery of form. She appreciated his lyricism and economy of expression, his objectivity, and his nuanced renderings of feeling through the evocation of natural settings. Her return to his fiction more than a decade after her absorption in Dostoevsky, Chekhov, and Tolstoy had waned reflects an important shift in Woolf's literary tastes and ambitions. Turgenev appealed to her just at the point when she had completed her most ambitious experimental work (*The Waves*, 1931) and relished a return to a more traditional form (*The Years*, 1937).

Rather than the intense and tumultuous flux of emotions that characterize Dostoevsky's fiction—"the seething whirlpools, gyrating sandstorms, waterspouts which hiss and boil and suck us in"—Turgenev's stories succeeded, in her judgment, through the author's understated renderings of character and experience.[21] His novels grew on Woolf, as she suggested they grow on his readers, as a result of their emotional authenticity and technical mastery. While composing *The Pargiters*, the novel that eventually became *The Years*, she read or reread eleven of Turgenev's novels for her own pleasure and interest, jotting thirty-three pages of notes on her reading. At the same time, a diary entry indicates that she was actively mulling over Turgenev's approach to form in contrast to Dostoevsky's.[22] She found the comparison valuable; it is clear that she had come to prefer Turgenev's artistic restraint, his sensitivity to beauty, and his lyrical sensibility over Dostoevsky's "hot, scalding, mixed, marvelous, terrible, oppressive" representations of the human soul.[23]

Woolf's concentrated rereading of Turgenev formed the basis for her only published essay on a single Russian writer: "The Novels of Turgenev," published in 1933. The essay is an appreciative analysis of the writer's artistic achievements, ranging from his powers of observation, his eye for the exact detail, and his masterful rendering of natural scenes that subtly suggest his characters' feelings. Woolf also praised Turgenev's economy of expression, his narrative objectivity, and his nuanced representations of Russian life and character. Moreover, as evidenced both in diary entries and in her own novel in progress at the time, Woolf strove to emulate Turgenev's balance between realism and lyricism—between what she termed "fact" and "vision"—in *The Years*.

OF THE MANY STRANDS OF READING that entered and affected Virginia Woolf's prodigious and original imagination, Russian literature is only one. Yet in my view it is an absolutely fundamental one. The major Russian writers to whom Woolf was deeply attracted during the impressionable and pivotal years of her developing career as a writer left indelible marks that cross all boundaries of her fictional and critical writing. They stimulated her thinking about new narrative possibilities and opportunities that challenged inherited literary conventions. They inspired her to test and stretch the boundaries of fiction for her own purposes, developing stream-of-consciousness narration and other techniques that came to define her signature style. Employing narrative methods different from those of the British and Continental traditions in which she was steeped, they provoked new sites in her imagination where, as she explained it, "the accent falls a little differently; the emphasis is upon something hitherto ignored; at once a different outline of form becomes necessary, difficult for us to grasp, incomprehensible to our predecessors."[24] One might highlight this famous passage, which Woolf retained in the version of the essay published six years later and titled "Modern Fiction," by stressing that the "accent" she heard was Russian.

One way to assess the magnitude of Virginia Woolf's response to the Russians is to try to imagine what her oeuvre might have been like without the fortuitous and decisive convergence, at a crucial moment in her literary maturation, of her dissatisfaction with traditional literary models and her engagement with the corpus of the giants of nineteenth-century Russian literature. As early as 1908, she had expressed her wish to show "all the traces of the minds [*sic*] passage through the world; & achieve in the end, some kind of whole made of shivering fragments."[25] The Russian writers entered her imaginative experience just as she began to seek more effective methods for realizing that ambition. They were the catalysts for Woolf's vital leap to "a new form for a new novel."[26] The rest is history.

For fear of undue influence, some writers resist reading the work of other writers while they are composing their own creative work. By contrast, Woolf's lifelong habit of reading and writing about other writers during her composition process fed her imagination, stimulating her thinking about specific matters of form, subject, character, and technique as well as larger ideas concerning the art of fiction and the meaning of experience. The narrator of her story "The Shooting Party"—the title of which she borrowed from Chekhov's story of the same name—observes, "There is nothing that does not leave some residue."[27] For Virginia Woolf, the imaginative residue of the Russian writers, demonstrable in both her fiction and her critical writing from the beginning to the end of her career, was inestimably decisive, transformative, and enduring.

Spring Semester 2010

1. Virginia Woolf, "The Russian Point of View," in *The Essays of Virginia Woolf: Vol. 4, 1925–1928,* ed. Andrew McNeillie (London, 1984), p. 185.

2. Ibid., p. 182.

3. Virginia Woolf, "Modern Novels," in *The Essays of Virginia Woolf: Vol. 3, 1919–1924,* ed. Andrew McNeillie (London, 1988), p. 35.

4. Virginia Woolf, "Modern Fiction," in *Essays: Vol. 4,* p. 160.

5. Virginia Woolf, "More Dostoevsky," in *The Essays of Virginia Woolf: Vol. 2, 1912–1918,* ed. Andrew McNeillie (London, 1987), p. 85.

6. Fyodor Dostoevsky, *An Honest Thief,* trans. Constance Garnett (1919; Westport, Conn., 1975), p. 206.

7. Virginia Woolf, *Mrs. Dalloway* (1925; New York, 1990), p. 186.

8. Virginia Woolf, "An Introduction to *Mrs. Dalloway,*" *Essays: Vol. 4,* p. 549.

9. Woolf, "Russian Point of View," p. 186.

10. Ibid., 184.

11. Virginia Woolf, *Jacob's Room* (1922; New York, 1950), p. 49.

12. Ibid., p. 141.

13. Ibid.

14. Virginia Woolf, "Tchekhov on Pope," unpublished review, 1925.

15. *The Diary of Virginia Woolf: Vol. 5, 1936–1941,* ed. Anne Olivier Bell (London, 1984), p. 273.

16. Virginia Woolf, "Tolstoy's 'The Cossacks,'" *Essays: Vol. 2,* p. 78

17. Virginia Woolf, "Mr. Bennett and Mrs. Brown," in *The Captain's Death Bed and Other Essays* (London, 1950), p. 103.

18. Virginia Woolf, "The Cinema," in *Essays: Vol. 4,* p. 350.

19. Virginia Woolf, *To the Lighthouse* (1927; New York, 1989), p. 108.

20. Woolf, "Russian Point of View," p. 187.

21. Ibid., p. 178.

22. *The Diary of Virginia Woolf: Vol. 4, 1931–1935,* ed. Anne Olivier Bell (London, 1982), p. 172.

23. Woolf, "Russian Point of View," p. 187.

24. Woolf, "Modern Novels," p. 33.

25. Virginia Woolf, *A Passionate Apprentice: The Early Journals, 1897–1909,* ed. Mitchell Leaska (London, 1990), p. 393.

26. *The Diary of Virginia Woolf: Vol. 2, 1920–1924,* ed. Anne Olivier Bell (London, 1978), p. 13.

27. Virginia Woolf, "The Shooting Party," in *The Complete Shorter Fiction of Virginia Woolf,* ed. Susan Dick (London, 1985), p. 260.

6

General Henry Wilson, Ireland, and the Great War

SAMUEL R. WILLIAMSON, JR.

At one point just before the First World War, Henry Wilson received a postcard addressed simply: "To the ugliest man in the British army." The card had reached its intended recipient. Standing just over six feet, with a huge head and a wide mouth that made him look a bit like a horse when he laughed, which he did often, General Henry Hughes Wilson worked hard to prepare the small British Expeditionary Force (BEF) of 150,000 men (in six divisions and a cavalry division) for a European war that he believed would come and would require British participation. But he did more than prepare the army. In the July 1914 crisis, he conspired, as he had easily done for most of his career, to maneuver the Liberal government, which he profoundly despised, to enter the war. And then he ensured that the government would adopt the war plans that he had arranged with the French since 1910, despite major reservations by generals senior to him.

Henry Wilson's career and what it says about British civil-military relations and the Irish question before the Great War have, since the publication of his indiscreet diaries in the 1920s, received occasional attention from historians. But almost all studies that examine British entry into the war have missed the key role that Wilson played in mobilizing the leading members of the Tory party to pressure the undecided British Cabinet to intervene.[1] How could a single officer be so influential, and how he could encourage the virtual mutiny of British officers over the Irish question in the spring of 1914 and still remain in office? The answers may prompt some revision of our understanding of civil-military relations in Britain both before and during a major war.

WILSON WAS AN ANGLO-IRISH OFFICER with deep family ties in Ulster, even though he was born on 5 May 1864, in County Longford, not far from Dublin. The Wilson family was part of the Protestant Ascendancy, having done well in shipping in Belfast and then becoming modest landowners in central Ireland. Although he would lead a comfortable life as an army officer, Wilson never had much money and indeed often sublet houses that he and his wife occupied during the high social season in London to earn money. The family and Wilson were members of the Church of Ireland—the Anglican Church in Ireland—and he was strongly anti-Catholic, or more precisely, strongly anti–Irish Catholic. Educated by French governesses until the age of thirteen, he acquired a tolerable command of French and an abiding love for France. He then attended the Marlborough School for three years and prepared for exams to enter the army, since, as the second son, he would not inherit the family lands. It was not easy: he failed the entrance exams for the Royal Military Academy twice and Sandhurst three times.

Indeed, his entry into the army typified much of his later career: in both, he used personal connections and the backdoor to attain his goals. In this case, he went into the Longford militia, thanks to his social connections, as a second lieutenant and trained for two years. Eventually, he passed the army exams, fifty-eighth on the list, in July 1884 and joined the prestigious Rifle Brigade.

In early 1885, he was sent to India, and then dispatched to Burma a year later. In May 1887, he received a severe wound to his right eye and returned home to recover. He never returned to India, successfully evading any further postings. After recuperation, he married Cecil Wray in October 1891; they had no children. When finished with the staff course, he did a stint in military intelligence and staff duty before going to South Africa and the Boer War in October 1899. There he did well and, equally importantly, became a part of the entourage of Lord Roberts, the successful commander and later a powerful patron for Wilson. On returning, he held a series of staff positions in the War Office as the British army, in the wake of the early disasters in South Africa, finally installed a General Staff system. He was promoted to the rank of colonel in charge of military education, and then in 1907 became commandant of the Staff College with the rank of brigadier general, an astonishingly rapid rise for the army of the day.

At the Staff College, Wilson worked hard to prepare the younger officers for the possibility of a Continental war. In the process, he developed a coterie of officers who came to share his views. And while many agreed with the need for some form of conscription and thus a much larger British army, few skirted the edges of public debate as often as Wilson, who steadily fed Lord Roberts information on why Britain needed more troops and thus compulsory service.

In August 1910, Wilson became the director of military operations (DMO), in charge of war planning and intelligence operations. From that point forward, he worked tirelessly to prepare the small BEF for war in support of France. To do that, he revamped and renewed secret military conversations with the French. To understand the importance of this step requires, however, a brief note on the evolution of Anglo-French relations after 1900.

BY THE END OF THE NINETEENTH CENTURY, the Boer War, Russian ambitions in the Far East, and growing German assertiveness had created strategic concerns in London. Splendid isolation no longer looked quite so splendid. The Anglo-Japanese alliance helped ease some of the concerns. And assisted by King Edward VII's love of Paris and its ladies, tentative steps for an easing of colonial frictions led in April 1904 to the signing of the Anglo-French Entente Cordiale, a colonial understanding that ratified Britain's position in Egypt and assured France of British diplomatic support in its quest for control of Morocco.

Then in the spring of 1905, amid signs of growing concern in London over German naval plans, the Wilhelmstrasse decided to challenge the French position in Morocco and the entente. It was a mistake; the British drew a bit closer to France. Even a change of administrations, with the Liberals under Sir Henry Campbell-Bannerman coming to power, did not diminish British support.

In December 1905 and January 1906, British and French military officials started informal conversations about what the British might do in the event of war. These conversations had the approval of the Prime Minister, Foreign Secretary Sir Edward Grey, War Minister Richard Haldane, and a very few others. The Liberal Cabinet as a whole did not learn of the talks until the fall of 1911. At every stage, London made clear to the French that the British were not committed by the talks to intervene, only to discuss matters.

Already in 1904–5, the British army had begun to think of involvement on the Continent. The entente pushed that view along, as did the obvious fact that the army needed a new raison d'etre after Russia's defeat by Japan lessened the threat to India, a threat still further reduced by the Anglo-Russian agreement of 1907. Gradually, the senior army leadership viewed a Continental war as the equal of its imperial commitments. Some members of the new Committee of Imperial Defence (CID) also accepted that idea, though First Sea Lord Admiral Sir John Fisher worked to block this at every point. Nonetheless, there were some desultory talks with the French military between 1907 and Wilson's arrival as the new DMO in 1910.

Wilson's often-indiscreet diary put it well on 25 October 1910, after his first months as DMO: "I am very dissatisfied with the state of affairs in every respect. No rail arrangements for concentration and movements of Expeditionary Force or Territorials [the reserve troops]. No proper arrangements for horse supply, no arrangements for safeguarding our arsenal at Woolwich. A lot of time spent writing beautiful but useless minutes. I'll break all this somehow."[2]

Over the next four years, Wilson did exactly that. Often browbeating his superior officers, whom he usually held in low esteem, he managed to transform war planning. By the end of 1912, he had the rail schedules arranged, troop movements coordinated, even medals prepared to give to those who in the merchant fleet would take the army across the channel. He argued for more realism in field training and pressed repeatedly for conscription, since he knew the army was too small to make a major contribution to a European war.

But he also devoted attention to relations with the French army. Already acquainted with General Ferdinand Foch, the commandant of the French Staff School, Wilson traveled to France soon after his appointment to discuss the essentially nonexistent military arrangements with France. He started by asking a French officer how many British troops would be needed. The reply was crisp and simple: "a single private soldier—and we would take care that he was killed."

If Berlin's ill-advised diplomacy prompted the initial Anglo-French military talks, the so-called Agadir incident on 1 July 1911, in Morocco (sparked by the arrival of a German gunboat in that port) acted like an accelerant on a smoldering fire. Suddenly, a Franco-German clash appeared possible. This crisis allowed Wilson to jump-start his talks with France and to get the CID to think officially of possible intervention with France. It also brought his activities into the gun sights of the radicals in the Liberal Cabinet.

In July, without any authorization from civilian authorities, Wilson negotiated an agreement with Paris on British assistance. He then explained these actions to a few members of the CID on

23 August and sought to show how six British divisions would make the crucial difference between victory and defeat for France. His assumptions were simple: the Germans would invade through lower Belgium, staying south of the Meuse and Sambre rivers with roughly fifty-one divisions; the French would confront them with forty or more divisions, and the six additional British divisions would give them virtual parity with the attacking Germans. With some variation, these assumptions guided his planning right down to August 1914. For their part, the Germans did not oblige in 1914: they used reserve troops as part of the Belgian invasion force, and their First and Second armies nearly enveloped the deployed British troops. At the Battle of Mons, the Germans possessed a two-to-one superiority in forces.

Word of the CID meeting, as well as the fact of the military talks with France, soon reached the radicals in the Cabinet, who had a healthy dislike of Wilson. Seeking to curb future talks, they got some assurances from Grey and Asquith that there were no commitments. Churchill's arrival at the Admiralty as First Lord, however, gave Henry Wilson a major ally. In 1912, Anglo-French naval talks began, with detailed arrangements to protect the English Channel. For its part, the French government, led by Premier, later President, Raymond Poincaré, tried repeatedly during 1912 to get Grey to convert the entente into an alliance, a step Grey resisted. One can argue that the military and naval conversations were a de facto form of an alliance; the test would come when it was time to decide for war. That came less than two years later.

In the interval, Wilson traveled often to France to perfect the arrangements. He and other officers cycled the Belgian border. Indefatigable in his efforts to know the terrain, Wilson probably had a better appreciation of the actual topography of the future war than any other European general. Still, he accepted French views about the likely size and thrust of German troops coming through Belgium, a failure for which his beloved BEF would pay dearly in August 1914.

BUT WILSON'S CONSIDERABLE ENERGIES were directed not only to preparing the British army for war and to making arrangements to assist France. He also worked to keep Home Rule from coming to Ireland or, if it came, to exclude at least the six counties in the north. In this effort, his preferred goal was to force the collapse of the Liberal government, whose leaders he called "dirty curs." In his contempt for the Liberals, shared fairly widely in officer circles, there was residual anger for their criticism of the army during the

Boer War. The Liberals had been harsh in their attacks on the conduct of the war and on the use of concentration camps by Kitchener
and others against the Boers. The army officers did not forget their
dislike when the Liberals returned to power in 1905–6 with a stunning majority, even though Haldane began significant and effective
reform efforts in the army.

After the second general election in late 1910, both major parties
had 272 MPs, with the Irish and Labour MPs giving the Liberals
their majority. When the House of Lords capitulated in late summer 1911 in a major constitutional crisis with the Commons, the
prospect of a Home Rule bill, following its passage three times by
the same Parliament, was a certainty. In practical terms, this meant
Home Rule in some form would come at some point during 1914.
Few understood this better than Henry Hughes Wilson.

The small world of London politics and clubs made it easy for
Wilson to establish ties with leading Tory and Unionist politicians
and journalists, including Leo Maxse of the *National Review*. In June
1912, he met Andrew Bonar Law, who had been elected leader of
the Tory party just months before. Of his initial impressions, Wilson
wrote in his diary: "I was very much pleased with his quiet, unosten-
tatious manner and his exceedingly logical and practical mind. . . .
He gives me the impression of being thoroughly honest and upright,
anxious and determined to do all in his power to save the country."

If Wilson's diaries are any indication, he saw Bonar Law frequently
thereafter, and one of Bonar Law's biographers called the general
his "unofficial military adviser."[3] This arrangement meant that in
the future, virtually no British army plan of any kind, whether it
involved Ireland or a war on the Continent, would be unknown to
the leader of the opposition party. Further, given Wilson's close association with Sir Arthur Nicolson of the Foreign Office, who had
come to dislike his own superior, Sir Edward Grey, this meant that
Bonar Law and his advisers were well informed about Liberal foreign policy plans.

From the end of 1913 through the onset of the July 1914 crisis, Henry Wilson was deeply immersed in the Irish question. He
worked on a series of fronts: first, he sought to ensure that the army
leadership did not commit itself to a policy of force against those
who would resist Home Rule. Second, he encouraged and supported
the creation of the Ulster Volunteer Force to provide active, local,
militia-like resistance to the government. And third, he had no hesi-
tance in encouraging a virtual mutiny among scores of British officers with strong ties to Ulster. A few examples will suffice.

On 4 November 1913, the same day he was promoted to major

general, Wilson talked with General Sir John French, chief of the General Staff:

> Sir John had a long talk with me about Ulster. He is evidently nervous that we are coming to civil war, and his attitude appears to be that he will obey the King's orders. He wanted to know what I would do. I told him that I could not fire on the North at the dictation of [John] Redmond [a leading Irish MP] and this is what the whole thing means.

In early December, after lunch with Fred Oliver, a leading Tory, Wilson talked of

> the irreparable damage which the present state of affairs is doing to the army, and the necessity of ending the disgraceful state we are in. . . . There is no time to be lost. Already all ranks are talking in a hostile manner of being employed against the north of Ireland.

In early January, he met with two leading generals for, as he put it, "a long and serious talk about Ulster, and whether we could not do something to keep the army out of it."

> We [the generals] realize our greatest difficulty is that poor Johnnie French is sitting in [War Minister] Seely's pocket and we understand has said that the army will be solid in obeying orders. This is most dangerous.[4]

As much as Wilson worried about the army and Ireland, he worried even more about those Anglo-Irish officers who might be ordered to carry out the desires of Liberal ministers. The issue came front and center in March 1914 when up to sixty officers prepared to resign rather than follow such orders (the Curragh incident). In the ensuing maneuvering to end this show of defiance, Wilson played such a prominent role that he further poisoned his relations with the Liberal leadership, though apparently not enough to be sacked. The general and Bonar Law were repeatedly in contact, and Wilson wrote in his diary that he thought of resigning. Eventually, the Liberal government managed to ease the situation. Among the Tory leadership, Wilson emerged as a hero, with Lord Milner saying "'the man who saved the Empire is Henry Wilson."[5] Even as he sought to prepare the BEF for war on the Continent, Wilson saw no contradiction in taking steps that cast doubt on whether the army would obey orders given by a Liberal government.

In the weeks after the Curragh incident, the Irish question simmered. Meanwhile, in Europe there were new Russo-German tensions, yet also some signs of a thaw in Anglo-German relations; even the Austro-Serbian friction appeared controlled. All that abruptly changed on 28 June when two shots by a Serbian-trained Bosnian Serb gunman felled the Archduke Franz Ferdinand and his wife, Sophie, in Sarajevo, Bosnia. The death of the heir apparent to the Habsburg throne soon brought an end to the peace of Europe.

IN JULY 1914, THE IRISH QUESTION and the threat of war on the Continent merged as issues in British politics. It has been customary for decades to say that internal politics played little role in decisions by the European governments to go to war in 1914. Closer study suggests that domestic unease in all the Great Powers except France played a large role in shaping the attitudes of decision makers, whether it was the Habsburg leadership in Vienna worried about losing control of Bosnia-Herzegovina if it did not act, or the Germans and their own domestic troubles, or London finding that the Continent offered a way out of Ireland. "What a real piece of luck this has been as regards Ireland—just averted a Civil War and when it is over we may all be tired of fighting," wrote a senior British general.[6]

Sir Edward Grey and the Foreign Office monitored developments on the Continent, yet there was little sense of urgency at the Foreign Office until the actual delivery of the Habsburg ultimatum late on Thursday, 23 July, with its forty-eight hour deadline. Outside the Foreign Office, attention centered not on Europe, but once more on Ireland and the prospect that Home Rule was about to be granted to Ireland without the kind of arrangements for Ulster that either the Irish or the Tory MPs could accept. The Liberal Cabinet, in almost constant session, focused entirely on Ireland. Even after Grey read the Austrian ultimatum to the Cabinet on Friday, 24 July, the group adjourned for the weekend without any discussion of Europe.

Ironically, Henry Wilson, who was obsessed by the Irish question, paid no attention to the European situation until Saturday, 25 July, and even then did not view it as serious. Confidently, he wrote: "My own opinion is that if Germany does not mobilize to-day there will be no war." The next day, Monday, with no sign of German action, he concluded, "I think there will be no war," though the French military attaché, Comte Eugene de la Panouse, had told him that Paris had learned the Austrians would move. The rest of his diary entry discusses riot deaths in Dublin and gunrunning at Howth.

Although Wilson may have taken things rather jauntily, Winston Churchill did not. On that Sunday, 26 July, he canceled orders that would have sent the naval reservists home after their annual maneuvers, and ordered a series of precautionary measures. The next day, even as Wilson remained relatively undisturbed, the Cabinet for the first time spent some time on the European situation and approved of the steps taken by Churchill. That day, it should be noted, Austria-Hungary declared war on Serbia, and shots were fired between Habsburg and Serbian troops near Belgrade; the war had started.

On Wednesday, 29 July, Asquith and the Cabinet discussed the European situation at length, having gotten agreement from the party leaders to suspend any action about Ireland for the moment. In the Cabinet there were sharp divisions and no support for intervention in a Continental war. But, to the apparent surprise of Wilson, the Cabinet ordered the start of the "Precautionary Period" to mobilization. Of this action he wrote: "I don't know why we are doing it, because there is nothing moving in Germany. We shall see. Anyhow this is more like business than I expected of this Government." That compliment, it should be added, was the last Asquith and Grey would receive from the general. Meanwhile, that night, British ships in the south of England sailed without lights through the Channel to their battle stations in the North Sea before the Germans or the Russians had mobilized.

On Thursday, Wilson judged the situation more seriously, given Berlin's maladroit attempt to get the British to agree to a violation of Belgium. Still, he was calm, almost casual.

Then on Friday, 31 July, Wilson's casual approach turned desperate and frenetic; for the next five days, he worked with little rest to get the government to commit first to help France and then to accept his plan of deployment. His frantic pace reflected the fact that Russia's mobilization on 30 July meant that the Germans would respond if Russia did not stop its preparations.

The Cabinet met again on that Friday. Once more, the group as a whole refused to commit Britain to a course of action. The most Grey could get was authorization to tell both France and Germany that a violation of Belgian neutrality would be regarded as a cause of war. A deeply disappointed Grey so informed French ambassador Paul Cambon of this news and seriously began to consider resigning, since he felt so strongly that Britain ought to support France.

Later that day, after news of Russian mobilization reached him, Wilson lamented that we are "doing nothing." He told the French attaché that France ought to break relations with Britain. But most of his anger was directed at the Liberals: "No C.I.D. has been held, no military opinion has been asked for by this Cabinet who are deciding the question of war." And "Squiffy," as Wilson derisively called Asquith, refused to stop training or order mobilization. "An awful day."

But Wilson was ever resourceful. That same day, he met Johnnie Baird, a Tory MP, and informed him of the situation, asking him to write Bonar Law and get him return to London to see Asquith. Nor did Wilson stop there. As his biographer C. E. Callwell noted, Wilson's home "became for the moment the centre of a movement of vital importance" for "bringing pressure upon the Government to support France in the struggle that had become inevitable."[7]

On Saturday, 1 August, aided by Leo Maxse and his longtime friend General Henry Rawlinson, Wilson organized what he called a "pogrom" to pressure the Cabinet. His choice of the word "pogrom" represented his true feelings about the Liberal government and his own narrow view of others. During that Saturday, Wilson contacted Leopold Amery, George Lloyd, and the *Times* editor Henry Wickham Steed, and got someone to contact Bonar Law and bring him back to London.

While pursuing the Tory leadership, Wilson found time to go to the French embassy to discuss the situation. He feared that should the Germans respect Belgium, there would be no British help. On this point, they could only wait. And meanwhile, the Cabinet, which met again that Saturday, refused to promise to intervene. Grey grew more frustrated, and his own inclination to resign increased. If he left, the Cabinet would collapse. Still, Asquith, for his part, waited patiently to see what would actually happen on the Continent while writing love notes to Venetia Stanley.

At 11 p.m. that Saturday night, on the eve of the meeting of the Cabinet the next day, Wilson went to Lansdowne House to see Lord Lansdowne (the former British foreign secretary), Bonar Law, the Duke of Devonshire, and Lord Edmund Talbot. The group agreed that Bonar Law would write Asquith and pledge Tory support for France; the letter stated that "any hesitation in now supporting France and Russia would be fatal to the honour and future security of the United Kingdom."[8]

This letter reached Asquith in the midst of two long Cabinet sessions that Sunday. Its effect cannot be overstressed; in essence, the Tory leadership made the strongest possible accusation that failure to intervene would hurt the national interest. The further threat suggested that if the Cabinet remained divided and Grey and Churchill and even Asquith departed, the Tories would be ready to form a new government that would help France. Such an action would force the Liberal ministers out, many of them with no prospect of immediate income. Given this possibility, and backed by the vociferous demands of the *Times* and other newspapers, the Cabinet found itself under siege: from the Tories, from the French, from the European situation, and from one of their own generals, Henry Wilson. Of the last's actions, Leo Maxse later wrote: "Speaking as one knowing what he did in the opening days of that sultry August, I remain lost in admiration of his wonderful nerve and verve and unrelaxing grip of a formidable situation."[9]

At the end of the Sunday sessions, with Lloyd George swinging to intervention, the Cabinet agreed to treat any German attack on the French coasts as an act of war and to restate its position on Belgium. Wilson remained angry at the Cabinet's distinction between the French coasts and the French border, but thought the Germans would attack Belgium and thus solve the problem of getting help to the French.

By nightfall on Monday, 3 August, Wilson and the French could rest more easily. The Germans had been obliging in their designs on the Belgians; Luxembourg had been seized; and military action on the Belgian frontier was under way. That afternoon, Sir Edward Grey had given a long address to the House of Commons, never once mentioning Russia but making it clear that London would defend Belgian neutrality and assist the French, though he said all this would be done without much damage to Britain—implying that the navy would do most of the work. In his diary, Wilson's evident jubilation, despite the delay for mobilization till 4 August, was evident: "Saw M. Cambon in Arthur Nicolson's room. He held out both hands to me. So different from day before yesterday."

But Wilson had other work to do. He now had to convince the Cabinet and the military high command to accept his arrangements to assist France. On Tuesday, 4 August, the day that Britain would, at 11 p.m., declare itself at war with Germany, Wilson briefed General French, the projected BEF commander, and General Archie Murray on the plans for France. Although he had called General French "a fool" just days before for talking of going to Antwerp, Wilson now found him an apt pupil.[10] And his coterie of Conservative friends— Milner, Baird, Lord Lovat, Amery, Maxse, and others—pressed the government to accept Wilson's plans. While pleased with news that Lord Kitchener would be the new minister of war, Wilson still castigated Grey for delays about the mobilization, calling them "sinful."

The key decisions to deploy the BEF came on Wednesday, 5 August. At this point, the long years of discussions between Wilson and the French staff became operative: he had a strategic plan ready to implement and could point to assurances given the French staff, whereas others could offer only suggestions, not real solutions. That morning Wilson briefed Generals French and Haig, the latter scheduled to command the I Corps. Somewhat to Wilson's consternation,

Haig thought they should wait to go to the Continent, a view that Wilson brushed aside by saying it was to be a short war and intervention had to come immediately to make a difference.

A 4 p.m., the War Council met at 10 Downing Street, chaired by Asquith and with all of the senior leadership present but Lloyd George. At one point, General French said they should just go to France and decide the destination later, since he thought the long-planned site at Maubeuge, on the Belgian border, might not be available. Kitchener and others talked of going to Amiens, all of which Wilson later said "led to our discussing strategy like idiots." Eventually, they agreed to send the troops to the arranged sites, though Kitchener wanted more conversation with Paris. And the group agreed in principle that all six divisions might go and one division would be ordered from India. Of this fateful session, the sarcastic general wrote: "An historic meeting of men, mostly entirely ignorant of their subject."

A day later, Kitchener angered Wilson with his decision to retain two divisions in Britain, thus sending only four infantry divisions and one of cavalry. This led to a confrontation with the Kitchener that did little good for Wilson's immediate career. Still, Wilson had the troops moving, and his arrangements went smoothly: no loss of life in the transport, 12,000 horses purchased in ten days, and no German awareness of the operation.

By 21–22 August, four BEF divisions had arrived at their deployed destination near Maubeuge, the Germans still unaware of their presence. That changed on the 22nd, when patrols ran into each other. Interestingly, the Prussian General Staff had considered the prospect of British intervention and discounted it. And ironically, the French general Joseph Joffre, despite all of his talks with Wilson over the years, had no great expectation of effective help from the British. Still, the British were in place, and when troops of the German First Army confronted them at Mons, the rapidity of fire was so great that the Germans believed the British had machine guns; they did not. The pressure of German numbers soon forced the British into retreat, but thanks to Henry Wilson and Kitchener, rather than withdraw to the Channel ports as would happen in 1940, the British troops were realigned with a new French division. By late August, these troops had forged a salient wedge between the German First and Second armies, which had swung east of Paris. It was this British presence, not actual military combat, that led General Moltke to decide to pull back and adjust his troops, in turn allowing the Battle of the Marne to take place. In a fashion far different from Wilson's expectations, the British had made a decisive contribution to the early outcome of the war, even if it was more from their presence than their fighting. From that point, the race to the sea began.

General Wilson spent much of the first months of the war as a senior staff officer, often in communication with the French. In 1916, he took over the IV Corps for a time, without noticeable success. He then returned to staff duty, and in early 1918 became chief of the Imperial General Staff, working effectively with the French leadership.

At the end of the war Wilson received a hereditary baronetcy and the military title of field marshal, the youngest commoner since Wellington to be so honored. He also got a grant of 10,000 pounds. And he continued as chief of staff, finding himself once more in the middle of the Irish question. This time, the six counties would be excluded from Home Rule. But Wilson's strident views were no secret, and he managed to alienate many Irish zealots. On 22 June 1922, two of them murdered him on his front door stoop just months after his retirement from the army and his election to Parliament.

WHAT DOES THE EXAMPLE OF HENRY WILSON say about the larger topic of civil-military relations, particularly in Britain? Answers to this question almost always reflect the political disposition of those asking and answering the question: conservatives go one way, liberals another, and my approach will be in the latter category. Civilian control has long been the norm in Britain and the United States, though Winston Churchill was more militaristic than many of his generals and admirals. Nor have civilian or military leaders been hesitant to deal with rank insubordination, though the higher the rank, the more careful civilians have been about dramatic changes. Still, Henry Wilson was certainly insubordinate, clearly overstepping his authority and openly working with members of an opposing political party to challenge the views and actions of the government in power. In most cases, this would have led even to a general's dismissal.

Why not in Wilson's case? First, his professional reputation gave him a certain aura that could not be easily dented. He was a superb professional strategist, and while he got some major things wrong about the German attack in 1914, his mistakes pale in comparison to those made by Joffre, Moltke, and Conrad von Hötzendorf. Second, he carefully cultivated political friends and allies, and this made it risky to sanction him for his behavior. If Asquith had sacked Wilson, it would have prompted a huge political firestorm, one the Prime Minister did not need. Third, the esteem he got from the French could not be ignored, however much the radicals in the

Cabinet might have wanted to do so. Fourth, the British army and its officers represented the Empire. The British public still gave credence to the army's role in defending the Empire and to those who led it, even after the Boer War debacle. To dismiss senior officers for what might be perceived as political reasons carried its own risks, certainly for a Liberal government just barely in control of its own destiny. The press would charge the Liberals with undermining national security and morale just as they had done to the army during the Boer War.

Still, there were some unpleasant consequences from Wilson's tactics and dominance. First, Asquith and then Lloyd George became gun shy about relieving British army leaders during the Great War; Churchill would not make the same mistake in the Second World War. A further consequence flowed from this as well. There was both a premium placed on conformity and skepticism about new tactics, equipment, and training, a skepticism only slowly overcome with the development of the early tanks, the coordinated use of airplanes, and new battlefield maneuvers.

Henry Wilson prepared Britain for war on the Continent, but his tactics and maneuvers shredded many operative concepts of civil-military relations. In the end, almost 900,000 British soldiers died in the Great War, far more than the single soldier the French had desired. The consequences of those losses would reverberate for generations—indeed, they still do. Wilson got his war and he got his six counties.

Spring Semester 2010

1. The most recent study—Keith Jeffrey, *Field Marshal Sir Henry Wilson: A Political Soldier* (Oxford, 2006)—almost totally ignores the July 1914 crisis.

2. C. E. Callwell, *Field-Marshal Sir Henry Wilson: His Life and Diaries,* 2 vols. (London, 1927). Unless otherwise noted, all quotations come from volume 1. The original diaries are now in the Imperial War Museum, London.

3. R. J. Q. Adams, *Bonar Law* (Stanford, Calif., 1999), p. 170.

4. Omitted in the printed diary.

5. Quoted in Callwell, *Wilson,* p. 144.

6. Quoted in Zara S. Steiner and Keith Neilson, *Britain and the Origins of the First World War* (2nd. edn., New York, 2003), p. 244.

7. Callwell, *Wilson,* p. 153.

8. Quoted in Samuel R. Williamson, Jr., *The Politics of Grand Strategy: Britain and France Prepare for War, 1904–1914* (Cambridge, Mass., 1969), p. 354.

9. Quoted in Callwell, *Wilson,* p. 155.

10. Omitted in the printed diary.

Somerset Maugham

SELINA HASTINGS

For much of his long life—he lived to be almost ninety-two—Somerset Maugham was the most famous writer in the world. He was known everywhere for his superb short stories and for his novels; the immensely acclaimed *Of Human Bondage* became one of the most widely read works of fiction of the twentieth century. His books, which were translated into almost every known tongue, filmed, and dramatized, sold in the millions, bringing him celebrity and enormous wealth. Wherever he went, he was pursued by journalists, eager for information: this extraordinary man seemed to know everyone, from Henry James to Winston Churchill, D. H. Lawrence to Charlie Chaplin. His magnificent villa in the south of France, much photographed and written about, was a byword for luxury and elegance. On the Riviera, as in London and New York, Maugham, always elegantly dressed, looking every inch the conventional English gentleman.

And yet conventional he was not. In Maugham's outwardly respectable existence there was a great deal he was determined to keep hidden, and in the latter part of his life, when he began to be besieged by would-be biographers, he did his utmost to make sure his privacy would remain intact. Evening after evening at the Villa Mauresque, Maugham went systematically through his papers, destroying hundreds of letters, throwing every last scrap of personal correspondence onto the fire. He also wrote to his friends, asking them to destroy any letters of his in their possession; and he issued strict instructions to his literary executors that no biography should be authorized, no access to his papers allowed, and all requests for information be firmly refused.

And what were these areas of experience that it was so important to keep concealed? Mainly, they had to do with his homosexuality, for Maugham lived in an era when, in Britain, homosexual practice was against the law. He was twenty-one in 1895, at the time of the trial of Oscar Wilde, an event that traumatized a generation of men who were not by nature inclined toward marriage. And although Maugham himself did marry, and fathered a child, his relations with his wife, Syrie, were wretchedly unhappy. Indeed, it was partly to escape Syrie that he undertook those long journeys in the South Pacific and the Far East that were to inspire some of his best-loved fiction. His companion on these journeys was a man who was the great love of his life, a dissolute charmer called Gerald Haxton.

Maugham met Haxton in 1914, when he was forty and Gerald was twenty-two. By this stage, Maugham was already famous, not yet from his novels but from having made a great name for himself as a playwright on both sides of the Atlantic. This was a success that had come to him after long years of struggle. He had been on the point of giving up trying to make a career as a writer when, by a fluke, a play of his, *Lady Frederick,* which had been turned down by no fewer than seventeen London managements, was put on to fill a gap at the Royal Court Theatre and, literally overnight, became a sensation. Audiences in 1907 were as shocked and thrilled by *Lady Frederick* as were audiences sixty years later when faced with full-frontal nudity on the stage in *Hair.* Within twelve months, Maugham, in his mid-thirties, had four plays running concurrently in the West End, a record that remained unbroken for more than a generation. He was also well on his way to becoming a very rich man.

For a long period at the beginning of his career, however, Maugham was seriously short of money. He had not been born into poverty. His first few years were spent in the pleasant surroundings of a large, comfortable apartment in Paris, just off the Champs-Elysées. Born in 1874, Maugham was the youngest of four boys. His father was a legal adviser to the British Embassy in Paris, and his adored mother was a beauty, with a large circle of friends. But by the age of ten, Maugham had lost both his parents, and his happy childhood was over. He was dispatched to England to be brought up by an uncle, the Reverend Henry Maugham, vicar of Whitstable, in Kent. The vicar was not a bad man, but he was narrow-minded, self-centered, and hadn't the faintest notion of how to cope with a child. Maugham was sent as a boarder to the King's School, Canterbury, where he was badly bullied: small for his age, he had never played cricket or football, knew nothing of current schoolboy customs or slang, and, having been brought up speaking French, was still not entirely at ease with the English language. Most damaging of all, he had developed a stammer, which was a huge joke to his classmates and an agony to him. On leaving school, Maugham decided somewhat bizarrely to train as a doctor: he knew even then that he wanted to write; he also wanted to travel; and he thought that if worse came to worst, then at least he could get a job as a ship's doctor and so see the world.

And this is very nearly what happened. In October 1897, after five years as a medical student at St. Thomas's Hospital, Maugham received his diploma, qualifying him to practice as surgeon and physician. A month earlier, his first written work had been published, a novel called *Liza of Lambeth,* inspired by the appalling poverty of the Lambeth slums, which he had come to know well while doing his rounds. ("I learned pretty well everything I know about human nature in the 5 years I spent at St Thomas's Hospital," he was later to say.)[1] The novel enjoyed a modest success, and Maugham believed he was now well launched on a literary career. Nothing if not industrious, he had finished a second novel even before the first made its appearance, but the second novel did far less well than *Liza,* and for the next ten years, Maugham struggled to make ends meet. He won some critical acclaim, and through one or two fortuitous contacts, with figures such as Edmund Gosse and Augustus Hare, he was taken up by some fashionable hostesses, who were pleased to have such a promising young writer as Somerset Maugham at their dinners and weekend parties. It was seated at their tables that Maugham met such famous figures as Edith Wharton, Henry James, and Thomas Hardy, and also Winston Churchill, with whom he was to form a lifelong friendship.

The critic Desmond MacCarthy memorably said of Maugham that he moved through London society "with the reserve and detachment of a professional man of letters."[2] Here, too, Maugham was undercover, an observer rather than a participant, and like the trained clinician that he was, he made detailed notes of his social encounters, relishing the opportunity to observe the upper classes in their natural habitat. It was at the end of a dazzling dinner of Lady St. Helier's, for instance, that Maugham found himself sitting next to the elderly Duke of Abercorn. "Do you like cigars?" the duke asked him, taking out of his pocket a large cigar case. "Very much," said Maugham, who could rarely afford them. "So do I," continued the duke, selecting one and inspecting it carefully. "And when I come to dinner," he continued lighting up, "I always bring my own." He snapped the case shut and returned it to his pocket. "I advise you to do the same." Maugham's fellow guests on such occasions were invariably well off, while he was poor, obliged to economize where he could. Dining out meant dressing in white tie and tails, with kid gloves and a silk top hat, and since cabs were beyond his means, Maugham usually traveled by bus. When invited to the country for a Friday to Monday, greater expenditure was unavoidable, with half sovereigns to be dispensed to the butler, to the footman who brought the morning tea, and often to a second footman who unpacked his bag and acted as valet. At a large house party, young bachelors were sometimes obliged to share a bed, which not infrequently led to sex. "Often it turned out to be very pleasant," Maugham recalled.[3]

Looking back on the days of his young manhood, Maugham used to say, "I tried to persuade myself that I was three-quarters normal and only a quarter queer—whereas really it was the other way round."[4] Maugham adored women; he wrote about them with exceptional sympathy and understanding, many of his closest friends were women, and of the two serious love affairs of his life, one was with a beautiful actress called Sue Jones, whose portrait he drew as Rosie in that wicked and wonderful novel *Cakes and Ale.* But Maugham was basically homosexual, a fact he found it essential to conceal while living in England, the country with the most punitive laws against homosexual practice of any country in Europe. Maugham made great efforts to pass as "normal," as he put it. Both his surviving brothers were deeply respectable, both were married with children, and both were lawyers, one, indeed, became Lord Chancellor, a distinction for which, on retirement, he was rewarded with a hereditary peerage. This all mattered very much to Maugham. During the thirty or so years that he lived in England, he was, on the whole, careful to conduct himself with decorum, going abroad with his boyfriends, and in London making his contacts in safe houses, under the eye of sympathetic hostesses like Ada Leverson. She had been a faithful friend to Oscar Wilde, who called her his "Sphinx," and during the early 1900s was regarded as the patron of a mainly homosexual coterie that included, as well as Somerset Maugham, Robbie Ross, Reggie Turner, and Lord Alfred Douglas. Ada was attracted to effeminate young men—she had once tried, unsuccessfully, to seduce Aubrey Beardsley—and for a time she became very close to Maugham. In one of her novels, she drew a portrait of him as Hereford Vaughan, whose private life remains frustratingly mysterious to the many unattached young ladies hoping to ensnare him.

IT WAS DURING THE FIRST WORLD WAR that Maugham's habit of leading a double life took on a new momentum. In 1914, he had just turned forty and was riding very high indeed, one of the richest and most popular playwrights in Britain and America; he had also just finished a novel, *Of Human Bondage,* that was to sell in the millions and become regarded as a classic for more than fifty years. His private life, however, was far from happy. To his great grief, the long relationship with Sue Jones had recently ended, and he was currently consoling himself with a married woman who was living apart from her wealthy and much older husband. Syrie Wellcome was lively and fun, and for a time Maugham enjoyed what he regarded as no more than a brief, light-hearted affair, until Syrie began putting pressure on him to marry her. Alarmed, Maugham made it clear there was to be no question of that, and he took himself off to Capri in the hope that in his absence, Syrie would put the idea out of her head. But Syrie was nothing if not determined, and at the beginning of August she followed him to the island, her arrival coinciding with Britain's declaration of war against Germany. Maugham returned immediately to London to join a detachment of Red Cross volunteers about to be dispatched to the front, but before he left, Syrie told him she was pregnant. Maugham was horrified: he felt he had been deliberately trapped. The idea of marrying Syrie appalled him, and yet he wanted to behave honorably, and so he told her that when the time came, he would not abandon her. And with that, Syrie was obliged to be content.

It was only a little time later, and not long after Maugham arrived with his unit in France, that he encountered the man who was to be the great love of his life. Gerald Haxton was a handsome American, a charming, gregarious fellow almost twenty years younger than Maugham. He was also in France as a Red Cross volunteer, and the two met while working in the same makeshift hospital, Gerald recognizing the well-known playwright, whose picture he had seen in the paper. One night after they had come off duty, he and Maugham found themselves standing on a balcony overlooking the garden, talking of what they would do when the war was over. Maugham said he wanted to write and to travel: what did Gerald want? "From you or from life?" the young man asked provocatively. "Perhaps both," Maugham replied. "They might turn out to be the same thing."[5] Soon after this, their units were separated, but Maugham knew he had found what he wanted, and for the next thirty years, Gerald Haxton remained the center of his existence. After the war, they met whenever they could, which was not always easy: by this time, Maugham was a married man with a high profile in London society, while Gerald, because of an unfortunate incident with another man in a Covent Garden hotel, had been declared an undesirable alien and forbidden ever to set foot on British soil. Thus, during the long years of his miserable marriage to Syrie, Maugham escaped at every opportunity to join Gerald on the Continent, taking him on his long journeys to the South Pacific and the Far East, and after Maugham's divorce, he installed him in the Villa Mauresque, the house he bought for himself in the south of France.

Maugham's friends were divided in their view of Gerald. Some saw him as a benevolent charmer whose good humor did much to counter the older man's irritability and bouts of depression: "[He] charmed the birds from the trees . . . [and] Willie was always enraptured by him," said the writer Arthur Marshall, an opinion seconded by the novelist Hugh Walpole, who wrote in his diary that Haxton was "charming, full of kindness and shrewdness mixed."[6] There were others, however, who regarded Gerald almost as the devil incarnate. "Shifty," "disreputable," "a cad," and "just this side of being a crook" are the words and phrases that repeatedly occur; the writer Peter Quennell, who memorably described Haxton as being "very masculine . . . with a hard tarty face," was one of many who judged his influence to have been entirely deleterious, holding him responsible for introducing the previously fastidious Maugham to some of the most sordid areas of the homosexual underworld.[7] But perhaps most revealing is the portrait Maugham himself drew of Gerald as Rowley Flint in his novella *Up at the Villa:* "[Rowley] had an air of dissipation and people who didn't like him said he looked shifty . . . [but] what Rowley Flint had which explained everything was sex appeal . . . There was something that swept you off your feet, a sort of gentleness behind the roughness of his manner, a thrilling warmth behind his mockery . . . and the sensuality of his mouth and the caress in his grey eyes."[8]

All this apart, Gerald was important to Maugham professionally. With his stammer and his innate reserve, Maugham found it difficult to talk easily to people he didn't know. And yet as a writer of fiction, he depended on other people, on strangers, to provide him with his material. And this is where Gerald quickly made himself invaluable. On board ship or drinking in a bar or sitting smoking on a hotel verandah, Gerald naturally fell into conversation, effortlessly making friends with casual acquaintances, with whom he was more than happy to pass hours drinking, talking, and playing poker. And afterward, he would report back to Maugham the stories they had to tell.

His talents in this direction were evident on the very first trip he and Maugham took together, to the South Pacific in 1916. On the long sea voyage from San Francisco to Tahiti, the ship called in at Hawaii, where the two men stayed for nearly three weeks, exploring the islands and, with the help of Gerald's sociability, uncovering the often extraordinary histories of the traders, half-castes, doctors, and missionaries with whom they fell into conversation.

On their last night in Honolulu, there was a police raid in the red-light district, and the following day, a few minutes before the ship was due to sail, a young woman came hurrying up the gangplank, clearly in a state of panic. She was a Miss Sadie Thompson, it turned out, a prostitute fleeing the police. Once at sea, however, she quickly regained her composure, and antagonized her fellow passengers— among them a couple of missionaries—by playing ragtime loudly on her gramophone and throwing drunken parties in her cabin for the ship's crew. This interlude was to be turned into Maugham's most famous short story, "Rain," which made its first appearance in book form in his collection *The Trembling of a Leaf.* "Rain," which was to earn its author more than $1 million in royalties, was endlessly reprinted; it was also reworked as a play, turned into a musical, and filmed no fewer than three times, with Gloria Swanson, Joan Crawford, and Rita Hayworth in the part of Sadie.

Maugham returned from the South Pacific to New York in 1917, taking reluctant leave of Gerald, who had decided to enlist. Maugham, too, was to be involved in war work, though of a rather different nature, a continuation of an enterprise he had first undertaken in Switzerland in 1915. At the end of 1914, he had left his job in the Red Cross to come back to England, mainly because he had to deal with the fact that Syrie was shortly to give birth to his child and was expecting him to marry her. Such a change in circumstance was not at all to his liking, but there seemed no honorable way out, and Maugham was resigned to doing the decent thing. He did not, however, wish to stay any longer than he could help, and thus accepted with alacrity when approached by a mysterious Major Wallinger with a proposal that he should do some undercover work for British intelligence in Geneva.

Here Maugham had the perfect cover, that of a writer retiring to the peace and quiet of a neutral country in order to write. The whole idea of becoming a spy appealed to him enormously. He had no difficulty playing a part; he always preferred listening to talking, and his fascination with other people's lives had developed in him an unusual level of perception. In Switzerland, Maugham (code name "Somerville") found that his own duties were, on the whole, fairly safe and routine, mainly involved with issuing instructions to agents and debriefing them on their return from sorties into Germany. Having made careful note of what he was told and adding his own observations, he would then write a detailed report and transmit it in code. Apart from an increased watchfulness, and the fact that at all times he carried a small revolver in his overcoat pocket, to Maugham there was little about the work that differentiated it from any routine office job. The regularity of his timetable led to a certain tedium in an existence that Maugham described as being in many respects "as orderly and monotonous as a city clerk's."[9]

The situation was very different on his second mission, which was to Russia, in 1917. On this occasion, Maugham had been recruited to act as an unofficial liaison between the Russian leader, Alexander Kerensky, and the British government. Britain, desperate to keep Russia in the war, was mounting a secret operation designed to offer support to Kerensky, who was committed to continuing the fight but whose position, under attack by Lenin and his Bolsheviks, was beginning to look worryingly insecure.

When Maugham arrived in Petrograd at the end of August, he found the city in a state of turmoil. Six months previously, the February Revolution had forced the abdication of the czar, igniting an anarchic period of riot and confusion. The day after he arrived, Maugham duly presented himself at the British Embassy. Only the vaguest explanation had been provided by London for Maugham's presence in Petrograd, but it was expected nonetheless that the embassy should offer him any assistance he required, specifically in the transmission of reports, to be sent in code via the British consul in New York. This did not go down at all well with the ambassador, Sir George Buchanan, who received Maugham with frigid courtesy, acidulously making clear that the well-known writer was a far from welcome visitor. Here was this inexperienced amateur, as Buchanan saw it, who not only was to be allowed direct access to Kerensky himself, but whose encrypted cables were to be sent on by the embassy in a code it could not read and without the ambassador being made privy to their content. It was this last, in particular, that Sir George regarded as a grave affront. "I realized," wrote Maugham after the interview was over, "that I could not count on much help in that quarter."[10]

Maugham's impression on first meeting Kerensky was that his position was too perilous to merit Allied support, an impression that did not change in further encounters, although he continued to confer with the Russian premier and his colleagues. For Kerensky, the Englishman was becoming an increasingly crucial contact in his dealings with the Allied powers. The American ambassador, a former grain merchant from St. Louis, rarely put his head above the parapet, while Buchanan, in Kerensky's view, was proving impossibly obdurate; it wasn't long before the Russian leader's only direct line to Downing Street was that provided sub rosa by Somerset Maugham.

As before in Switzerland, Maugham had a team of agents under his control, to be employed as he thought fit, and as before, much time was spent diligently filing his reports and spending long evenings in his hotel bedroom, encrypting the information he had gathered during the day. The novelist Hugh Walpole, also in Petrograd at this time, was intrigued by Maugham's observations on the rapidly changing political scene. "He watched Russia as we would watch a play, finding the theme, and then intent on observing how the master artist would develop it," he wrote.[11] But now the play was drawing to a close. By mid-October, it was obvious to all that the Bolsheviks would soon be in power, and since Maugham, "the secret agent of reactionary imperialism," was a marked man, it was decided to recall him.[12]

Maugham left Petrograd on 22 October 1917, two days before the outbreak of Lenin's Bolshevik Revolution. He never returned to Russia, but his natural affinity for intelligence work was revealed to a wide public when he wrote a series of stories about his activities, known as the "Ashenden" stories after the name he gave his protagonist, closely modeled on himself. Interestingly, Maugham was the first to write about the business of espionage as in actuality it was, depicting the world of undercover intelligence as not only morally dubious but also frequently boring. Maugham was never tempted to glamorize his assignments, never lost the cool, clinical eye that rested so dispassionately on his surroundings, and it is this clear-eyed vision that largely accounts for the extraordinary impact that *Ashenden* made on the writing of espionage fiction. Up till then, spy stories had been unashamedly escapist and melodramatic, and thus, Maugham's realistic approach came as a shock to many readers and set the tone for an entirely new generation of British spy fiction. "The modern spy story began with Somerset Maugham's *Ashenden*," wrote the critic and crime writer Julian Symons, a statement with which many distinguished followers of the genre agreed.[13] Among them was John Le Carré, who credited Maugham with having significantly influenced his own work, saying that his predecessor "was the first person to write about espionage in a mood of disenchantment and almost prosaic reality."[14]

Ashenden was eventually published in 1928, having been held up for ten years by a Foreign Office veto. There had originally been thirty-one stories, but when Maugham showed them to Winston Churchill in draft, Churchill insisted on fourteen being destroyed, since he considered them in breach of the Official Secrets Act. From that time on, *Ashenden* has continued to flourish: it has been made into a film, *The Secret Agent* by Alfred Hitchcock, and for several years was required reading for entrants into MI5 (the British counterintelligence and security agency) and MI6 (the foreign-intelligence service), as well as inspiring a study of British spy fiction on the part of Soviet military intelligence. But perhaps the ultimate accolade was awarded during the Second World War, when the *Ashenden* stories were referred to in a broadcast by Joseph Goebbels, the German minister for propaganda, who cited them as a typical example of British cynicism and brutality.

AFTER THE END OF THE WAR, Maugham's work in espionage was temporarily laid aside, and yet, in an important sense, he continued to live undercover. As a married man with a small daughter, he led a life that to outward appearances seemed that of a fairly conventional husband and father. Mr. and Mrs. Somerset Maugham were a fashionable couple, they entertained lavishly, everybody wanted to know them, and in the relatively small society of 1920s London, almost everyone did. Yet in private, the strain on Maugham of maintaining a double life, of dividing himself between Syrie, who increasingly bored and repelled him, and Gerald Haxton, to whom he was wholly in thrall, was beginning to seem untenable. Maugham still looked on London as his base: it was his home, the center of his social and professional life; and yet it was also where he felt most repressed and confined. Gerald, representing freedom and adventure, remained on the other side of the Channel, and it was not possible for Maugham to endure his absence for long. Knowing this, Syrie was passionately jealous, and night after night the most fearful rows went on behind closed doors.

For more than a decade, Maugham sought to escape his miserable marital situation in travel. He was never happier than when he was on the high seas, sailing to a distant and preferably unfamiliar destination. "I can't see a ship without wanting to get on it," he used to say, and in the many voyages undertaken over the years, he was a passenger on every variety of vessel, from the great transatlantic liners to pearl luggers sailing the Indian Ocean and the rusty little traders laden with bananas and copra that plied regularly between the islands of the South Pacific.

Maugham loved to explore, loved to be on the move, and always found in travel not only a source of inspiration for his writing but also an enormous sense of freedom, freedom from social, domestic, and moral constraints, and freedom as well from the limitations of his own sometimes suffocating sense of self. He identified strongly with William Hazlitt's "Gentleman in the Parlour," a title he gave to an account of his journey through Burma and Siam in 1922. Travel, wrote Hazlitt, enables us "to shake off the trammels of the world and of public opinion—to lose our importunate, tormenting, everlasting personal identity in the elements of nature, and become the creature of the moment, clear of all ties . . . to be known by no other title than The Gentleman in the Parlour!"[15]

Time and again Maugham's stories are set against the background of a ship at sea: "Mr Know-All," in which the narrator shares a cabin with the insufferable Mr. Kelada while crossing from New York; "Winter Cruise," in which Miss Reid, a feisty spinster, drives everyone mad with her constant chatter onboard a small German freighter in the Caribbean; and "P&O," in which Mrs. Hamlyn returns home from the Far East, a long voyage that gives her plenty of time to observe her fellow travelers:

> The approach of Christmas gave them an occupation, for someone had suggested that there should be a fancy-dress dance on Christmas day . . . [and] a meeting was held of the first-class passengers to decide whether the second-class passengers should be invited . . . The ladies said that the second-class passengers would only feel ill-at-ease. On Christmas day it was to be expected that they would drink more than was good for them and unpleasantness might ensue. Everyone who spoke insisted that . . . no one would be so snobbish as to think there was any difference between first and second-class passengers as far as that went, but it would really be kinder to the second-class passengers not to put them in a false position.[16]

Maugham was often a passenger on ships like these, en route to Hong Kong or Singapore. For many of his readers, Somerset Maugham is identified with the British Empire and the Far East. Just as Kipling belongs to India and the Raj, so Maugham is associated with the Malay Archipelago, and much of the best of his fiction stands as testimony to his fascinated exploration of this long-vanished world. Those famous tales of his set on rubber estates, on remote outstations, in the card rooms of the local club, those stories of incest and adultery, of footsteps in the jungle and murder on the verandah, are what remain in the minds of many as the very image and epitome of Maugham's fictional territory. As Cyril Connolly once wrote, "If all else perish, there will remain a story-teller's world from Singapore to the Marquesas that is exclusively and forever

Maugham, a world of veranda and prahu which we enter, as we do that of Conan Doyle's Baker Street, with a sense of happy and eternal homecoming."[17]

Home for Maugham, however, meant a return to Syrie in London and a domesticity that he found increasingly intolerable. In 1928, Maugham finally managed to procure the divorce for which he had longed for eleven years. "I made a mistake when I married her," he wrote bitterly. "We . . . had nothing in common and . . . I brought happiness neither to her nor to myself."[18] As soon as he was free of his wife, he bought a house in the south of France, the Villa Mauresque, where he was to spend the remaining nearly forty years of his life. On Cap Ferrat, in the warmth and light of the Riviera, Maugham was at liberty at last to lead the life he wanted, and the Mauresque became a byword for luxury and comfort and, among Maugham's homosexual coterie at least, an unusually liberated way of life.

And yet even here, Maugham to an extent remained under cover. He was a generous and genial host, but behind the apparent ease of manner, a formidable discipline was carefully concealed. In a sense, the way of life at the Mauresque summed up the two sides of his nature, on one side luxe and warmth and sensuousness, on the other the austerity of the artist and a rigorous self-control. While his guests slept late and idled by the pool, Maugham followed a strict and unvarying daily routine that nothing was allowed to disarrange. Every morning he awoke early and spent the first hour or so reading before his breakfast was brought to him in bed. At eight thirty he had his bath, and at nine, he retired to his rooftop study, well away from the rest of the house, and here he remained until just before one, when he came downstairs to join his guests for a cocktail, never more than one, on the terrace before lunch.

For Maugham, writing was not just what he did: it was where he lived. "I have never been able to persuade myself that anything else mattered," he wrote in his memoir, *The Summing Up*.[19] While at work, he was completely in control, in a world of his own making, and in extreme old age he stated that the happiest hours of his life had been experienced while seated at his desk when his writing was going well and "word followed word till the luncheon gong forced me to put an end to the days' work."[20] While in the middle of a novel, Maugham said, his characters were more real to him than the characters of real life, more vivid and more meaningful than any in the physical world outside. The words did not always flow, and sometimes a single page had to be written and rewritten, but however difficult, the experience never failed to be wholly absorbing. Yet in the final analysis, the actual process of creation, "the most enthralling of human activities," as Maugham described it, was impossible to pin down.[21] The precise moment of alchemical reaction remained a mystery, explicable only as the work of the subconscious, or as he put it, of "the useful little imp that dwells in your fountain pen and does for you all your best writing."[22]

ALMOST UNTIL THE END, MAUGHAM remained extraordinarily hardworking and productive. He had also, for more than half a century, been extremely famous, and in his last twenty years or so, he was plagued by would-be biographers, all keen to unravel his extraordinary story. Such a man, such a life presented an irresistible subject, but Maugham was determined to allow none of it, and he went to great lengths to protect himself. He instructed his literary executors that after his death, they should continue to refuse information and access to all applicants and deny permission for the publication of his letters. Further to cover his tracks, Maugham burnt every scrap of documentary evidence he could lay his hands on. For years, he had been ruthless with shredding his own correspondence, and in a series of great bonfires at the Mauresque, Maugham threw into the flames every fragment he could find. He also wrote to all his old friends, asking them to tear up any correspondence of his they might have—which, of course, ensured not only that this correspondence was kept, but also that it was sold, for very large sums, to American universities.

In 1955, when he was eighty-one, he was asked in a newspaper interview whether he liked the idea of having his biography written. No, he did not. It would be a pointless exercise, in his view. "The lives of modern writers are not interesting in themselves," he said dismissively. "A life of myself is bound to be dull . . . [and] I don't want to be associated with dullness."[23] There was little danger of that. Maugham's life was extraordinary. Not only is he one of the great storytellers of our time, but there is also an enormous amount to be learned from Maugham's own story, from his life. It is the truth that is important: the life throws light on the work, and Maugham's work, much of it now overlooked or forgotten, deserves to be lit. And after all, nothing can hurt him now.

Spring Semester 2010

1. Somerset Maugham to Barbara Kurz, April 1961 (Howard Gotlieb Archival Research Center, University of Boston).

2. Desmond McCarthy, *William Somerset Maugham: The English Maupassant* (London, 1934), p. 4.

3. Quoted by Raymond Mortimer in an interview by Robert Calder, 2 Nov. 1972 (Neil Jenman Collection, New South Wales).

4. Robin Maugham, *Escape from the Shadows* (London, 1972), p. 232.

5. Robin Maugham, *Conversations with Willie* (London, 1978), p. 18.

6. Arthur Marshall, interview by Robert Calder (Neil Jenman Collection); Hugh Walpole, MS diary (Harry Ransom Center, University of Texas at Austin).

7. Peter Quennell, interview by Robert Calder (Neil Jenman Collection).

8. W. Somerset Maugham, *Up at the Villa* (1941; New York, 2000), p. 17.

9. W. Somerset Maugham, *Ashenden* (1928; New York, 2000), p. 109.

10. W. Somerset Maugham, "Looking Back" (unpublished MS), p. 80.

11. Hugh Walpole, "William Somerset Maugham," *Vanity Fair*, 1920.

12. Rhodri Jeffreys-Jones, *American Espionage: From Secret Service to CIA* (New York, 1977), p. 96.

13. Julian Symons, *New York Times Book Review*, 13 Sept. 1981.

14. Quoted in Ted Morgan, *Maugham* (New York, 1980), p. 313.

15. Quoted in W. Somerset Maugham, *The Gentleman in the Parlour* (1933; New York, 2001), p. 4.

16. W. Somerset Maugham, *The Casuarina Tree* (1926; Oxford, 1985), p. 55.

17. Cyril Connolly, *Sunday Times*, 19 Dec. 1965.

18. Maugham, "Looking Back," p. 110.

19. W. Somerset Maugham, *The Summing Up* (1938; New York, 2001), p. 229.

20. Maugham, "Looking Back," p. 5.

21. Maugham, *Summing Up*, p. 222.

22. W. Somerset Maugham, *Plays*, vol. 5 (London, 1934), p. viii.

23. Quoted in the *Sunday Express*, 16 Apr. 1955.

8

Olivia Manning

PHYLLIS LASSNER

F rom a *New York Times* story on 15 August 2010, with a Calcutta dateline:

> Entering the crumbling mansion of the Lawrence D'Souza Old Age Home here is a visit to a vanishing world.
>
> Breakfast tea from a cup and saucer, Agatha Christie murder mysteries, a weekly visit from the hairdresser, who sets a dowager's delicate hair in a 1940s-style wave. Sometimes, a tailor comes to make the old-style garments beloved by Anglo-Indian women of a certain age. . . .
>
> "On Sundays, we listen to jive, although we don't dance much anymore," said Sybil Martyr, a 96-year-old retired school teacher, with a crisp English accent.
>
> "We're museum pieces," she said.

Museum pieces—ornamental shards of a culture that have been stored away and forgotten, perhaps, many might feel, in the best interests of all. But there is a contrary view, and this lecture attempts to restore to view a colonial site a little farther west: the Middle East, particularly Palestine and Egypt, where the sun set a little later on the British Empire. There are women, perhaps even Sybil Martyr herself, who have stories to tell that might very well complicate, even challenge what has become conventional wisdom—that it is the colonized who, because it is their experience, know the truth of colonial racial oppression and of how and why the sun had to set on the British Empire.

As the Empire was ending, post-colonial subjects found their way
to the imperial epicenter and altered the landscape of British culture
in significant ways. Not the least of which was the inclusion of race
as a category of analysis. And yet despite this inclusion—indeed, this
highly charged emphasis—it remains startling that the specifically
racialized decade of the 1940s has found no points of convergence
with post-colonial studies. Most significantly, despite the fact that
the Second World War was launched by the Axis powers as an imperial conquest based on racialist ideology and precipitated the end of
all European empires, there has been little attempt to integrate this
cataclysmic event into the racially defined and ever-expanding post-
colonial and transnational narratives. If, as post-colonial critics argue, "modernity, in all its incompleteness and instability was made
through colonialism," where is that most globally destabilizing event
of modernity, the Second World War?[1]

It is in the writing of British women who refused to be ignored in
the story of the end of empire and its relation to the Second World
War and racial modernity. These writers argued that because the
war was the defining moment leading to the end of empire, it could
no longer remain absent from modern cultural history. In the shadows of a global imperial battle, British women writers constructed
their own racial analyses and gendered verdicts of the end of empire. And yet despite a deluge of theory and analysis of colonial and
post-colonial experience, representation, and its gendered amend-
ments, the white colonial woman writer remains invisible or marginalized. An illustration of this is the case of Doris Lessing and Nadine
Gordimer. Despite, or perhaps because of, their prominence, they
are often dismissed for exhibiting false consciousness, that is, even
as they represent the evils of apartheid, they are condemned either
for the failure to represent the consciousness of the colonized or for
exploiting that consciousness for the sake of white colonial creativity.
Damned if they do and damned if they don't, these women writers
and others never fail to speak self-consciously from their privileged
social positions and critique them. Their novels and memoirs fully
recognize their status even as their own racial, economic, and gendered positions may have denied them privilege. In the case of the
Caribbean writer Phyllis Shand Allfrey, despite years of working tirelessly on behalf of Dominica's independence and workers' rights, she
was ousted from a governmental position because she was a white
woman. And so, just as traditional literary canons had criteria for
ignoring the troublesome figures of women writers, so we now have
post-canonical, post-colonial criteria for setting boundaries and perhaps settling scores. The result reduces the complex cultural and

political identities and agendas of white women colonial writers to models of complicity with imperial racial ideologies.

Now many post-colonial critics argue for the necessity of complicating such oppositions as oppressor and victim. After all, the category of victim denies women the ability to act on their own sense of selves, and victimhood assumes their passivity. As a remedy, feminist critics have analyzed the voices of colonized women. In the very act of recognizing the right of colonized women to represent themselves, however, post-colonial critics have not extended the same license to such colonial women as Elspeth Huxley, who grew up in British Kenya, or Rumer Godden, who was raised in British India. But these and other colonial women writers also had crucial stories to tell. Instead, colonial women are treated with equal doses of righteous indignation, depicted either as victims of men who coerced them from the manicured greens of Tunbridge Wells to the heat and dust of the Vale of Kashmir, or as agents of the imperial project, loading their Liberty chintzes onto the bent backs of their blacks. Settler writers in particular, such as Huxley, are seen as having succumbed to the lure of adventure, profit, and power, and of being duped into believing they could be authentically British. Such criticism does not accept the possibility that a colonial writer can have a political identity with integrity equal to that of the critic.

Viewing the colonial woman as a life-writing subject with complicated identity politics of her own offers new strategies for the production of colonial and post-colonial knowledge. The positions of second-generation settler writers such as Rumer Godden and Elspeth Huxley, and of Phyllis Shand Allfrey, whose family roots in the Caribbean date from the seventeenth century, questioned the terms "national identity" and "cultural identity," because these writers did not have just one of each. Though they grew up in colonial homes, were British subjects, and lived in Britain as adults, all three settler writers identify with the spaces and historical crises that defined their migrations. There was no homeland to endow them with stabilizing citizenship. Each one, moreover, abandoned the colonial culture in which she was reared to become a writer who questioned the very ethos of colonial settlement. Because England was an unknown and alien place until they were adults, these writers saw English political and social culture from an in-between distance. Alienation provided them with the recognition that British superiority was merely an arbitrary sign that lost its grip under imaginative scrutiny. Another group of writers, including Phyllis Bottome, Olivia Manning, and Muriel Spark, were also British citizens, but most of their writing, political, and emotional lives were spent in

destabilizing circumstances, on the move from Central Europe to
the Middle and Far East. It was from these crisis-ridden places that
they recognized the convergences and differences between the British Empire and its would-be conqueror, the Third Reich.

Many of these writers plotted fictional as well as autobiographical
relationships in which the values, felt experiences, and insights of
the colonizer and colonized not only intersect, but also intertwine in
clashes, even in their attempts at mutual understanding. In Phyllis
Bottome's novel of colonial Jamaica, *Under the Skin* (1950), seething
racial tensions in a school of mixed-race students and staff explode
in a murder plot against a well-intentioned English headmistress.
Elspeth Huxley's childhood memoir *The Flame Trees of Thika* (1959)
depicts the inevitable failure of English settlers to dominate the Ki-
kuyu social justice system. These and other writers used their imaginative renderings of historical, social, and political contexts to raise
critical questions about colonial identities, colonial subjects, and
their cross-critical perspectives.

These women wrote to understand and critique the Empire while
sometimes struggling, and failing, to find a place for themselves
within or outside it. In all cases, they provided a critical response to
the complaint that they were beset by nostalgia for an idyllic colonial
Eden. Among their many critical insights, these women viewed relationships between colonial subjects and objects as an intertwined
history of cultural transformation that remains a haunting and anxious force. For example, even in its humane critique of colonialism,
Rumer Godden's 1946 novel of India, *The River,* expresses a desire
for the British presence to have been benign, a desire that could not
be met in the hybrid identities of the soon-to-be post-colonial state,
no matter how fruitfully they were negotiated. Through a variety of
tragicomic colonial encounters, British women writers resisted treating the narration of imperial history, in the words of one critic, "as a
romantic . . . compensation for its tragic acts and consequences."[2]

Instead, their fictions show how the lingering effects of colonialism can be understood by reflecting back on the protracted demise
of the Empire. In representing that lingering denouement as a defining moment instead of an anticlimax, many of these women's
novels show how the intensity of feeling on both sides of the colonial
divide could produce a reverberating violence even as the world was
engaged in its most violent war.

A CASE STUDY: THE ANGLO-IRISH Olivia Manning writing about the
end of the British Empire in the Middle East. In her own words:
"Christmas 1941: a feast without food. In the Middle East, the dis-

posed of Europe gave thanks for Pearl Harbour and waited for the war to turn round."[3] Of all the exotic sites of imperial imagination, the Middle East is closest to the heart of Western civilization. And yet despite its sacred and profane history, despite the proliferation of books by writers from all over the Middle East being translated into English, its colonial and post-colonial literature by British writers, especially women, is mostly absent. This is not to say that this writing isn't read. Muriel Spark's prominence guarantees that her novel of Israel and Jordan, *The Mandelbaum Gate* (1965), is always cited by scholars, but it is also considered peculiar. Olivia Manning's *Levant Trilogy* (1977–80) has been in print ever since its Masterpiece Theater production introduced Kenneth Branagh and Emma Thompson as the exiled Guy and Harriet Pringle. But like an anti-Orientalist dream come true, such films as Agatha Christie's *Death on the Nile* (1937), are easily accused of offering more lessons in vintage couture than in history.

Olivia Manning, whose writing life was propelled by world war and the end of empire, set the tone for her career with her 1937 novel, *The Wind Changes,* which depicts the Irish rebellion against British rule and provides witness to the Empire's final blows. Manning's finest moments as a novelist are expressed in her dramatization of Britain's greatest threat, the Nazi siege of Europe and the Middle East, as she and her husband flee the Nazis across the Balkans to Cairo and Jerusalem, where the Allies were under attack in the desert. The scope and passion of her epic construction of the war are narrated from the perspective of an outsider, not only to the indigenous cultures around her, but to the British mission, from which she chose to remain aloof. She could not, however, be accused of detachment, for this perspective enabled her to develop empathy for those oppressed by any imperial force. Nowhere did this become clearer than in the Middle East, where refugees from Nazi-occupied Europe found themselves competing for safe ground with those who could barely remember when the land was not colonized.

The novels that compose Manning's Middle East saga had to wait to be written until the war was over and she could stop running. But as she told her friend Kay Dick, "I write out of experience. I have no fantasy. I don't think anything I've experienced has ever been wasted."[4] In her experience of the Middle East, it is Cairo and Jerusalem that capture her imagination. The Jerusalem of Manning's 1951 novel, *School for Love,* may be considered an icon for many, representing universal love and peace as the holiest site for three monotheistic religions, but as she points out, its very sanctity has inspired world-class battles for political sovereignty. In the time of the novel, despite Britain's military successes across the Middle East and North Africa, Jerusalem represents a precarious sanctuary as the capital of British Mandatory Palestine. The city's crowded spaces may be home to colonized Arabs and to Jews fleeing Hitler's death camps, but it also encapsulates the imperial battle between European titans for control of the entire Middle East. Because there are no battles within the novel, the war can be seen as merely a gloomy backdrop for the sad tale of an orphaned English boy—a warning that his odyssey into adulthood, with its awakening of social consciousness, may run aground on the alien rocky hills of colonial space. *School for Love* casts its love as an accomplice to both global and local racial violence. The novel stages the fate of individual consciousness and of colonialism through Felix, stranded in Jerusalem since his parents' deaths in Iraq. As he confronts enigmatic and conflicting political realities, and since he has neither the resources nor the power to be responsible for himself, Felix could easily represent Palestine itself.

And like Palestine, he becomes the target of projected hopes for a triumphant and restorative post-war future while also embodying the failed promises of triumphalist imperial power. In wartime Palestine, Felix's fate is caught up in the recognition that the British Empire is being bankrupted by a war to save not its privilege, but its bare bones. Despite military and diplomatic strategies to maintain control over global influence and resources, the only sustainable future for Manning's British colonials is imprinted on a one-way ticket back to a dissolving imperial power. In her political imagination, writing this novel in 1950, two years after Arab nations fused their rage against the UN partition of Palestine and invaded Israel, it was the British presence that exacerbated the tensions that led to the Arab-Israel War of 1948.

Of course, Britain's presence in the Middle East did not end with Palestine, but as Manning shows in her novels *Artist among the Missing* (1949) and *The Levant Trilogy*, Britain's ambivalence extended to Egypt as well. We can hear her anxiously prescient voice in her novel of wartime Egypt and Palestine, *Artist among the Missing*. With its multicultural tableau, this novel relates indigenous Middle Eastern political tensions to the Second World War battles for the Middle East, and to the global reaches of imperial racism. As the Third Reich challenges the British Empire in the western desert, the global war between them not only expands territorially but also includes the fate of those, like the Jews, who have no way of escaping the war on themselves, or those, like the Arabs, who have no say about the war being waged on their soil. *Artist among the Missing* locates the Empire's most nervous center in the character of Geoffrey Lynd, who "must represent for [those serving under him] all the evils of British imperialism."[5] The artist of the title, Geoffrey suffers from a kind of shell-shocked depression. Since it forms the novel's defining consciousness and perspective, this malady of mind becomes bound up with the body politic to implicate the artistic imagination. Four years after the Allies' victory, this novel assessed the conflict between the necessity of defeating the fascist Axis and the necessity of sustaining British imperialism.

Throughout her fiction of the Second World War, Manning elaborates and analyzes this conflict as both incitement and entrapment for the creative and critical imagination, as both opposition and interrelationship between the political and the artistic. These novels evaluate the political bind as follows. The fascist mandate called for eradicating freedom by exterminating those it racialized as poisonous Others. The humanistic freedom for which the British were fighting included the colonial right to elevate the lives of those it racialized as inferior Others, even as it exploited them. As novelist and witness, Manning had to decide whether her own representations of these Others exploited them as well and, even more dangerously, represented them in ways that risked replicating the racial and ethnic stereotypes that put these Others in harm's way. Despite the hindsight gained, and the shifting geopolitics that passed, during the thirty years between the publication of *Artist among the Missing* and *The Levant Trilogy*, Manning's political imagination continued to translate the political-artistic bind into a vision of imperial devolution. That vision intensified as she replayed the British defeat of German forces in the western desert in the light of increasing knowledge of the Holocaust. But instead of declaring a moral victory for the British, she showed them mired in the politics and moral ambivalence generated by their own waning power. In her role as artist, Manning ultimately decided that British ambivalence became the prison house of Others.

The depression that drove Manning's vision in 1949, and that overwhelms Geoffrey Lynd in *Artist Among the Missing*, also served as a critique reflecting Britain's sense of its "unsustainable" Empire in the Middle East—what has been called "imperial fatigue." In *The Levant Trilogy*, the depression from which Harriet Pringle suffers not only registers the war's immediate emotional and life-threatening urgencies, but also figures Manning's deep concerns about victory. In this trilogy, which followed *The Balkan Trilogy* (1960–5), the centrality of Harriet's depression alternates with that of a young British soldier, Simon Boulderstone. In the thick of the prolonged battle at El Alamein, Simon becomes disoriented and depressed himself as the streams of tanks and infantry that he follows lose their way in the dust that they stir up and that comes from the debris and smoke of the fallen. As a signal carrier, Simon represents an instrument of the Allies' efforts to give their war aims coherence and meaning. The queries and responses he carries back and forth between temporary headquarters and the front are designed specifically to synthesize and then create the information necessary to coordinate the next battle moves. For Manning, the question arises whether any meaning at all can be created between the promises of a war for freedom, its exploited subjects, and its maimed and dead. But as the questions Simon carries to the front turn out to be no longer relevant, the meanings of the means of war evaporate like water in the desert. Manning's trilogy disassembles the professed meanings of war by showing how they became as lost as the soldiers, Hitler's victims, and the exploited North Africans. All these are made invisible by the battles that envelop them. Meanings apart from official war aims do emerge, however, in the alternating narratives that connect the plight of Hitler's designated victims and the colonized landscape. Just as the desert landscape seems to disappear under the weight and breadth of the war's tanks and infantry, it mounts its own resistance in the form of rising, blinding sands. In effect, these are storms against a war that in this desert land promises only to reset the boundaries and alternate the names of imperial victors, like the ebb and flow of ancient empires.

In Manning's vision, El Alamein is a center of action that, even as it becomes the site of British victory, destabilizes the imperial presence. Although Manning does not tamper with the historic outcome of the battle, the novel embeds a fear that represents a different outcome—what would have happened if the Allies had lost at El Alamein? Like the rest of Europe and beyond, they would have become the colonized Other of the Third Reich. It is this fear that drives the Allies across the desert and produces the anxiety that accompanies its victory. As Manning projects the historical knowledge and perspective of the 1970s back onto her wartime fiction, she introduces another Other, one whose presence had been made invisible by the world war. Positioned like searchlights in the desert, the Egyptians emerge within and between the brutal slaughter of the battle lines. In effect, they put the lie to imperial myths: how the isolated courage of the Allies came to the rescue of empty, harsh lands neglected by natives too ignorant to know how to cultivate and govern them. In Manning's trilogy, the Egyptians claim their land. Iqal, Harriet's translator at the American Embassy, is one of the voices in an Egyptian chorus that serves as critical commentary. He questions the legitimacy of the occupier's fear: "What do you British do with my country, Mrs. Pringle? You come here to rule yet when the enemy is at the gate, you run away." Asked how he feels "about a German occupation," he shows how the continuous history of imperial occupation has eroded differences between the current combatants.

> What do these Germans promise us?—they promise freedom and national sovereignty. What are those things? And what are these Germans? They are invaders like all the invaders that have come here for one thousand four hundred year. They come, they go, the English no worse than others. But to govern ourselves!—that we have forgotten, so how do we do it? And why should we believe these Germans, eh? For myself, I am brushing up my German to be on the safe side, but all the time I am asking myself, "Better the devil we know."[6]

If the natives became invisible in the desert's imperial battles, Manning gave them voice. On a train to Alexandria, Harriet responds to "the gleeful yells of the porters" with her own political protest: "Even when poor, diseased and hungry, they maintained their gaiety, speeding the old conquerors off without malice. No doubt they would welcome the new in the same way." Now Harriet can easily be considered as patronizing of the Egyptians as the British ambassador of the time, Lord Killearn, who assessed them as "essentially a docile and friendly people, but they are like children in many respects."[7] Though Harriet's mockery is directed at the combatants, its sarcasm requires and exploits the assumption that the Egyptians deserve their fate because they lack the resolve of their more mature saviors: they will accommodate any conqueror. The novel, however, questions this assumption by celebrating Harriet's consistent sympathy for the Egyptians and her criticism of the British Empire. The Egyptians are caught between combatants, not only in this world war, but also between this war and others the West has brought to North Africa. The victory against the Afrika Korps is decisive for the Allies, but it registers differently through the lens of the local Egyptians. Guy Pringle, a British Council lecturer and Harriet's husband, realizes that by "lecturing on English literature, teaching the English language, he had been peddling the idea of empire to a country that only wanted one thing; to be rid of the British for good and all." Manning goes on to make the point even more starkly: "And, to add to the absurdity of the situation, he himself had no belief in empire."[8]

Manning provides a critical guide to the problems of representing indigenous peoples, not only by creative writers but also by their critics. Post-colonial critics complain that white colonial and even anticolonial writers turn indigenous peoples into exotic, eroticized objects. This complaint reduces the white colonial woman writer to the same problematic single dimension. What these critics fail to see is that Manning's irony always targets the British. This is a self-conscious strategy that indicts the British themselves as responsible for the voices and political implications they create. Even as characters like Harriet and Guy Pringle and Geoffrey Lynd are presented sympathetically as voices of conscience, their complicity with imperialism is not excused or considered irrelevant, as though they are innocent bystanders.

THE LITTLE CRITICAL WORK ON *The Levant Trilogy* is divided. On the one hand, critics applaud Manning's complex treatment of both Simon's desert war and the Pringles' marriage. But no attention is given to Harriet's implication in and understanding of the relationship between the meanings of colonial racism, the war, and those Others caught in the middle. For far too long, critics have assumed that female protagonists and women novelists are driven by interpersonal relationships and individual erotic experience rather than by the critical social and political issues of their day. As though in response, Manning asks how the marriage plot is affected by a war story. If colonialism is added into the critical mix, as Manning's plotting demands, it becomes possible to see how the subjugated position of the colonized sheds light on the character and condition of a modern married heroine. As post-colonial critics now recognize, to designate the colonized as powerless is to pursue the endgame of the imperial project. Rather than reducing the colonized to the position of victim, critics now recognize not only their resistance but also the maneuvers that one could too easily call complicit with colonial power. That is, by not judging the accommodation strategies of the colonized, it has become possible to see their political moves as satisfying the fundamental need to survive and to maintain an indigenous cultural and social order. In this light, the relationship between colonized and colonizer is far more intimate than a simple opposition of power and powerlessness. From this perspective, Harriet, within her depressed state, represents a robust critical selfhood even as she succumbs to her husband's charismatic powers.

The trilogy links the depressed Englishwoman's lack of options with the survival strategies of her elated Egyptian porters through their historical contexts: they include clashing empires, the fate of a colonized people and land, and the emotional and political costs of imperialism. Harriet tries to save herself from the emotional emptiness of her marriage by escaping to Damascus, but like the porters who wait patiently for the next wave of interchangeable conquerors,

Harriet returns to Guy. The Englishwoman and the Egyptian porters are granted very different subjectivities, however. In a 1967 essay about her stay in Cairo, Manning notes the Egyptians' response
to the ebb and flow of German and British offensives and retreats:

> They had been ruled by outsiders for 2000 years and were still
> ready to believe that a new master could mean a good time for all.
> And now the old master was on the run. Speeding us away, they
> shouted their derisive amusement, letting us know we were done
> for. They could have behaved a great deal worse.[9]

Unlike Harriet, whose developing political consciousness betrays
her depressed behavior, the Egyptians are given a consistently resistant political strategy, one concealed by their good cheer. Nonetheless, because their service to the British and their characters are
presented as one and the same, Manning can be accused of denying the Egyptians the integrity of a complex experience. But unlike Guy's English lessons, which promise civilization but efface the
students' culture, the language of the native retains its integrity
precisely because it is never uttered. The effect is that the native's
language and the experience it represents remain beyond the pale
of colonial appropriation.

Manning's strategy, like that of other British women writers, is
problematic for many post-colonial readers. The white woman
writer transcribing the native voice is easily interpreted as a censor.
Instead, the novel represents the Egyptians as launching a critique
of its author's self-conscious anticolonial questions. Expressing Manning's own political critique, her own "gleeful yells," the Egyptian
porters assert a reality that remains out of reach to both the English
characters and their author. At the end of *The Levant Trilogy*, with
the Allies' victory, the spoils belong to the colonized, who regain
their nation after the British are forced to retreat from both Palestine and Egypt. As Manning's coda states:

> Two more years were to pass before the war ended. Then at last,
> peace, precarious peace, came down upon the world and the sur-
> vivors could go home. Like the stray figures left on the stage at the
> end of a great tragedy, they had now to tidy up the ruins of war
> and in their hearts bury the noble dead.[10]

As "stray figures," the British were not only pushed to the margins
of imperial history, but also recast as bit players or stagehands.
Their agency was confined to discovering some coherence in the
tiny spaces between the end of the heroism that defeated fascism,
the end of the Empire, and the beginning of mourning both.

1. Antoinette Burton, "The Unfinished Business of Colonial Modernities," in *Gender, Sexuality, and Colonial Modernities,* ed. Antoinette Gordon (London, 1999), p. 1.

2. Simon Gikandi, *Maps of Englishness: Writing Identity in the Culture of Colonialism* (New York, 1996), p. 103.

3. Olivia Manning, "The Tragedy of the Struma," *Observer,* 1 Mar. 1970.

4. Kay Dick, *Friends and Friendship: Conversations and Reflections* (London, 1974), p. 31.

5. Olivia Manning, *Artist among the Missing* (1949; London, 1975), p. 46.

6. Olivia Manning, *The Levant Trilogy* (Harmondsworth, 1982), p. 74.

7. Quoted in Wm. Roger Louis, *The British Empire in the Middle East, 1945–51: Arab Nationalism, the United States, and Post-War Imperialism* (Oxford, 1985), p. 226.

8. Manning, *Levant Trilogy,* pp. 513–14.

9. Olivia Manning, "Cairo: Back from the Blue," *Sunday Times Magazine,* 17 Sept. 1967, p. 53.

10. Manning, *Levant Trilogy,* p. 571.

Yale, Cambridge, and Julian Bell

PETER STANSKY

I made my first visit to England in the summer of 1950, when I was eighteen, between my freshman and sophomore years in college. I had been on a youth hostel trip to France, Switzerland, and Italy. It was a quite extraordinary visit, only five years after the end of the Second World War. Rather impulsively, my two best friends on the trip, two splendid Smith undergraduates, and I decided to extend the trip on our own for two weeks in England. A major reason for this was that Alice had an English cousin, Hugh Alexander, and he would put up his cousin and her classmate. I was more or less on my own, but it made the visit so much more interesting to have at least that connection with an Englishman. In effect, although I only saw him a few times, Hugh Alexander would come to play, somewhat inadvertently, a significant role in my life. He was a civil servant and a chess champion, writing a column about the game in the *Sunday Times*. He had been a central figure at Bletchley Park, the great code-breaking center. At that point, the role of Bletchley was still secret, its story not revealed until the 1970s. But most importantly for his effect upon me, he was a Kingsman, having received his BA at King's College, Cambridge, in 1928. When he took the three of us to visit Cambridge, naturally he emphasized his own college. If I had to locate a particular event, I suspect that this was the crucial seed of my interest in England. My time in London was also important, despite my problems at the bed and breakfast where I was staying off the Finchley Road. The geyser to supply hot water, and its needing to be fed with shillings to keep it going, defeated me, as did the primitive toaster that generally resulted in one side burnt and the other untouched. Because the geyser was so perplexing and seemed continually on the verge of explosion, I attempted to bathe only once. I also traveled about a bit, hitchhiking to Winchester, Stonehenge, and Salisbury. Somewhat to my surprise, I was seen as an old hand at hosteling, being asked by the hostel warden at Winchester to advise some neophytes. On the other hand, my general scruffiness was adversely and legitimately commented on by the butler at the home of Sir Louis Sterling, the record magnate, where I had been asked to dinner. He was the brother of a close family friend in New York, where Sir Louis had been born.

When I returned to the United States, my interest in England was reinforced by the Anglophilia of Yale, although, surprisingly, I never took a course in English history, not even the legendary one given by Lewis Curtis. Another great influence was my classmate Russell Thomas. His father, with the wonderful name of Thomas Thomas, had participated in the Versailles Conference and was a Harvard classmate of T. S. Eliot's elder brother, giving the family a connection with the Anglo-American literary world. Russell was also the nephew of the famous editor Maxwell Perkins, who had worked with Ernest Hemingway, F. Scott Fitzgerald, and Thomas Wolfe. Through these connections and his own interests, Russell knew a great deal about the English and American literary scenes. He displayed his extraordinary range of knowledge with the particular mixture of serious ideas and gossip that characterized that world. We would have tea almost every day at the Elizabethan Club at Yale, and also drunken conversations with our friends about once a week, when we consumed quite disgusting amounts of cheap sherry. As an undergraduate, I worked mostly in Continental history. I had taken the freshman European survey with lectures by Sherman Kent and Basil Henning. I was somewhat put off by the Waspy, tweedy, and intellectually not all that distinguished proponents of British history at Yale. I had much more pleasure in the junior intensive history seminar taught by the European intellectual historian Leonard Krieger. It was there that I wrote my first paper on an Englishman and the Spanish Civil War. (The war always had a rather mythic pull for me, arising from listening innumerable times to records of the wonderful songs of the International Brigade while growing up.) My paper was about John Cornford, a young man killed on his twenty-first birthday or the day after while fighting with the International Brigade. I was particularly intrigued that Bernard Knox, who gave a spellbinding course at Yale on the Greek plays—I still have the books for it—had fought alongside Cornford in Spain. (That charismatic figure died on July 22, 2010, at the age of ninety-five.)

I also had an odd experience of the growing strength of McCarthyism in the early 1950s. Knox had written the chapter on Cornford in Spain in the Cornford memorial book, published in 1938, so it was no secret that he had been there and had fought along with Cornford in the International Brigade. I mentioned this in my paper, which presumably no one would see but Professor Krieger. Nevertheless, as I remember, he told me that it was a bad idea to put such information in print, even in a paper that only he was likely to see, and that somehow I might get Knox in trouble. This was, after all, the dreadful period of the Second Red Scare. Fifteen years later, when William Abrahams and I wrote *Journey to the Frontier* about Cornford and Julian Bell, Knox himself still felt sufficiently uneasy about the political situation that he asked us to put him in the book under a pseudonym. It would be some years before he wrote a series of splendid essays about the civil war himself. At Yale, I wrote a senior essay on four Englishmen and their involvement in the civil war: Cornford, Julian Bell, George Orwell, and Stephen Spender. Knox recorded in one of his published essays that a Yale student, presumably me, had turned to him once and exclaimed: "You're my thesis," but the memory doesn't quite ring true to my style. That is not to say that it didn't happen.

What to do after graduating from Yale? Law school? Graduate school in history? I wasn't sure, but I thought an exciting temporary solution would be to study in England. Besides being potentially an extraordinary experience, it would provide time and experience that could help me to try to make up my mind about my future. I applied for the scholarships available for study in England at the time. Not surprisingly, I didn't receive one of Yale's endorsements for the Rhodes Scholarship, but even if I had, there was no way I would have won one. At that point, Woodrow Wilson Fellowships could take one to England, but I felt I had blown the interview by mispronouncing the last name of Walter Bagehot. Marshalls came into existence the following year, and I am sure I wouldn't have won one. The Ehrman Fellowship to King's alternated between the University of California at Berkeley and Yale, and my graduating year it was Berkeley's turn. Delightfully, the next year, when it was Yale's turn, it was awarded to Standish Meacham, who had a career as a modern British historian at the University of Texas. Although we were contemporaries at Yale, it was not until we were together at King's that we became good friends. The Mellon Fellowship to Clare College was won by one of the stars of our class, Jim Thomson. My parents, far from wealthy, with great generosity offered to stake me to study in England. The fees were very low. I think that my father felt that this might lead me ultimately to study law, but if he did, he never said so explicitly. I applied to King's as an affiliated student (someone who could do a BA degree in two years rather than three) and was turned down. I was so upset that I burned the letter. But lo and behold, about a week later I received a telegram reversing the decision and saying that room had been found. Perhaps I should have asked at some point whether there was a reason that this had happened, but I never did. My theory was that Hugh Alexander had intervened—I presume that I had written to him that I was applying—with the senior tutor in charge of admissions, his old friend and Cambridge contemporary Patrick Wilkinson. If true, it was an introduction to one characteristic of the English system. It contrives with a surprising amount of success to look as if friends and influence do not count, but in so many ways they can make a crucial difference.

I WENT TO ENGLAND FOR A TWO-YEAR STAY, from 1953 to 1955, as an undergraduate at King's College. Those two years were crucial for my shaping as an historian of the country. Like almost any other place in England, it was a fine location for the study of class. And I doubt whether I could have come to a more appropriate place than Cambridge to acquire an awareness of the intellectual aristocracy. In 1955, Noel Annan, one of my teachers at Cambridge, published his famous essay "The Intellectual Aristocracy." It deals with the intersection of the personal and the intellectual, or the convergence of ideas and gossip. I already had a proclivity for looking into areas where the personal, the social, the political, and the intellectual converged and combined, but it was reinforced by my two years at King's. I also think that it was particularly valuable to be there as an undergraduate, to live my first year in college in a room with an overwhelming view out of my ground-floor window across the great lawn to Clare College. On my right, I could see the chapel, and on the left, the Cam. I remember coming out the first night into the front quad and wondering whether I was really there. At that time, there weren't any so-called taught MA courses. So the choices were either to acquire a second BA or, if accepted into the program, to plunge into writing a dissertation for a PhD. There was no way I was prepared to do the latter, and indeed I certainly didn't want to do so at that point.

Because there was still military conscription in England and men did their military service before going to university, there was no age difference between the British undergraduates and me. I am sure that college life was far different from what it had been before the war, but it was also far more traditional than it has become. King's was still an all-male college. There was still rationing, but barely, and I had to acquire a ration book for butter and bacon, if I remember correctly. We still had to wear gowns to dinner, to tutorials, and when we were out of our college at night. I did a two-year Part II of the Historical Tripos and had fine supervision in weekly tutorials, about two-thirds of the time with the solid and more traditional teaching of Christopher Morris and John Saltmarsh, but also with Noel Annan and Eric Hobsbawm as well as Arthur Hibbert and Ian Stephens. The English teaching system, at least as I experienced it, was a combination of the professional and the personal. I had known some teachers well at Yale, Charles Blitzer and Howard Lamar most notably. There were a few graduate students and younger faculty who lived in the Yale residential colleges and whom one came to know somewhat. There were affiliated senior faculty members, some of whom would turn up from time to time to have lunch. But it was very rare to come to know a faculty member so well that he became a friend (and in those days it was almost exclusively hes), much less a mentor. In England, it somehow worked out that a person could be both. In the United States, except at the graduate level, I think it is comparatively rare that the student-teacher relationship can be a professional friendship. That was what it tended to be in England, and very much so at King's. What I did not realize for some time was that King's was even more unusual in the closeness of the relationship of the dons and the students, although it certainly existed in other Oxford and Cambridge colleges. Perhaps it owed something to the college's tradition of homoeroticism, although I was not aware of any affairs taking place among students or between dons and students. Perhaps it was my naïveté, but it was also the 1950s. I remember with a degree of excitement meeting Thom Gunn and Mike Kitay as a couple in my second year in Cambridge.

One aspect that may have been unique to King's was that many of the fellows, rather than eating on their own in a separate room or space, as was the custom in other colleges, had lunch with the undergraduates. And then after lunch, generally one of the undergraduates would offer the group, including the dons present, coffee in his rooms. And there were still a fair number of bachelor dons who lived in college. There was the colorful but slightly silly provost, Sir John Sheppard, who had been a fringe member of the Bloomsbury group. Some of the more famous figures who lived in college tended not to come into lunch: Dadie Rylands, the English don famously interested in the theater, and the great economist, A. C. Pigou, who allegedly was friendly only with undergraduates who were mountain climbers. There was the great bibliographer who was librarian of the college, A. N. L. "Tim" Munby. And scientists as well, such as the biologist Kenneth Harrison, who was more interested, I think, in the stained glass of the chapel than his subject. The most famous figure of all who lived at King's was not an academic at all, E. M. Forster. He frequently came to lunch, and took a small role at the play readings of the Ten Club, of which I became the secretary. The undergraduates I knew best were my fellow historians, among them James Cargill Thompson, who died far too young but made his mark as an historian of the Reformation; Neal Ascherson; and Tam Dalyell, who was then, I believe, head of the university Tory Club and had not yet launched upon his splendid career, unusual for a Scottish laird, as a radical Labour MP and ultimately Father of the House.

At King's there was a very welcoming Yale person whom I hadn't known in New Haven—Bob Evans—and it was through him that I rapidly met my circle of friends. Through him, I also came to know Frances Cornford, the poet, the granddaughter of Charles Darwin, and the mother of John Cornford. During term, she had an almost weekly small "at home." There we discussed serious topics with, I suspect, the excessive earnestness of the young. It was a pleasure and a privilege to be on the fringes of the "intellectual aristocracy" through her and some of the dons I knew at King's. And I also went to a fair number of lectures. I remember particularly those in European history by Herbert Butterfield, Denis Mack Smith, and Denis Brogan, and ones in British history by J. H. Plumb. I did a Tripos paper, "The Expansion of England," which had an associated seminar given by Jack Gallagher. There were tour de force lectures by Noel Annan.

Not having grown up in England or its Empire, I had much to learn about the country. But there were also advantages to being an outsider. This was most important in being apart from the English class system and the English obsession with the subject. At least then, the ideal for the English, it seemed to me, was to emerge from the womb knowing all the indicia of class. It is something that one is supposed to know, not learn. The English tend not to know or care about the American class system, but take it as a given that others should be interested in the ramifications of theirs. Only the bumptious Jasper Rose, then a young fellow of King's, once asked me a question no English person would direct to another: "What are you, middle class?"

I cannot pin down exactly how being in England for two academic years was helpful to me in becoming an historian of that country. I became aware of some of the paradoxes of the country. King's, in its chapel, had the greatest ecclesiastical building in Cambridge, and one of the greatest in the world. Quite a few of us went to services from time to time for the glory of the singing, and as members of the college, we wore surplices. But the college was also famously irreligious. Shane Leslie, a Catholic convert and Winston Churchill's cousin, wrote a novel about Cambridge, *The Cantab,* in which he remarked how much finer a college St. Catharine's, the college next door, was than King's. St. Catherine's was the college that God forgot, in contrast to King's, the college that forgot God. This attitude had some unfortunate consequences. A year or so after I left, the religious dean committed suicide by jumping off the chapel roof, allegedly because he couldn't stand the college's atheism. It was almost as if the college had deliberately appointed a sweet but not very bright man. His successor was a person with much more intellectual power, Alec Vidler.

One aspect of England that I learned at Cambridge is that odd combination of respectability and radicalism: the domestic radical. It is, I believe, an extraordinary strength, but also a source of profound irritation. There is smallness of scale, and that can lead to a failure of imagination, what Forster called the undeveloped heart. It can be reflected in the considerable accomplishments but also the limitations of the Arts and Crafts movement and even of Bloomsbury. It was what drove Ezra Pound and Wyndham Lewis wild. It inspired the famous remark of, I think, John Strachey's that when the communist revolution came, half the Cabinet would be Old Etonians. England would change, but it would stay the same. Indeed, the key to the success and paradox of English life is that it stays the same through changing. It was being in Cambridge that helped me understand that combination of a deeply hierarchical society paradoxically allied to an egalitarianism that, to a degree and at times reluctantly, rewards talent, wherever it may be found. (Although it is true that many talented people may be missed.) And by doing so, it defangs the troublemakers. It is a society that would like ideally to disguise the innovative as traditional. For instance, in my work on the London Blitz, I was very struck with the use of the term "the people's war." It would appear to be a term that reached out toward the progressive, but in practice, it often supported traditional values and excluded rather than included.

WHILE AT CAMBRIDGE, I HAD NOT solved the problem that had led me to go there in the first place. What should I do with my life? I thought I would cut through the dilemma by going into publishing.

I returned to Manhattan in the late summer of 1955 and took two part-time jobs, one helping a book designer and the other selling books, at an excessive markup, at the British Book Centre, owned by Captain Maxwell. (I met him only once, when he asked me whether I was related to a Jerusalem bookseller.) I was offered a job at the University of Texas Press as well as the chance to do some teaching there; Harry Ransom, the chancellor and inspirer of the great collection of British manuscripts found in the humanities center named after him, liked those who had had an English experience. But that kind offer led me to conclude that if I were to end up at a university, I would prefer to be a member of the faculty. The Harvard Graduate School, which might easily have been sick of my continually applying, being accepted, and then withdrawing, treated me very indulgently and said that I might enter as early as February 1956, the second semester of the academic year. One reason I finally decided to go to an American graduate school was that I had been advised that I should study with those who could help me with my career in the United States. Ironically, my eventual mentor, David Owen, was on leave that first semester, and I worked with the distinguished H. L. Beales, from the London School of Economics, and two fine assistant professors who were about to go elsewhere.

I returned to England in the summer of 1958, when I was looking for a dissertation topic. I completed my Harvard history PhD in 1961; my dissertation was published as *Ambitions and Strategies: The Struggle for the Leadership of the Liberal Party in the 1890s*. That same year, 1961, I met William Abrahams, and we were to be together until his death in 1998. He was a poet and novelist but was now turning to the career in which he would achieve his greatest reputation: being one of the most prominent book editors of the twentieth century. I met Billy, as he was known to everyone, just as I was completing my dissertation; we were introduced by two common friends, Richard Poirier and David Kalstone. He was flatteringly interested in my work, and me. I mentioned to him that that during my dissertation research, I had read quite a bit of amusing correspondence about the question of who should succeed Lord Tennyson as poet laureate. The Liberals couldn't decide, ruling out Swinburne on the basis of his personal life and William Morris on the basis of his politics. When Salisbury became Prime Minister, he didn't take the task seriously and appointed Alfred Austin, perhaps the worst poet who ever held the post. The piece that Billy and I wrote together was published in *History Today*, my first publication other than a few book reviews.

Having worked together well on that, Billy then asked whether there was something further that we might do together. I brought out for his consideration the senior essay I had written at Yale on four Englishmen—Cornford, Bell, Orwell, and Spender—who had been involved with the Spanish Civil War. That became our next project. We originally intended to write on all four, and started to do work with that aim in mind. Only Stephen Spender was still alive, and Billy knew him somewhat already. As we went forward, it became clear both intellectually and practically that doing all four in the same volume was too large an undertaking. There was a dramatic difference between the two young men, Cornford and Bell, who had been killed in Spain, and Orwell and Spender. In the 1930s, they were already established writers, even though Orwell had not yet achieved the worldwide fame that he enjoyed in the last few years of his sadly short life. Eventually, we would write one book on the two who had died, *Journey to the Frontier* (1966), and two on Orwell's writings and life through the Spanish Civil War, *The Unknown Orwell* (1972) and *Orwell: The Transformation* (1979).

NOW, MORE THAN FORTY YEARS LATER, I have decided to return to the life of Julian Bell. I have observed with admiration that Sir Michael Holroyd has published two subsequent versions of his great life of Lytton Strachey. (It was published just after the decriminalization of homosexuality in Britain, when all could at last be told.) But I have felt up to now that I couldn't revise an already published text. Once I have written on a subject, I find the idea of reconsidering it, let alone rewriting it, rather uncongenial.

But my attitude toward this question changed in the summer of 2004. The previous year, I had published *Sassoon: The Worlds of Philip and Sybil*. If less literary than some of my previous work, and far less concerned with radical figures, it combined my interests in society, politics, and art, with a comparatively new interest in Anglo-Jewry. (Although I had considered the Anglo-Jewish peerage as a possible thesis topic years before.) Now I was at work on quite a different project: the Blitz, in particular the first day of the bombing, September 7, 1940.

While in England in the summer of 2004 to do research on the book, I participated in several events associated with what is considered the hundredth anniversary of the beginning of Bloomsbury. In 1904, the four Stephen children, all in their twenties, scandalized their elders after the death of their father, Sir Leslie, by leaving Kensington and taking a house together, without a chaperone, in the respectable but nondescript area of Bloomsbury, hence eventually and inadvertently creating a term in literary history. In *Journey to the Frontier*, Billy and I had written on the second generation of Bloomsbury as represented by Julian Bell, who was Vanessa Bell's son and Virginia Woolf's nephew. I had also written on my own about the very early years of Bloomsbury in *On or about December 1910* (1996). In that study, I explored as deeply as I could the Bloomsbury events that lay behind Virginia Woolf's famous and somewhat tongue-in-cheek remark: "On or about December 1910, human character changed."

Julian Bell was on my mind in 2004 as I chaired a session largely concerned with him at the first International Virginia Woolf Conference held outside the United States, at the Senate House of the University of London, appropriately in the Bloomsbury district. Patricia Laurence had just published *Lily Briscoe's Chinese Eyes* on Bloomsbury and China, which paid much attention to Julian's year and a half teaching at Wuhan University. A novel by Hong Ying, *K*, had come out, based on Julian's affair there with Ling Shuhoa. I also met William Beekman, a prominent Bloomsbury collector who had a particular interest in Julian and who owned many of the surviving letters that Virginia Woolf wrote to him. Marking the anniversary was not only the Virginia Woolf conference but also associated events, a day visit to Charleston, most notably marked by a splendid interview with Olivier Bell, Julian's sister-in-law. Her husband, Quentin Bell, was sadly missed. Then the climax of the celebration was a grand dinner at King's College, Cambridge, Julian's college as well as Forster's, Roger Fry's, John Maynard Keynes's (and mine). There Dadie Rylands had given Virginia Woolf the lunch immortalized in *A Room of One's Own,* and she had not been allowed to walk on the grass.

There was a reception before the dinner, on the great lawn at the back of the Gibbs building at King's, on a ravishing summer evening—England at its best, with a view of the Cam, of Clare College, of the building where Dadie Rylands had his rooms, and of Bodley's, where I had lived my first undergraduate year. There was a small display of photocopies from the King's Archives to be looked at during the reception. Included was a letter from Duncan Grant to Julian, saying that he must do what he thought best, but pointing out how much pain his going to Spain would cause his mother. And there was a copy of the few notes that Vanessa had jotted down about Julian's life. She never really recovered from his death. These two documents, which had not been available years before, made me realize how much new material was likely to have surfaced in the forty years since Billy Abrahams and I had initially, with the extraordinary cooperation of Quentin and Olivier Bell, looked into Julian's life. It suddenly occurred to me that when I had finished my study of the Blitz, I might well turn, or rather return, to the life of Julian Bell. I was going back to London by coach after the dinner, but just before hurrying to catch it, I had a message that Olivier would like to speak to me for a moment. She was wondering, in reaction to Patricia Laurence's interest in doing a biography of Julian (some years later, she would publish a pamphlet about him, *The Violent Pacifist*) whether there should be another life of Julian. After all, as she kindly said, there was *Journey to the Frontier*. Pat Laurence had spoken to me earlier about this possibility, and I had urged her, if she wished, to go ahead, it not occurring to me that I might be interested myself. That idea, almost a revelation, had come to me on the lawn at King's. I hurriedly indicated to Olivier that I would write. As indeed I eventually did, although I knew that it wouldn't be for some time.

In the spring of 2006, I spent some time in the Berg Collection of the New York Public Library, where I read the papers of Ling Shuhoa, Julian's Chinese mistress, which Pat Laurence had used in her work. That summer, I spent a few days in Cambridge, read some material, and acquired a sense of how much had come to light since I had first looked at material on Julian. In February and March 2007, I spent five weeks in Cambridge and read in the King's Archive. I also reread *Journey to the Frontier*. I thought that the book had held up well, and I wondered, as had Olivier Bell, whether another version was necessary. Julian's life was one of promise and beginnings, very sadly cut short by an early death, five months after his twenty-ninth birthday. What he had accomplished in his short life in his writings, his poetry, and his ideas was not without interest. He was, no doubt, a minor figure. But nowadays we are interested in such lives, not only of those of proven accomplishments and importance.

And then there was the matter of Bloomsbury. Interest in Bloomsbury can become excessive. There are those who can never get enough about the Bloomsbury figures, and there are others who loathe the very idea and are sick of what they sometimes refer to as the "industry." Julian himself had somewhat mixed feelings about his situation. Though at its center, he was not a very important Bloomsbury figure. At the heart of Bloomsbury were the two sisters, Vanessa and Virginia, and Vanessa's children. Their husbands, Clive Bell and Leonard Woolf, at times felt a sense of exclusion. Julian's closest relationship was with his mother, and he was a great supporter of Bloomsbury's values in many senses. But in other ways, he turned against them. He also felt that its politics had to be updated to deal with the contemporary situation of the 1930s. He enjoyed being a child of Bloomsbury, and the status and advantages that it gave him. But he also wanted to be his own person. And although he felt driven to prove his worth to Virginia and Leonard, he might not have minded if they had been a little less honest in telling him their views of his writings.

On rereading *Journey to the Frontier*, I was impressed at how good it was. Because I believe the voice of the book is more Billy's than mine (and hence, I do not believe I have made an immodest statement), I have had doubts about how to proceed with the project of writing a fuller life of Julian Bell. I do not wish to rewrite and destroy the original text. In some ways, it is an historical document that I believed deserves to be preserved. But then how should I proceed? My thinking will perhaps strike some as misguided and self-indulgent. My thought was to rewrite the original text about Julian only to an extent and to provide some account of the search for Julian Bell as it took place over a span of more than fifty years. But I also incorporated and discussed the extensive and, I believe, important new material that has become available. The text in the new book is almost twice as long as the original.

Much of the new material is personal. Bloomsbury has always maintained an intriguing relationship between the private and the public. As pioneers of the modern, freeing themselves from what they saw as Victorian conventions, its members believed that they should live the lives that they wished. But that was not to say that there were not many personal problems and difficulties. A willingness and an effort to be "honest" about personal relations does not necessarily lead to personal happiness, particularly since it might involve informing others of your opinion about their characters and actions. On the other hand, Bloomsbury was not postmodern. This has led some to accuse it of hypocrisy. It did not necessarily believe that private life, which, in theory (although sometimes not in fact), was to be as free as one might wish, should become public. Angelica Bell felt that she was badly treated in not being told until she was eighteen that Duncan Grant, and not Clive Bell, was her father. Duncan Grant, who led exactly the sexual life that he wished, felt uneasy about the possibility that all would be revealed in Michael Holroyd's pathbreaking life of Lytton Strachey, even though it was published after the decriminalization of homosexuality. Members of Bloomsbury were upper-middle-class figures who sometimes felt that those in the know should know and that those not in the know should not. During the writing of *Journey to the Frontier*, Quentin and Olivier Bell couldn't have been more helpful to us, but didn't feel it was appropriate to tell us all the ramifications of Julian's love life. And much of the material documenting it had not yet come to light. Now Julian's life can be told in much more depth and detail. And that is what I have attempted to do.

Fall Semester 2010

10

Lunching on Olympus

STEVEN ISENBERG

The British writers W. H. Auden, E. M. Forster, Philip Larkin, and William Empson paid respectful attention to one another. Larkin wrote, "English Auden was a superb and magnetic wide-angled poet, but the poetry was in the blaming and the warning." Empson thought Auden a "wonderful poet" and put Larkin among the "very good poets." Auden wrote a sonnet for Forster, and Empson wrote a poem called "Just a Smack at Auden." Forster's novels were touchstones for Auden, who cabled "Morgan" Forster on his eightieth birthday these good wishes: "May you long continue what you already are stop old famous loved yet not yet a sacred cow." Empson thought Forster's *Aspects of the Novel*—lectures he had heard as a student at Cambridge—"a model."

For me, the four have another thing in common, the unlikely and unexpected occasions of my having met each of them for lunch. Those visits are always with me, and while I kept no diary and so remember fewer of their words than I wish, the memories I do have are testimony to their humanity and kindness.

> *Oh, don't bother much about that.*
> W. H. Auden

IT ALL BEGAN WITH AUDEN in New York in 1962. I had recently graduated from Berkeley and started to work at McGraw-Hill as a reader of manuscripts that senior editors wanted cleared out. Unauthorized and unanticipated by my boss, I looked Auden up in the telephone book and called him at home. I said I was in McGraw-Hill's trade editorial department and had recently been a student of and reader for Mark Schorer, the head of the English Department at Berkeley. I wondered whether we could meet to discuss his writing a biography. I had come up with this because even though Auden was not our author, I had been told that exclusivity clauses in publishing contracts sometimes omit a genre in which the author had never written.

Auden said he didn't write biographies, but was curious about whom I had in mind as a potential subject. E. M. Forster, I said, or Thomas Mann, or—the third is fuzzy in my memory, but it was either Carl Jung or Hermann Hesse. "Forster is alive," he said. "Well, perhaps, that one might wait," I replied, and somehow I got from there to setting a date for lunch. I chose the Oak Room at the Plaza Hotel because I had looked in there once and it seemed Old World, serious, and comfortable.

A few days later, my boss, Ed Kuhn, the head of the trade editorial department, summoned me to his office. "I have just had a call," he said, "from Bennett Cerf [I knew who he was from the television panel show *What's My Line?*], the head of Random House, asking who the hell you were. I couldn't imagine why he had heard of you and why he sounded so damn put out. Cerf asked, 'What does he do for you? He is poaching on one of our authors.' I asked Cerf who that was. 'W. H. Auden. He is trying to get him to write a biography.' I told Cerf you were just a kid out of college, and I had no idea about this, and Cerf said, 'Well, Auden is having lunch with him.'"

For McGraw-Hill to publish W. H. Auden was virtually unthinkable. We had brought out Schorer's biography of Sinclair Lewis, but our biggest-selling authors were Eugene Burdick with *Fail-Safe* (cowritten with Harvey Wheeler) and Robert Ruark with *Uhuru*. So it was on a few counts that Kuhn was astonished. I could tell Cerf and Kuhn had enjoyed a laugh at my expense. Nevertheless, the whole matter pricked Kuhn's pride. Why shouldn't his house be a place for the likes of Auden?

Kuhn asked what biographies I had suggested. I told him. He was even more stunned after I got out one name. "How much Auden have you read?" he asked. "Not much," I admitted. He told me to take afternoons off for the next several days to read Auden so the lunch would have less danger of being embarrassing. I asked him whether he would like to come with us. "No," he said, "that wasn't what Auden had in mind"—and if he went, Cerf would be on the telephone again, and this time it wouldn't be so amusing.

The day before the lunch, though, Kuhn appeared in my office and suggested I include John Starr, a senior editor who had taken a shine to me. Starr was a friend and editor of Richard Condon, the author of *The Manchurian Candidate,* and that was as much as I knew about his literary taste. He was a seasoned hand at picking up a check on the lunch circuit and had been especially kind to me, so I was happy to ask him. It wouldn't hurt to bring along someone with the bona fides of adulthood and publishing experience.

We waited for Auden in the leathery den of the Oak Room. Neither of us had ever seen him in person. He came in carrying a pile of newspapers, which seemed to include lots of cutout crossword-puzzle pages from *The Times* of London. He wore a tweedy sports coat and pants, his shirt and tie were dominated by academic brown and allied shades. His face was like a plowed field.

We never spoke of biographies at all. Or of his writing anything for us. Auden and Starr began talking about good food and wine. The substance of it was beyond me, but they were at ease and familiar with one another's distinctions and discriminations. They didn't show off; they were just appreciative critics. They then spoke of the Second World War. Starr had served as an army officer in Europe, while Auden had famously emigrated from England to New York in 1939. In 1940 he wrote "In Memory of W. B. Yeats," set amidst the backdrop of war:

> In the nightmare of the dark
> All the dogs of Europe bark,
> And the living nations wait,
> Each sequestered in its hate

Again, I was separated from the talk by age and experience, having been born in 1940, but they made me feel included. I had a front-row seat; I had made the lunch happen, and they were both happy to be together talking.

Then Auden asked me about Berkeley. I had just done my senior paper on Yeats and said something about his mysticism. "Oh," he said, "don't bother much about that. Just a contrivance, a device, a stage, more than anything else." I gathered from the familiar tone that he knew Yeats, about whom "In Memory" says:

> You were silly like us: your gift survived it all;
> The parish of rich women, physical decay,
> Yourself; mad Ireland hurt you into poetry.

As the lunch drew to its close, we asked Auden what he liked best about New York, and he said Jewish jokes. He asked whether we knew any. I said I was from Los Angeles and couldn't really do a good accent, but my aunt from Brooklyn and my father told some good jokes. He laughed at the couple I told him, and then he told one of his favorites. A man from the Upper West Side goes to his psychiatrist. The doctor listens and tells him he is depressed and hostile. The doctor suggests a hobby or a pet, something to bring him out of it. The man says he lives in a small apartment; it would be difficult. The doctor says even a small pet would do. After several weeks, the doctor noted improvement and asked whether the man had bought a pet. "Yes," the man said. "What kind?" "Bees," he replied. "Bees?" the doctor said, puzzled. "I thought you said you had a small apartment. Where do you keep them?" "In a cigar box," said the patient. "But how do they breathe?" the doctor asked. "How do they breathe?" said the patient. "Fuck 'em."

> *I will tell you when it's time to go.*
> E. M. Forster

In 1965, while I was a student at Oxford, NBC was trying to make a television show about the Genizah Scrolls from Cairo (an archaeological find second only to the Dead Sea Scrolls). But NBC wasn't having any luck in getting access to the Genizah archives in the Cambridge University library. Fortunately for me, someone at a dinner party in New York said he knew a student at Oxford who might help. So I got the job of producing the show.

In the course of visiting Cambridge, I arranged an introduction to the professor of Near Eastern languages and literature, and through him to the curator of the scrolls. Once the curator had gotten used to both the astounding news that television existed and the bemusing fact that I was American, he granted me some kind of honorary Oxbridge status, and so the scrolls—actually scraps of parchment journals—were seen on television for the first time.

Because the show's sponsor was the Jewish Theological Seminary, the professor asked me whether I was religious. I said I had had a bar mitzvah and been confirmed, but after that I had gone to services rarely—so, no, I wasn't religious. He probed a bit further, laughed, and said, "You are a pagan. Would you like to meet another one?" I had no idea whom he had in mind, but said yes. He knew I was reading English at Oxford, and perhaps that explained his next words: "Write me when you have read all of E. M. Forster, and I will ask him to see you."

Some months later I did, and I received a short note from Forster proposing a day and time when I might visit him and saying he hoped I had other business, since it seemed a long trip to make only to see him. One gray, chilly March day in 1966, I planned to take the train down to London and then up to Cambridge. As I was leaving the college, I ran into my tutor, Christopher Ricks. "Remember, you are meeting an old man," he said, "so you should leave after about twenty minutes."

At ten the next morning, I walked into King's College, one of the grandest Oxbridge colleges, whose cathedral-sized chapel is one of the most famous buildings in Europe. The porter gave me the staircase and room numbers and directions. I walked up the wooden stairs—five flights (a lot, I thought, for an old man—Forster was then eighty-six)—and knocked on the door.

It opened to reveal a small, slightly stooped, demure man, smartly but modestly dressed, who welcomed me in and offered me a chair. It felt straight away as if I were a visitor rather than a student having come for a tutorial. He asked my plans for the day, once again saying it was an awfully long way to come just to see him. I said I had no other plans and that compared to my travel from California, this trip was short. The visit with him more than justified it.

He seemed to want me to ask questions, but first he talked about living in college and how generous King's had been to him and how much enjoyment he reaped from it and how convenient it was. He asked after my college at Oxford, Worcester—where were my rooms and did I enjoy it?

He asked what I had been reading lately. I said Dickens and George Eliot and that I was going to do the special paper on the novel in my exams. This to the man who wrote *Aspects of the Novel*. I asked Forster if we could talk about Lawrence, and he responded "David or T. E.?" He told me that in his bedroom he had several letters from D. H. Lawrence. I told him my mother had picked "Lawrence" as my middle name after Lawrence of Arabia, and he laughed happily at that. But I found that I didn't have much more to ask him. It was one of those moments, as in all these meetings, when my self-doubt was playing as hard inside me as my excitement.

I was hoping he would get out the D. H. Lawrence letters, but suddenly it occurred to me that it was getting to be around the twenty-minute mark. I said that he had been kind to see me and that I ought to be going and leave him to his work and reading.

"Someone told you that you are going to see an old man and you ought to leave after a short time," he said, and my expression told him that that was just what had happened.

"Anyone who says that should also remember when you go to see someone old, it may be the last time. Please stay, if you can, and I will tell you when it's time to go."

That exchange stays with me because of its simple kindness. I remember the moment better than anything else that was said, other than his asking me "Did you ever know Gide?"

"I know who he was," I replied.

"No," Forster said, "did you ever have lunch with him?"

I almost laughed out loud at the absurdity, but I just said no, and no more was said of André Gide.

Forster asked me to open the mail piled on a nearby table and to go through it, setting aside anything personal or seemingly important for him to look at. And then, since it was nearing eleven, he suggested that we go to the Senior Combination Room for coffee. He put on his overcoat, as I did mine, and slowly but surely he descended the staircase. We walked through the college—it was out of term, so not many students were around—and went into the SCR lounge. It was populated only by a few extraordinary-looking old men, bent under the weight of age and the burdens of study. No one spoke, and everyone sat so as to have no need to converse.

We were served our coffee and biscuits, and after a short time, Forster got up and led me outside. It was cold and clear. He suggested a walk along the River Cam. "Would that suit you?" he asked. "Of course," I said. As we began to walk, he laced his arm through mine. Can you imagine how I felt—a boy from my circumstances, so American, so unfinished—walking along the backs of the Cambridge colleges with the man who wrote *A Passage to India* and *Howards End* on my arm as a silent companion?

At some point, Forster began to remark on things he loved about particular colleges—their gardens and parts of the river. I followed his lead, and we wound up walking down the main street of the town; soon we were in front of Heffers, the university's bookstore. Only then did I realize I hadn't brought a book for him to sign. I asked him whether I could run in and buy one. He said yes and that he would wait outside.

I ran in, totally unfamiliar with the store and suddenly worried about leaving Forster in the street alone. I don't know what I thought would happen, but I imagined headlines reporting an accident: "Forster Accompanied and Then Abandoned by a Visiting American Student." I couldn't find the novels section, but I caught sight of a hardbound edition of Lionel Trilling's book on Forster and bought it in a desperate rush.

We then walked back to King's and up to his room. "Now it is time for me to go," I said, and I told him how grateful I was for his kindness. He asked where I would go, and I said back to Oxford. He said, "Let me sign your book," and without explanation, I showed him the Trilling. He smiled and drew a line through the title—his name—and signed his name.

> *I never like to be more than five miles from home.*
> Philip Larkin

FIFTEEN YEARS LATER, WHEN MY FAMILY paid a summer visit to Christopher Ricks in England, he had the idea that I ought to try to see Philip Larkin, offering to write Larkin and ask whether he would see me. The year before in New York, I had set up a lecture that Ricks had given about the poet. I asked Ricks whether he would come with me. Absolutely not, he said. He wanted to ask for me—that would make him happy. I do not have a copy of Ricks's letter to Larkin, but I do have a copy of Larkin's answer:

28 June 1982

Dear Christopher,

Thanks for your letter—this is the fourth week of having the painters in, which is why I haven't replied.

It's true I generally decline, with such gentleness as I can muster, self-proposed visits by chaps like yours, but I suppose I can break my own rules.

On condition that

i. You name your man, & he isn't someone I detest;

ii. It's understood that this isn't a precedent but a single exception;

iii. This is a private meeting and not an interview—very important this—

iv. He realizes I am seriously deaf & hard to talk to;

v. The meeting doesn't last more than an hour or two; then I should be willing to oblige you.

Venue doubtful: I shall be in London in July. *Here* less trouble, but makes [rule] v. harder to observe. However, I leave this rather doubtful ball in your court.

Your life sounds exciting. If it isn't the Faculty, it's the College! Must be wearing.

Kind regards,

Yours, Philip

A day was set, and with every Larkin rule in mind, I drove to Hull, where Larkin was university librarian. On campus, I was directed to the library, and asked for the librarian's office. Larkin's secretary promptly announced my arrival, and I was summoned into a large office. From behind his desk, a taller, balder, more affable Larkin than I had imagined came to shake my hand.

"Good morning, Professor Isenberg."

"Good morning. Thank you for letting me come to see you. But first, I am not a professor."

"Well, I see you are young, but surely you must be at least an associate professor."

"No, I'm not an academic."

Larkin's smile widened with open delight. "Good. But somehow I got the impression of Ricks giving a lecture you helped arrange."

"I will tell you about the setting—I think you would like it."

"Please do. But what is your job now?"

"I have just begun working in newspapers."

His face showed less of a smile.

"What do you do?"

"I'm assistant to the publisher of *Newsday,* a large newspaper in Long Island, New York, where I'm learning the business and hope one day to run one."

"Good," he said, his face brightening again. "You're neither a reporter nor an academic." "Come," he said, "I propose we go for a pub lunch in the country. I will be happy to drive."

We walked out to his car, which was some sort of mini–station wagon. Larkin had large thick glasses, and I was apprehensive about his driving skills, but he wouldn't hear of me driving. "That would make me an awful host, and anyway I would have to keep giving you directions, and as a publisher, you are a direction giver."

His tone and manner were anything but that of the Larkin of despair and loneliness; he was fast, funny, and friendly. I laughed often and was struck by the precise and fresh turns of phrase in his conversation.

At the pub, we had beer. I am a slight drinker; Larkin went at a seasoned Englishman's lunchtime pace. I told him about the evening of the Ricks lecture, and he was pleased.

He was, by his own admission, wary of Americans; they wanted either to ask academic questions about his poems or to try to get him to visit America. He said he was the sort of Englishman who did not want to go anywhere else. He told me of going to Germany to get an award. When he went to the hotel's front desk in the morning to ask for a newspaper, he discovered that "although they tell you the people in those places speak English, they don't."

At some point, I asked him about contemporary poets. He was jokey and dismissive, refusing to be caught up in "Ted Hughes worship," as he put it, "or anything like that."

He told me he had a friend who had visited New York and been mugged outside the New York Public Library on 42nd Street. I told him that when he came, I would get my younger brother, who was a strong guy and a criminologist, and knew a lot of policemen, to see that he was protected. "You see," he laughed, "you are working on trying to get me there."

He seemed in no rush to begin lunch, and I started to fear the rule about an hour or two. I didn't want to drink too much without eating, but I had another beer with him.

When we did sit down, I remember two things I said. I misquoted a word in a snatch of a John Betjeman poem, and he corrected me, gently. (At the end of our visit, he gave me an edition of Betjeman's poems and signed it: "For Stephen (or even Steven), commemorating a delightful day, Kindest regards, Philip.") Second, I said that the way he wrote about death and growing old, staring them in the face, summoning un-shopworn, unexhausted everyday words, all newly woven and unflinching, ironically, gave me a certain comfort against my own fears. He listened quietly.

He then raised the matter of going to see well-known people and asked had I done it before. I told him of going to see Forster.

He told me that when he was young, he had gone to see Forster, too. Forster had entertained a circle—literally—of young men. Every ten minutes or so, he made them change chairs so someone new sat on his right. Larkin said he had taken the manuscript of his first novel, *Jill,* and tried to press it on Forster to read, but he wouldn't take it. Larkin laughed at himself. It was an embarrassing and amusing memory—not painful, though I got the clear impression he would have been happier if Forster had taken and read his manuscript. I think he told me this story to put me at greater ease— we both knew it takes nerve to arrange one of these meetings, and there is a certain nervousness once you are there.

He had another tale of meeting the famous. When he was librarian of Belfast University, the Queen visited, and he was introduced to her. He told her an Irish joke, which he said was sort of a triple faux pas—telling the Queen a joke, an Irish one, and doing it in Northern Ireland.

At some point, the chemistry felt right, so I did take up the question of a visit to America. What stops you? I asked. He said, "I don't like to be in hotels, and I really don't know anyone." I said, "Here's a proposition. You know Ricks—he always stays at my home. Get him to vouch for us. Why don't you stay with us at our apartment? It overlooks Central Park. There's my wife and our son, who's nine. You don't have to talk to us. You can come and go as you please, invite anyone over you like."

He said, "The idea sounds appealing," and I thought that if I could get him on a plane that day, he would do it. Then he said, "I never like to be more than five miles from home."

Well, here's another idea, I said. Why don't you fly to New York? We'll get a helicopter to take you to Manhattan, take you to see whatever you want, and then take you back to the airport, and you can fly home.

"Oh," he said, "I like that very much. But you can't do that."

"Oh yes, I can," I said. I told him of a friend who was the head of the Port Authority.

"They run the airports, and my newspaper will find a way to get it done."

He roared. "That's the best offer I have ever had." Years later, I read that Larkin said he would like to go to China—if he could come back the same day.

It is faces we remember, and his was big, enlarged by his baldness and the glasses and the animated intensity of his speech. For all his poems, which often showed a glum, lonely, and struggling self, the man I met was strong, confident, terrifically alive, welcoming, relaxed, engaged, engaging. He had another beer, finished his lunch, and insisted we have something sweet. I tried to pay; he wouldn't allow it.

As he drove back, I was thinking how much he had drunk and how narrow the country roads were. I must have given off some whiff of apprehension, because he turned to me and said, "I hope we don't have an accident or the headline in your paper will be 'Our Beloved Assistant Publisher Dies with Unknown English Poet.'"

My boy, it is just like a symphony.
William Empson

A YEAR LATER, RICKS ASKED ME whether I would like to join him on a visit to William Empson in London. I was staying with a friend in Hampstead Heath, quite near Empson's home, so Ricks and I met late on a Saturday morning, planning to take Empson out to lunch, somewhere close by and informal.

The eccentricity of Empson's genius was almost as well known as his important critical works: *Seven Types of Ambiguity, Some Versions of Pastoral,* and *Milton's God.* Robert Lowell, then the American poet of highest standing, had once written to Empson that he was "the most intelligent poet writing in our language and perhaps the best. I put you with Hardy and Graves and Auden and Philip Larkin." A prized possession of mine is a recording of Empson reading his poems in a tone of voice that I believe no other human being can match, even if that person also combined Wykehamist, Cantabrigian, and Chinese accents.

Ricks is said by Empson's biographer, John Haffenden, to be Empson's "greatest fan and friend," and Empson himself once said gruffly to Ricks's mother, "Your son saved me." This invitation was a great privilege for me.

We were met at the door by Empson himself, unkempt white hair and beard prominent. His shirt and pants were a faded gray and looked to have been worn unwashed for several days. The sitting room itself was strewn with newspapers and was visibly dusty; it looked as unkempt as Empson. Almost at once, I could tell I was going to have a very hard time understanding him. I had to listen for key words. He said his wife was away, so we would have to put up with him. In honor of "our American guest," he would make Bloody Marys. He was a skinny man whose clothes hung on him, and as he walked about, he continually hooked his thumbs in the front of his pants and stretched them forward. Ricks and I had to avoid each other's eyes. Empson picked out of the kitchen sink three large glasses that may have been washed within the week. On the counter was a large open can of tomato juice with a rusted top. He poured juice into each glass and, after that, generous amounts of something that could have been either gin or vodka—I couldn't see. Then he sprinkled on something that might have been Worcestershire sauce and dredged up browned celery stalks from a bin. And then he stood back to admire his work and repeatedly stretched and fanned his pants.

Bading us keep our seats, he served his magic drink, which I knew I was meant to praise as thoroughly authentic, even if not hygienic. The real challenge was to drink some of this warm slop—no ice cube ever was evident—without spluttering. We toasted Empson and set to work. It had to be done in slow sips; every chance for him to offer a second one had to be eliminated.

Ricks and Empson had a few things to talk about, and they laughed together. I was concentrating on getting enough of the drink down to be neither insulting nor sick. By now, Ricks and I were having a harder time with the drinks and the pants stretching—it was just so outrageously funny, but we contained ourselves. I tell my classes that I believe America has weird and idiosyncratic people, but only England has naturally, fully formed eccentrics. Empson is the paradigm. (Recently, Ricks remarked of Auden, Forster, Empson, and Larkin that because they were centric in so many ways, their eccentricities were all the more interesting.)

I told him about meeting Auden and being astonished by his wrinkled face. "It was all those sailors," said Empson, who had written of

Auden and Dylan Thomas that they were the only contemporaries "you could call poets of genius."

After a time, Empson said he wanted to make us lunch, and we would eat in the garden, since it was such a fine day. Glancing again at the kitchen, I almost pleaded that he let us take him out to the closest place he enjoyed. Ricks added his solicitation. Empson wouldn't hear of it.

He went into the kitchen. I asked whether I could help. He said I could set the table outside. I began a search for silverware, plates, and glasses. We were to switch to beer, warm of course. He provided no direction, so I had to look in cabinets and drawers. It gave me the chance to rinse and towel everything as unobtrusively as possible. He said we needed soup bowls and spoons, and knives for cheese. I found three rolls, butter, and cheese. The rolls had seen a better day, but I hoped they could be buttered into edibility.

Ricks was ordered to stay seated, and then the soup making began. First, Empson produced a large, dirty pot, which I had no chance to rinse. He ran water into it and set it to boil. From strange corners he found an onion, leeks, parsley, and some of the browned celery. He threw in some other things, but by then I couldn't look. At least it was all floating in hot water.

After a time, Empson told me to bring the bowls to him, and he ladled out full portions for each of us, stopping between scoops to make pants adjustments. We sat outside in the lovely air and quiet garden, which did not have much beyond grass and some shrubbery. We were at a wooden table, with Empson at its head. He was obviously proud of his culinary work. There was no choice but to get it all down. Tasting it, I was shocked to find it was good. I didn't know what it was, but I was so relieved that I would be able to eat it at all that I blurted out my compliments.

"My boy," Empson said, "it is just like a symphony. You get the right instruments together—here, the ingredients—and the conductor then blends it all together." We laughed at his delight.

He told us that when he had taught for a semester in America at a small college, he was assigned to teach Shakespeare to a class full of engineers (perhaps because he had taken the first part of his Cambridge degree in maths). Without slighting them, he said they knew nothing, not even what the Avon was. But what he liked best about them was that they were so well disciplined by their engineering training that they looked up every word they didn't know—so they met the first test of close reading.

I left with his voice even clearer in my head than on my old Caedmon recording of him reading his poems, my favorite being a Gertrude Stein pastiche, "Poem about a Ball in the Nineteenth Century":

> Feather, feather, if it was a feather, feathers for fair, or to be fair, aroused. Round to be airy, feather, if it was airy, very, aviary, fairy, peacock to be well surrounded. Well-aired, amoving, to peacock, cared for, share dancing inner to be among aware.

THERE THEN: VISITS TO FOUR MEN who lived and died by, with, and for the English language. What most remains for me, beyond their words and genius, is their generosity. Today, Christopher Ricks is the Oxford Professor of Poetry, just as Auden was more than a half century ago, finishing his five-year appointment in 1961, the year before our luncheon.

As I have grown older, read more, and now teach, becoming what J. D. Salinger called a "lifetime English major," how many times I have wished for another meeting with each of them, because I have so much more to ask. And to hear again how each was so indelibly himself, to say some thanks to them for their part in making my teaching years full, to show them how much these meetings meant to me.

Spring Semester 2006

A version of this lecture appeared in the *American Scholar* (Winter 2009), and was later chosen for inclusion in *The Best American Essays 2010*.

11

Maurice Bowra

G. W. BOWERSOCK

As Warden of Wadham College in Oxford, President of the British Academy, the author of well-known books on ancient Greek literature, and a conversationalist of legendary brilliance, Maurice Bowra seemed, in the middle of the last century, the very embodiment of Oxford life. Enjoying a huge international reputation as scholar, wit, and administrator, he was duly elected into prestigious academies and awarded honorary degrees in both Europe and America. George VI knighted him in 1951. Yet few who were not alive at that time know his name today. For those of the younger generation who are aware of him at all, his career conjures up the Oxford of *Brideshead Revisited,* and it has been said that he was the model for Mr. Samgrass. A few of his bright remarks linger on among the chattering classes: "Buggers can't be choosers" or "Where there's death there's hope" or "He is a man who has no public virtues and no private parts." But for the most part, he has sunk into oblivion, to emerge from time to time in an obituary or in the voluminous correspondence of Isaiah Berlin.

Wadham College, which Bowra led from 1938 until 1970 and elevated from a long tradition of mediocrity into one of glittering prominence, commissioned a new biography by Leslie Mitchell, an "old boy" of Wadham and a historian of modern England and France. Mitchell knew his subject personally and had access to the archives of many of the notable figures with whom Bowra had been in contact. He has a deep sympathy for the contradictions and anxieties that drove Bowra to almost frenetic activity in Oxford, but unfortunately he has no comprehension of ancient Greek culture and the world of classical scholars, whose rejection drove Bowra into administration in the first place and then consigned his publications to the trash heap soon after his death. Once he was dead, the verbal assaults that Bowra hurled at his detractors came no more.

Bowra's incandescent talk was admired wherever he went, and he never failed to deliver. In commemorating him for *The Times,* Isaiah Berlin wrote, "His wit was verbal and cumulative. The words came in short, sharp bursts of precisely aimed, concentrated fire, as image, pun, metaphor, parody, seemed spontaneously to generate one another in a succession of marvelously imagined patterns, sometimes rising to high, wildly comical fantasy." Anyone who has ever listened to Berlin himself cannot but think that he is describing his own way of talking, and yet the description of Bowra's wit is nonetheless right on target. Bowra and Berlin were very old friends, and the peculiarly dazzling logorrhea that characterized both of them doubtless arose from decades of conversation together.

ALTHOUGH BOWRA WAS BORN IN CHINA, where his father worked in the Chinese customs service, he soon came back to England and was given an impeccable classical education at Cheltenham. Although his exotic origins may have encouraged a lifelong interest in foreign literatures, Bowra was irreproachably British in background and manner, and for someone like Isaiah Berlin, born of a Jewish family in Riga and arriving in Oxford by way of St. Petersburg, Bowra must have provided a seductive model of sophistication. Berlin saw Bowra as "a major liberating influence," and many years later, in 1952, he poured out his gratitude to the Warden of Wadham with perhaps excessive self-depreciation:

> As you know, I take a low view of myself and all I do and friendship means more to me—and always has—than anything else at all . . . It is not merely love and admiration for you that I feel, though these emotions are genuine enough; but I owe you a transformation of my entire mode of life and attitude towards it. It is a trite way of putting it perhaps, but you did "liberate" me . . . I do not for a moment suppose that you were aware of the strength and emancipating power of your mere presence, but if I am anything to anybody the . . . responsibility is largely yours.

This liberating force of Bowra must have been real, although I never felt it myself on the few occasions when I met him, toward the end of his life. Even John Sparrow, the Warden of All Souls College, whom Bowra often annoyed mightily, wrote affectingly in verse

> You made us what we are;
> Our jokes, our joys, our hopes, our hatreds too,
> The outrageous things we do, or want to do—
> How much of all of them we owe to you!

For anyone bright enough to respond to the challenges of Bowra's manner, he was clearly charismatic, and in the 1920s and early 1930s, he overtly surrounded himself with young admirers, who always ran the risk of banishment from the charmed circle. Among his undergraduate guests were Kenneth Clark, John Betjeman, Hugh Gaitskill, Evelyn Waugh, and Cecil Day-Lewis. Both Isaiah Berlin and John Sparrow survived and profited from this quite literally intoxicating society. Yet the pied-piper aspect of Bowra itself sprang from deep fears of rejection and failure, and he tells, as Berlin himself did in his address at the memorial service in 1971, that H. W. B. Joseph, a demanding philosopher to whom the young Bowra was assigned for tutorials at New College, nearly destroyed his pupil's confidence by constantly challenging and mocking his assertions. It was only by dropping philosophy at this stage that Bowra managed to recover his equilibrium and go on to a successful undergraduate career in classics. But the sense of inadequacy and failure never left him, and in a notorious episode in 1936, it changed the entire course of his life.

Gilbert Murray, whose name among English speakers was synonymous with Greek literature in the early twentieth century, was about to retire from the Regius Professorship of Greek at Oxford. He had taught the young Bowra and apparently led him to believe that he might well become the next Regius. But to the surprise of almost everyone, Bowra himself above all, the electors to the chair chose an Irish scholar of Neoplatonic philosophy, E. R. Dodds. This was someone completely outside the circle of Oxford academics in which Bowra had already found a niche, and his friends could only assume that Murray had dropped his support of Bowra.

At any rate, the outcome of the election was devastating. Bowra promptly went off to be a visiting professor in America, where he was offered a chair at Harvard. But, Oxonian to the core, he returned and decided instead to accept the Wardenship of Wadham as a new vocation in the absence of a chair of Greek. This whole episode was absolutely crucial in determining Bowra's future career. It left him with a feeling, which Joseph had first instilled in him, of being second-rate—a feeling that impelled him to prove himself over and over again in a series of books on Greek as well as modern literature. What happened in the summer of 1936 can be explained only by reference to classical scholarship at the time. In the previous year, Bowra had published a critical edition of the poems of Pindar in the highly esteemed series Oxford Classical Texts, and this was obviously meant to be the major scholarly work that would ensure his elevation to the Regius chair. Unfortunately, the edition of Pindar had the opposite effect.

A review of Bowra's book appeared in the distinguished German periodical *Gnomon,* which all professional classicists consulted with respect. One of the journal's founders, Eduard Fraenkel, had recently arrived in Oxford as a Jewish refugee from Germany, and he may well have had early warning of the review of Bowra's *Pindar* that was about to appear. But it would certainly have been available in print before the electors met in 1936. Murray must have seen it, and Bowra, who read German with facility, would have seen it too. The reviewer, Alexander Turyn (then in Warsaw), found the text of the poems marginally acceptable because it simply reproduced another scholar's published text, but he pronounced Bowra's own scholarship "completely worthless" (*vollkommen wertlos*). Another person who must have read that review was Arthur Darby Nock at Harvard, to whom Murray had written for an opinion about his successor. Nock told me explicitly in 1962 that he had written against the election of Bowra and had put forward the name of Dodds, whose work he had known through his own on late antique philosophy. In his autobiography, Bowra's cool reference to Nock during his brief stay at Harvard in late 1936 suggests to me that he had some knowledge of what had gone on behind the scenes.

Curiously, the choice of Dodds as professor proved to be an inspired one. His great book *The Greeks and the Irrational* is, without question, one of the acknowledged masterpieces of classical learning in the twentieth century, and his edition of Euripides' *Bacchae* reigns supreme even now. No less curiously, the bitter disappointment that drove Bowra into the Wardenship of Wadham proved to be the making of the Bowra that acquired such renown in post-war Oxford. The electors to the Regius chair achieved far more than they imagined.

Bowra never again attempted to do a critical edition of a Greek author. In a memorial that appeared in the *Proceedings of the British Academy,* Dodds's successor in the Regius chair, Hugh Lloyd-Jones, wrote candidly:

Bowra was not suited to be a textual critic. He lacked the accuracy and caution expected of an editor, and he had been denied the gift of textual divination . . . His Oxford text of Pindar (1935), though its apparatus criticus contains some useful matter, has not enough positive merits to compensate for its numerous inaccuracies.

After becoming Warden of Wadham, Bowra devoted himself entirely to expository books about literature, apart from his autobiographical *Memories*, which he strangely refused to carry beyond the 1930s.

The published oeuvre remains something of a mystery to this day because it is uniformly so dull. Anyone with knowledge of Bowra's conversation and wit, and of the poetic parodies that lacerated the reputations of his contemporaries, will find it difficult to imagine why his academic prose was so utterly undistinguished. As Lloyd-Jones wrote:

> Those who knew only Bowra's writings may find it hard to understand, but no person who knew him at all well can fail to be surprised that nothing that he ever wrote gives the faintest inkling of the impression which he made in conversation . . . Even where he avoids cliché, what he wrote seems flat and pedestrian beside the brilliance of what he said. To this deficiency of style corresponds a deficiency of content.

I think that the reason for this bizarre situation is that Bowra at his best was pure artifice, whereas scholarship was—and is—not. His coruscating brilliance in speech, his puns and put-downs, were simply not enough for serious work. Unlike A. E. Housman, he was incapable of uniting wit with scholarship, and Housman could do it only in print.

It is here that we must look for what made Bowra ultimately so different from Isaiah Berlin, who professed that he had learned so much from him. Oxford's two greatest talkers were old friends. They both could dazzle audiences, and both had a profound interest in foreign cultures. Berlin's sovereign command of Russian language and literature could hardly be matched by Bowra's readings of Russian poetry, but it is impressive that both promoted this literature in an Anglophone environment. But what gradually became clear in the relationship between these two men was Berlin's interest in ideas and his breadth of human sympathy. Bowra had neither.

Perhaps the memory of Joseph's tutorials and the abiding feeling of being second-rate kept Bowra away from anything that remotely resembled philosophical thought. His steely carapace of wit and parody constantly prevented him from showing or accepting human warmth. As the years passed, the brilliance of Berlin never faded as he reached out to an ever-larger band of friends and intellectuals whose horizons were all but imperceptible to Bowra. A telling case was Berlin's regard for the critic Edmund Wilson, of whom Bowra greatly disapproved. In writing to Noel Annan, Berlin confided, "I secretly see Mr Edmund Wilson with whom (don't tell Maurice) my relations are becoming quite warm." Berlin's correspondence, vastly enlarged after he took up the Dictaphone, displays a beguiling openness to people of all sorts and to philosophical ideas. The difference is encapsulated in the titles of books: Berlin's *Historical Inevitability* or *Two Concepts of Liberty*, by comparison with Bowra's *The Greek Experience* or *Heroic Poetry*.

Not that Bowra was imperceptive. His suspicion of the attractive German Rhodes Scholar Adam von Trott, who left golden memories at Balliol before the war, was not irrational, despite von Trott's terrible execution after the plot to kill Hitler. As Mitchell observes, "For some reason, Bowra had a visceral distrust of the man." When von Trott appeared in Oxford to assure Bowra that the members of the German opposition would remove Hitler on their own, provided the Nazis could be left in control of the Sudetenland and Austria, Bowra smelled a rat. The signs that von Trott ultimately turned against Hitler are compelling, but equally so are those of his earlier complicity with the Nazis. Even Berlin seems to have questioned the widespread opinion that von Trott was a martyr. In 1951, David Astor, the editor of the *Observer*, who had admired von Trott since their time together at Balliol, viciously attacked Bowra when he received his knighthood. Berlin rightly saw in Astor's hostility a wholly unwarranted belief that Bowra was somehow responsible for bringing about von Trott's death. It is true that Bowra had written to Felix Frankfurter that he had doubts about von Trott's commitment to oppose Hitler. British intelligence intercepted his letter and presumably made use of it. It would have put von Trott into an impossible position, but Bowra may have been right. Justin Cartwright has recently fictionalized the story in *The Song before It Is Sung* (2007).

Although Bowra may have had some indirect influence on war policy, as in the von Trott case, he was not called upon to serve in diplomacy or intelligence, as so many Oxford colleagues were. This meant that he had to endure considerable isolation in Oxford when term was out, and he clearly resented Isaiah Berlin's posting to the British Embassy in Washington, where, according to Bowra, he was "pillowed on pink, satin sheets." Many noted Oxonians were breaking codes in Bletchley or picking up rumors in foreign places (John Betjeman in Dublin, Ronald Syme in Istanbul). Bowra, an old soldier from the previous war, was "deeply anxious to do some war job," as he admitted to Frederick Lindemann. His friends tried to help, but without success. His apparent though not flamboyant homosexuality may have rendered him untrustworthy, although if he had possessed desirable technical skills, as Alan Turing (another homosexual) had in breaking the Germans' Enigma code, Bowra might have been employed in the war effort. Leslie Mitchell is probably right in saying in his biography, "Establishment figures, so long mocked and teased in dinner party stories and scurrilous verse, took a terrible revenge."

That scurrilous verse was notorious. When Lloyd-Jones wrote his British Academy memorial in 1972, he tempered his account of Bowra's boring prose by alluding to his scabrous poetry: "His least inhibited writing was his occasional verse, and it is sad that little of this is likely to be published while those who can recognize its allusions are alive." By a strange irony, Henry Hardy, the indefatigable editor of Isaiah Berlin's letters, published Bowra's "unpublishable" verse in 2005 from a manuscript left with John Sparrow at All Souls College.

Under the title *New Bats in Old Belfries,* Bowra's clever, brittle, and obscene parodies can now be read and assessed. Almost all are directed at his contemporaries, and the ones maligning his enemies are unspeakably vicious and small minded. Even his friends could not have been altogether pleased with how they were commemorated. His epithalamium on the marriage of Kenneth Clark begins:

> Angels of St. James's Park,
> Make the bed for Kenneth Clark:
> Make it when such loves are sealed
> Broad as any battlefield.
> When he strips him for the fight,
> Help him in his work tonight.
> See that all the night till morn
> No preventative is torn;
> Many a useless child may live
> From a torn preventative.

Bowra's parody of John Betjeman's "Dorset," under the title "Major Prophet," is about none other than Isaiah Berlin. It is hardly an affectionate tribute, although tribute it is:

> See the young girls' enraptured faces
> To the adagio listening.

> Oh, hark, for sex-appeal is calling
> And ripples down those bended necks.
> The master calls them to attention,
> Unveils the mysteries of sex.

The abundant sexual content of Bowra's poems is so consistently puerile, however smartly phrased, that one has to wonder about his emotional maturity. He had been initiated into gay sex in Germany in 1932 through his friend Adrian Bishop, a Wildean character who finally became an Anglican monk to expiate his sins. Bowra's most elaborate verse parody, "Old Croaker," taking off from T. S. Eliot's "East Coker" and alluding along the way to Milton and Yeats, among others, was a grotesque celebration of Bishop's debauchery:

> I will arise and go now and go to have a pee,
> Way down in Innisfree.
> That's where I wish to be
> With a Corporal on my knee.
> Oh is it town or gown or tousled hair,
> A tousled boy-scout's hair
> Inside the WC?

Yet despite his flings in Germany, Bowra's sexual extravagance in Oxford was largely verbal, and as his reputation as the Warden of Wadham grew, he became increasingly sensitive to being labeled a homosexual—to such an extent that he refused to meet with Jean Genet, who had come to Oxford to receive an honorary degree.

BOWRA'S PUBESCENT SEXUALITY and sharply honed wit seemed to leave little room for such feelings as tenderness or compassion, to say nothing of love. Yet there is one hint of such emotion in the aftermath of his German experience of 1932. He had been introduced to members of the circle of the poetic guru Stefan George, who exalted the boy he called Maximin into the muse of his poetry. (Oddly, Mitchell insists on spelling the poet's surname without the final *e*, but then his German seems shaky, since he translates *wahrscheinlich* as "truly" instead of "probably.") Bowra went on to introduce George's work to Anglophone readers, and in 1934 he met in Oxford one of the poet's most distinguished disciples, the medieval historian Ernst Kantorowicz, the author of a magisterial biography of Frederick the Second and the influential study *The King's Two Bodies*. A personal friendship of such intensity and longevity ensued that it is reasonable to suspect that the two became lovers.

Kantorowicz prescribed that all Bowra's letters to him be destroyed upon his death, and so we are deprived of seeing what Bowra wrote, but a letter from Kantorowicz to Bowra survives, with thanks for a photo of the young Bowra in his "buggerable days." This might, of course, be simple playfulness, but it is remarkable that a transatlantic relationship between the two, including European travel together, lasted for several decades—when Kantorowicz was in California at Berkeley and then at the Institute for Advanced Study in Princeton. As an executor of his estate, Ralph Giesey has testified that when Kantorowicz died in 1963, there were three photographs beside his bed. One was of his mother, another of Stefan George, and the third of Maurice Bowra. This is the only glimpse we have today of any kind of deep emotional attachment in the entire course of Bowra's life. Soon after Kantorowicz's death, Bowra wrote to Felix Frankfurter, "My own debt to him is incalculable. He stirred my intelligence, bolstered my morale, amused me with dazzling paradoxes and intuitions and formulations."

For those of Bowra's old friends who outlived him, he was difficult in his last years. He became deaf and demanding. Even so generous and forgiving a person as Isaiah Berlin clearly had problems in coping with him as time passed. In 1954, Berlin wrote to John Sparrow that he avoided invitations when he knew that Bowra would also be present. "I cramp his style," wrote Berlin, "and he knows it—there is nothing I can do about that." Life beyond the Warden's lodgings at Wadham was inconceivable for Bowra, who had depended for decades upon college servants. The college prorogued his position for two extra years and then provided rooms for him in a new college building. But it is scarcely surprising that he could not tolerate his new existence, and death came swiftly after he left the Wardenship in 1970.

Tacitus wrote, in the biography of his father-in-law, Agricola, that persons like himself who lived on into a different kind of world from the one in which they grew up not only outlived other people but themselves as well: *non modo aliorum sed etiam nostri superstites sumus.* This might well be applied to Bowra: he survived himself. When he died, the glamorous and witty soirées belonged to an irrecoverable past. The naughty poems were already gathering dust. Meanwhile, Isaiah Berlin, with his irrepressible intellect, his passion for ideas, and his friends all over the world, was triumphantly building a reputation to which Bowra could never have aspired. Yet another of his old friends, John Sparrow, revealed a heartbreaking glimpse of the affection that might have been, when he imagined that on Judgment

Day, Bowra himself would divide the dead between the celestial and the nether realms:

> Send us to Hell or Heaven or where you will,
> Promise us only you'll be with us still:
> Without you, Heaven would be too dull to bear,
> and Hell will not be Hell if you are there.

Mitchell's biography of Bowra serves as a requiem for the Oxford of *Brideshead*.

Fall Semester 2011

A version of this lecture appeared in the *New Republic,* 5 October 2009.

12

Hugh Trevor-Roper

NEAL ASCHERSON

ight years after his death, Hugh Trevor-Roper's reputation is still a cauldron of discord. He would have enjoyed that. Steaming in the mix are the resentments of those he expertly wounded, the awe of colleagues at the breadth and depth of his learning, dismay at his serial failures to complete a full-length work of history, delight in the Gibbonian wit and elegance of his writing, and—still a major ingredient—schadenfreude over his awful humiliation in the matter of the Hitler diaries.

In his lifetime, nobody was sure how to take him. Those who supposed they had his measure soon found that they were wrong. The fogeyish camorra who ran Peterhouse in the 1980s chose him as Master because they assumed he was a semi-fascist ultra like themselves. But as the Cambridge historian Michael Postan put it, "They are such fools: they thought they were electing a Tory and never realized that they were electing a Whig." Mrs. Thatcher imagined that the scholar who had written *The Last Days of Hitler* would share her hostility to a reunified Germany. But at the infamous Chequers meeting on Germany in 1990, Trevor-Roper faced her down and tore her arguments to pieces.

The historian John Habakkuk was an editor of the *Economic History Review* in 1952 when Trevor-Roper's onslaught against R. H. Tawney landed on his desk. He mused: "I find it difficult to decide whether T-R is a fundamentally nice person in the grip of a prose style in which it is impossible to be polite, or a fundamentally unpleasant person . . . using rudeness as a disguise for nastiness." Habakkuk's first guess was very sharp. Perhaps Trevor-Roper was essentially a nice person. But the niceness was not apparent to many people who had to judge Trevor-Roper by what and how he wrote.

The prose style he adopted—or which adopted him—owed something to his idol Gibbon but more to Carlyle (whose ideas he despised). Especially in reviews of other historians' work, he could be pitilessly sarcastic, annihilating in his mockery. In his demolition of Arnold Toynbee, for example, Trevor-Roper accused the saintly old windbag of regarding himself as a messiah, complete with "the youthful Temptations; the missionary Journeys; the Miracles; the Revelations; the Agony." Reviewing a biography of Sir William Stephenson, a figure in British wartime intelligence, he declined even to list its inaccuracies: "To make such a charge against this biographer would be unfair. It would be like urging a jellyfish to grit its teeth and dig in its heels." In his 1951 campaign to "liquidate Stone" (the young historian Lawrence Stone), he composed what was later described as "one of the most vitriolic attacks ever made by one historian on another." Victims constantly used the word "malicious" about his choice of language, and Trevor-Roper himself often talked gleefully about his own "malice." Yet the glitter of his style could tempt him into absurdity, as when he asserted that eighteenth-century Scots—smarting from the loss of independence—turned "to discover and appreciate their native literature": "Unfortunately, when they looked for it, they could not find it. There was none."

But it was not just a prose style that gripped Hugh Trevor-Roper and came to dictate his posture in the world. It was a whole style of living and behaving. In the 1950s, there still existed in Britain a few fairylands of ancient privilege and exclusiveness, almost immune to social change, innocently convinced of their own superiority. One of these was the remnant of the old territorial aristocracy, the upper class that had been inconvenienced by austerity and the postwar lack of servants but that still held on to its country seats and its influence. Another was the world of the two "historic" English universities—the "top" colleges of Oxford in particular.

Trevor-Roper was captured by the second, and married into the first. Enemies invariably called him "arrogant." But it seems that he was never quite confident that he belonged in either world; he took on their manner with an exaggerated relish that suggests insecurity. In this, he was unlike the much tougher A. J. P. Taylor, who came to Oxford from middle-class Lancashire and was able to view the place with affectionate detachment. Taylor got on sturdily with his work. Trevor-Roper let himself be drawn into energy-sapping college intrigues, academic beauty contests, and professional vendettas. Other scholars took part in all that, but still managed to finish their books. For all his brilliance, and his bursts of intensive research, Trevor-Roper allowed his diligent affectation of an Old Oxford style to dilute his sense of purpose. I have wondered whether this man, who had such driving intellectual curiosity, such a genius for asking the question that no other historian had noticed, wouldn't have done better in a different sort of university. Edinburgh would have been right for him if he hadn't had such a blistering phobia about the "Scotch." Manchester, Liverpool, or University College London would have let him concentrate. Perhaps he should never have gone to Oxford. Perhaps it maimed him.

But that leads on to a separate question. It has been the general view that Trevor-Roper somehow did not "fulfill his promise": he never completed the great work about early modern England that everyone expected from him. He left behind a long trail of aborted books, writings that are now being tidied up, edited, and steadily published. Even Mrs. Thatcher scolded him for weak book productivity. "On the stocks? *On the stocks?* A fat lot of good that is! In the shops, that is where we need it!"

And yet who is to say that success as a historian is to be measured by hardcovers in Blackwell's? Trevor-Roper's natural distance was the long essay in a historical journal, the lead book review, the lecture series polished up for publication, the heavyweight foreign-page reporting in the *Observer* or the *Sunday Times.* On that scale, he produced his best and most influential work, launching challenges and controversies that permanently altered interpretations of the English and European past. In his abandoned books, he would put all his energies into a few brilliant chapters and then lose interest. The only full-length book of history he published in his lifetime was his first: *Archbishop Laud* (1940). The others were almost all journal supplements or compilations of one kind or another. The book for which he was best known, *The Last Days of Hitler* (1947), was reportage and detective work rather than conventional history.

HE EMERGED FROM AN ANCIENT gentry family that had come down in the world. His father was a small-town doctor in Northumbria; his mother was soured by anxieties about class and status. The young Hugh was put through the conventional sequence of grim prep schools—chilblains, ignorance, and the cane—and then Charterhouse, where, as he recalled, the "missing element was thought." But he was an excellent examinee; he read furiously, began to think for himself, and, on long walks in the holidays, grew to know the

Borders and their rough history. Adam Sisman, in his 2010 biography of Trevor-Roper, is not the first commentator to suggest that his antipathy to Scotland began in local patriotism. He soaked up a romantic English version of Border mythology in which the noble English were victims and the raiding Scots barbarous invaders.

In 1932, he won a classics scholarship to Christ Church. The ambience when Trevor-Roper arrived resembled that of Regency Eton: young bloods pursuing their habits of drinking, gambling, and fighting while treating the dons rather like elderly servants who could be trusted not to make them open a book. In the midst of all this lurked the minority of brainy scholarship boys, clad in long gowns but usually lacking grandeur in their social origins. At first intimidated, Trevor-Roper soon took to the Christ Church style. He drank, betted, smashed glass, and threw food about with the best of them. Well, not quite the best: he was not posh enough for the Bullingdon. The Gridiron Club was the place where he caroused, on wild nights that could end in ritual debaggings and dunkings in fountains. All this sits oddly with the later image of an austere, disciplinarian Regius professor. But Trevor-Roper was always a highly physical creature. He was a phenomenal walker, whether in the Borders or the Peloponnese, and would appear in college after "a short stroll" of thirty-eight miles in the Cotswolds. Above all, he developed a lifelong passion for hunting. Horses rolled on him; he lost his spectacles in ditches. But an alluring meet could take precedence over a lecture, or even duties in wartime intelligence.

Though he attended chapel services with a surplice over his hunting gear, Trevor-Roper soon lost what faith he had ever had. Recoiling from an encounter with Father D'Arcy, the Jesuit soul fisher of pre-war Oxford, he became not so much an atheist as a militant anticlerical, as hard on Roman Catholics as on Calvinist fundamentalists. He tried Freemasonry, but soon dropped his Masonic kit over a bridge. He was for a time seriously interested in Marxism, and although he soon rejected its "prophetic" claims, he retained for the rest of his career an awareness of social and economic change as determinants in history, an attitude that marked him off from conventional "Tory historians."

His first visit to Germany, in 1935, left him with an impression of the Nazis as vulgar and coarse. But he seems to have been indifferent to politics until the Munich crisis in 1938. Disgusted with British appeasement and with socialist "weakness" over the prospect of war, he read *Mein Kampf* and took it seriously as a coherent program. This was a view he stuck to; he would never accept later interpretations—

by A. J. P. Taylor in particular—that reduced Hitler to a mere opportunist who made up his actions as he went along.

During the war, Trevor-Roper worked in intelligence, at first in the Radio Security Service. This outfit initially fell under MI8, but was later transferred to the Secret Intelligence Service (MI6) and its huge Ultra decrypting operation at Bletchley Park. He was brilliant at his job, but his insistence on the importance of interpreting Nazi signals traffic, rather than just warehousing facts, often enraged his superiors. Other accounts have described some of the exotic figures who commanded Britain's secret world, but Trevor-Roper's private notes on them are startling. Felix Cowgill, in charge of counterintelligence, was a "purblind, disastrous megalomaniac." He rather fancied Colonel Gambier-Parry, who went hunting "in a risqué chocolate uniform," but despised his sidekick, Ted Maltby, as a "farting exhibitionist" resembling "those baboons on Monkey Hill, exhibiting to all in turn their great iridescent blue bottoms." Not surprisingly, such men came to hate him. One of them even tried to frame him as a traitor who was passing the Ultra secret to Nazi agents in Ireland—a charge that could have landed him in front of a firing squad. In spite of them, Trevor-Roper enjoyed himself. He went twice to enjoy the unrationed plenty of neutral Ireland, where the police regarded him as a "British spy" and raided his hotel room. And he continued to hunt most weeks with the Whaddon or the Bicester. Once, the Whaddon hounds chased a fox past the sentries and into Bletchley Park itself, and Trevor-Roper, the only hunter with a security pass, had to round them up.

He achieved some big "scoops of interpretation." These included the first news of the deepening political feud between Admiral Canaris of the Abwehr and Heinrich Himmler's SS. When his superiors tried to suppress his ideas, he often went over their heads to contacts in Churchill's inner circle, like Frederick Lindemann. This made him even less popular. But he emerged from the intelligence war with some important and lasting friendships, including those with Gilbert Ryle, Stuart Hampshire, Guy Liddell, and Dick White, who, after the war, became the head of MI5 and then MI6—an invaluable contact. And Trevor-Roper enjoyed the company of Kim Philby, whom he found the most intelligent and sophisticated of his colleagues.

After the war, he interrogated Nazi prisoners in the British zone of Germany. Dick White was now ensconced in a confiscated schloss with a first-class chef, and "over the third bottle of hock," the two men hit on a seductive idea. Trevor-Roper should use his historian's skills and prove to the world, once and for all, that Hitler really was dead. In Berlin, he explored the derelict bunker and then set off in a jeep across Germany to find witnesses. He enjoyed these "delightful journeys, motoring through the deciduous golden groves of Schleswig-Holstein" along empty roads. But this was September 1945! Trevor-Roper's lofty indifference to a shattered country whose cities lay in ruins, whose people were approaching starvation, and where millions of homeless refugees and "displaced persons" were wandering in search of food and shelter is hard to understand or forgive.

His work, however, was a success. His report in November established the Führer's death beyond doubt and won him a lasting reputation as a "Hitler expert." He assembled his research into a best-selling book, *The Last Days of Hitler,* which earned him enough money for "a Sardanapalian beano" in Oxford. But the praise was not quite unanimous. Catholics were upset by his contempt for the behavior of the Church under Hitler, and especially by his drawing attention to Goebbels's Jesuit education. Here began his long-running vendetta with Evelyn Waugh. And the book abounded in withering generalizations about "the German national character," views popular at the time but now embarrassing to read.

Back in Oxford, he found that he was resented by some older dons. The bitchiest of all the sniping came from Maurice Bowra, who wrote to Waugh that "Trevor-Roper is a fearful man, short-sighted, with dripping eyes, shows off all the time, sucks up to me, boasts, is far from poor owing to his awful book, on every page of which there is a howler." Understandably, Trevor-Roper enjoyed escaping to wider worlds: the *Observer* hired him to report on politics in western Europe (driving a Bentley with his friend Robert Blake) and then in Czechoslovakia (a Lagonda with the young Alan Clark). In Tuscany, on the first of these jaunts, he met Bernard Berenson, the art collector and maestro of highly paid authentication. Berenson became an intimate friend, and their correspondence over the years—witty and very frank—is a rich source. But, unexpectedly, Sisman himself comes downstage to pitch an authorial mud pie: "It was possible to see Berenson as an old fraud, a man who had squandered his talents in the pursuit of money, and whose personality had shrivelled in the process of trying to defend the indefensible." Maybe, but it wasn't possible for Trevor-Roper to see him like that.

IN 1957, HE FINALLY BECAME REGIUS PROFESSOR of Modern History, after a much-publicized contest with Taylor. It is a myth that they were deadly enemies. The two men had vivid disagreements—not least over Hitler and his intentions, as described by Taylor in *The*

Origins of the Second World War—but respected each other's gifts and stayed on remarkably affectionate terms. Before and after his appointment, Trevor-Roper plunged into a succession of historical controversies. Some of these were mere "liquidations" of an opponent, without much resonance for the understanding of history. But others showed Trevor-Roper at his most convincing and powerful as he challenged received interpretations of the past.

He tried to refute the thesis that England's seventeenth-century crisis derived from the "rise of the gentry" and the social-economic decay of the aristocracy. The reverse was true, he argued: the gentry at the end of the sixteenth century were in decline. He suggested that the "Marxisant" class analysis of the period was too crude; the real conflict was between what he called Court and Country, and by the 1640s, the English Court had become the most arrogant and intolerably expensive power structure in Europe. In sometimes-brutal polemics, he attacked the whole *Religion and the Rise of Capitalism* orthodoxy established by R. H. Tawney and Max Weber. The question for him was not why capitalism emerged in Protestant countries, but why it did not emerge in Catholic Europe after the Counter-Reformation. Widening his focus, he denounced another received version: that the intellectual pedigree of the Enlightenment led back to Calvin's Reformation in Geneva. The European Enlightenment did have religious roots, he admitted, but they lay among heretics, dissenters, and independent thinkers of all faiths, not in an elect obsessed with sin and predestination. This led him to ask another question: how could the Scottish Enlightenment have happened in a country he insisted on describing as absurdly primitive? It was a question that older Scottish historians, darkly suspicious of the Enlightenment as an "English import," had avoided. Remarkably, Trevor-Roper did not take this view, but suggested—on rather daringly slim evidence—that the thinkers who made Hume, Ferguson, and Adam Smith possible were Scottish, but "heretics" to the Presbyterian mainstream: liberal Catholic exiles, Jacobites, and Episcopalian intellectuals from Scotland's Northeast.

This, and his irrepressible sneering at all things Caledonian, annoyed the Scots. It was meant to. Trevor-Roper's anti-Scottish sentiment, evident even in the letters he wrote as a boy from a Scottish prep school, was not entirely rational. *The Invention of Scotland* (2008), a posthumous selection of some of his essays on the country, is fun to read but spoiled by ignorance of the background, unfamiliarity with recent Scottish research, and malicious interpretation. The fact is that he was out of his depth, as he often was when he stepped beyond about 1760. Trevor-Roper, like most English historians of his time, had a tin ear for nationalism ("atavistic, tribal") and no insight into romantic cultural politics. His elaborate essay on the Ossian fraud does not even mention that similar fragments of ancient verse were cooked up into "epics" in a dozen European countries over the next hundred years.

Trevor-Roper's own politics remained Whiggish, unpredictable. Students, noting his snobbish style and grand contacts, supposed him a Tory. But in the strict sense, he never was. Over Suez in 1956, he called Anthony Eden a "vain, ineffectual Man of Blood," and reviled "the world of lower-middle-class conservatives who have no intelligence but a deep belief in violence as a sign of self-importance." He attended the first Congress for Cultural Freedom in Berlin, in 1950, but was repelled by its fanatical anticommunist rhetoric, which reminded him of Nazi rallies. He was never a Cold Warrior, and although he seems to have kept MI5 informed of colleagues he suspected of communist sympathies, he retained a deep respect for Eric Hobsbawm, a Party member, as a historian and helped him get a U.S. visa. Neither was he such a Little Englander as he seemed. Visiting Paris, he was enthralled by the work of Fernand Braudel and the *Annales* School, and complained that they were "totally excluded from Oxford which remains, in historical matters, a retrograde provincial backwater."

THE BOOKS CONTINUED NOT TO APPEAR. There were at least nine unfinished works, including a "huge book, in three volumes" on the Puritan Revolution, which he may have meant to be his defining achievement. Trevor-Roper confessed in a letter: "I am interested in too many things, and I write so slowly, so painfully slowly, that by the time I have written a chapter I have got interested in something else." This doesn't feel like the whole story. Trevor-Roper was as busy and efficient as anybody else, but ultimately he worked for his own pleasure. He loved the process of research for its own sake, and then avoided the drudgery of writing it up by turning to some other delicious, irresistible train of discoveries. And it could be that the "brilliant examinee syndrome," the private terror of public failure, had something to do with it as well. No book, no devastating book review.

He married Lady Alexandra Haig, daughter of the Field Marshal. Tall and commanding, she was miserably married to an admiral when she and Trevor-Roper fell in love. Their letters survive, and are very touching. It was a strange match—a sardonic bachelor don and an effusive but conventional aristocrat. They could madden each other, but the passionate bond between them was tough enough to withstand her extravagance, his reluctance to show emotion, and the sniggers of camp Oxford. Xandra was perilously unselfconscious. When two guests said that they had spent the previous night in Birmingham, she responded: "Birmingham? Whose place is that?"

By the mid-1950s, Trevor-Roper was regarded as the English-speaking world's leading expert on Nazi documents. *Hitler's Table Talk* (1953) was published with a long Trevor-Roper introduction ("The Mind of Adolf Hitler"), soon followed by another introduction to *The Bormann Letters*. Newspaper editors hungry for "Nazi revelations" jostled to sign him up, and journalism took an increasing share of his time. In the Third Reich trade, he began to meet a number of shady, greedy figures—among them, the Nazi-nostalgic François Genoud, Himmler's masseur Felix Kersten, and the young David Irving—to whom he initially gave more trust than they deserved. Trevor-Roper had a curious weakness for con men. He found them fascinating. But he overestimated his ability to see through them and underestimated the damage they could do.

Those interested in Trevor-Roper must confront a classic problem: an acute case of hindsight. Knowledge of the end—his authentication of the fake Hitler diaries—can seem to point to many previous episodes converging toward that awful Hamburg press conference on 25 April 1983. The omens are easy to pick out. Trevor-Roper, although he had seen plenty of forgeries (some of Kersten's Nazi "archives," for instance), grew dangerously confident that he could identify a fake. And he could be perversely uncritical when on a research trail that excited him. In 1964, he ploughed through the 20,000 pages of *The Warren Report*'s evidence and concluded that this "vast and slovenly" report had got it wrong: Kennedy had probably been the victim of a conspiracy. He refused to retreat even when his *Sunday Times* article to that effect ("Kennedy Murder Inquiry Is Suspect") was torn apart by critics. Adam Sisman comments: "The episode demonstrated both the positive and the negative sides of Hugh as a controversialist: his independence of mind, his boldness and his determination, but also his rashness, poor judgment, obstinacy and, perhaps, arrogance."

Arrogance and poor judgment were to show up in his relations with Rupert Murdoch and his gang. Trevor-Roper (by then Lord Dacre of Glanton) had been a director of *The Times* for seven years when Murdoch took over Times Newspapers in 1981. He had no illusions about Murdoch: "He aims to moronise and Americanise the population . . . wants to destroy our institutions, to rot them with a daily corrosive acid." Yet he did almost nothing as Murdoch tore up his agreements with the directors, threatened to sack six hundred staff members, and imposed his own standards of journalism. Instead, he stayed on the board for another six years. Perhaps he felt that as an "independent" director, he was a superior being who should not descend to the squabbles of tycoons and journalists. If so, it is hard to forgive—much harder than his behavior over the diaries. That failure, which blighted the rest of his life, was caused less by hubris than by two sorts of ignorance.

The first was that, without realizing it, he had lost touch with modern Germany. Unlike David Irving, he knew little about recent research into Nazi documentation or about the new market in convincing forgeries. At a different level, he did not grasp how hysterical and dishonest West German media bosses and journalists could be. He relied on his experience of Germans from the post-war "Occupation Time," thirty years before, which was now irrelevant. His second ignorance was about journalism. Again, he thought he knew about newspapers and the media because he knew "presentable" editors who printed his articles. He had no idea of the frantic haste, secrecy, and pressure of a big exclusive, in which there is no room for second thoughts. His first glance at the diaries suggested to him that they could be real, but a first glance was all he got. His instinct was not to authenticate them until he had taken more time to reflect, to examine, to wait for the ink and paper tests to be confirmed. But that was not on offer. His mistake was to allow himself to be hurried into stating that the diaries were genuine. When he did change his mind, the *Sunday Times* presses were already rolling. Murdoch said: "Fuck Dacre. Publish." Within a week, Hugh Trevor-Roper became the butt of the world's reading public.

He made many wrong calls in his life. But that one deserves sympathy. A sort of innocence, rather than his famous arrogance, brought the catastrophe about. Most of the journalists and academics who jeered at him must also have privately muttered: "There, but for the grace of God . . ." And in fact, though his public credibility was wrecked, his professional reputation did not suffer much. His friends stood by him.

Meanwhile, he was suffering a different kind of torment. In 1979, Trevor-Roper was astonished and pleased to be offered the Mastership of Peterhouse, Cambridge. He did not realize that the invitation was a labyrinthine ploy, devised by Maurice Cowling, to give the college a head so reactionary that he would be the willing prisoner of its extreme Right ruling clique. But like many princes of darkness, Cowling was so devious that he tripped over his own bootlaces: Lord Dacre, far from being a romantic Tory ultra, turned out to be an anticlerical Whig with a preference for free speech over superstition. He did not find it normal that fellows should wear mourning on the anniversary of General Franco's death, attend parties in SS uniform, or insult black and Jewish guests at high table. For the next seven years, Trevor-Roper battled to suppress the insurgency of the Cowling clique ("a strong mind trapped in its own glutinous frustrations") and to bring the college back to a condition in which students might actually want to go there. Neither side won the struggle, which soon became a campaign to drive Trevor-Roper out of the college by grotesque rudeness and insubordination. He hung on for his seven-year term and achieved some reforms, but left fearing that Peterhouse would "revert to its old condition of mouldering anarchy permeated by destructive intrigue." When he and Xandra celebrated their thirtieth wedding anniversary, he invited five duchesses to the party but not a single Peterhouse fellow. He affected to regard Cambridge as a "torpid, introverted village" among "dreary fens."

In 1987, he and Xandra retired to a spacious old house in Didcot. He published several more volumes of essays, all generously praised by critics, but failing eyesight prevented him from completing his memoirs. Xandra began to drift away into Alzheimer's, and Trevor-Roper cared for her tenderly. He survived Xandra's death in 1997 by six lonely years.

FEW HISTORIANS HAVE ATTRACTED so much abuse in their lifetimes. Bowra called Trevor-Roper "a robot, without human experience . . . no desire to like or be liked." Isaiah Berlin said that "he doesn't have any human perceptions; he's all glass and rubber." It can't be denied that his behavior invited that sort of venom, and sometimes deliberately. But these psychograms were inaccurate. The odd creature inside the spiky shell was all too vulnerable. Ved Mehta, interviewing Trevor-Roper for the *New Yorker*, was reminded of "a literary critic who has no love for writers." But Mehta also recognized that this supercilious professor was part of a larger, very English intellectual fashion: "going for the largest game, creating an intellectual sensation, striking a posture, sometimes at the expense of truth . . . generally enjoying the fun of going against the grain." That was a smarter insight than the robot cliché. Fun—the delight of raising hell by turning dogma on its head or asking the unpardonable question—was what Trevor-Roper was about. At his memorial meeting in Christ Church, his friend Blair Worden said: "His avowed aim, and his certain achievement, was to make history live." And that, for all his faults and failures, he did.

Fall Semester 2011

A version of this lecture appeared in the *London Review of Books,* 19 August 2010.

13

Nye Bevan

KENNETH O. MORGAN

Nye Bevan is firmly established in the socialist pantheon as a hero of Labour. This is not surprising. He was not only a prophet but also a great constructive pioneer. His National Health Service remains as a symbol of social solidarity. What is far more surprising is that Nye should have become in time a hero for New Labour. At a centenary event in Congress House in November 1997, the legacy of Bevan was hailed not only by old Bevanites like Michael Foot and Barbara Castle, but also by Chancellor Gordon Brown. Brown returned to his reverence for Bevan again in addressing the Bevan Foundation (23 May 2002), when he recalled Bevan's speech of 1946 introducing the National Health Service Bill.

More remarkably still, Tony Blair has often placed Bevan in the great line of Labour succession. Nye, the scourge of the capitalist ruling class, has become a pivot of the Progressive Alliance. In a foreword to Geoffrey Goodman's centenary celebration of Bevan, *The State of the Nation,* Blair acclaimed not only Bevan's "ideas and personality and rhetoric," not only his managerial skill in creating the National Health Service, but also his call for "passion in action," as embodied in Bevan's political testament, *In Place of Fear.*[1] Even Edmund Dell's account of the labor movement, *A Strange Eventful History,* which is fiercely critical of the revisionists Hugh Gaitskell and Anthony Crosland, found rare words of favor for the visionary and inspirational qualities of Nye Bevan.

In the 1980s, commentators contrasted Nye Bevan's "passionate parliamentarianism" and the Bevanite "legitimate Left" of the 1950s, with the anti-parliamentary extremism of the Bennites and "hard Left." Nye Bevan, it seems, has been reinvented as a mainstream patriot who defended Britain's manufacture of nuclear weapons and whose National Health Service represented social citizenship, everyman's idea of what it meant to be British. The ultimate radical has been transplanted into the center ground.

Is this justified? Is this reinvention of Nye credible, or is it yet another example of a dissenting radical going legitimate in hindsight? Bevan was never an establishment figure. Even the Tories whose company he enjoyed were offbeat mavericks like Lord Beaverbrook and Brendan Bracken. He was the most abused, as well as the most idolized, politician of his time. A product of the socialist cauldron of South Wales, he was a ferocious critic of conventional capitalist wisdom. Baldwin, Chamberlain, and even Lloyd George were savaged. He was, along with Stafford Cripps, expelled from the parliamentary Labour Party for advocating a Popular Front in 1939, and almost was again in 1944 for uncomradely attacks on Ernest Bevin and the unions. The Bevanites were accused by the party right of fomenting civil war. In 1955, he was expelled again, and almost terminally, for anti-party and anti-union activities, Clement Attlee's prudence and the whims of union members of the Labour National Executive saving him at the last. The later reconciliation with Gaitskell was always a shotgun marriage.

Even his record as architect of the National Health Service led him into trouble. His enemies denounced him as the "Minister of Disease," a "Tito from Tonypandy" (deliberately mispronounced and also inaccurate, since Bevan actually came from the equally alliterative Tredegar). His fateful remark when launching the NHS in July 1948 that the Tories were "lower than vermin" became a defining moment in Britain's version of the class war.[2] He received abuse, packets of excrement addressed to the resident of "Vermin Villa," a kick in the pants in White's Club from a deranged landowner appropriately named Strangeways.

And yet this stormy petrel does seem, half a century later, a more centrist politician than his contemporaries allowed. From his emergence in the 1920s, he usually chose the mainstream, even if under protest. Not for Nye the impotence of Jimmy Maxton and the Clydesiders of the Independent Labour Party (ILP). He retained a restless urge for power—even if "you always saw its coat-tails disappearing round the corner."[3]

BEVAN GREW UP IN THE CLASS TURMOIL of South Wales in 1910–26, between the Tonypandy riots and the General Strike. Those were the stormy years of the Plebs League and the Central Labour College evangelizing in the valleys; of the government's "betrayal" over the Sankey Commission's proposals for nationalization of the mines and the climbdown by fellow unionists of the Triple Alliance on Black Friday (15 April 1921); and of the titanic coal strikes of 1921 and 1926. This was capitalism raw and in crisis. Born in 1897 and sent down the mines in 1911, the young Bevan imbibed a rich variety of philosophies. He read the novels of Jack London and the revolutionary ideas of the German Joseph Dietzgen and the American Daniel de Leon. He was excited by the quasi syndicalism of the Rhondda-based Plebs League and its Marxist missionaries, particularly the charismatic ideologue Noah Ablett. They produced that passionate pamphlet, *The Miners' Next Step,* published by the Unofficial Reform Committee at Tonypandy. The young Bevan's ideas centered on direct action by the miners themselves. His views crystallized in his years at the Central Labour College in London in 1919–21, a workers' seminary for other young socialists like Jim Griffiths, Morgan Phillips, and Ness Edwards. He appeared to be the prototype of the young industrial rebel, focusing on direct action at the point of production to win for the workers the surplus value that was rightfully theirs. His work as dispute agent for the miners confirmed for him the deep injustices of the benefit system and the wage cuts that afflicted those miners not thrown out of work.

But it is highly relevant that these years still kept Bevan somewhere within the mainstream. The miners' strike of 1921, and even more the general strike of 1926, confirmed for him the sheer futility of an industrial struggle doomed to defeat by the anti-strike apparatus. For all his anti-capitalist rhetoric, Bevan forswore strategies such as the Minority Movement's effort to link up the Miners' Federation rank and file with communist allies. Still more did he reject the path that took another comrade, Arthur Horner, into the cul de sac of the Communist Party. While Bevan never wholly abandoned the mirage of industrial direct action, by the mid-1920s he was essentially an orthodox parliamentary socialist. He became a member of the Tredegar Urban District Council as early as 1922; he worked on the Tredegar Medical Aid Society (which influenced his ideas on the NHS after 1945); in 1928, he became a member of the Labour-controlled Monmouthshire county council as councillor for Ebbw Vale. To complete the process, his friend Archie Lush began a campaign to de-select the local MP, the passive Evan Davies. The miners balloted strongly in favor of Bevan, and in 1929 he was easily returned as Member of Parliament for Ebbw Vale. He remained its representative for the rest of his life.

Bevan began as an angry MP on the left. A controversial early speech on the coal industry featured a ferocious attack on the great figure of Lloyd George—"better dearer coal than cheaper colliers"— that shook that veteran, perhaps as an uncomfortable echo of his own youthful onslaughts on Joe Chamberlain.[4] Bevan was foremost, along with the Clydesiders, in denouncing the second Labour government under Ramsay MacDonald, and even more MacDonald's perceived treachery in forming a National Government with the Tories and Liberals in August 1931.

Bizarrely, the eloquent young Welshman then fell into strange company. He became friendly with the Marxist intellectual John Strachey. Through him, he briefly followed Sir Oswald Mosley's call for corporate planning, public works, tariffs, and revival of the home market. More personally, he was taken up by Lord Beaverbrook, and hobnobbed socially with such intimates as Brendan Bracken, who derided him as "Bollinger Bolshevik, Ritzy Robespierre and Lounge-lizard Lenin."[5] This stylish bohemian seemed far removed from the austerity of his native mining valleys. Very seldom did he have lunch with other South Wales Labour MPs, many of them elderly union officials.

Yet he always remained anchored within the Labour movement, never joining fringe bodies like the Socialist League. This was a source of passionate debate with his wife, Jennie Lee, a Marxist who kept to the ILP until 1944. Bevan affectionately chided her as "his Salvation Army lassie" who preferred cherishing the "virginity" of her pure little sect when it disaffiliated from the Labour Party in 1932 rather than joining the broad church of the British Labour movement. He told her: "Why don't you get into a nunnery and be done with it? . . . I tell you, it is the Labour Party or it is nothing."[6]

In South Wales, this was a bleak time of mass unemployment and the means test, of wage cuts and hunger marches. Bevan toyed with a variety of approaches, including a bizarre idea for setting up Workers Freedom Groups as a kind of local defense militia.[7] In 1937, he joined the Unity Campaign that was associated with Sir Stafford Cripps and condemned by the Labour Party hierarchy. But he was generally housed within the Social Democratic broad church. When the international crisis built up in the later 1930s, Bevan called for a united nationwide response. From the standpoint of the Popular Front, which indeed was to lead to his expulsion from the parliamentary party, along with Cripps and George Strauss in

1939, his fundamental cry was always for a broader unity. In the columns of the democratic-socialist newspaper *Tribune,* on whose editorial board he sat from 1937, his approach was patriotic as well as socialist. Earlier than many, he called for armed resistance to fascism. He condemned Munich, on the distinctive grounds that it represented a crisis for the ruling capitalist class. In *Tribune,* he became, remarkably, an advocate of the view that Winston Churchill should be brought into the government. In March 1938, he passionately backed up a speech by Churchill calling for resistance to the dictators.

During the war, he appeared most detached from mainstream Labour views. He rejoined the parliamentary party almost immediately, but then began a prolonged campaign of opposition to many of the policies of the Churchill coalition. In the wartime years, he moved from bit player to enjoying top billing as the "squalid nuisance" of Churchillian oratory. He was remarkably effective in challenging the coalition's strategic decisions, calling for a second front to assist Britain's Russian allies rather than to prop up the empire in North Africa, condemning carpet bombing by the RAF as ineffective as well as inhumane, and criticizing interference in the civil war in Greece. At home, he denounced the coalition for obstructing the advent of socialism. His anonymous tract *Why Not Trust the Tories?* (1944) laid waste the policies of a Tory-run government on social welfare, employment, and industrial planning. He refused to criticize strikes and stoppages by some miners and other trade unionists, and attacked Bevin and "jaded, irresponsible, cynical trade union leaders" for imposing penal restrictions on the right to strike.[8] These led to a great crisis in May 1944 when union leaders tried to throw him out of the party altogether. Bevan was certainly among those (like Orwell in "The Lion and the Unicorn") who saw the war as "a radical moment," a unique opportunity for social transformation.

But Bevan always sought revolution via the ballot box. He saw the war years as having made free institutions, especially the Commons, even more powerful as an instrument of the popular will. *Why Not Trust the Tories?* is a passionate affirmation of free assembly, ending with his evocation of Colonel Rainboro of the Levellers proclaiming his egalitarian message at the 1647 Putney debates. At the height of his alleged extremism as an enemy of the consensus, he always saw democracy as his essential strategy for change. It was never likely in 1944, with victory in Europe in sight, and Jennie Lee on the verge of rejoining the Labour Party, that Bevan would favor the impotence of exclusion. After penning an apology that kept him in the fold, he stood for the National Executive constituency section and was elected, coming fifth out of seven. From then on, he had a crucial power base within the party. In the 1945 election, he bent his oratory to striving for the triumph of democratic socialism. He caught the attention of Attlee as a dynamic force who ought to be accommodated somewhere in a Labour government. He was indeed one of the very few Labour leaders who foresaw the popular uprising that would sweep Churchill ignominiously out of office in July 1945. Bevan, unexpectedly sent to the Health Ministry, would carry that movement forward.

AS A MINISTER IN THE ATTLEE government, Bevan was a remarkable success. More than almost any other minister, he could point to a record of great legislative achievement. But he was effective in large measure because he went with the grain of political realities. He was a broadly centrist minister most of the time, causing no great trouble for his colleagues. His National Health Service, marked by years of deadlock with the British Medical Association, was a triumph of relativist philosophy. At times, Bevan lost his temper, as when he denounced the BMA representatives as "a small group of politically poisoned people."[9] They, and especially the serpentine Charles Hill, erstwhile "radio doctor," replied in kind. Later on there was "vermin." But he always left leads open. In the end, his ability to persuade and beguile his opponents, notably the Royal Colleges and Lord Moran of the Royal College of Physicians, "corkscrew Charlie" to his intimates, was decisive.

The National Health Service had been only roughly conceived when Bevan became a minister, and the early key decisions were all essentially his. His charm and commitment won the devotion of his civil service staff from Sir Wilson Jameson downwards. The broad concept of a service financed from general taxation and freely available at the point of delivery had been enshrined in the Beveridge Report during the war. Bevan's most radical innovation was to take the hospitals into national ownership and control. This led to fierce opposition from Herbert Morrison and Chuter Ede, backed by Arthur Greenwood, Tom Williams, and A. V. Alexander, who wanted control to remain with the local authorities. At the key Cabinet meeting on 20 December 1945, Bevan just managed to get his way with the support of the venerable Lord Addison, himself a former medical man of great authority as well as the first Minister of Health in 1919, and, most crucially of all, the personal backing of Attlee. Bevan argued that local authorities lacked the resources to take over the voluntary hospitals and that only central control could ensure a properly national service effective in all parts of Britain. He just carried the day.[10] Bevan's proposal reflected the most effectively argued solution among the technocrats, which was also open to the weakest political objection from the personnel within the health service. It was the least speculative approach available to him, though whether it was more appropriate than local control and accountability has been much contested from that day to this.

In other key respects, Bevan's health service contained many concessions. Of course, he made compromises galore with the doctors, later acknowledging that he "stuffed their mouths with gold." He retained private practice in full, and "pay beds" in the hospitals. He never tried to create a fully salaried medical profession. The final settlement, negotiated via Moran and Sir Alfred Webb-Johnson of the Royal College of Surgeons, made the state element only a small part (£4,300) of doctors' remuneration. The sale of practices was indeed ended, but £160 million was provided to compensate GPs for the change. A process of two-tier health provision, with the basic national system left underfunded and circumvented by privately funded medical schemes run by the British United Provident Association and others, was already underway.

The NHS was a skein of compromises that greatly disappointed some on the left. Radicals like Dr. Stark Murray of the Socialist Medical Association were left in dark disillusion. The SMA felt that the opportunity for creating a truly national service had been lost. In particular, its own cherished scheme for neighborhood health centers had been largely set aside. It ended up as a marginalized and largely ineffective pressure group. On the right, Bevan's creation was commonly attacked for its inadequate financial provision. This led to a succession of supplementary estimates from 1949 and to rows between Bevan and Cripps over the possibility of imposing charges for medical prescriptions. But it should be emphasized, too, how Bevan's achievement was equally attacked at the time as a sellout to private specialists and practitioners, almost a betrayal of the values of socialism.

In other aspects of his role as a minister, Bevan again found that his socialist aspirations were hemmed in. His policy on housing, successful in building one million new homes (far more than was often acknowledged), was relatively traditional. He left the initiative firmly in the hands of the local authorities and rejected proposals for more challenging policies such as a new Housing Corporation, put forward by Douglas Jay and others. While Bevan concentrated on the public provision of council housing for rent, and on severely restricting housing for sale, he was also compelled to mirror the pattern of the existing class system—for instance, in creating special categories of better housing stock to minister to the needs of middle-class managers. On the other hand, Bevan's insistence that local-authority housing should be marked by high standards of construction and levels of comfort for council-house tenants shows him at his most imaginative.

Elsewhere, Bevan was not a troublemaker. He liked neither Ernie Bevin nor a Cold War foreign policy. Bevan especially disliked what he saw as a violently anti-Jewish policy in Palestine. On the other hand, the realities of international tension between the West and Stalin's Russia stirred Bevan as powerfully as other ministers. He was not and never had been a fellow traveler. His anti-communism was beyond doubt. Stalin's attack on the socialist experiment in Tito's Yugoslavia helped shape his responses. He was a strong champion of NATO's coming into being, even while insisting that it was progressive ideas, not massive armaments, that would defeat communism in the end. On the Berlin blockade in 1948–9, Bevan was one of the hawks. He called for Allied tanks to drive a route through the Soviet zone to West Berlin in order to provide food and essential supplies for its citizens. Most striking of all, Bevan raised no protest when news came out almost accidentally that Britain was manufacturing nuclear weapons. Indeed, he would have favored this policy, if only to ensure that the Americans alone did not control a nuclear arsenal directed against the Kremlin. Not for Bevan the quasi-pacifist evasions of Labour foreign policy throughout the 1930s, even beyond Munich. He accepted Britain's atomic bomb, its worldwide defense network based on military conscription, and all the arms budgets until the fateful new policy of early 1951. Britain's socialist middle way needed to be defended against all corners. No mirage of a "socialist foreign policy" here.

At home, Bevan was well content with the main thrust of policy making under Attlee. He supported, of course, the policy of nationalization, and fought strongly alongside Hugh Dalton and (surprisingly perhaps) Bevin for iron and steel to be kept on the list in late 1947. But as an old syndicalist of the Plebs League days, he recognized that industrial democracy, let alone any form of workers' control, had become casualties of centralism, and that public ownership should be made to work better, including for consumers, before it was blithely extended. Bevan went along with the remainder of the welfare legislation, even if it reflected the centrist liberalism of Beveridge. For all his rhetoric, Bevan, like Herbert Morrison, was, from 1948, an advocate of consolidation, making the foundations more secure before pushing on to the next phase of the socialist advance. At the Dorking party colloquium in May 1950, Morrison and Bevan voiced virtually the same conclusions at that transitional moment.

Elsewhere, too, Bevan was markedly more circumspect than, say, Tony Benn in the 1970s. He did not lend support to backbench revolts against the government on domestic or external issues, even when they often included Jennie Lee and close friends like Michael Foot. For a time, *Tribune* came perilously close to being an organ of the party faithful. Nor did Bevan encourage dissent at party conferences. This later champion of the left-wing constituency rank and file slapped down critics at the 1947 party conference who wanted him to change policy over tied cottages.

Likewise, he condemned unofficial strikers on the docks and in the gas industry. Bevan had no difficulty, when he was on the Cabinet Emergencies Committee in 1948–9, in supporting the use of troops to break strikes. He gave his backing to the Attorney General, Hartley Shawcross, in exploring legal weapons to be used against stevedores encouraging disaffection on the London docks.[11] This was also Bevan's own approach during his ill-starred three months as Minister of Labour in January–April 1951. Never, down to Gaitskell's budget proposals at that time, did Bevan openly oppose his own government's domestic policies. Even the necessary retreats in the period 1948–50—rationing, a wage freeze, devaluation of the pound (which Bevan vigorously defended on socialist grounds in a memorable speech in the Commons)—were all defensible. In any event, they were the work of the new Chancellor, Sir Stafford Cripps, an old ally from Popular Front/*Tribune* days before the war.

It is not his record in the Attlee government but rather the way he left it that is largely responsible for Bevan's later reputation as an irreconcilable of the Far Left. In an historic episode, Bevan clashed furiously with the new Chancellor, Hugh Gaitskell, initially about the scale of his proposed £4,700 million rearmament program for 1951–4, and then fatally over the charges to be imposed on the health service to help pay for it. After announcing, almost casually, in a speech at Bermondsey on 3 April 1951 that he was resigning as a matter of principle, he left the Cabinet on 22 April, along with Harold Wilson (a critic of the arms program on economic grounds) and the lesser figure of John Freeman. Bevan's disastrous resignation speech included bitter criticism of Gaitskell (whom Michael Foot in *Tribune* compared to the traitor Philip Snowden in 1931, the ultimate comparison in terms of Labour mythology). A "party within a party" (so-called) came into being, with its own manifesto, *Keep Left,* in July 1951, and the Bevanites were born. Labour lost the 1951 general election, plunged into four years of civil war, and gained a reputation for being divided and unelectable that lingered into the 1990s.

CLEARLY, RESIGNATION IN SUCH circumstances indelibly stamps a politician as a divisive, perhaps destructive, force. Gaitskell and Dalton freely compared their former colleague to Mosley, even to Hitler. A series of ministers, Attlee, Gaitskell, Dalton, Gordon Walker, Shinwell, and others, spread the total untruth that Bevan had previously voiced no concern at the new rearmament program. Others claimed that Bevan was basically consumed by personal jealousy of Gaitskell, a public school upstart who had entered the Commons only in 1945. "He's nothing, nothing, nothing," Bevan exclaimed.[12] Clearly, he felt a real sense of grievance toward Attlee, never the best Premier in promoting or removing ministers. Gaitskell was pushed into the Treasury, and Morrison was promoted to the Foreign Office in place of Bevan. Bevan, denied promotion to these two key posts, was given little in return. He was not moved on to the Colonial Office, apparently because of his excessive sympathy for black Africans, while his move to the Ministry of Labour was at best a move sideways. After Bevan's achievements at Health, Attlee had given him a curmudgeonly reward.

But this is not why Bevan resigned, and it would be unfair toward both him and Gaitskell to lay the main emphasis on personal jealousies. Bevan resigned not because he suddenly cast considerations of loyalty to the winds, but because Gaitskell's budget raised grave issues that went beyond previous policies. On those issues, it was Bevan, not Gaitskell, who was proved demonstrably right. Contrary to statements in some later memoirs, Bevan twice declared at length in Cabinet meetings that Gaitskell's proposed rearmament program was impractical and unaffordable. On 1 August 1950, while supporting the Anglo-American position in resisting the North Korean invasion of the South, Bevan condemned the £3,600 million program.[13] On 25 January 1951, just after Attlee's talks in Washington had led to a massive increase in Britain's rearmament burden to £4,700 million, heavier per capita than in the United States itself, Bevan argued that it was quite impractical. He offered major economic objections—the effect on exports and inflation, the bottlenecks in supplies, the disruption of labor, the shortage of machine tools. Gaitskell responded, in effect, that Britain had no option but to back America to the hilt.[14] It was the supposed Celtic firebrand Bevan who offered reasoned economic arguments, and the rational economist Gaitskell who spoke as a politician, underpinned by emotion. Bevan steered clear of financial controversies in a fine Commons speech of 15 February defending British involvement in Korea. But it was well known that he opposed the arms program and that helping to finance it by imposing charges on the health service would be a resigning matter.

Other ministers did not help. Attlee was ill at a crucial moment, leaving the Cabinet in the hands of Morrison, Bevan's archenemy. Attlee's letter from his sickbed, unhelpfully and unhistorically comparing Bevan's actions with Lord Randolph Churchill's fatal resignation from the Salisbury government in December 1886, made matters worse. The crisis could have been avoided. The gap between ministers was the tiny sum of £13 million (£23 million in a full year). Many tried to bridge the narrow gulf—the aged Lord Addison, the dying Ernest Bevin, junior ministers like Alfred Robens, Michael Stewart, and James Callaghan. But almost fatalistically, the majority willed Bevan to leave them, and he did. His resignation did not show him up as a fellow-traveling extremist. Rather, it showed that the inexperienced and dogmatic Gaitskell, for all his statistical expertise, had got his sums fatally wrong. Indeed, his one and only budget, in 1951, was financially inadequate as well as politically disastrous. It discouraged investment and failed to address inflation. When Churchill returned to power in late October, he took Bevan's side. The arms program was proved by Ian Bancroft and other civil servants to be quite impractical; they were scornful of Gaitskell's calculations. Labour's original arms program was cut by Churchill by more than a third and phased over four years, not three. They were all Bevanites now, it seemed, but the outcome was disastrous for Bevan's career.

The years of internecine controversy while in opposition, 1951–5, were a painful period that did great harm to Labour's standing. But again, a careful assessment of Bevan's record may lead to a revision of the conventional wisdom. His dissent was fierce and consistent—but on foreign and defense policy only. On domestic matters, Bevan and Gaitskell, both of whom favored nationalization and greater equality, were never far apart. The great debate was fought out primarily within the parliamentary party. There were rhetorical broadsides from the Bevanites, who filled six out of seven places in the constituencies section of the National Executive. But they did not necessarily emanate from Bevan. Indeed, it was his followers like Foot and Castle who were the main protagonists. Bevan himself, however, seemed to keep his distance from his followers. He might have observed, echoing Marx, that, above all, he was no Bevanite.

The great debates were almost wholly about foreign affairs. These were years when, especially after the death of Stalin in 1953, coexistence and conciliation seemingly gripped the international mind. Bevan argued strongly that the United States was now turning NATO, a necessary military alliance, into an ideological anticommunist crusade, notably in relation to China. He warned in similar terms about the formation of the Southeast Asia Treaty Organization (SEATO) in early 1955. There were at least grounds for rational debate, but reason was set aside, not least by an impassioned and aging Bevan himself. For a third time, in 1955, he was almost expelled by the comrades, after attacking Attlee fiercely in the Commons over the formation of SEATO.

Yet Bevan in these years was still cleaving to the broad center ground. Nothing confirms this more strongly than his volume *In Place of Fear* (1952), taken to be a supreme testament to the Bevanite outlook at that time. It is certainly a fascinating book, even if disjointed, really a series of essays written over a period of many years. But it is also very far from being an extremist text. It is a civilized, qualified statement of the socialist case for parliamentary democracy. It expresses a view of socialism rooted in its time, with nationalization central to it, but that was standard before Crosland's *Future of Socialism* (1956). It is open to criticism on many fronts, not least for its unrealistic assumption that world trade patterns in no way "limit the application of socialist policies to the British economy."[15] Indeed, the economic argument of the book, neither Keynesian nor Marxist, is somewhat rudimentary.

But the main thrust of Bevan's argument concerns applications, and here it is immediately recognizable within the mainstream Labour tradition. Financially, there is a strong commitment to public expenditure, Labour's main mantra down to 1997 and far from lost thereafter. Public spending was the essential tool to remove the injustices of an unequal society; the NHS was financed from public taxation, not by a poll tax. Politically, the essential route to socialism was the parliamentary one, "government by discussion." As Jennie Lee later wrote, Bevan wrote as a "passionate parliamentarian" and a libertarian.[16] Parliamentary socialism was the path to power. Emotionally and morally, he saw democratic socialism as a vibrant creed with values of its own: libertarian, pluralist, an extension of the creed of the Levellers and Tom Paine and Bevan's favorite philosopher, the Uruguayan Jose Enrique Rodo. Socialism was precisely defined, it had its own lineage—and it was great fun. Not for Bevan the joyless desiccation of the Webb-Cole tradition. His own honeymoon was spent in sunny Torremolinos, very different from the

Webbs' working honeymoon to investigate trade societies in Dublin. *In Place of Fear* is the testament of a humane libertarian. It retains all the poignant magic of a socialist classic.

BEVAN'S LOCATION IN THE MAINSTREAM was finally confirmed in his last phase. After Gaitskell's election as party leader in 1955, there was a partial reconciliation. Bevan, with his record of disaffection, never had a chance of succeeding Attlee. But he was still inspirational in party and country, with an international reputation through his friendships with figures such as Jawaharlal Nehru, Pietro Nenni, Milovan Djilas, David Ben-Gurion, and Pierre Mendès-France. Gaitskell wisely brought him into the Shadow Cabinet as Colonial spokesman in February 1956. He had little time to make much of an impact there, though one revealing episode came that April when Bevan, along with George Brown, led the way in challenging Nikita Khrushchev over the treatment of Soviet dissidents. Khrushchev sneered that if these were the Labourites, he was for the Conservatives. At the time of Suez, while Bevan strafed Eden and Selwyn Lloyd with ridicule for their humiliating failure over the invasion—"using the bugle of advance to cover his retreat"—the old Zionist appeared more restrained than Gaitskell in condemning the government.

As shadow foreign secretary, he, along with Gaitskell, took up the cause of "disengagement" in Europe, notably the Polish Rapacki plan for a nuclear-free zone in central Europe, including in time, perhaps, a reunified, though disarmed, Germany and the return of the Oder-Neisse territories in the East. Bevan was broadly optimistic about East-West relations in the later 1950s. He was convinced that the Soviet Union was moving toward a firmer acceptance of détente and, less convincingly, that it was being transformed into a more open society. In general, Labour, with Bevan as its spokesman, maintained its traditional pro-NATO stance. In Bevan's report to Labour's Foreign Affairs Group in November 1957, he included one particularly Delphic phrase: "France is a verb without a noun; America is a noun without a verb."[17]

The most dramatic instance of Bevan's orthodoxy, the one that caused most pain to friends and disciples, came at the 1957 party conference. With opposition growing to British nuclear weapons, and the Campaign for Nuclear Disarmament set to be launched at Easter 1958, Bevan emotionally defended the possession of nuclear weapons. Britain should retain them as a bargaining counter. It should not send a Labour Foreign Secretary "naked into the conference chamber."[18] Other countries, including Russia, wanted Britain to retain nuclear weapons. A moralistic gesture by Britain to give up its own nuclear stockpile would be futile. It would have no effect on the thermonuclear weapons remaining in the hands of other countries, nor would it slow down the progress of a nuclear arsenal in coming states such as China. Unilateralism would be simply "an emotional spasm," the negation of political reality, about which he had lectured Jennie Lee in the past. Bevan became uneasy when pressed by Frank Cousins on whether Britain would engage in "first use" of the bomb, or whether having the bomb was compatible with nontesting. In the end, he and Gaitskell came up with the half-formed notion of the "non-nuclear club." But his rejection of unilateralism was highly symbolic. In a supreme crisis, he threw himself behind the leadership, behind a tradition of British participation in world collective security. His friends in the Campaign for Nuclear Disarmament could never move him from that.

Bevan's occupation of the center, even right-wing, ground in defense policy made him, more than most, a force for unity. In 1959, he became deputy party leader. His status was confirmed dramatically in the party conference of October 1959, just after a humbling electoral defeat at the hands of Macmillan's Tories. The conference was preceded by Gaitskell announcing, on no clear evidence, that Labour's defeat was due in part to Clause Four in the party constitution, which committed the party to unending nationalization. This produced uproar in the ranks. Bevan strode gallantly to the rescue. Like others on the left, he recognized the need for an updated socialism, attuned to modern circumstances, with an emphasis on social equality and strategies for economic growth. At the 1959 party conference, he saved his leader's bacon with a brilliantly evasive speech that aimed to reconcile the views of Gaitskell and Barbara Castle over public ownership. He quoted Lenin on capturing "the commanding heights of the economy." He cited Euclid as evidence that two things equal to a third thing were equal to each other.[19] Unity was preserved; the Clause Four issue disappeared for another thirty-five years. It was all due to Nye, the great compromiser. A few months later cancer killed him.

Just before his election as leader in February 1963, Harold Wilson took his ex-Bevanite colleagues over to the wall to toast the portrait of Nye, the man who ought to have led the party instead. Nye Bevan was not really Labour's lost leader, and his mantle was an elusive, ambiguous garment. Yet he still remains a giant in Labour's Valhalla—but a giant as much of the center ground as of the left. Throughout his career, he cleaved to the majority view on domestic politics, foreign policy, and the imperatives of democracy.

Does he then deserve his emerging role as an icon for New Labour? His socialism was of his time, conceived within a very different global economy and a polarized class structure. But New Labour still retained its socialist ingredient in the 1990s, however well disguised. Within it, Bevan and his Health Service convey the essence of the idea of community, of a commitment to public service, of a measured incremental socialism that "made one freedom safe by adding another to it."[20] So Tony Blair's enthusiasm for the "solidarity, social justice and co-operation" embodied in Nye's philosophy is not so bizarre.[21] Aneurin Bevan was a socialist for all seasons. A latimer for the oldest, finest values, he may take his appointed place in the world of the new.

Fall Semester 2010

1. Tony Blair, foreword to Geoffrey Goodman, *The State of the Nation: The Political Legacy of Aneurin Bevan* (London, 1997), pp. 4–6.

2. *Manchester Guardian*, 6 July 1948.

3. Aneurin Bevan, speech in the House of Commons, 15 Dec. 1943.

4. *Parliamentary Debates*, 3rd ser., Vol. 235, 2462–8 (27 Feb. 1930).

5. Quoted in Charles Edward Lysaght, *Brendan Bracken* (London, 1979), p. 150.

6. Patricia Hollis, *Jennie Lee* (Oxford, 1997), p. 64, citing a letter from Bevan to Jennie Lee.

7. Hywel Francis and Dai Smith, *The Fed* (London, 1981), pp. 192ff.

8. Michael Foot, *Aneurin Bevan*, 2 vols. (London, 1962), Vol. I, pp. 412–15.

9. Peter Jenkins, "Bevan's Fight with the BMA," in Michael Sissons and Philip French, eds., *Age of Austerity* (London, 1963), p. 230.

10. Cabinet Minutes, 18 Oct., 20 Dec. 1945 (National Archives, Cabinet Minutes, CAB 128/1).

11. Cabinet Emergency Committee, Minutes, 28 June 1948 (CAB 134/175); also see minutes of the Committee for 21 June, and 4, 6, 7, 20, and 22 July 1949 (CAB 134/176).

12. Brian Brivati, *Hugh Gaitskell* (London, 1996), p. 116, citing the recollections of John Strachey in his obituary of Gaitskell in 1963.

13. Cabinet Minutes, 1 Aug. 1950 (CAB 128/18).

14. Cabinet Minutes, 25 Jan. 1951 (CAB 128/19).

15. Aneurin Bevan, *In Place of Fear* (London, 1952), p. 51.

16. Jennie Lee, foreword to Bevan, *In Place of Fear,* p. 13.

17. Richard Crossman, *The Backbench Diaries of Richard Crossman,* ed. Janet Morgan (London, 1981), p. 633 (entry of 26 Nov. 1957).

18. *The Times,* 4 Oct. 1957.

19. Annual Conference Report of the Labour Party, 1959, pp. 151–5.

20. Bevan, *In Place of Fear,* p. 130.

21. Tony Blair, foreword to Goodman, *State of the Nation.*

14

The Third Man

DONNA KORNHABER

I first saw Sir Carol Reed's 1949 tour de force, *The Third Man*, as a student in film school at New York University almost fifteen years ago, and I remember quite clearly it being categorized by my teachers as something between a Hitchcock film and a film noir—a rather fuzzy definition. *The Third Man* has been a notoriously difficult film to assign to a genre, though generations of film scholars have tried, and it has been even more difficult to account for its lasting success. But lasting success it has had. In fact, according to the British Film Institute, it is the greatest British film ever made. (According to the American Film Institute, it is the fifty-seventh greatest *American* film ever made. The fact that neither of these two august bodies can agree on whether the film is in fact British or American is only part of the problem.)

Why does this film work, and how does it manage to sustain dramatic tension to the end? These questions have been asked before. Indeed, much of the critical and scholarly literature on *The Third Man* seems to question whether it is even possible to understand what makes the film so great and so endlessly watchable. In his excellent introduction to the Criterion edition of the film, the director and film historian Peter Bogdanovich wonders whether *The Third Man* isn't just a "happy accident," much like *Casablanca*—the improbable result of fortuitous circumstance.[1] Throw together some great performances by great actors in their prime, many of whom couldn't stand one another and at least one of whom tried to sabotage the film; a couple of behind-the-scenes blow-ups between hot-headed collaborators and several logistical considerations that just happened to result in genius artistic decisions; and a gorgeous city gorgeously photographed by three different lead cinematographers with very different visual styles—somehow you end up with a great work of art, equal parts unmatchable and inexplicable.

This is all true. But unlike *Casablanca,* a bona fide romantic drama by every measure, *The Third Man* does not neatly fit into any one generic box. Does it have Hitchcockian elements? Yes. Is it, in its own way, a revision of the noir ideal? Yes. Does it have something else, something special going for it, alongside these correspondences, that makes it work? Yes. From the start, *The Third Man* simply had too many cooks in the kitchen to be Carol Reed's film alone. In the words of Bogdanovich, "*The Third Man* is one of the best, if not the greatest, non-auteur film ever made."[2] Like the occupied city that it depicts, this is a film controlled by four distinct powers: the British impresario film producer Alexander Korda (the founder of London Films and owner of British Lion Films), the American powerhouse producer David O. Selznick (forever emboldened by back-to-back Academy Award wins for *Gone With the Wind* and *Rebecca*), the British director Carol Reed (regarded as one of the best filmmakers working during his lifetime, though not much talked about today), and the novelist Graham Greene (screenwriter for *The Third Man,* which he penned between *The Heart of the Matter* and *The End of the Affair*). And then there is Orson Welles (or as I like to think of him in the context of this list, the Fifth Man), whose role in the film as an actor may be small, but whose directorial influence and legacy looms large over the visual style of the film, much like his shadow on a Viennese cobblestone street. *The Third Man* is the story of a post-war city subject to competing powers, and it was a film that was likewise subject to competing powers. Nonetheless, it is an astonishing confluence of substance and style, content and circumstance, which can be felt and seen in almost every shot and situation of the film.

Reed opens the picture with a wide establishing shot of the skyline, the word "Vienna" spelled out in large block letters as a caption. We see the points and domes of various landmarks, and although we can see some damage to the rooftops, for the most part it seems as though at least the formidable outline, and perhaps even the formidable idea, of Vienna has survived the war. And then the narration begins, undercutting the hope proffered by the still-lovely profile of the skyline: the speaker is a fast talker with a British accent, sardonic, and with no clear moral orientation. The editing continues at a fast clip, beginning with an image of the famous Strauss statue and culminating in a gentle low-angle shot of a snow-capped Mozart glaring down at us from his perch. Or is he glaring down at something else—perhaps at the very next image we see, the weathered faces of local racketeers (in neorealist style, these were local Viennese plucked off the street and dropped into the film for their "worn" look). These faces are followed by a series of headless medium shots—arms and hands busy trading in illegalities. We move then to a series of separate shots of each of the four occupied zones of Vienna—American, British, Soviet, and French—the graphics of their identifying signs woefully outclassed by the backdrop of Vienna's ornate architecture, and here we see that the city itself has been dismembered, much like its headless racketeers. The footage next transitions into something different—handheld, seemingly less constructed and more documentarian. A series of long shots shows us the rubbled results of the city being, as the narrator says, "bombed about a bit." As the narrator mentions Holly Martins and "Lime, Harry Lime," we see the train that our protagonist, Holly Martins, is arriving on, the shot positioned as just another image cut in quickly among the documentary footage.

It is an opening sequence that hits like a burst of cold air. And it is also a complete lie. The opening is strangely, even gloriously, unattached to what happens in the rest of the film. It is not just that the roughish speaker (voiced by the director, Carol Reed, himself) never appears and that we never learn who is telling us this story or why. It is that in many ways, Vienna itself never directly arrives, at least not as promised here. Those brief visions of four-nation control are just about the only images of Vienna's political and military situation that appear in the film. The British officials investigating Lime play a major role, of course; and their Russian counterparts play a minor one. The Americans and the French, on the other hand, never appear again and are almost never mentioned. Even the iconic locales implied by the opening caption "Vienna" never appear. And the visual style of the opening—the quick cuts matched with formal symmetry, and then the handheld, almost neorealistic shots of the soldiers and rubble that mimic newsreel footage? Neither of them becomes a defining visual motif of the film. It is as if they are from another movie entirely, perhaps one by Roberto Rossellini.

The opening, in other words, seems like a brilliant patch job. And in point of fact, that is what it is. While *The Third Man* in its finished form has become inseparable from its Viennese setting, originally the film was supposed to take place in London. In 1947, Greene, Reed, and Korda had just finished collaborating on *The Fallen Idol* when they agreed to work together on another picture.

Greene suggested the germ of an idea he had been toying with for a while about a man who accidentally discovers that his supposedly deceased friend isn't actually dead. After the basic story had been developed, Korda insisted it be relocated to Continental Europe. There was a substantial untapped film market in post-war Europe, but currency regulations demanded that a film be at least partially made on the Continent in order to be distributed there. Korda had had a string of offices across Europe before the war; only the ones in Vienna and Rome were still functional. Thus, he demanded that Reed and Greene reset their story in one of those two cities so that the film could be distributed in Europe; they could choose which one. It was Greene who decided that *The Third Man* would take place in Vienna, but not because of the city itself. While visiting the city on a joint research trip to Austria and Italy sponsored by Korda, Greene was introduced to a young Viennese writer and journalist named Peter Smollett. Smollett had a series of unpublished short stories, which he showed to Greene in hopes of getting help finding a publisher. Among them was a story about the underground trade in penicillin. In Smollett's story, Greene saw a means of linking his already developed outline with a topic specific to Vienna. After the initial script was completed, Greene had Korda hire Smollett (for a pittance) to add local color and detail—effectively outsourcing the better part of his screenwriting duties.

And yet, how different *The Third Man* would be if it were not set in Vienna, how almost unimaginable that would be. Without Vienna, gone is the juxtaposition of a stately imperial past with a bombed-out, criminal present. Perhaps more importantly, Vienna brings a prevalent, almost overwhelming sense of ambiguity to the film. For while Austria was classified by the Allies as a victim of Nazi aggression despite its alliance with Germany, the country and its citizens were inevitably viewed with some suspicion after the war: Vienna in the post-war occupation walked a thin line. Add to that the tension of four-nation control and the result was a city whose social and political life was as layered and intricate as its underworld. Yet to self-consciously try to capture the essence of such a place would have been a fool's project, bound to the kind overstatement and solemnity that could kill a picture. There was perhaps no better means of capturing Vienna at the time than to do so offhandedly: to tell the story off-the-cuff, like the narrator in the opening, or just because it happened to fit—as it did for Graham Greene. *The Third Man* is a story that was squeezed into Vienna because of an agenda that had nothing to do with it. And it is, paradoxically, an essential part of what helps the film capture the essence of the place: the story has its own independent aims and agenda to pursue, like the narrator of the opening and like everyone else in Vienna at the time.

AT LEAST, THAT IS THE IMPRESSION you would have gotten if you had seen the film when it premiered in the UK and in Europe. In the United States, you might have gotten an altogether different impression. In the American opening of the film, recut by Selznick, the imagery is exactly the same. But gone is the mysterious voice of indeterminate origin and unknown agenda. And gone is its narrative ambiguity. And in its place: narrative certainty—and perhaps moral certainty as well. The interlocutor is Holly Martins himself, telling us how his tale begins. We are meant to think that he is a good guy—interested, sympathetic—and harboring none of the playful condescension detectable when the same lines are spoken by the unidentified and probably criminal narrator of the UK opening. But before condemning Selznick too quickly for tinkering with Reed's art, we must give him some credit. The idea for that gripping, documentary-style opening—however wonderfully executed by Reed—belonged to a Benzedrine-crunching Selznick during one of many all-night script conferences held in Los Angeles. And it was Selznick who made Holly Martins an American. (A few of his other, less-useful notes on the script, which Reed and Graham dutifully disregarded, indicate that Harry Lime should wear green socks and that the title should be changed to *Night in Vienna*.)

To imagine a version of *The Third Man* without any American characters—that is, without Selznick—is to imagine a very different film. For many, the essence of *The Third Man* lies in its boiled-down tale of misguided American adventurism: Holly Martins, a writer of "cheap novelette" westerns, as they're called by Major Calloway, is emblematic of American overconfidence, simplicity, and moral certainty. Yet that there are any Americans in the film at all is another by-product of box-office concerns, again related to international distribution. Just as he wanted access to the untapped European film market, Korda also wanted access to the lucrative American film market, and to gain American distribution rights, he brought on Selznick as a co-producer. Selznick, in turn, demanded script approval in order to make sure that the film he was backing could make money in America. And the first draft of *The Third Man* was a no-go for him. Rightly or wrongly, Selznick believed that American audiences would have no interest in a film without Americans: at a minimum, they would want the hero to be American. And if Holly had to be American, so did Harry, or else their school-days friendship made no sense.

It is hard to overstate the importance of this change. What Reed and Greene did with their newfound American characters is certainly nothing Selznick had anticipated. The film became, at least in part, a parody of American attitudes, its only American characters being, in the words of the film historian Charles Drazin, "a villain and a fool."[3] And the fact that these Americans were imposed on the story from without makes them, in a way, all the more apropos. The contempt that the British authorities show for Holly and his bungling insistence on clearing his friend's name takes on a delightfully political edge because of the difference in nationalities. Yet it is not in the least didactic: these political animosities are embedded entirely inside personal disputes, since, in the original version of the script, there was only the personal—originally, all the characters were British. A mere shift in nationality gave *The Third Man* a political dimension where none had been present before, one automatically contained within the interpersonal dynamics of the story.

Selznick's impact on the characters in *The Third Man* was not simply a matter of making them American—it was also a matter of deciding which American actors would play them. In the all-important role of Holly, Selznick insisted on Joseph Cotten. Carol Reed was holding out for Jimmy Stewart, but the timing didn't work out. For Selznick, pushing Cotten was in part an artistic choice, since he had worked with him before and was fond of him as an actor. But it was also a shrewd financial move: Selznick had Cotten under contract already, and so it wouldn't cost him a thing to use him in the picture. Jimmy Stewart's being busy was just luck, since casting him would have changed the tenor of the film immensely. By 1948, Stewart's film persona, carefully cultivated in pictures like *Mr. Smith Goes to Washington, The Shop around the Corner,* and *It's a Wonderful Life,* was one of virtue, folksy charm, and pluck—among the qualities American audiences most liked to see in themselves. It would have been difficult, even impossible, for Reed to paint Stewart as a dangerously out-of-touch interloper, and surely impossible for audiences to accept that the female lead would so momentously turn down his advances, as Holly's love interest, Anna, does in the film's tremendous closing scene. Cotten was another matter entirely. He was well known enough, but primarily for playing characters who were both charming and somewhat shady. For filmgoers at the time, there was something potentially dangerous beneath Cotten's innocence—and *The Third Man* does a masterly job of exploiting this.

Selznick also showed either great judgment or great luck in pushing Alida Valli for the role of Anna, Harry's abandoned lover and Holly's ill-considered new love interest. For Reed and Korda, the role called for something more like the typical heroine of a film noir, someone brash and potentially dangerous. But Selznick saw something different in the role, this time for reasons more artistic than financial. As with Cotten, he had the young Italian actress under contract and could loan her to the picture at no cost. But Selznick also saw a way to make the film better suit the new star he was trying to promote. Because of the overwhelming success of *Gone with the Wind* and the strong figure of Scarlett O'Hara at its center, one of Selznick's first instincts when he saw the script for *The Third Man* was to build up the female part to make her more independent, strong-willed, self-reliant, and morally certain—that is, more like Scarlett O'Hara. In the final version of the film, Anna has a notably willful quality that isn't in the earlier drafts: she is a woman of conviction who will not be swayed in her belief in Harry, by persuasion or by force, no matter what the evidence. This was Selznick's doing. Early in the process, Selznick demanded that the production team have a woman involved in refashioning the part of Anna, and he brought in his trusted story editor Barbara Keon to make detailed suggestions. The result is a character who seems utterly, wonderfully at odds with the film around her, putting the breaks on the male characters' intentions at every turn, as though she had been thrown against her will into their narrative—which, in a sense, she was. But changing her part also inflected the character of the picture. The film critic Roger Ebert puts it this way:

> *The Third Man* is like the exhausted aftermath of *Casablanca* . . . The hero doesn't get the girl in either movie—but in *Casablanca,* Ilsa stays with the resistance leader to help in his fight, while in *The Third Man,* Anna remains loyal to a rat. Yet Harry Lime saved Anna, a displaced person who faced certain death. Holly will never understand what Anna did to survive the war, and Anna has absolutely no desire to tell him.[4]

The one area of casting where Selznick seems to have miscalculated lay in the part of Harry Lime. It was Reed who insisted that the role be played by Orson Welles. Selznick resisted—after the box-office failure of *Citizen Kane* (1941), he regarded Welles as box-office "poison"—but since he wouldn't have to pay Welles's salary, which Korda offered to cover, he eventually relented, acknowledging that Welles would at least add some "prestige value" to the picture. Welles's casting wasn't an accident; as soon as Lime was turned into an American, Reed knew he wanted Welles. But the depths of Welles's performance and the way in which it dominates the film were the result of a lucky coincidence. For Reed hadn't at all anticipated the pairing of Welles and Cotten, but it turned out to be one of the most thematically resonant reunions in film. Welles and Cotten were in fact old associates—Cotten was originally a member of Welles's Mercury Theatre Company—and they had made cinematic history together in *Citizen Kane.* There, Cotten played opposite Welles as Jedediah Leland, Kane's longtime friend and business associate who grows disillusioned with Kane's utter lack of morals. When we last see Leland on screen in *Kane,* he is an elderly man painfully remembering a hard friendship. For audiences at the time and for film buffs today, the reunion of Welles and Cotten onscreen in *The Third Man* was a kind of fascinating refraction of their earlier relationship in *Kane.* As Drazin puts it, "Somewhere in our cinematic unconscious there's Jed Leland . . . coming to terms with the bitter realization that his friend Charles Foster Kane has betrayed his youthful principles."[5]

Although his performance is one of the most remembered aspects of the picture, Welles has only a few minutes of screen time in *The Third Man.* But what time he does have he fills with an absolutely beguiling frenetic energy. In Cotten and Welles's famous exchange at the fairground—Welles's first true scene in the film, where Harry is confronted by his old friend Holly on his turning to a life of crime—one quickly notices all the "business" that Welles invents for himself: the constant return to indigestion pills (which was his addition to the script) and the distracted drawing of Anna's name on the window of the Ferris wheel car in which they are riding. Welles's Lime has to constantly be in motion, and yet that motion seems to add up to nothing at all: it is an externalization of the paradox of Lime, the man who is everywhere and nowhere, a merciless charmer and a merciless killer. Welles is smiling throughout the scene, but his smile tells you no more than the Mona Lisa's—we don't know whether he is happy to see Holly or about to kill him.

It is a nervous, energetic, and brilliantly uncomfortable performance—and in many ways, it is utterly a product of the circumstances of the film. Welles was supremely uncomfortable throughout the filming of *The Third Man.* For one thing, he was the bane of the cast and crew when he finally arrived in Vienna for his scenes. Welles had had financial disagreements with Korda in the past— Korda had promised to produce several Welles films, but none had ever come to fruition—and so he made it a point to make his work on *The Third Man* as difficult as possible. (He had agreed to take part in the film only in order to earn enough money to finance his film version of *Othello,* for which, characteristically, he was having trouble raising money.) Welles refused to arrive to Vienna on time, so Reed had to send a production assistant to Italy to track him down and deliver him in person. As a result, nearly every shot of Harry Lime that does not show his face was done with a stand-in for Welles before he showed up on location. To make matters worse, Welles almost shut down filming by refusing to perform in the Vienna sewers, as had been planned; he insisted instead that a re-creation of the sewers be built for him in London, even though the cast and crew had been filming in the dank underground for weeks. Welles the actor was as anticipated on set as Lime the character is in the film itself. But unlike Lime, when Welles did finally arrive, the irritation was palpable.

And so was Welles's discomfort. For Welles also felt that he had something to prove, in particular in acting opposite Cotten. Though they were longtime friends and collaborators, Cotten had made it known publicly after *Kane* that while he thought Welles was a brilliant director, he was not convinced he was a great actor. Welles, who was fast becoming more comfortable behind the camera than in front of it, did not entirely disagree. Paired again with Cotten now, and with the whole production stalled on his behalf, he felt tremendous pressure to perform. The result was an explosion of energy channeled into the figure of Harry Lime and a delicious embodiment of the rakish magnetism that everyone ascribes to the character.

BUT WELLES ALSO MARKED *THE THIRD MAN* in another way: the cinematography—the lighting and camera choices used throughout the film. In fact, *The Third Man* might be regarded as the greatest film such as Orson Welles never directed, so influenced was it by his earlier work, in particular *Citizen Kane,* but also by later films such as *The Stranger* (1946) and *The Lady from Shanghai* (1947). There are many ways in which this is true, but there are perhaps two main lines of influence between Welles and Reed: the dutch, or tilted, camera angle, and the mobile frame. Reed was a master craftsman himself, and without detracting from his powers, it is reasonable to say that *The Third Man,* a film in which the tilted camera dominates, is more than literate in Welles's earlier experiments. Welles began his career as a virtuosic theatre actor and director, so for him, the camera was far more than a framing and recording device: it was an artistic tool unavailable in the theatre, one that could be used to shock the viewer into awareness or to distort or upend expectations. Tilting the camera, also known as "canting" or "dutching" the frame, was a proven method of doing this, as was using a moving camera or a mobile frame—the former technique originating for the most part in German expressionism, the latter with the film pioneer D. W. Griffith. Used occasionally and strategically in *Citizen Kane,* and most often in conjunction with high-contrast, low-key lighting that enabled deep focus, a disorienting technique in which multiple planes are in focus simultaneously, the dutch angle and the mobile frame worked to create unprecedented narrative and thematic flourishes. In *The Third Man,* however, these flourishes became de rigueur. Techniques that Welles used only at key moments serve in *The Third Man* as a kind of visual ideology. This is less true in the case of the mobile frame, which is employed more sparingly, along Welles's model. But whereas Reed and company sought to follow Welles's example in the occasional use of the moving camera, they certainly managed to outdo him in the use of canted angles.

The canted, or dutch, angles begin innocuously enough in *The Third Man:* the first view of the porter on the staircase, and then a scene in which Holly gets drunk in a bar after attending what he believes is Harry's funeral. In the bar scene, the distortion of the frame mirrors Holly's intoxication and seems a visual echo of the scene's content. But what about when we meet the porter? Reed once commented that in his use of dutch angles, he "wanted to convey the impression that crooked things were happening."[6] But what of the overuse? Once the canting begins in the film, it doesn't stop. Much as in *Kane,* these shots are skillfully used to communicate unease and disorientation; but they are also used to underscore dramatic tension, to underscore the romantic subplot, to underscore the introduction of new information, and sometimes to underscore nothing discernible at all (figure 14.1). Canted angles are so pervasive in *The Third Man* that the film has become almost definitional for the technique. The dutched angles of *The Third Man*—used at all times, in all places, for all reasons—provide a continual visual reminder of the fraught tension permeating post-war Vienna. And they are conspiratorial: they demand that we, the viewers, hold in question everything shown us, and they refuse to allow us to normalize what we see. But like any good conspiratorial view, they also provide a sense of consistency and structure, ominous though it may be, even as they try to destabilize. What Welles started as a flourish, Reed turned into a language.

But like so many other aspects of *The Third Man,* this language was achieved largely through circumstance. In this case, the circumstance was snow. Because so much of the film takes place at night, Reed and Korda decided to shoot in Vienna in the late fall, when the nights would be longest without the logistical problems of snowfall. It was a dangerous proposition, though, for if the first snow came early, it would wreak havoc on the continuity of scenes that were not shot in order. Thus, in an effort to try to beat the impending Viennese winter, Reed directed three different film crews on an eighteen-hour daily cycle (he slept for three hours, twice a day): one shot at night, one shot during the day, and one shot in the sewers. Whereas a typical film crew team will have a lead cinematographer and a supplementary B-unit to shoot nonessential footage, Reed's filming schedule meant that *The Third Man* had three lead cinematographers, all shooting essential footage. So although the unmistakable visual style of *The Third Man* was an artistic choice, it seems that it was also a practical cover-up: having everyone shoot dutch angles almost all the time—forcing them all to conform to an overriding visual motif—was a way to minimize and eclipse subtle differences between the techniques of the three cinematographers.

This is not to say there was not artistry behind the film's visual decisions. In fact, credit for the motif usually goes to Reed's night-unit cinematographer, Robert Krasker, who was a great admirer of Gregg Tolland, Welles's groundbreaking cinematographer on *Kane,* and a passionate advocate of his inventions and techniques. (In contrast, Reed's day-unit cinematographer, Hans Schneeberger, was a practiced traditionalist and was decidedly unenthusiastic about the new techniques. His shots are among some of the most visually subversive—that is, subversively level—in the film.) Regardless of individual perspectives, however, the execution of this tilted vision was a joint affair. Though it was Krasker who won the Academy Award for Best Black and White Cinematography in 1950, the film's most famous canted angles—showing Harry Lime in a darkened doorway—were in fact shot by John Wilcox, a fourth cinematographer on the film, who was the head of nonessential photography for the sewer unit.

The insistence on canted angles in *The Third Man* turns Vienna into an expressionist nightmare, one that the film and the characters must try to contain and control. But it bears pointing out that this is a nightmare that was largely of Reed's creation: it is an impossible Vienna that Reed committed to film, one that he envisioned but that never truly existed. This is not a metaphor, but a literal description of how Reed put together a city to suit his artistic vision for the film. Consider the pivotal moment when Holly first realizes that Harry is still alive and then chases him down a darkened Viennese street (figure 14.2). How perfectly Vienna conforms to the needs of the film in this famous sequence, offering layered cityscapes and atmospheric streets and ominous plazas. Except, of course, no city is perfect—not even Vienna. What Reed created for this sequence is a composite of how Vienna should be for the purposes of his film. The chase takes place, in the film, over the course of about three blocks. In reality, the three streets that Holly and Harry pass through are located miles apart in the city, each one selected and cut together for a particular visual element that Reed was seeking: an atmospheric doorway, a sharp corner, an appropriate canvas of buildings for Harry's exaggerated shadows. The final plaza, where Harry disappears, is Am Hof, the largest square in Vienna, located almost half a mile away from where he starts. In fact, even the components of the real Vienna weren't quite right for Reed and his crew. In an unusual move for a location shoot, Reed had his crew fill a truck with baroque-style accoutrements to be inserted into scenes that needed touching up. The fountain in the middle of the plaza where Holly splashes water in frustration after losing Harry's trail, for instance, is a Reed addition (figure 14.3). To anyone who knows the city, such juxtapositions might give the impression of a place not in control of its own identity, and this would be correct; in *The Third Man,* Vienna is a city under artistic as well as political occupation.

Part of the genius of Reed's direction, though, is that he was shrewd enough to allow moments of resistance to this occupation, building in destabilizing elements that point to the unstable circumstance of Vienna itself. Perhaps the most famous of these moments is the final shot of the film: a prolonged long shot in which Holly patiently waits for Anna after Harry's funeral, only to see her walk right by him without so much as an acknowledgment (figure 14.4). It is a brilliant moment, and a brilliant acceptance of ideas that were not Reed's own. The substance of the shot belongs to Selznick, who insisted that so grand a heroine as the Anna he created would never debase herself to pursue a relationship with her dead lover's traitorous friend. The reality of the shot belongs to Cotten, who created a character that might plausibly think that waiting for Anna was a good idea and that Anna might plausibly walk right by. The framing of the shot belongs to Hans Schneeberger, Reed's day-unit cinematographer, who believed in classical framing and shot composition, in stark contrast to Robert Krasker's canted angles. And the location of the shot belongs to Vienna: it is the main entrance to the Central Cemetery, with no Reed-imposed additions or alterations. The shot, brilliantly, is a contradiction: of the story Reed meant to tell, of the actor he meant to hire, of the visual style that he demanded, and of the cityscape he tried to reconstruct. And it is practically eternal: a long, staid meditation to end a film composed of short, off-kilter shots. It is a bold decision: a wink to the audience and a visual acknowledgment of the different ways the film might have gone if circumstances had been different.

In a sense, then, we might take Orson Welles's most famous lines in the film (another of his own interpolations) as a kind of epigram for all of *The Third Man:*

> In Italy for 30 years under the Borgias they had warfare, terror, murder, and bloodshed, but they produced Michelangelo, Leonardo da Vinci, and the Renaissance. In Switzerland they had brotherly love—they had 500 years of democracy and peace, and what did that produce? The cuckoo clock.

Peace and good planning might lead to perfect construction, yes. But that is something different from success. There are any number of films noir that function as perfectly as cuckoo clocks, well-oiled machines in every respect. But it takes strife and struggle to produce great art: it must be an attempt to build order and meaning out of chaos. The creation of *The Third Man* was not so violent as all that, but it was no easy or straightforward affair. Its genius is not so much the genius of perfect construction as the genius of matching circumstance to substance, and accident to artistry. Its genius is the genius of using the moment it was given.

Fall Semester 2010

1.   *The Third Man,* DVD, dir. Carol Reed (1949; New York: Criterion Collection, 2002).

2.   Ibid.

3.   Charles Drazin, *In Search of The Third Man* (London, 1999), p. 34.

4.   Roger Ebert, "The Third Man," *Chicago Sun Times,* http://rogerebert.sun times.com.

5.   Drazin, *In Search of The Third Man,* p. 34.

6.   Quoted in Bill Hare, "The Third Man: Classic for the Ages," Film Noir Foundation, http://noiroftheweek.com.

Figure 14.1
Harry Lime (Orson Welles) framed by a canted angle in The Third
Man, directed by Carol Reed (1949). Photo courtesy of Canal + Im-
age UK Ltd.

Figure 14.2
Holly Martins (Joseph Cotten) chasing Harry Lime through the too-perfectly atmospheric streets of Vienna. Photo courtesy of Canal + Image UK Ltd.

Figure 14.3
Holly Martins in Am Hof Square, resting on fountain supplied by
the film production. Photo courtesy of Canal + Image UK Ltd.

Figure 14.4
Holly Martins waiting hopefully but in vain for Anna Schmidt
(Alida Valli) in the final scene of The Third Man. Photo courtesy of
Canal + Image UK Ltd.

15

Harold Macmillan and the Wind of Change

JOANNA LEWIS

These are my principles and if you don't like them, here are some others.
Groucho Marx

If I stay, there will be trouble / If I go, it could be double
The Clash, "Should I Stay or Should I Go Now?"

When Prime Minister Harold Macmillan stepped off his plane at Lusaka Airport on 21 January 1960 to begin a four-day tour of Northern Rhodesia, he was met by a persistent drizzle. The rain was a sign of what was to come. Once inside the terminal, women protestors from the African National Congress (ANC), led by the Tonga firebrand Harry Nkumbula, forced officials and police to usher him into his car through a side exit. He never did quite escape Harry's "babes." They stood in pairs along the official route of the cavalcade, along with other nationalist protestors, dancing and singing, "whooping and waving." Placards read "No difference South Africa and Federation" and "Give us 1 man 1 vote."[1] Standing among the throng at the airport was Peregrine Worsthorne, special correspondent for the *Daily Telegraph*. When the brass band struck up "God Save the Queen," few Africans stood to attention or took their hands out of their pockets, he noted.[2] From here on, Macmillan endured a mixture of black protest and white indifference. On his way to the Copperbelt region the next day, one local newspaper, the *Northern News*, reported that he was met by "soggy banners" and a "half-hearted welcome." Six Africans had lined his route from the airport, and it was left to a puny, fifteen-person local choir to fill the football stadium with joyful song. One mining town could not even muster any flag-waving white school-children; only two shops in Kitwe had any bunting. At Ndola, a man lunged menacingly toward him. During a tour of a mine, Macmillan mysteriously lost his wallet. It was never found.

Meanwhile, aboveground, Lady Dorothy slipped and fell, requiring five stitches to her lower leg. At the Savoy Hotel, where the official party was given a luncheon, four sticks of gelignite wired together with detonators attached to two three-foot fuses were found hidden among a pile of coal next to the boiler. Among the forty members of the British press corps on the trip, the incident was dismissed as not representing any real threat to Macmillan's life, the *Daily Mail* and the *Daily Mirror* being exceptions. Macmillan joked about it afterward as the work of "a crank," though a police commissioner conceded that a political motive could not be ruled out. Outside the hotel, a thousand protestors organized by Kenneth Kaunda's United National Independence Party (UNIP) waved banners and shouted "freedom" in an attempt to stop the Prime Minister from exiting. One poster threatened violence: "Your friends are shooting us in cold blood—for the sake of freedom we shall give them more."[3] In vain, settlers tried to drown out cries of "Release Banda" and "To hell with Roy Welensky" with "Good Old Mac." Security was subsequently tightened. Tensions ran high. Two Africans tried to join the congregation at St. Andrew's Church in Livingstone, where Macmillan was reading the second lesson on Sunday. When they refused to show police what was inside their briefcases, they were turned away.

The visit to Northern Rhodesia was an uncomfortable moment for the British Prime Minister. Yet the final leg of the tour, following Macmillan's address to the South African parliament, was a complete triumph. Not surprisingly, therefore, the role and impact of his South African visit has also dominated the historiography, for in comparison, Northern Rhodesia appears parochial, insignificant, and obscure. Macmillan does not mention those days he spent in Northern Rhodesia in his memoirs. Yet it was a part of an extraordinarily complex and tense moment in the endgame of British decolonization, one that could have gone very differently because of the potential for violence and because British policy could have gone in another direction. It can be seen as the culmination of what the historian John Darwin calls "the final strange phase of British imperialism: the zig-zags and u-turns after the Second World War."[4]

Macmillan's address to the South African parliament, generally called the "wind of change" speech, was one of the most admired political speeches of the twentieth century. Like the speech, the rest of the African tour was a tightly orchestrated media event. Just how orchestrated becomes clear from the press coverage and the paper trail left by Macmillan's Northern Rhodesian visit. The buildup to the visit; the many groups that tried to meet with Macmillan; the carefully stage-managed media visit choreographed around keeping Africa at a safe distance—all provide rich evidence of the volatile, potentially explosive local dramas that played out as the British Government attempted to impose its colonial endgame on African colonies populated by white settlers and competing black nationalists. This lecture looks at how those on the ground experienced Macmillan and the wind of change as he made his way through "a dense and deadly political jungle," as the *Daily Telegraph* sympathetically put it.[5]

HAROLD MACMILLAN BECAME PRIME MINISTER in the wake of the resignation of Antony Eden after the humiliation of the Suez crisis in 1956, an event that threw into question Britain's capacity to go it alone with an independent Middle East policy; more generally, the fiasco had shown that military intervention in major strategic areas was unlikely to succeed without U.S. support. This was not the only problem facing Britain: its finances were precarious, especially in the face of a balance-of-payments crisis. In addition, France and Belgium were seen as outmaneuvering Britain, their longtime imperial rival, in their response to African nationalist protests in areas with white settlers, and in their fast-track timetables for independence. Britain had been used to occupying that sort of forward position, and now it faced being usurped—or worse in its eyes—being classed in the same league as the Portuguese. Macmillan also had to repair relations with the United States, whose view of the Empire as a bulwark against communism was fading fast. For a collapsing imperial star, life in the universe of the Cold War was becoming decidedly chilly.

Macmillan was able to read these trends and to convert them into a decisive policy in Africa. He had decided in November 1959 that he would do a tour. Its purpose was to provide an international stage for Britain's views and policies on the future of Africa. Macmillan was like a company director promoting his own product; unsurprisingly for the scion of a publishing-house dynasty, his first stop was Ghana, with its highly literate, book-reading public. Macmillan discussed his speech with Kwame Nkrumah, the Ghanaian Prime

Minister. Three sub-principles shaped the tour: offering a fillip to the Commonwealth; easing the racial tensions surrounding the contested but now preferred model of multiracialism (which was a particularly acute problem in the increasingly unworkable federated states of Nyasaland, Northern Rhodesia, and Southern Rhodesia); and not alienating South Africa. Originally South Africa was to be the first visit, but the South African parliament was not sitting at the first date proposed, hence it became the last port of call. So on 5 January, Macmillan, his wife, and a team of advisers and journalists left for Ghana, Nigeria, the Federation, and South Africa.

The speech in South Africa was to be the major speech of the four scheduled on the tour. It went through multiple drafts; it was multi-authored. The phrase "wind of change" first appeared in Ghana, penned originally by a Colonial Office civil servant, James Robertson, as part of a theme on "the importance of Africa today"; it was reworked and inserted into Macmillan's text by David Hunt of the Commonwealth Relations Office. But it was not taken up by the press. In South Africa, Macmillan read:

> The wind of change is blowing through this continent, and whether we like it or not, this growth of national consciousness is a political fact. We must all accept it as a fact, and our national policies must take account of it.[6]

Hugely influential in the writing of the speech for South Africa was the British High Commissioner there, Sir John Maud, who flew to London to discuss the speech. Along with John Johnston, the Deputy High Commissioner, he stressed the need for South Africa to see itself in a global context; the need to understand that Africa was of world interest; and the need to see that national consciousness was "awakening . . . across the world."[7] Yet equally important was the desire not to offend the supporters of apartheid. Like the decolonization process that was to follow, it was a fast turnaround from ideas to events.

THE SPEECH HAS DEEPLY ROOTED ITSELF in British historical memory. It left far less to the imagination than previous similar efforts and made a lot of people feel a great deal better. What has been underestimated is that in just more than forty minutes, Macmillan restored the liberal image of the British Empire at home: most people in Britain, most of the time, had believed in that image and preferred it that way. For at the heart of the speech was, as the headlines ran, "a rejection of the idea of any inherent superiority of one race over an other." The *Daily Mail*'s sensationalist headline was "TOAST

OF AFRICANS: Macmillan's Speech Stirs a Continent"; likewise from *The Times,* "Mr Macmillan Dispels the Apartheid Taboo."[8] (Yet he did not actually mention the word.)

Naturally, much of the historiography stresses the brilliance, the bravery of Macmillan, his erudition, charming diplomacy, and so on. Those points are not refuted here. The drama unfolding on and off the page still feels Shakespearean. He had been violently sick before giving the speech (not untypical). A leader of a political party built upon stopping change was now signaling change, ahead of what many in his party believed in, because of some hard thinking about where imperial and national interest now lay. Some of those he had shown the speech to beforehand hated it: amusingly, the Tory extremist Julian Amery judged it to be a truly terrible speech and strongly cautioned against it ever seeing the light of day. By any reasonable standard, it is a great political speech. His rhetoric cloaks the imminent end of empire in dignified, continuous, principled, and unbroken British rule. And all this effort for an audience he was not actually addressing—the Americans. It was a long speech: part seduction, part lesson in global history, part philosophical treatise.

Approval ratings of the speech were high. The South African MPs appreciated Macmillan's candor and his willingness to criticize them to their faces. Finally, here was someone who had broken free from the constraints of discretion, according to Peregrine Worsthorne. Describing the atmosphere in the lobby afterward, he said it was as if a boil had been lanced: "That Britain disapproved of apartheid came as no surprise. What had caused anxiety was the fear that Britain might be preparing to do something about it."[9] Nothing, it seemed, and their world had not ended. Hendrik Verwoerd, the South African Prime Minister, was able to show how gracious a South African response to criticism could be. Macmillan was later cheered when he left Cape Town while wearing an Afrikaner bush hat. Meanwhile, back at home, James Callaghan, the shadow Colonial Office spokesman, approved of speaking out against "the evil policies of apartheid": "We had asked him to do this before Christmas," he insisted.[10] It saw everyone off, and his speech rightly deserves its place in the history of great speeches.

Yet the principles Macmillan espoused in speech were not original; his statements were abstract; the words were not his. The iconic phrasing—elemental forces across an Africa that could never be tamed—was, by 1960, pretty hackneyed. The speech did not dent apartheid. Just months later, the Sharpeville Massacre took place. The Southern Rhodesians were emboldened enough to go it alone in 1965 via a violent nationalist movement. Has it been too easy to view the rapid end of British rule as having occurred through the efforts of "Supermac"? Many contemporary cartoons depicted him as David facing a Goliath representing either a large black man (the raw masculine force of nationalism) or a stocky, aggressive white settler. African nationalism was constantly depicted in cartoon form as angry, virile, impatient. In contrast, colonial officials were aging, wobbly-kneed Lilliputians. Have we been led too readily by the orderliness of the official record? All colonial governments were sent copies of the speech. The tour file in the Zambian National Archive closes with the speech; therefore, it is placed on top. The speech being placed on top creates a sense of a definitive moment that shows Macmillan coming out on top. But if one goes behind it and looks more closely at the previous days in Northern Rhodesia, a messier paper trail suggests a moment in the end of empire in Africa that was sometimes chaotic, embarrassing, grubby, and farcical.

IN THE ARCHIVES OF THE AFRICAN nationalist parties of this period, there is little to suggest that Macmillan's visit to Northern Rhodesia or his speech in South Africa made any great impact upon them. In December 1959, the President-General of UNIP wrote to the Conservative Overseas Bureau to inform it of the new party and its aims, namely, to end the Federation on "the absolute principle of non-violence," though warning that sometimes things got out of hand when argument failed.[11] He was sure they would meet Mr. Macmillan, he continued, when he visited in January, and they would discuss their constitutional proposals. He left little doubt about the disdain felt for British colonial rule:

> It is a pity he will be a guest of the prime minister of settlers—a person whom Africans have no reason whatever to trust for justice and fair dealing. It is a pity too that he will even visit damned (according to Africans) South Africa where systematic exploitation and humiliation of the natives is going on (while Britain refuses even to condemn this).

Meeting UNIP was not on Macmillan's agenda; it was only after UNIP called a press conference that a meeting was hastily fitted in. Kaunda had, until ten days before, been serving a nine-month prison sentence for sedition and had been President of the banned Zambia African Congress. Little else seems to have survived from UNIP's meeting. The delegation called for an end to the Federation and for immediate self-government.

As for the ANC, all that survives are two lines in a letter from John Michello, the national secretary, to D. K. Mwinga at Katete. He described the meeting at which the four-man ANC delegation presented Macmillan with a petition as "a very historic moment."[12]

Why so marginal? There are three main reasons. Bitter local struggles for dominance were taking place between two nationalist parties: the liberals, represented by the ANC, and the new unitary-state nationalists, UNIP. Their limited resources made it difficult to fight more than one battle at a time. In letters to fellow ANC officials about his tour of the Copperbelt in February 1960, Michello provides firsthand evidence of the hand-to-mouth daily struggle of a party activist. The extent of UNIP's influence was his first concern, but he was pleased to report people being "roused beyond our expectations" against federation. Michello begged for money to be collected so that they could buy paper and post their petition to Macmillan and the Labour party; they were desperately in need of propaganda. And finally, he asked his correspondent to find his only suit, for he was badly in need of it: "You know I have only one trousers," he wrote, "and so [you] can imagine what embarrassment I am encountering."[13]

Second, the climate the parties were operating in was still a hostile one with regard to African politics in general. Kaunda and Munukayumbwa Sipalo had just been released from jail. Both met with Macmillan after UNIP issued a statement to the visiting press corps. Two weeks before meeting Macmillan, the ANC had its offices raided by police. Papers, a typewriter, and duplicators were taken away. The very day Macmillan was touring the Copperbelt, the offices—a two-room hut—were again raided, this time for the purpose of questioning Mainza Chona. To the shock and embarrassment of the police, they learned that after protesting at Ndola, he had then left for Tunis to attend an all-African congress.

The third reason is that Macmillan chose to publicly address the white community only. And when he spoke to anyone, he stuck to general platitudes about principles of merit, partnership, and the need for everyone to support the forthcoming Monckton Commission—an attempt to keep the Federation show on the road by setting up an inquiry and encouraging Africans to give their views, thus encouraging them to believe that the principle of partnership was developing. His public mission in Northern Rhodesia was to stop the African boycott of the commission. When Macmillan met Nkumbula, the latter apparently told him and his delegation that the partnership policy behind the Federation was apartheid in another name and that the African members on the commission (to include the paramount chiefs) were "stooges." UNIP was less direct and more conciliatory. Its delegation asked for the release of

Hastings Banda, the leader of the Nyasaland African Congress, and for the Prime Minister to do his duty to "develop us to a stage when we are going to rule ourselves."[14] For both, the visit was just a minor interlude in their ongoing struggles and campaigns. By February, the ANC, for example, had prepared a new "Memorandum on Constitutional Change" for presentation to Iain Macleod on his forthcoming visit.

SO WHAT DID MACMILLAN FEEL he should say to a small white-settler community in Northern Rhodesia, and how was this different from what he went on to say in South Africa? There was no mention of wind; instead, "a tide of change" was "flowing strenuously" and could not "be stemmed." That tide was not given the name "nationalism," but was described as "the steady natural growth of new countries into civilization and nationhood." The Monckton Commission was described as a stock-taking exercise of "the great and new conception of partnership between the races." It was a challenging exercise, he conceded, but a boycott would be "distressing." He offered them a bribe—money in the form of a grant for development. But, he warned, there was a limit: "I can't say look here old fellow, let me give you some of my overdraft"; moreover, it was an "illusion" that fifty million people in Britain could produce savings for export. He urged the settlers to make fullest use of all their manpower. He came closest to condemning the color bar by arguing, toward the end of his speech, that "an equal opportunity should be afforded to every man in the country, be he black or white, to make their fullest contribution," adding that he was confident that partnership would work and that Northern Rhodesia would move toward a constitution based on nonracial principles.[15] In other words, the settlers could not expect to be cast free.

The *Central African Post* (22 January) interpreted the speech thus: "Message to all parties and races: cooperate with the Monckton Commission appeals Macmillan." The *Northern News* (23 January) was not enthusiastic. "Least said soonest mended" was its headline; and its verdict was that Macmillan's speeches were "a lesson in political adroitness—the art of speaking well and saying nothing." Unsurprisingly, the response from the white community was largely negative. White settler communities often assumed positions of hostility: their very identities and genealogies were usually defined in opposition to something; they represented to themselves the best of what had been lost elsewhere; and they proudly paraded their parochialism and anachronism because "they know best, they know Africans the best."

At the civic luncheon in Macmillan's honor held on the day he arrived, the closest to a state occasion on this trip, the Lusaka white community represented there could barely contain its simmering resentment toward the British Government. Macmillan was introduced by the mayor, Councillor Harold Mitchell, who was another Scot and a resident for thirty years. His introduction was diplomatically described by Macmillan later as full of "provocative remarks," but it delighted the audience.[16] Mitchell's speech received much more coverage than any Macmillan made on his tour. Mitchell derided the visit as another one of those fact-finding missions they had learned to put up with. His tone may have encouraged shouts from the audience after the speech: one woman blurted out, "He's not as good as Verwoerd but give him a clap"; another telephoned the *Central African Post* afterward to call him "a disgrace."[17]

The *Central African Post* focused on the mayor's speech. The speech reflected the lack of a white "wind of change," particularly on race. The white settlers were worried: the mayor admitted that they as a community would not be able to play their full part in the prosperity of the country. He disdainfully referred to the wishes of the "illiterate masses," but added that "the vast majority of white Northern Rhodesians will not care if a blackman or a white man represents them in parliament . . . once the standards of education and civilization of the African are the same as the European." Higher wages were not the only answer; education was key, and he criticized the British government for failing to educate African women, for it was "women who were the driving force of civilization." He then finished with the warning that any legislation to enforce social integration would be "doomed to failure" and "as evil and inhuman as segregation laws."[18]

As the *Post* put it, Macmillan had heard some "plain speaking." Its editorial on the day focused on how to make the Federation work:

> Britain is leaving it to us to make it work. But the white community was stalling, sticking to its old racist platitudes. The ten or fifteen years guarantee they wanted before any kind of self-government would be brokered had not been offered.[19]

Less still was there any reassurance of an independent Federation before the northern territories were African-governed.

WHAT OF THOSE PEOPLE MACMILLAN refused to see? Three memoranda or petitions were presented at Government House, Lusaka, on the day of Macmillan's arrival. The *Times* headline for the day was "Mr Macmillan Hears All Sides in Northern Rhodesia."[20] The

Guardian carried the same message. That was not true. Each group of petitioners sought an audience with Macmillan; each was denied. The memorandum from the African Railway Workers Union claimed to represent 22,000 members in Northern and Southern Rhodesia; a separate one was submitted by the Broken Hill branch; a seven-page memorandum from the Northern Rhodesia Trade Union Congress (TUC), signed by Jonas Ponde and Matthew Mwendapole, claimed to represent 75,000 men.

The memoranda speak separately, but their voices are, in effect, joined in their opposition to the Federation. The Broken Hill workers put it in bold: they wanted "UNIVERSAL ADULT SUFFRAGE OF ONE MAN ONE VOTE" and the same constitution as existed in Britain; they also reminded the Premier that they had laid down their lives in the Second World War to protect Britain. They called for an end to further European migration and for France to stop nuclear tests in the Sahara. Second, the disparity between African wages and European ones was high on their agendas: on the railways, monthly wages were £45.72 for a European but only £6.18 for an African doing the same job.

These memoranda provide insight into the huge wounds from racial discrimination lived with daily, a common testimony that was no longer possible for those ruling the empire to claim ignorance of. There was no threat of violence; perhaps they did not feel the need for one. As the authors of the African Railway Workers Union memo point out, African wages were below the poverty line, and were set in complete ignorance of a cost of living, since there was no African consumer price index to work from. Ponde and Mwendapole regretted the "lopsided development" of Northern Rhodesia, with its tiny enclaves of industrialization surrounded by pre-industrial economies. As they put it, a small group of people enjoyed exceptional wealth, political power, and prestige, and was resistant to changes that would help the economy. Their privileges in health and education meant they possessed "more than average energy and social skills, by which to influence events," whereas half of African schoolchildren in towns had no access to basic education.[21]

Furthermore, the effects of daily-experienced abuse and a recent worsening in race relations come through these carefully crafted petitions, suggesting the importance of the color bar in fueling demands for independence. Trade unionists wrote how every European "treats himself as an employer when he is an employee just as the African is," adding that race relations had recently deteriorated to the point that there was "much less contact now . . . between the two major races." The explanation was that racial discrimination in the workplace had worsened and thus affected social relations in general. Color-bar practices had become more pronounced in all public places. And any Europeans prepared to take a risk and go against this hardening of attitudes faced "a social cost . . . sufficiently heavy as to dissuade" them "from taking the risk."[22]

Interviews with a few Zambians who remember this period seem to indicate that no one knew of the "wind of change" speech nor remembered it. For William Chipango, who worked in the late 1950s as a railway employee and was an active trade unionist, his single memory of late-colonial rule is of the humiliation of the color bar.[23] He recalled first and most vividly the practice of Africans in Livingstone having to go to the back of shops to purchase items: they gave their orders, paid their money, and received the merchandise through a small hatch, which was often restricted further with wire mesh. At independence, a wave of white residents left to live across the border in Southern Rhodesia, unable to stomach Africans in charge. That was also the memory of two cousins, Wamu Lewamba and Wakumeto Sililo, then young boys, whose parents made a living by fishing on the Zambezi just above the town.[24] Their memory of colonial rule, drawn from the visits the family made from the countryside to sell their produce in the town's market, is of the color bar and what their parents said about it.

Sparse as these living testimonies are, their veracity and representativeness can be buttressed by left-wing British journalists who accompanied Macmillan on his tour. Sydney Jacobson, the *Daily Mirror*'s correspondent, could not take the "hypocrisy" he had witnessed in the Rhodesias any more after he left the North for Blantyre, Nyasaland. The piece he filed for his paper on 27 January was a plea that Macmillan be made aware of the reality of the color bar.[25] Thus far he had been shielded from it; Jacobson suggested that Macmillan was the hapless victim of "window dressing." He listed hotels he had visited that had dropped the color bar for the duration of the visit. Similarly, Macmillan read the lesson at the Anglican church in Livingstone, St. Andrew's, where Africans were not allowed to worship (they had a tiny "black chapel" in a separate building behind the whitewashed church). But for that day, they were allowed to sit in the audience. In Livingstone, one European told Jacobson that if he wanted to take an African friend to the cinema, he had to ring up the District Commissioner first for permission and then, if that was granted, he had to warn the cinema. He would be given a seat in a special box away from the white audience, while his African companions had to endure further embarrassment from the film-certification announcement: "Not suitable for children under twelve or for Africans."

What Macmillan chose not to do, and Jacobson hugely regretted that he did not, was to have made in both Rhodesias a "blunt denunciation of the colour bar and all it means in the day-to-day lives of Africans here." His words on this, Jacobson insisted, would have counted for a lot. Finally, he closed his "memo" with his view of what lay at the heart of the political ferment he had witnessed: "the desire of the African to walk the streets in dignity in his own country."[26]

Even on the right, there was criticism of Macmillan's snobbery and distance with regard to Africans. He showed no "spontaneous human touch," regretted the *Telegraph,* when it came to African protestors until the end of his tour, when he acknowledged a group at Livingstone Airport. Usually, he "looked the other way, or avoided passing by."[27] His wave and acknowledgment were apparently met with smiles and good-natured laughter.

Instead, meetings behind the scenes were the order of the day. Throughout Macmillan's tour, he met quietly or secretly with representatives from the big mining companies and other businessmen. When summing up the tour, Peregrine Worsthorne at the *Telegraph* quoted Sir Ronald Prain, the chairman of the Rhodesian Selection Trust, making him the most powerful force in Northern Rhodesia. Prain commented that "there were only two things of permanence in Africa today: the natives and big business." This "ruthless realism" accepted black nationalism as a reality, in a tradition that went back to Cecil Rhodes. By no longer adopting the "paternalist haut en bas" white approach, big business was bridging the gap between the races. Prain was comparatively enlightened, best known "for the major role he played in dismantling racial barriers to employment on the Copperbelt during the 1950s."[28] His private meetings with Macmillan and Macleod fostered their desire to move faster on decolonization. His views, also made to U.S. shareholders and publicly, were the Conservative Government's wind of change, particularly with regard to his impatience with Europeans wanting to maintain the industrial color bar on both jobs and higher wages for Africans.

IN THEIR RAWNESS AND AUTHENTICITY, in their pain and anger, the memoranda written by self-educated, morally righteous, labouring African men highlight the role of race in the wind of change across Africa, a neglected aspect in the study of British decolonization in Africa. After 1945, organized trade unionism in the British Empire was in the vanguard of exposing degrading working conditions and low wages. In the Copperbelt, their agitation and militancy extracted concessions, exposed Europeans as overpaid, and resulted in a state of emergency in 1956. Macmillan never read their petitions; he never addressed all of Northern Rhodesia about the color bar; and in his condemnation of South Africa's white-minority rule, the word "apartheid" was never mentioned. Macmillan met the nationalist parties in Northern Rhodesia only hesitatingly and rather at the last minute. Perhaps a Labour Prime Minister would have had more time for trade union representatives.

This lack of inclusion and recognition fed into the bigger process that resulted in a rushed independence. The British authorities deferred to those so-called nationalist parties that seemed to offer stable rule in their support for established business interests: the upshot was a monolithic face and a conservative approach to governance. Decolonization was an act of exclusion as much as inclusion.

In addition, Macmillan's tour increased political repression. The botched attempt to blow up the Savoy Hotel where Macmillan luncheoned provided an occasion for the chief secretary to drum up support for a new Public Security Bill to replace the emergency ordinances that Kaunda and others had fallen foul of. But in effect, it simply made emergency powers part of the normal law. The bill banned printed material considered prejudicial to public security, banned meetings, restricted the movement of individuals, and, in certain circumstances, allowed the governor to detain suspects without trial. Not surprisingly, the one-party state of Kaunda's UNIP, which emerged by the 1970s, found these precedents for how to deal with opposition rather attractive. For example, in 1965, William Chipango, mentioned earlier, who had helped write the railway workers' memoranda, became Livingstone's first black mayor. But he resented UNIP officials for slowly but surely taking control of the apparatus of government in Southern Province, and bitterly resented Kaunda's style of politics. Three years after independence, he found himself jailed for treason, tortured, and fighting for his version of freedom for the next twenty years.

All this supports a number of general hypotheses about African nationalism and the rapid handover of power to nationalist parties in the early 1960s. First, the emotional issue of race made African nationalism highly distinctive from other post-imperial nationalisms outside the continent. African nationalism was a very moral ism, which gave its parties decisive discursive power, masking old and new conflicts. These conflicts were huge. It was an enormous challenge to forge cohesion from parties run on a shoestring, in areas lacking a territorial consciousness but riven by linguistic and religious differences, "tribalism," and regionalism. Africans remained a people with "predominantly local concerns"; very few Europeans involved in this phase of African history had any clear idea about the real force behind nationalism, and they overestimated its strength and cohesion.[29] British officials rushed to deal with those national-party para-bureaucracies that gave the impression of cohesion (partly because they were much better at using the media than some of their local rivals). They looked like the best bet for supporting big business. In this regard, the "wind of change" was also one of continuity. Macmillan's rapprochement with the new "modern" men of the hastily constructed nationalist parties, who were trying to paper over huge divisions and weaknesses, made business sense to the companies and political sense to the nationalists.

For imperial racial paternalists, nationalism was easier to talk about than race. Macmillan's half-hearted nod at racial rule reflected a generational view of the limits of African capabilities and a lack of empathy with regard to the cruelties of the color bar. It was an embodiment of the "schizophrenic" tradition in British liberalism, allowing people to simultaneously occupy positions that were "both racist and liberal."[30] Temperamentally, Macmillan was a Victorian, and the British Empire remained essentially a Victorian empire. He wound it up in line with Victorian racial paternalisms and British financial interests. His actions reveal the continuity behind the "wind of change" with regard to the role that "gentlemanly capitalists" (in P. J. Cain and A. G. Hopkins's celebrated phrase), for all their philanthropic guises, played in the Scramble for Africa. And the passivity of government. As a junior minister, Winston Churchill feared the British "disturbed rather than governed Africa."[31] That innate sense of powerlessness must have surely run down through the generations and haunted Northern Rhodesia's administrators in the late 1950s.

The Monckton Commission found in favor of the African majority and recommended a multiracial electorate in its report of November 1960. Northern Rhodesia's whites had to make the decision, like Macmillan, "to stay or go now." Many left for Southern Rhodesia and South Africa, helping in various ways to prolong white-minority rule. Northern Rhodesia became Zambia in 1964. Outside of UNIP, an independent Zambia for many Africans meant exclusion and oppression by authoritarian, chauvinistic rule. Macmillan came out of it all the best, with his great speech. Rhetoric aside, it showed his courage in disregarding the wishes of his own party. It restored Britain's self-image as a liberal colonial power. It discharged the Empire from the messy and financially costly process of planned and prepared-for decolonization in not-yet-multiracial societies. Imperial decline had never had it so good.

Spring Semester 2011

1. *Central African Post,* 22 Jan. 1960 (Zambia National Archives, hereafter cited as ZNA).

2. "Macmillan Plea Ignored; Africans Go on with Boycott," *Daily Telegraph,* 22 Jan. 1960.

3. "Macmillan Bomb Scare," *Daily Mail,* 23 Jan. 1960.

4. John Darwin, *The Empire Project: The Rise and Fall of the British World System, 1830–1970* (Cambridge, 2010), p. 14.

5. *Daily Telegraph,* 6 Feb. 1960.

6. Harold Macmillan, speech at Cape Town, 3 Feb. 1960 (copy in ZNA, NR 11/84).

7. Ibid.

8. *Daily Mail,* 4 Feb. 1960; *The Times,* 8 Feb. 1960.

9. *Daily Telegraph,* Feb. 1960.

10. *Daily Mail,* 4 Feb. 1960.

11. M. M. Chona to R. D. Milne (UNIP/6/7/3).

12. J.E. Michello to D. K. Mwinga, 9 Feb. 1960 (UNIP Archives, ANC 2/12).

13. J.E. Michello to B. I. Lombe, 14 Feb. 1960.

14. *Northern News,* 22 Jan. 1960.

15. Quotations from Macmillan's speech as reported in the *Central African Post,* 22 Jan. 1960.

16. Ibid.

17. Ibid.

18. Ibid.

19. Ibid.

20. *The Times,* 22 Jan. 1960.

21. Northern Rhodesia TUC, Memorandum, signed by Jonas Ponde and Matthew Mwendapole, 21 Jan. 1960 (ZNA, NR 11/84).

22. Ibid.

23. William Chipango, interview by the author, Livingstone, Zambia, 22 June 2009.

24. Wamu Lewamba and Wakumeto Sililo, interview by the author, Lusaka, Zambia, 16 June 2009.

25. Sydney Jacobson, "A Memo to Macmillan: They Are Hiding the Colour Bar from You Says the Man from the Mirror," *Daily Mirror,* 27 Jan. 1960.

26. Ibid.

27. "African Chiefs Respond to Premier's Appeal," *Daily Telegraph,* 25 Jan. 1960.

28. L. J. Butler, "Business and British Decolonisation: Sir Ronald Prain, the Mining Industry and the Central African Federation," *Journal of Imperial and Commonwealth History,* 35, 3 (Sept. 2007), p. 460.

29. John Iliffe, *Africans: The History of a Continent* (Cambridge, 2009 edn.), pp. 267, 251–72.

30. Richard Weight, *Patriots: National Identity in Britain, 1940–2000* (London, 2003 edn.), pp. 426–39.

31. Quoted in John Lonsdale, "Nationalism in Sub-Saharan Africa," in John Breuilly, ed., *Oxford Handbook on the History of Nationalism* (Oxford, forthcoming).

16

The End of the Dutch, Belgian, and Portuguese Colonial Empires

CRAWFORD YOUNG

In the age of European imperial expansion that opened at the close of the fifteenth century and lasted for more than four centuries, three of the smallest countries emerged with some of the largest colonial domains. Portugal and the Netherlands pioneered the construction of far-flung seaborne mercantile empires in the sixteenth and seventeenth centuries. By the twentieth century, the original maritime imperial expansion had evolved into large African territorial conquests and scattered Asian enclaves for Portugal; for the Netherlands, the vast archipelago colony that became Indonesia, sprawling 3,600 miles from east to west, as well as much smaller Caribbean holdings. Belgium, through the extraordinary skill of King Leopold II in the predatory diplomacy of African partition, acquired by inheritance from its monarch a large part of central Africa. All three countries came to attach great value to their imperial domains and entered the era of decolonization determined to retain them into an indefinite future. But in contrast to the British Empire, the empires of these smaller colonial powers all ended disastrously. This lecture establishes the comparative historical context.

In part, their tenacious resistance to decolonization showed merely the territorial possessiveness that is inherent to states: a domain once inscribed as a sovereign possession is rarely voluntarily abandoned. Only military defeat, external imposition, or irresistible challenge by a subject population can annul territorial possessiveness. The three cases at hand differed from those of the larger colonial powers in their delay in drawing the inevitable inferences from the factors overriding territorial possessiveness.

In all three instances, the end of empire came suddenly and unexpectedly. The process was disorderly, accompanied during and after the transition by protracted violence and international crisis. In different ways, the troubled course of decolonization escaped the control of the colonizer, who far too long had resisted the implacable logic of global trends and events.

Each in its own fashion, the three small imperial centers had come to view their overseas empires as critical to their national well-being or even identity. The vast scale of their overseas holdings dwarfed the modest dimensions of the metropole, multiplying the significance of the three states as international actors. Embedded but deceptive public ideologies clothed the colonial mission with an apparent success and moral worth that persisted until an unexpected collapse. Thus, the loss of empire was traumatic, associated with a national crisis. Their small size made them singularly vulnerable to external pressures as a changing international normative discourse grew increasingly hostile to colonial rule.

THE DUTCH MERCANTILE ROLE IN ASIA dates from 1595, formalized with the charter of the United East India Company in 1602. The Dutch transformed their mercantile domain into a full-fledged despotic colonial state only after 1816, largely based on the exploitation of Java through the nineteenth century. By 1831, a system of high land taxation and obligatory crops, the "Cultures System," was generating sufficient revenue to meet colonial administrative expenses and export a surplus to contribute to the Netherlands metropolitan budget. Between 1831 and 1850, colonial proceeds provided 19 percent of the Dutch budget, and 32 percent between 1851 and 1860. This revenue windfall embedded within the Dutch national psyche a presumption that the East Indies holdings were an indispensable resource for the Netherlands.

The Cultures System was modified after 1870, replaced by a "Liberal System," and then about 1900 by an "Ethical System," which was the first one to incorporate into policy a vision of welfare of the subject. The exploitative nature of colonial subjugation remained, and the economic crisis of the 1930s resulted in a reversion to more despotic practices.

Until the later part of the nineteenth century, effective Dutch occupation was mostly limited to Java, the Moluccas, and some of the Sumatran north coast. The completion of colonial conquest extended into the 1920s, with the final subjugation of Papua. Though the colonial budget no longer generated a surplus transferable to the Netherlands, Indonesia was a critical source of foreign exchange and national wealth.

Nationalism became a social force in the early twentieth century, taking form around the precocious naturalization of a concept of Indonesia. Strikingly, the new political leadership, although mostly ethnic Javanese steeped in a richly elaborated historical culture, chose the larger "Indonesia" idiom as the frame for challenging colonial rule. They also made the crucial choice to foster the coastal trading language of the region, Malay, as a national language, reframed as Indonesian.

Indonesian national organizations emerged by 1908, at first moderate, but by the 1920s including more radical Islamic, communist, and nationalist streams. A large communist uprising in 1926–7 shook the colonial establishment, and coping with nationalism became a major Dutch preoccupation thereafter, oscillating between management and repression. A 1936 Indonesia advisory council petition for autonomy within a dual kingdom was firmly rejected.

However, the destruction of Dutch colonial rule came from without, not from within. The fateful transformative event was the Japanese invasion in January 1942. The isolated Dutch Indies establishment, with few means of resisting the invasion, surrendered two months later. Although the Japanese maintained the indirect-rule structures of village administration at the local level, they liquidated the superstructure of alien authority. Their primary aim was access to critical raw materials for the war effort, above all oil and rubber. The ruthlessness of their rule and the hardships occasioned by the occupation antagonized many. But they trained military forces that would subsequently provide the trained and armed personnel to ensure the core of an independent Indonesian army. The Japanese did not organize a puppet state, as in Burma and the Philippines, but did offer a collaborative role to the two leading Indonesian nationalist figures, Sukarno and Mohammed Hatta.

By 1944, as the tides of war were running heavily against Japan, Indonesian nationalists found the Japanese occupiers receptive to pleas for support for independence. On 17 July 1945, Japan promised independence, and Sukarno and his allies began to make preparations. On 17 August, three days after Emperor Hirohito's surrender broadcast, Sukarno, in a very brief and laconic statement, declared Indonesia a sovereign republic. Sukarno and Hatta quickly formed a government and adopted a constitution; they won support in most of Java, but some of the outer islands were reluctant to accept their authority.

The Dutch, however, clung to dreams of full restoration. The East Indies was a vital economic resource for a Netherlands economy crippled by the German occupation and the war effort. Their determination was reinforced by the conviction that Sukarno and Hatta were untrustworthy Japanese collaborators and unacceptable partners. But the first Dutch troops could be landed only in December 1945. As soon as sufficient forces had landed, a reconquest offensive began. Although they enjoyed initial success, capturing the key towns of Jakarta, Bandung, and Jogyakarta over the following weeks, the Republic of Indonesia, despite internal tensions, was already too well established to be easily overcome. In core areas of the archipelago, the Republic enjoyed strong support, especially in Java, Madura, and much of Sumatra. In the outer islands, however, a number of rulers were reluctant to back the Republic. Some groups had experienced intense Christian mission activity and had relatively large elites who harbored apprehensions about the religious intentions of the Muslim majority (90 percent of the population).

Strong international pressure for negotiations quickly built up. A compromise truce accord was signed, reluctantly by both sides, in November 1946, confirming the Republic's authority only in Java, Sumatra, and Madura; the Dutch plan was to gather under their umbrella an assemblage of outer-island territories. A federated united state of Indonesia was promised by January 1949; the Republic would be one of the federated states, with Queen Wilhelmina as titular head of a Netherlands-Indonesia union of sovereign states. But each side distrusted the other, and hoped for a more complete victory.

The Dutch launched two additional major military offensives, in July 1947 and December 1948. On both occasions, intense international pressure compelled their suspension, even after substantial success. The second offensive not only reconquered key Java centers, but also captured Sukarno and most other Indonesian leaders.

The Republic faced its own major challenges, beginning with ongoing conflicts within the leadership. Among the Muslim organizations, there was restiveness concerning the refusal of Sukarno to declare Indonesia an Islamic state and his insistence on religious neutrality. More-radical Islamic groups revolted in west Java in March 1948; the resulting Darul Islam insurgency was contained after serious fighting, but skirmishing spread to the outer islands and dragged on until 1962.

An even larger insurrection exploded in August 1948 in central Java, led by the Communist Party of Indonesia (Partai Komunis Indonesia, or PKI). Although decimated by its crushing defeat in 1926–7, the PKI regained momentum after the war. The PKI insurgency was defeated by November 1948, but only after a number of pitched battles and thousands of casualties. The communist uprising was critical in inscribing a Cold War template on unfolding Indonesian events, particularly for the United States. The success of the Republic in subduing the PKI revolt led America to see new merit in the Indonesian regime, and added urgency to reaching a definitive settlement regarding independence.

Confronted with an American threat to suspend Marshall Plan assistance unless a final agreement on Indonesian independence was reached, the Netherlands abandoned the dream of colonial restoration. A final accord, signed in November 1949, provided for full acknowledgment of Indonesian sovereignty over the entire archipelago, except Papua, as a united federation. The culmination of the Indonesian revolution took place on 17 August 1950, five years after the original declaration of independence, with the federal structure of the 1949 accord abandoned and Indonesia reconfigured as a unitary republic.

There remained the unfinished business of Papua, called West Irian by Indonesian nationalists. In 1957, the continued deadlock over its status helped provoke Indonesian nationalization of all Dutch enterprises without compensation as well as the expulsion of the remaining Dutch population, erasing what remained of the three centuries of Dutch presence. In turn, these punitive measures fortified Dutch determination to guarantee the Papuan population a choice other than incorporation into Indonesia. But in the face of continued international support for Indonesian claims to all the territory of the former Dutch East Indies, and small-scale military invasions by Indonesian forces, the Netherlands reluctantly agreed in 1962 to a brief UN interregnum, which led to the area's incorporation into Indonesia. But to this day the culturally distinct Papua remains a restive and reluctant subject of Indonesia, whose hold is reinforced by substantial immigration there from core areas of the Republic.

The end of empire in the East Indies was a severe trauma for the Netherlands, well captured by Arend Lijphart:

> The agonies of the decolonization process are well exemplified by the painful and reluctant withdrawal of the Netherlands from its colonies . . . Holland acted with an intense emotional commitment,

manifested in pathological feelings of self-righteousness, resentment, and pseudo-moral convictions. These emotions started to decrease in intensity in the late 1950s, but protracted and ultimately unsuccessful resistance to decolonization still left the country internally divided, frustrated, and humiliated.[1]

BELGIUM WAS AN EARLIER INSTANCE of painful territorial loss by the Netherlands. The country was created in 1830 through a successful revolt of the Netherlands' southern provinces. The secession created a new binational country lacking a national narrative and clear identity. Upon this uncertain social base, a unitary state with French as the primary language was erected.

In 1865, Leopold II ascended the throne, convinced that his country required the invigoration of colonial territories. The Belgian political and economic elites did not share his imperial appetites; Belgium lacked the naval and military power to nurture such ambitions. Leopold, however, was undeterred; with the explorer Henry Morton Stanley as his prime agent, a zone of influence was stitched together in the Congo basin, based on a host of treaties with local rulers. At the Congress of Berlin in 1885, in a remarkable diplomatic tour de force, Leopold managed to secure international blessing for his claim to personal sovereignty over nearly a million square miles of central Africa, with the pledge to guarantee free trade and impose no customs while also combating slavery and fostering Christian mission activity. Thus was born the Congo Free State.

To finance his vast proprietary domains and achieve the "effective occupation" that the Berlin Congress reconfirmed as requisite for secure colonial title, Leopold had to find a revenue flow. This was accomplished by forced deliveries of wild rubber, imposition of a state ivory monopoly, and the renting of sovereignty to several major chartered companies, the whole underwritten by ruthless brutality and innumerable atrocities. By the 1890s, revenues were beginning to flow.

By 1903, Belgium and Leopold had become the target of an international campaign against the grotesque abuses of the Congo Free State, led by Britain and an array of humanitarian organizations. To parry these external pressures, in 1908, a year before Leopold's death, Belgium formally assumed sovereignty over the Congo. The first imperative was to regularize and reform colonial administration, bringing its practices more closely into line with what, by the standards of the time, was "normal" colonial exploitation.

The stain of Leopoldian atrocities was largely removed; in the decades that followed, Belgium fashioned a remarkably dense, coercive, and thorough paternalistic superstructure of hegemony. By the 1950s, European personnel in the administration numbered 10,000; when one adds the 6,000 European missionaries, and the mines and plantations that blanketed the territory, the infrastructure of domination was imposing.

The first post-war decade was a golden age for the Belgian colony, which now basked in an image of success. The foreign-exchange earnings of colonial exports were a crucial resource for post-war Belgian recovery. The commodity price boom that continued almost until independence brought a remarkable expansion of colonial revenues. In the period from 1939 to 1950, state revenues increased elevenfold, then again tripled in the final colonial decade. The fiscal bonanza made possible major state investment in social infrastructure—education and health notably—that earlier had been largely delegated to the missions. In 1955, King Baudouin made a triumphant royal tour of the colony, its image for the Belgian public and many others as a model of paternal governance still intact. Before an enthusiastic crowd of 70,000 in the colonial capital, Baudouin declared, "Belgium and Congo form a single nation."[2]

Although there was some subdued conversation in colonial circles about the eventual destiny of the Belgian Congo and the participation of the African subject in its governance, the dominant assumption until the mid-1950s was that some form of reformed linkage to Belgium was permanent. Any change in status was presumed to lie in so remote a future that no immediate preparatory steps were required. The main grievance of the emergent elite at the time was that they encountered pervasive racism and obstacles to their social promotion on an equal basis with Europeans. The latter was addressed by a 1952 decree providing "immatriculation" to the handful who survived a humiliating administrative test of their mastery of the cultural codes of the colonizer.

Mesmerized by the successful image of the colony, Belgian officials up to the mid-1950s felt relatively little pressure from the international system, domestic opinion, or the Congolese subject still in thrall to colonial mythology. The nationalist hero Patrice Lumumba himself, in a posthumously published manuscript written in 1955, expressed admiration for the grandiose achievement of Leopold II in constructing the Congo, and endorsed the project of a Belgo-Congolese Union as its fulfillment.[3] Only the future will tell, he then wrote, when the Congo has reached "the more advanced degree of civilization and the required political maturity" to advance to self-government.[4]

Fissures had begun to appear in the colonial monolith by 1956. The powerful Catholic Church defected in 1956; a conclave of bishops in the Congo declared their support for Congolese "emancipation." An unusual Socialist-Liberal coalition took power in 1956, determined to introduce a state school system into the colony to compete with the Catholic schools. As well, growing Flemish-French tensions in Belgium spilled into the Congo. The accelerating decolonization elsewhere in Africa, and the potential costs of combating it, became daily more evident.

Notwithstanding these changes, a summons in 1955 by a Belgian professor, A. A. J. Van Bilsen, to develop a thirty-year plan for "emancipation" provoked a wave of indignation. The brevity of his timetable shocked the Belgian public, and he endured a torrent of abuse. In mid-1956, the public call for emancipation (in effect, a code word for independence) also came from the Congolese side. By 1958, political language across a broad spectrum had evolved to frame the core demand as swift independence.

The formation of political parties became legal in 1958, and they soon multiplied, mostly based in the six provincial capitals. Politicization of the populace proceeded rapidly, especially in the cities. The critical decolonization trigger, however, waited until January 1959, when Leopoldville (now Kinshasa) exploded in days of mass rioting. Although the eruption was unplanned and leaderless, its sheer scale was unprecedented, as was the incapacity of the security forces to quickly subdue it. Controlled gradualism was upended, and from that point forward, Belgium lost the capacity to control the process and timetable. Later that year, the Belgian administration realized that its administrative control of the lower Congo and some other areas was fast weakening in the face of nationalist mobilization. But even yet, Brussels assumed the transitional timetable would be fifteen years.

The Leopoldville riots introduced a profound disjuncture, shattering colonial complacency. A week after the riots, King Baudouin, still imbued with the sense of a special royal role in the colony his grandfather had created, seized the initiative by making the first formal pledge of independence, "without undue delay or ill-considered precipitation."[5] An accompanying governmental declaration pledged negotiation with Congolese leaders. All restrictions on political activity were finally lifted, and political parties that had begun to form in 1958 proliferated rapidly. By the end of 1959, however, only a handful had any presence outside the provincial capitals; the administration still counted on its capacity to influence rural voters, in alliance with chiefs and moderate Congolese elites. By this time, the Belgian colonial minister, Auguste de Schrijver, had indicated a likely 1960 date for independence, though with an expectation that foreign affairs, defense, and finance would still remain under Belgian tutelage.

But the need for a formula for negotiating a way forward became increasingly urgent; the multiplying array of parties, mostly with ethnic clienteles, competed in the aggressiveness of their discourse. A unique formula to break the deadlock was proposed: the Round Table Conference, mainly composed of more than a dozen leading Congolese political parties and the Belgian government, which was joined by the three leading parties, including the opposition socialists.

To the surprise of the Belgian side, when the conference convened in January 1960, the Congolese participants formed a united front around the demand for immediate independence. After acceding to Congolese proposals for a 30 June 1960 date, the Belgians saw their hopes for some reserved powers for at least two years vanish when a socialist opposition participant supported the Congolese insistence that independence be total. Also abandoned were the hopes that the Belgian monarch would be head of state and that European residents could vote; the Eurafrican dream finally dissolved.

With their demands satisfied, the nationalist parties turned their attention to political organization; the first national elections were scheduled for May, and the rural areas mostly remained to be organized. A brief moment of relative good will ensued while the details of power transfer were settled. A provisional constitution was elaborated, closely adhering to the Belgian model, which few Congolese contested. The major contention was the demand by parties representing Katanga and the lower Congo for a federal structure; a mainly unitary state, strongly backed by Belgium and most Congo parties, prevailed. The colonial administration was scrupulous in the organization of the national and provincial elections to create the representative structures of the new state. Although dismayed at the electoral outcome, which saw its most aggressive tormenter, Lumumba, emerge as the primary victor, in the end the Belgian managers of the transition accepted the electoral verdict and brokered an arrangement that installed Lumumba as Prime Minister, and an early voice of independence, the Alliance des Bakongo leader Joseph Kasavubu, as president.

The stage was thus set for what became known as the *pari congolais* (Congolese gamble). Belgium still held some apparent trump cards.

Especially important was the overwhelming dominance of Europeans in the core armature of the state, the administration and the army. Of the 4,642 positions in the top three grades of the civil service, only three were held by Congolese, all recent appointees. The Congolese had only begun to acquire the university diplomas requisite for such posts; academic secondary schooling (except for seminaries) necessary for university admission became available only in the 1950s. The thousand officers in the army were exclusively European. Thus, the essence of the *pari congolais* was an exceptional form of decolonization in which the transfer of real power would occur well after independence, once an accelerated program to train qualified personnel had been completed. In retrospect, the hope of a harmonious collaboration between an entirely Congolese political sector of ministers and parliamentarians, and a wholly European operative armature of the state appears forlorn at best. The racism that saturated the colonial encounter, the accumulated frustrations of the subject, and the climate of mutual mistrust and uncertainty surrounding the sudden surge to independence all ensured the instability of the formula.

But by the time the settlement acceding to the demands of Congolese nationalists had been reached, Belgium had few options. The rapidity of the spread of nationalist protest, and loss of administrative control in important regions, raised the specter of ungovernability. The colonial army warned of the limits of its capacity to guarantee security. Most importantly, the long shadow of the Algerian war, and the costs and limits of military repression of nationalist challenge, hung heavily over Belgian officialdom and the Belgian public. So did the recollection of the fate of their Dutch neighbors' effort at military reconquest in the East Indies, pummeled into submission by international protest and the American threats to suspend Marshall Plan aid.

As Independence Day dawned on 30 June 1960, deep uncertainties weighed on the celebrations. Among Africans, soaring expectations of immediate rewards, encouraged by extravagant promises of the electoral campaign, mingled with vague apprehensions of an uncharted future. For Europeans, the aggressive tone of nationalist rhetoric intensified insecurities; the Belgian administration had blocked currency conversion, foreclosing the exit option for many settlers. The contradictory sentiments found reflection in the independence ceremonies; after King Baudouin delivered a paternalistic encomium to the grandiose achievement of Leopold II and the civilizing accomplishments of the colonial state, Prime Minister Lumumba seized the microphone for an unprogrammed, fiery recitation of African sufferings under the colonial yoke.

In the event, the decolonization settlement unraveled after only five days. Its architecture collapsed when its presumed strongest pillar, the army, dissolved in mutiny against its Belgian officer corps. On 11 July, the richest province and the source of half of governmental revenue, Katanga, declared its secession; European personnel remained to ensure its functioning. Thus, the fledgling Congo government found its elemental means of rule eviscerated: its administrative superstructure, its means of coercion, and its major source of revenue. Overnight, the Congo became the epicenter of a global emergency, with the Cold War as template; the *pari congolais* became the Congo crisis.

By 10 July, Belgian troops had intervened to protect the European population; to Congolese indignation, they also shielded the Katanga secession. On 14 July, the UN Security Council authorized a peacekeeping operation with both military and civilian components. Both the United States and Soviet Union activated their intelligence resources to support factions congenial to their interests. The new Congolese government, despite the frantic activity of its leaders, Kasavubu and Lumumba, was largely incapacitated. One of Lumumba's ministers offered an eloquent summary: "Though we sat so comfortably in our sumptuous official cars, driven by uniformed military chauffeurs, and looked as though we were ruling this large and beautiful country, we were in fact ruling nothing and a prey to whatever might happen."[6]

The collapse of the decolonization settlement became complete in early September when President Kasavubu, with American, Belgian, and UN connivance, ousted Lumumba on debatable constitutional grounds; in the ensuing constitutional void, de facto UN and international tutelage prevailed. The nadir was reached in January 1961, when the imprisoned Lumumba was transferred to Katanga, with external complicity, and assassinated. Although a modicum of legitimacy was restored with parliamentary confirmation of a new government in August 1961, and UN military action to crush the Katanga secession in January 1963 reunified the country, the costs to both Congo and Belgium of a botched decolonization were high.

Portuguese Africa came to a comparably disorderly end, but by a different avenue: protracted insurgencies met by intransigent resistance, followed by the radical disjuncture of regime change in Portugal via military intervention. The unexpected coup in 1974 that ousted the regime of Antonio Salazar and Marcelo Caetano ended an autocracy dating from 1926. Nearly five hundred years of Portuguese presence came to an abrupt and unplanned end, in circumstances that left in its wake nearly thirty years of bitter civil war in its most important colony, Angola.

Some distinctive attributes of the Portuguese colonial project deserve note. From its beginnings, Portuguese imperial doctrine gradually developed a notion of a globalized Lusitanian polity, which periodically received new stress. The 1822 constitution revived this notion, treating imperial possessions as overseas provinces; free persons were declared Portuguese citizens. Although in later constitutions more orthodox colonial terminology subsequently oscillated with the global Portugal mythology, the mystique of an intercontinental polity proved a durable illusion.

Also distinctive to the Lusitanian empire was the central role of the slave trade in its Atlantic development. Angola was a major source; the island outposts of São Tomé and Cape Verde were way stations and plantations; and Brazil was the insatiable market. The slave trade, a mainstay of the colonial economy well into the nineteenth century, was nominally abolished in 1836, but not finally ended until 1870. From this encounter emerged strongly creolized populations in São Tomé and Cape Verde; in Angola, an Afro-Portuguese intermediary population expanded the slave-trading networks progressively inland. Subsequently, the Verdeans and Afro-Portuguese played a crucial role in an eventual institutionalized colonial administration, sometimes holding top posts. In the revolt against colonial occupation, the mestizo populace was to play a crucial role.

By the nineteenth century, the days of imperial glory were long over; Portugal was a relatively poor and weak European country, shorn of its most profitable colony, Brazil, and lacking the state capacity and capital of its colonial competitors. Though Portugal maintained vaguely defined sovereign claims extending far inward from its coastal bases in Angola and Mozambique, its actual rule was far more circumscribed.

The intensifying Scramble for Africa in the last quarter of the nineteenth century forced the Portuguese hand: validation of its territorial claims was now contingent on effective occupation. But full conquest of the hinterlands of Portuguese Guinea, Angola, and Mozambique was completed only in the 1920s. The African subject became sharply demarcated as a "native," distinct from the "civilized" population of Europeans and mestizos, and subject to taxation and forced labor by a frequently venal administration.

The struggles with European rivals over colonial territorial demarcation redefined Portuguese nationalism, placing "colonialism firmly at the center of nationalist discourse for nearly a century" and engendering "the idea that every portion of national territory was sacred."[7] The authoritarian character of the Portuguese state as the first hints of decolonization appeared is yet another distinguishing feature; democratic institutions put in place by other major colonial occupants gave an entirely different dynamic to the end of empire.

Thus, while the pressures for African independence had become tangible elsewhere by 1950, Portugal moved to tighten its hold. In 1951, the empire was once again defined as a global polity, with the African (and Asian) territories reinscribed as "overseas provinces." All African subjects were decreed citizens in 1961, a status that in the authoritarian corporatism of Salazar's Estado Novo granted few political rights, with forced labor remaining a quotidian reality on the ground. And there were no inconvenient implications of an overseas majority in representative institutions. As the wars for independence broke out in the African territories in 1961, Salazar defiantly insisted: "We will not sell, we will not cede, we will not surrender, we will not share . . . the smallest item of our sovereignty."[8]

Ironically, only in the last two colonial decades did the African territories, especially Angola and Mozambique, begin to prosper economically. Salazar abandoned the closed imperial system and allowed in a flow of foreign capital. In Angola, the European population, still only 44,000 in 1940, had risen to 335,000 by the end of the colonial era, and to 200,000 in Mozambique. Oil production began in Angola in the late 1950s; diamond and coffee production soared. In Mozambique, cotton prices were at historic highs for much of this period, and South Africa paid a gold bounty for each Mozambican worker recruited for the mines.

Although the circumscribed educational opportunities restricted the size of African elites, a significant mestizo intelligentsia existed by the post-war years. Especially in Angola, Protestant mission education supplied future nationalist leadership. By the 1950s, currents of anti-colonial, nationalist doctrine elsewhere stirred aspirations in the Portuguese territories. The autocratic cast of the Portuguese state inhibited its open expression, but unrest percolated in small discussion groups, especially in the colonial capitals. Only the clandestine Far Left offered comradeship, and their ideological currents, radical socialist and Marxist-Leninist, flowed into emergent nationalist thought. Its revolutionary and multiracial cast attracted many mestizos and Indians as well as some radical whites. As they watched other African territories win independence, their frustration grew; the Portuguese dictatorship permitted no open challenge to colonial rule.

Left with no other alternative, armed liberation movements initiated uprisings that began in 1961 in Angola and spread to Guinea-Bissau in 1962 and Mozambique in 1964. The offshore isolation of the island colonies, Cape Verde and São Tomé, precluded revolt, though Verdean intellectuals, led by Amilcar Cabral, played a leading role in the Guinea-Bissau insurrection. Portugal responded only with reforms aimed at full integration of the overseas provinces, and with military force. By the early 1970s, the Portuguese had deployed 340,000 troops in the African territories, two-thirds of them African. A bitter array of guerrilla wars endured for thirteen years.

Although intellectuals supplied the top leadership, the circumstances of protracted guerrilla war compelled nationalist mobilization to follow a very different strategy from those that had succeeded in other parts of Africa. Portuguese security forces could maintain a firm grip on the major cities, and could count on the loyalty of many customary rulers; success in guerrilla struggle rested upon a capacity to persuade rural populations to join in risky combat, whose costs they would bear. In Guinea-Bissau, where Portuguese colonial occupation was weakest, insurgents had mostly confined the security forces to urban garrisons by the late 1960s and had created extensive "liberated zones" providing some basic services. The Mozambique liberation movement, the Frente de Libertação de Moçambique (FRELIMO), became increasingly unified and effective, eventually winning control of much of the north. In Angola, the struggle was hampered by competition among three sharply divided insurgent groups. Portuguese occupation was densest there, and the insurgency was at impasse when the 1974 coup suddenly transformed the situation.[9]

As time went by, although the warfare was of low intensity, Portugal tested the limits of the ability of a small state to resist the "end of empire" currents then flowing so powerfully in world politics. On the European front, Portugal had long neutralized Western pressures in support of staged decolonization through its charter membership in the North Atlantic Treaty Organization (NATO) from 1949. Lisbon skillfully used the strategic value of its Azores bases to deflect American pressure for change. But this shield had no value in the UN and other international forums, where Portugal increasingly became a target. In addition, colonial warfare and autocratic governance barred Portugal's entry to the European Community.

The deepening isolation of Portugal took its toll. But the imperial will also rotted from within as the wars became interminable. The army relied on conscript soldiers, with service obligations extending to four years; tens of thousands immigrated to France to escape the draft. The rank and file in Africa grew demoralized as the fighting continued with no end in sight. Over time, their disaffection seeped into the officer corps, setting the stage for the April 1974 military coup that destroyed the Estado Novo.

Although some coup leaders imagined that new and different overseas links might be retained, such an outcome held no appeal for the guerrilla movements. Portugal itself was soon consumed by ideological cleavage within both the junta and society at large. The transition to democracy promised for Portugal consumed metropolitan energies in the period that followed.

Meanwhile, the new junta quickly validated Guinea-Bissau's independence. In Mozambique, FRELIMO's ascendancy was well established, though resisted by many European and some Indian settlers; despite some transitional frictions, independence followed in June 1975. Cape Verde and São Tomé, though not scenes of guerrilla action, had dominant nationalist movements that could inherit sovereignty the same year, though in the latter case, the leadership had lived abroad for many years.

Angola, however, was a different story, with post-colonial disaster awaiting. The three competing movements, the Movimento para a Libertação de Angola (MPLA), the Frente Nacional para a Libertação de Angola (FNLA), and the União para Independência Total de Angola (UNITA), each had zones of ethno-regional support. Their rivalry was complicated by the importation of the Cold War; each movement had external allies and patrons (the Soviet Union and Cuba for the MPLA, Congo-Kinshasa and the United States for the FNLA, Zambia and South Africa for UNITA). The swiftly weakening Portuguese administration sought to broker a transitional coalition regime, as did the Organization of African Unity. But these efforts foundered on the deep mutual distrust of the movements. Arms began to flow in from outside sponsors, followed by external combatants and operatives (Cuban, Soviet, American, South African, Congolese), and by March 1975 civil war had broken out in Luanda. On 11 November 1975, in a forlorn end to its African empire, the last Portuguese governor simply announced that he was turning power over to "the Angolan people," boarded a waiting ship, and sailed away.

THE COMPARATIVE SCRUTINY of these three cases of outsized empires under the sovereignty of small, relatively weak states suggests several concluding observations. Riding with the tides of the times and adjusting to a changing international normative order seemed beyond the steering capacity of these polities. Empire, even though reluctantly assumed by Belgium, tended to find inscription in the inner recesses of national identity. The colonies acted as a transformative elixir dissolving the constraints of smallness in a world dominated by the large and powerful. The official mind, as well as the public at large, was mesmerized by the self-justifying promotional information diffused by colonial information offices.

In the post-war era, the rapidly changing international environment for empire subjected all remaining colonizers to substantial pressures. Up until the Second World War, colonial holdings were a wholly legitimate form of rule in dominant international society, subject only to ethical limits on the scope of coercion. Professions of benevolent intent toward the subject populace, unless flagrantly contradicted, sufficed to meet the legitimation imperative.

After the war, the international normative order evolved swiftly. For the three small states under review, once the loss of empire seemed inevitable, each sought some formula for organic post-colonial ties, though none succeeded. The Dutch lost all their Indonesian holdings, as well as residential rights for their citizens. In both the Belgian and Portuguese cases, the disorderly circumstances of independence led to the massive exodus of large settler populations, many abandoning possessions and property in panicked flight. Though Belgium became a significant external partner for Congo-Kinshasa over time, the relationship remains ambivalent and marked by episodes of tension. Portugal is only a minor player in post-colonial Lusophone Africa.

Decolonization almost invariably is a traumatic moment for the withdrawing occupant. But the trauma is even greater for a small state condemned to a diminished role in the world through the loss of empire. The therapy of time only slowly eases the attendant pain and humiliation.

Fall Semester 2010

1. Arend Lijphart, *The Trauma of Decolonization: The Dutch and West New Guinea* (New Haven, 1966), p. 285.

2. Quoted in Pierre de Vos, *La decolonization: Les évenéments du Congo de 1959 à 1967* (Brussels, 1975), p. 24.

3. Patrice Lumumba, *Le Congo, terre d'avenir, est-il menacé* (Brussels, 1961).

4. Cited in Jean Stengers, "Precipitous Decolonization: The Case of the Belgian Congo," in Prosser Gifford and Wm. Roger Louis, eds., *The Transfer of Power in Africa: Decolonization, 1940–1960* (New Haven, 1982), p. 314.

5. Quoted in de Vos, *La decolonization*, p. 33.

6. Thomas Kanza, *Conflict in the Congo* (Harmondsworth, 1972), p. 32.

7. Gervaise Clarence-Smith, *The Third Portuguese Empire, 1925–1975: A Study of Economic Imperialism* (Manchester, 1975), p. 83.

8. Quoted in Basil Davidson, "Portuguese-Speaking Africa," in Michael Crowder, ed., *Cambridge History of Africa*, Vol. 8, *From c. 1940 to c. 1975* (Cambridge, 1984), p. 760.

9. Among many sources, let me note Patrick Chabal, *A History of Postcolonial Lusophone Africa* (Bloomington, 2002); Allen Isaacman and Barbara Isaacman, *Mozambique: From Colonialism to Revolution, 1900–1982* (Boulder, Colo., 1983); René Pelissier, *La colonie du mintaure: Nationalismes et révolte en Angola, 1928–1961* (Montaments, France, 1978).

17

Life in the Zambian Copperbelt

JOHN BERRY

My late wife and I arrived in Zambia in mid-1966, twenty months after independence and eight months after Zambia had become a republic. I had returned home to England, after five years in the United States, with an American wife, a master's degree, two dollars, and tuppence in my pocket. After a determined effort, I had received three job offers, two in the UK paying £1,200 ($3,400) annually, which was about 40 percent of the going rate in America, and one in Zambia paying £1,325, but offering a house and furniture at a low rent, plus free round trips to Europe every three years and what seemed like a lot of vacation: fifty-five calendar days a year. I took a walk with my father, one of those "significant" parental interactions you remember for the rest of your life, and asked him how my wife and I could survive as a married couple in the UK on the salary offered. "Well, son, you can't." "But Dad, what do other people do?" "We-e-ell, Barnard made the down payment on his children's house, and Peterson pays the mortgage for his son-in-law," etc. "Well, Dad, would you do anything like that for us?" "Not b****y likely!"

Until independence, new employees of the Rhodesian Anglo American Corporation took a leisurely journey to Northern Rhodesia: a P&O liner to Cape Town, and then rail to the Copperbelt—the theory being that by the time they arrived, they had begun becoming acquainted with Africa. We flew out, and were thus from the beginning members of the despised class of "VC10-ers," newbies who had arrived since independence. After a brief stay at the ultramodern Edinburgh Hotel, where we ate crayfish meunière and steak for a week at about two dollars a meal, we were moved to The Gulch, a semicircle of semidetached bungalows where Zambian Anglo Mine Services placed its new employees until permanent housing became available.

Our next-door neighbor on one side was a Scottish lady, Mrs. Harvey, who refused on principle to employ any African servants. Her husband was an ineffective Old Etonian stuck in a minor administrative post at the mine. On the other side were the Davises, a young Orthodox Jewish couple from Johannesburg who had moved to Zambia because Rob was sure that he was being followed by the South African secret police because of his liberal political activities. They kept strict kosher, and when an implement got used for the wrong thing, Shelley buried it in the backyard. The house servant would promptly dig it up and return it to service, and when we suggested to him that this might not be a good thing to do, he put his finger to his lips and replied, "Bwana, what the donna does not know will not harm her!" Also in the close were Curt and Rosemarie Niggli, from Switzerland. He had been the previous geologist to come out, the last by boat, and they had been held up for a week in Rhodesia because the train had hit an elephant near Victoria Falls.

On our first night in Kitwe, we were invited to a *braai* (*braaivleis*, or barbeque) by my boss, Dr. Peter "Bwana Kalulu" Freeman. Pete had grown up on Williamson's Diamond Mine in Tanganyika. He was a short, energetic, and enthusiastic person who literally ran across outcrops in the field exclaiming continually, "Man, look at this!" Hence his African nickname of Bwana Rabbit. He had gotten his PhD at McGill, where he had married a rather stunning French Canadian, Thérèse. This was a farewell party for my predecessor, Dave Abraham.

The next morning, a Saturday, Dave drove me out to the West Limb of the Nkana Syncline, introduced me to the crew of Africans who would be working for me, and showed me a selection of the prospect pits that I would spend the next few years going down and describing. He explained a little about the local geology, and that was it—on Monday morning, I was on my own, with a couple hundred pits to log, 30 Africans to supervise, and total responsibility for a camp containing them and their families, about 150 people in all.

THE PROSPECT PITS WERE TWO FEET THREE INCHES in diameter, just large enough for my shoulders (fig. 17.1), and, in this area, as much as 60 feet deep. One I examined at Kansanshi, 150 miles west of the

Copperbelt, was 105 feet deep: not good, since the maximum legal depth was 65 feet and the inspector of mines was with me at the time. The pits were unlined: tropical soils will support themselves indefinitely as long as the opening is small and protected from running water. Each geologist had to log—describe the geology, make a cross-sectional drawing, and mark off sample intervals—at least eight pits a day. There were hundreds, maybe thousands, of pits in each project area: they were dug 25–50 feet apart on lines 500 feet apart. To log a pit, you were slowly lowered by five laborers on a one-inch rope that passed over a small pulley at the top of the pit. You sat on a ten-by-sixteen-inch plank supported by a knot in the end of the rope. The sampler, an African, followed later on a similar rig, scooping the dirt from each defined interval into a paper packet that was later sent for analysis for copper, cobalt, zinc, and lead.

If the results were encouraging, we then dug tunnels, about three feet high and two feet wide, between the pits in order to get more accurate information. You logged these crosscuts by wriggling through on your side. Again the sampler followed (fig. 17.2). Logging crosscuts was a mildly unpleasant business: snakes and other creatures regularly fell into the pits, and if there were a crosscut at the bottom, they could hide there. As you descended the pit, your body and face were progressively exposed to whatever was in the crosscut before you could actually see into it. Remnants of the mystique of the white man still survived from the colonial period, and it was absolutely vital not to show any sign of concern, much less fear, in these kinds of situations.

The other big hazard with pitting was gas, which seeped from the soil near certain termite (*Macrotermes* spp.) mounds, and was of two kinds, carbon dioxide and formic acid vapor. The former was rarely dangerous, since there was time to quickly finish the logging and be hauled back to the surface. But the first breath of the latter would make you dizzy, and the second render you unconscious. If you passed out in the pit, your head would slump against the wall, and then you would be jammed and impossible to pull out—therefore, rather quickly dead. Fortunately, the odor was so distinctive that no one ever actually died: the laborers knew that if you yelled "*bamwolo steric*" ("up, fast"), you were to be got out instantly.

This tedious and labor-intensive method of prospecting and geologic mapping was necessary because there are few rock outcrops in the Copperbelt. In the humid tropics, erosion is slow but chemical weathering is fast, with the result that the soil is up to sixty feet thick and the rocks are weathered soft down to about four hundred feet below surface. Therefore, you have to dig to reach anything that can be mapped or sampled. The pits were dug by hand because a rotary drill smears the inside wall of the borehole to a depth of several inches, whereas hand digging leaves the rocks and all their details pristinely exposed.

It took two men to dig a pit. The main tool was a heavy six-foot-long spear made from one of the drill steels used underground. Each end of this very tough tungsten-steel bar was hammered flat to make a sharp blade about a foot long and three inches wide. The other tools were a bricky's bucket (it has vertical sides) and a shovel with the handle cut off. The digger stabbed the steel blade into the bottom of the pit as he moved around barefoot in a tight circle (remember, his feet cover a quarter of the bottom of the pit). When he called "*bakati pansi,*" his partner lowered the bucket with the shovel inside. The digger filled the bucket, yelled "*bakati bamwolo,*" and resumed digging. The limitation on how fast they could dig was not the digger; it was how fast the bucket could be hauled up and down. Regulations said that the digger had to wear steel-toed mine boots, but to a man they refused—without boots, they could shinny in and out of the holes with ease; with them, it was hard if not impossible.

THE "BOSS-BOY" (A TERM THAT DIED SLOWLY) and the sampler had to be numerate and literate, and were paid as much as 60 kwacha (Kw) a month (almost $100). The unskilled laborers who hauled the geologist and sampler up were paid Kw1.00 a day ($42 a month). The pitters were paid an ngwee (a penny) a foot times their daily average footage: if they averaged the minimum of 11 feet a day, they got 11 ngwee a foot times 11 feet a day, or Kw1.21 a day. The overall average was about 17 feet a day (equal to 289 ngwee, or Kw2.89, or $3.95 per day [$103 per month], which was not far from the U.S. minimum wage at the time), and in good months or easy conditions, they could reach 25 feet a day (Kw6.25, or $8.75, a day, for $227.50 a month).

The workmen had few expenses, since the system was completely paternalistic. Before we started a job, we selected a site and laid out a camp consisting of a square of rectangular houses facing onto a large open space: the surveying constituted lesson one in industrial culture for the new men. One side of the square would have the geologists' and boss-boy's offices and a storeroom. The houses were built by the men themselves, and were made of wattle and daub with thatched roofs and packed dirt floors. Each was initially about twelve feet by twenty feet, with a central front door facing the square and two window openings, one either side of the door. The houses tended to grow through time as families expanded, and were really only for sleeping and storage: cooking was done outside in a charcoal stove or a clay fire pit, and bathing and laundry were done at the local creek—one of the essential requirements for siting a camp was that there be a suitable creek adjacent to it. Besides the cooking and laundry, the wives had gardens where they grew peanuts, rape, tomatoes, and various squashes. These *shambas* looked like nothing so much as graveyards, since they consisted of arrays of raised beds, each about eight feet by three feet, separated by narrow walkways. My favorite lunch was a large handful of freshly dug peanuts bought from a bowl balanced on the head of a woman passing by and then roasted in their shells on a small fire of dried grass stems.

Every payday (biweekly on Saturday mornings), we would fill one or two Land Rovers with everyone who wanted to go to town. Once a month, everyone would go to the flour mill to buy a two-hundred-pound sack of white maize flour (mealy meal), which, in the form of a porridge (*sadza* or *nshima*), was the staple diet. If someone became sick (and I had cases of kwashiorkor—severe malnutrition due to protein deficiency—leprosy, and elephantiasis in my camps at one time or another), we would take him (or her) to the doctor or hospital, which was usually free. If a workman was terminally ill, it was occasionally I who would have to find a way to tell him. If a close relative died, we often had to make an advance on the workman's pay to take care of funeral expenses. And, of course, there were several occasions when either I or the boss-boy had to bail people out of jail on the morning after payday.

We expatriates lived under the same paternalistic system: I have already mentioned that our fares home were paid at the end of each three-year contract and that we were provided a house and "hard furniture" for a nominal rent (£4 10s. ($6.30) and £5 ($7.00) a month respectively). The downside of the housing arrangement was that our contracts specified that "in consideration of the allowance for hard furniture we were to hold ourselves ready for transfer anywhere in Africa at 24 hours' notice." They meant it, too: while on a visit to Johannesburg, I nearly got transferred to Oranjemund in Namibia without even an opportunity to go home to Kitwe to pack our belongings! I was eventually to discover that although every expat got the furniture allowance, only the geologists had this clause in their contracts. We also had free medical care, provided by the Mine Hospital, a good pension scheme, and our retirement age was fifty-nine and a half. The company's policy was one of lifetime employment, even though our contracts were for only three years (that was a post-independence innovation). I, and I think most others, thrived under this system. It left us free to do our jobs and follow our hobbies without having to worry too much about the future or even the details of the present.

WHEREAS MUCH OF THE MINE LABOR force was second, even third generation, and had at least a sixth-grade education, my camp was the first stop on the route from the village to the money economy. Workers from many tribes coexisted in camp, which was thus also the first step in the proletarianization of these subsistence farmers, since many aspects of their native cultures were quickly lost. In particular, dietary customs were abandoned: the family of Lasson, one of my pitters, for example, ate nothing but mealy meal, and their children drank nothing but Fanta. This is typical, actually, of uprooted people of any ethnicity in the early stages of urbanization: my mother had to deal with people in Liverpool during the 1930s who ate nothing but bread-and-cheese sandwiches. Naturally, Lasson's children got very sick with kwashiorkor.

Aliki, my night watchman, a fifty-nine-year-old Second World War veteran, met Lasson's sick daughter Mary coming home in tears from the village one day. On inquiring, he found that she had dropped the bottle of oil ("salad") that she had been sent to buy. Aliki gave her a susu (a dime) to buy a replacement. Lasson later sued Aliki in the Local (formerly "Native") Court for trying to kill his children by witchcraft. He was successful, and I had to lend Aliki six dollars to pay the fine. The court's reasoning was that the children must have been sickened by witchery, and the witch must have been Aliki, since he was entirely unrelated to the child, therefore his only reason to be kind to her was to gain power over her, and also he was so old that he should have been dead by now anyway. Witchcraft was most definitely practiced in my camp: I came upon the remains of a major ceremony on a visit early one Sunday morning. From the evidence of the pregnant clay figurines and those that were stuck with thorns and then smashed, the practices seemed to be very similar to those of European witchcraft.

My last camp in Zambia was near Bwana Mkubwa, on the Zairean border in the north-central part of the country, in 1971–2. There was very little surface water in this area, so we were constrained to be on the same stream as, but a few hundred yards downstream from, a rather large African village. The result was that our water supply was highly contaminated with fecal and typhoid bacteria, and we had to both filter and boil all we used. Another result was that cooking was a near impossibility—as soon as food was opened, a swarm of flies from the village descended on us with a buzz we could hear from two hundred yards away. I was forced to eat mostly the German tins of fish that are sealed with a rubber ring: you boil the can, pop off the ring, and inhale the contents. We never even bothered with building a kitchen! But there was more abundant native food here than at any other camp: one morning I woke up to find the camp eerily silent—no men, no children, and no dogs. Only Samson, my watchman: "*Ayy, Samson, amabantu ili kwi?* Where is everybody—are they on strike?" "*Ahwi, Bwana, azikulo indaba,* no problem. They have taken the *imbwe,* the dogs, to look for mushrooms." These turned out to be truffles that grow in cavities in the large anthills and are harvested just a few days each year. I insisted on my share!

This camp was not far from the Tug Argan Barracks of the Fourth Battalion, Zambia Regiment. Tug Argan was a battle in a disastrous campaign in Somaliland in the Second World War in which the Northern Rhodesia Rifles distinguished themselves very well. Aliki had been there, but he was like most old soldiers in that I could never get him to talk about his experiences. The Ore Formation went right through the army's firing range, and we used to take a gunnery sergeant along for protection when we were digging or logging pits. Which was fine until the day we all got mortared. After that, I negotiated for a captain, and we never had any more confusion.

When I got really ill with malaria, I would go over to the barracks and the Zambian military doctor there would give me a shot in the butt that I don't want to think about even now, and a Camoquin pill that was designed for horses, and the whole thing would be over by morning. He was a wonderful chap, trained in Moscow and Edinburgh. All the officers were great company, but I hated to go over to their mess because it ran on the chit system, and there was no way I could reciprocate for the drinks they insisted on buying me.

It was they who told me that, with only 4,000 men (four battalions of 1,000 men each), stationed in three different places (Lusaka, Kabwe, Tug Argan, and the fourth battalion on patrol), they had lost control of some rather large areas where there were major camps of the Mozambican, Angolan, and Zimbabwean rebel movements. These had up to 2,000 guerillas in each camp, and there was an incident in which the geologist for the King Edward Mine south of Lusaka stumbled into one and was badly beaten. Perhaps this situation accounts for the fact that at the time when President Kenneth Kaunda, known as KK, was most rancorously preaching against Richard Nixon and Ted Heath, whom he felt had seriously snubbed him in October 1970, there were some strange incidents apparently involving the CIA. These included one in early 1971 in which Zambian border guards enticed their Mozambican colleagues over the border for a cigarette, and then promptly put them in handcuffs. They were taken to Lusaka, where they were apparently interrogated by Americans, according to my Goanese colleague Terence Faria, whose Portuguese-speaking uncle was called in to interpret for the Americans. Strange, if true.

I NEVER CEASED TO BE AMAZED BY KITWE, which neither my wife nor I had heard of before we arrived in Zambia. Here was a pleasant town of 100,000 people, of whom 15,000 were expatriates and the rest Africans. But the invention of the transistor radio, and the political mobilization leading to independence, had made every resident in the bush aware of the advantages of living in the money economy, and by 1968 people had begun to pour in from the bush to live in hastily erected shantytowns around the city's periphery, pushing the population to 250,000 by 1975.

The town had a bustling downtown with all the shops one could need, a couple of good hotels, two hospitals, good schools, and several very nice parks (fig. 17.3). There was a very good library, an excellent Little Theater, rugby clubs, golf courses, and a flying club. It seemed impossible to me, who had grown up in a rather dreary 1,300-year-old town of the same size in England, that until a few years before I was born, there had been nothing at Kitwe but tsetse-fly-ridden malarial bush. Kitwe itself was founded in 1936, although Nkana, the mine township across the railway tracks, went back all the way to 1932.

There were five other towns on the Copperbelt, including Ndola, which was as big as Kitwe. Altogether half a million people lived and worked on the Copperbelt, of whom almost all the Europeans and Indians were expats, and about 70 percent of the Africans were migrants, mostly from other parts of Zambia, but also from Zaire (Democratic Republic of the Congo), Rhodesia (Zimbabwe), and Malawi.

Probably close to a majority of the expats were of South African or Rhodesian origin, which meant there was a lot of racism: you had to be just as careful not to earn the reputation among your colleagues of being a *Kaffir-boetie* (Afrikaans for "Kaffir brother," or a white person who fraternized with blacks) as you did not to offend the wrong Zambian, which could get you deported overnight.

Then there were the Scots, who had an active Burns Society: the Burns Dinner would seat at least 300 people. Then came the English and Welsh, with the Irish in a distant fourth place. There were also a large number of Indians in Kitwe: they tended to run millinery shops and clothing stores, but the local photographer was

Indian as well. And the railway was beginning to hire the less expensive Indians rather than Europeans. Then there were a thousand Italians, followed by Greeks, many of whom ran grocery stores and restaurants. Among professionals there were a large number of Dutch (the majority of the geologists in fact), with a few Swiss and French. Then there were significant numbers of Canadians and a few Americans.

Most of our social life was either with the Little Theater or the Sporting Club of Nkana, aka the Italian Club. On our first visit to the theater, I ordered drinks from the bar, and a large, very overweight and ugly character sitting there remarked loudly, "Ah, Gott, not another bleddy Pongo (Englishman)!" The theater put on several plays each year, including musicals, and I remember their version of *Oliver!* as the best I have seen. The company competed annually at a festival in London, and often won. In the pantomime *Jack and the Beanstalk* in 1967, the large ugly character, Guy Hobbes, played the Widow Twankie, Jack's mother, and his obligatory striptease was a sight to see! I was one of two knockabout comics: the other was Dave Pownall, a personnel officer at the mine who has gone on to write hundreds of stage and television plays and to win various prizes on both sides of the Atlantic.

Thus Zambia provided a welcoming environment for many artistically inclined Britons: they could have a secure job with a paternalistic employer, a good salary, and little pressure to do overtime. Daily chores were taken care of by a gardener and a house servant at minimal expense. One chief geologist (Carl Mason) published books of poems and short stories, and the wildlife artist David Shepherd lived in Zambia. There were many other aspiring actors, artists, musicians, and photographers, most of whom did not succeed. But the cultural environment may be deduced from the successes of their children born in Zambia: the novelist Wilbur Smith, the architect Denise Scott Brown, the sculptor Tawny Gray, and various actresses (Thandie Newton, Julia Rose), singers (Rozalla), and sportsmen, including two Welsh international and three Springbok (South African) international rugby players.

The Italian Club, which was just down the road from the theater, held regular dances with live music as well as a running game of bocci. Many of the Italians in Kitwe were self-employed small businessmen. They tended to own the mechanics and the artisan businesses. Most had served in Somalia and never gone home to Italy. A typical example was Libero Zappia, a Calabrian who had drifted down through Kenya and Tanzania to Kitwe, where he owned the appliance and television shop. An American Franciscan priest, the man charged with translating the Bible into ChiKaonde, was also a habitué of the club. Father Ralph would drive in on the weekend from Mwinilunga, 300 miles of treacherous dirt road away, and after the band went home, he would bring out his huge accordion, on which he could play seemingly any song known to man, and start singing.

The headquarters of the Zambian Anglo Mine Services was a fine modern building called Mutondo House, but the Geology Department was banished to the third floor of a building in Kitwe's main square, Coronation Square (renamed Independence Square), since our muddy boots and dirty overalls were felt to be out of place in the executive suites. The ground floor of our building was occupied by the Place Pigalle Bar, owned by Madame Fufu, a Belgian lady from the Congo. On the two floors above this, she operated a rather discreet though garish bordello. She sold out to our draughtsman, a Dutchman, in 1967. Jan Plankman closed the bordello, but kept the Pigalle going, managing alcohol deliveries by yelling out the open window behind his drafting table. The next I heard of Madame Fufu was in 1983, when the Nevada newspapers reported that the federal government was trying to extradite her as an undesirable immigrant because she ran the best little whorehouse in Winnemucca. The state government had gone to bat for her on the grounds that what she was doing was perfectly legal in Nevada.

There was a serious riot two weeks after we arrived in 1966. Zambia had partially closed the border with Rhodesia because of the Unilateral Declaration of Independence, and that meant that everything that had come in or gone out by rail, including fuel and copper, now had to go by truck to Dar es Salaam, in Tanzania, along 1,500 miles of dirt road known as the "Hell Run." This required a huge fleet of trucks, for which drivers were recruited from all over southern Africa and Europe, but it also meant that we had a gasoline ration of ten imperial gallons a month. Much of the fuel arrived in fifty-five-gallon drums, which then had to be pumped by hand into the big storage tanks at the Kitwe fuel depot. One Sunday morning, someone was smoking as he pumped, and the depot caught fire. On one side of the fire, a heroic crew of Africans rushed practically into the flames to roll the drums away to safety. But on the other side of the fire, where the African townships were, agitators from the United National Independence Party (UNIP, the ruling party) were proclaiming that the fire had been started by racists from the south and that all Europeans were racists and should be killed. They started stoning cars on the Chingola Road, and a young pregnant lady from Chingola was killed. After this incident, our gasoline ration was eight gallons a month until late in 1968, when the Tazama pipeline from Dar es Salaam was completed.

ALTHOUGH THE COPPERBELT TOWNS are young, the flowering (if that is the right word) in the last thirty years of a modern industrial complex in the heart of Africa was the outcome of a much longer process.

The Copperbelt has, of course, a long pre-European mining history, although the mines in Katanga, across the Congolese border, were the most extensively worked, because they had very prominent green malachite outcroppings. The level of skill was very high: at Kansanshi and Bwana Mkubwa, the miners removed the hard copper-bearing vein material and absolutely nothing else. They sometimes went down 200 feet: only the presence of water stopped them, because they didn't have pumps. The copper was smelted and traded across Africa in the form of cast-copper crosses.

It was thirty-three years from Livingstone's first traverse of Barotseland in 1851 until the first European missionaries went to live in Northern Rhodesia and the first adventurers arrived in the Congo Free State to the north (1884). From then, it took only seventeen more years for the boundaries of the country, this last fragment of unknown Africa, to be decided in a series of treaties (to 1901), and for the first large-scale prospecting expedition, led by an American (the Burnham Expedition, 1895–6), to come back with reports of great mineral wealth.

There was another gap, of thirty-five years, from the Burnham Expedition to the opening of the first big mines in 1930. In 1895, technology for the profitable treatment of sulfide ores did not exist, and neither did the necessary financial resources. By 1930, the technology was there, and Johannesburg had the financial muscle, but the Great Depression delayed the start of large-scale copper production until the mid-1930s.

ZAMBIA'S RELATIVE POLITICAL SUCCESS since independence is partly accounted for by the experience that African leaders gained in the trade-union movement in the mines. The first African strike in the mines was in 1935, when only the Roan and the Nkana had reached production. This early industrial activism was in large part due to two things: first, much of the early Copperbelt labor force had had previous experience working in the mines of Katanga, Southern Rhodesia, and even South Africa. Second, the Jehovah's Witnesses had established an early presence in South Africa, brought by black preachers from the United States, and the movement had there

developed both educational institutions and an indigenous leadership that was, to some extent, anti-European (i.e., anti-white). From
there the movement spread northward to Nyasaland (Malawi) and
northeastern Rhodesia (eastern Zambia), where it became known
as the Watchtower sect and was very successful. Many early miners,
among them the most literate, who were clerks and shift bosses,
were members of the Watchtower sect and were politically and economically savvy. By the time I arrived in Zambia, the Watchtower,
though active, had been much reduced in power and membership
by the independence struggle, because of its members' refusals to
join political parties or to pledge allegiance. It remains to this day a
large and persecuted minority in Malawi.

The high pay of the European miners had been a sore point
with the Africans since the middle of the Second World War, when
they began to realize that many of them were smarter and harder-
working than the whites, even though the whites were paid seven
or eight times as much as they were. This realization was another
major driver of the development of African unionism, which in turn
led to the development and efficient organization of political movements for independence in the 1950s.

For a short time in the 1950s, a set of very farsighted leaders in
both the African and European mineworkers unions negotiated to
join forces against the mining companies, but this foundered because of racism among whites and distrust of whites by blacks. It
is fascinating to think what the future of Zambia would have been
if real interracial cooperation had flourished during the period of
Federation.

At the time of independence, the African Mineworkers Union insisted that a commission, the Brown Commission, be sent out from
Britain to determine a fair, nonracial wage scale. In 1966, the commission recommended an across-the-board increase of 22 percent
for African mineworkers and the abolition of racially based pay
scales. By 1970, expats and Africans were essentially on the same
wage scale, which was close to the British level. Both groups also
had free health care and dental care, essentially free housing, free
sporting and recreational facilities, and free schooling. As in segre-
gated states in America, the levels at which these services were provided were vastly different, meaning that the racially based income
difference in effect remained. The African townships were crowded,
barrack-like rows of little concrete cottages, two or three rooms at
most, and unheated. Europeans had housing that was similar to
housing in Canada or America, but much better than they could
have afforded in those countries. Even so, white South Africans by

1966 were leaving in droves rather than live under a black government: they were being replaced by southern Europeans and, on the railway, Indians. The lowest wages in the mines were Kw45 ($63 a month) before 1966, Kw55 ($77 a month) afterward. Skilled African workers earned $200 and $240 a month before and after, and supervisors $315 and $385.

By 1966, copper prices were beginning to boom, and the future of independent Zambia looked rosy. But geological conditions meant that most Zambian mines were high-cost underground mines. So when commodity prices worldwide dropped steeply in 1974, the Zambian mines quickly became economically unfeasible. But 51 percent of the mines had been nationalized in 1969 (the Mulungushi economic reforms, under which the insurance companies and savings and loans were also nationalized), and as part of the settlement, the mining companies were allowed to export their profits, which before had been prevented from doing by exchange controls. By 1974, the "evil" capitalists had got their money out and invested heavily in North America: Anglo had bought Hudson Bay Mining in Canada and Inspiration Copper in the United States.

By 1971, the political situation in Zambia, as well as conditions of racial harmony and levels of public health, were all beginning to deteriorate. Our small-businessman friends were becoming more and more nervous as the state increasingly sought to control the economy: I remember one occasion when people were lighting cigarettes with Kw10 bills, which could have got them deported. There was constant talk in the government and party press of Rhodesian and South African spy rings and saboteurs in Zambia, and this was having a negative effect on behavior toward whites in general. It was clear that Kaunda was drifting toward dictatorship, and in 1972 the Chona Commission gave him the green light to declare a one-party state. This caused a lot of resentment and anger among those who supported multiparty politics, leading to a string of treason trials, beginning with the prosecution of John Njapau, a former Member of Parliament for Mwinilunga, who was accused of leading a movement to carve a revived Lunda Empire out of northwestern Zambia, northeastern Angola, and southern Zaire. In 1972, the management contracts between the mining companies and the government were terminated: this was, in effect, the complete nationalization of the mines. Fortunately, by then we had just left.

Northern Rhodesia had been a sort of Camelot for a fairly cultured and cosmopolitan society of expatriates, many of whom took advantage of their privileged economic position to indulge heavily in cultural and sporting activities. There were few changes in the first six years after Zambian independence that made a serious difference to this life of privilege as far as employed expatriates were concerned, but more changes that affected small businessmen. This corner of the Empire thus remained an idyllic spot for expats until 1972, after which conditions rapidly deteriorated because of the institution of a one-party state, the nationalization of most big business, and, eventually, a serious deterioration in trade conditions.

Spring Semester 2010

Figure 17.1
Sampler in a prospect pit, Kawiri, Zambia, 1969. Photo by the author.

Figure 17.2
Mr. Chrishimba Chilufwe in a prospecting crosscut through the
Ore Shale, South Orebody Extension, Nkana, Zambia, 1970. Photo
by the author.

Figure 17.3
The north side of Makuta Avenue, Kitwe, 1967. One of the two supermarkets is on the left end; the butcher's shop is on the right end of the block. Photo by the author.

Figure 17.4
The author, *right*, preparing to log a prospect pit with his sampler, Edward Kamfolomo Mulenga, *left*, and the leader of his pit crew, Chrishimba, *center*. West Limb, Nkana Syncline, Zambia, 1960.

18

Margaret Thatcher and the End of the Cold War

ARCHIE BROWN

Margaret Thatcher played a part in the end of the Cold War quite different from what might have been predicted—by her, by her most committed supporters, or by her political enemies. Who would have imagined that she would form a political friendship and cordial relations with the General Secretary of the Central Committee of the Communist Party of the Soviet Union? Of course, when that General Secretary was Mikhail Gorbachev, this meant a Soviet leader very different from any of his predecessors. What made the relationship especially significant, particularly in the earliest years of the reformation of the Soviet Union—Gorbachev's perestroika—is that Margaret Thatcher was, of all Western leaders, the closest to the American President, Ronald Reagan.

When Thatcher became British Prime Minister in 1979, she had already taken a hard line on the communist world, and some of her political allies strengthened her suspicions of the British diplomatic service. Throughout her eleven years at 10 Downing Street, she retained a strong distrust of the Foreign Office. She thought its officials were too accommodating of communist regimes, even viewing the Foreign and Commonwealth Office (FCO), in the words of her Foreign Policy Adviser, Sir Percy Cradock, as a bunch of "defeatists, even collaborators."[1] She was in complete accord with Ronald Reagan's rhetorical attacks on the Soviet Union and communism, which were a feature especially of the first term of his presidency. Sir Rodric Braithwaite, who was British Ambassador to Moscow from 1988 to 1992, recalled in his memoir of British-Soviet relations that when it was suggested to Thatcher, early in her Prime Ministership (1980), that she might wish to be briefed by people from the Foreign Office with knowledge of the Soviet Union, she responded: "Foreign Office? Foreign Office? What do they know about Russia?"[2]

Thatcher's attitude to the FCO had been encouraged by some of her informal advisers, people such as Brian Crozier, who were obsessed with Soviet disinformation and the KGB and oblivious of the various undercurrents within the Communist Party of the Soviet Union. Crozier, on his own account, had frequent meetings with Thatcher both before she became Prime Minister and after. From the outset of Gorbachev's General Secretaryship, Crozier was among Thatcher's advisers who took the view that what was called "the new thinking" was another Soviet deception—"the most ambitious Soviet deception of all."[3] Even after the Soviet Union had ceased to exist, Crozier failed to understand how Gorbachev's thinking had evolved, especially during his time as Soviet leader. Crozier did not criticize Thatcher directly, but was clearly disappointed by her more nuanced view of developments in the Soviet Union in the second half of the 1980s, when she realized that Gorbachev was serious about making fundamental change to the system he had inherited.

Thatcher had other advisers on the communist world with a broader outlook than Crozier's, but what they had in common was extreme skepticism that anything good was likely to happen in the Soviet Union. They were brought together by Hugh Thomas (now Lord Thomas), and their meetings are discussed in a book by one of the participants, George Urban. Urban was a much more sophisticated analyst of communist countries than Crozier, but he is critical of the extent to which Thatcher came to identify with Gorbachev. He says: "I shared her respect for this untypical and personable Soviet leader . . . . Yet such was Margaret Thatcher's faith in Gorbachev that she was slow to recognize his vanishing support and his limitations as an engine of reform."[4] Percy Cradock, Thatcher's Foreign Policy Adviser from 1984 until her fall in 1990, went so far as to complain that she "was *dangerously* attached to Gorbachev in his domestic role" (italics added). From 1987 onward, he "found it harder to talk about Gorbachev with her entirely objectively."[5] The Soviet leader was becoming for Thatcher, Cradock argues, "something of an icon," and he believed that her judgment had become "flawed by personal sympathies."[6]

Crozier, Urban, and Cradock were mistaken. Thatcher's recognition that Gorbachev was a different kind of Soviet leader and that serious change was underway in the Soviet Union should be counted as her most valuable contribution to international politics. It was all the more important because she was able to bolster the belief of President Reagan in the possibility of change in the Soviet Union while helping to bring him round to the view that Gorbachev would be the principal agent of transformation. When she first entered 10 Downing Street, Thatcher was much more skeptical than the British Foreign Office about the desirability of engaging with the Soviet Union and of the prospects for change there. Before she left office, those positions had been reversed.

Rodric Braithwaite has reported that the Foreign Office was not very happy when, at Thatcher's instigation, Gorbachev made his third visit to Britain, in the spring of 1989. They had become warier than the Prime Minister of developments in the USSR and were worried that she was stoking "Gorbymania," which they feared had a hold on European public opinion.[7] What, then, led to Thatcher's change of mind, and of what consequence was it in the ending of the Cold War?

THE YEAR 1983 WAS A SIGNIFICANT ONE both for American policy toward the Soviet Union and for the start of a rethinking of British policy. The Cold War got so icy in that year that a nuclear war could have begun by accident. This was the year in which Reagan announced his Strategic Defense Initiative—his aim of developing an ambitious antimissile defense system (or "Star Wars," as it became popularly known). It was also the year—indeed, the same month (March)—in which he described the Soviet Union as an "evil empire," which was predictably ill received in Moscow. In fact, the Soviet leader at the time, Yuri Andropov (who had earlier headed the KGB for fifteen years), believed that Reagan was trying to prepare the American people psychologically for war. The Russians suspected that a NATO exercise being held in 1983 might even be a cover for a surprise nuclear strike on the Soviet Union.

The double agent Oleg Gordievsky, a colonel in the KGB based in the Soviet Embassy in London, was working for the British secret service, MI6. One of the most useful things he did for the cause of peace was to warn his British employers that in Moscow the threat of a Western attack on the Soviet Union was being taken seriously.[8] That was no joke, for if the Soviet leaders had become completely convinced that a Western surprise attack was in the offing, they would have been tempted to get their own surprise attack in first.

Another way in which nuclear war could have started accidentally was through the technological failure of early-warning systems. If they malfunctioned, suggesting that a nuclear attack was already underway, this could have led to a nuclear response. So, whatever our present discontents, we should not be nostalgic for the days of the Cold War. It was better than hot war, but it was an inherently dangerous state of affairs. What happened in 1983, following Gordievsky's warning, was that the NATO exercise was altered to make it absolutely plain that it could in no way be part of a preparation for a real attack by the West on the Soviet Union.

Many in the Reagan administration took the view that no genuine reformer could ever emerge as leader of the Soviet Union and that negotiations would be a waste of time. That was essentially the view of the CIA chief, Bill Casey, and of the Defense Department under Caspar Weinberger. The State Department, under George Shultz, had a more nuanced approach and a willingness to engage with its superpower rival. Shultz himself was influenced by Jack Matlock, the Soviet specialist on the National Security Council who subsequently became an outstanding American Ambassador to Moscow from 1987 to 1991. Reagan's speeches sent out mixed and inconsistent signals, but the policy of the State Department under Shultz's leadership—which met with much resistance within the administration—was that the United States should negotiate from strength, but it *should* seek to negotiate with the Soviet Union. Even in the first half of the 1980s, President Reagan, too, was not against having summit talks with Soviet leaders, but as he not unreasonably complained: "These guys keep dying on me." True enough, Leonid Brezhnev died in November 1982, age seventy-six; Yury Andropov died in February 1984, age sixty-nine; and just thirteen months later, Konstantin Chernenko died in March 1985, age seventy-three.

In Britain in 1983, there was alarm within the Foreign Office about the growing East-West polarization and the lack of dialogue, all of which increased the danger of confrontation. The problem for them was Thatcher's dismissive attitude toward the FCO, even though she made exceptions for some of its individual members who had served her well. Moreover, she was on particularly bad terms with the Foreign Secretary, Francis Pym. Thatcher had appointed him in April 1982, and in June 1983 she unceremoniously fired him. As Pym observed: "Whatever else may be said of it, my meeting with the Prime Minister on the evening of Friday, 10 June 1983 was brief and to the point. 'Francis', she said, 'I want a new Foreign Secretary'."[9] Pym had been concerned about the lack of East-West dialogue and was critical of Thatcher's decision not to attend Brezhnev's funeral the previous December. The new Foreign Secretary was someone who, at that time, was much more an ally of the Prime Minister, Sir Geoffrey Howe. He had, however, been Chancellor of the Exchequer hitherto, and while he was feeling his way into his new job, he was in no position to dominate British foreign policy. Indeed, given Thatcher's personality, he was not allowed to dominate it subsequently either. (Howe, of course, was to have the last word. It was his resignation from the government headed by Thatcher that triggered the crisis in the Conservative Cabinet and parliamentary party that led to her forced resignation in November 1990.)

The people who played an especially important role in persuading Thatcher that, given the international situation, it was time to take a fresh look at British foreign policy and, most specifically, at relations with the Soviet Union and Eastern Europe were her two senior advisers in 1983—her Private Secretary, John Coles (who, much later, as Sir John Coles became head of the British diplomatic service) and her Foreign Policy Adviser, Sir Anthony Parsons, who had been Britain's man at the UN. These advisers were themselves career diplomats from the Foreign Office, although once such people move to 10 Downing Street, their primary loyalty is to the Prime Minister. (Neither Coles nor Parsons, however, became anything like so inextricably linked with Thatcher as did Charles Powell, who succeeded Coles as Private Secretary in mid-1984.)

Coles and Parsons helped bring Thatcher to the view that it would be a good thing to hold a seminar on the Soviet Union and Eastern Europe and to reappraise Britain's relations with the communist bloc. That meeting, held at the Prime Minister's country residence, Chequers, on 8–9 September 1983, turned out to be highly significant. When, some years later, I asked Parsons how he would rate its importance, he said: "It changed British foreign policy." More recently, Sir Malcolm Rifkind, who in 1983 was the minister of state at the Foreign Office responsible for relations with the Soviet Union (later Foreign Secretary in John Major's government), told me that he agreed with that assessment.[10]

A lot of argument went into deciding the composition of the seminar participants. It had been agreed that they would be experts, but Thatcher was initially presented with a list of names of people from the Foreign Office. The Prime Minister was having none of that. She wrote on the suggested list:

> This is NOT the way I want it. I am not interested in gathering in every junior minister, or everyone who has ever dealt with the subject at the FO. The FO must do their preparation before. I want

also some people who have really studied Russia—the Russian mind—and who have had some experience of living there. More than half the people on the list know less than I do.[11]

The Foreign Office, for its part, was worried that if outsiders were invited, they would consist of some of the people who advised Thatcher in her political seminars, people like Crozier, whom they regarded as extremists. In fact, the eight outside specialists were chosen in a process in which the Prime Minister was very much involved but which produced scholars who were neither part of the Foreign Office list of candidates nor part of Thatcher's political advisory circle. They were people who had complementary expertise on different aspects of the Soviet Union and Eastern Europe. Each of the academics wrote a six-to-eight-page paper, which Thatcher read and annotated while she was staying at Balmoral in August as guest of the Queen. The Foreign Office and the Ministry of Defence each submitted much longer papers for the seminar, which were also read in advance by the Prime Minister. The Foreign Office paper came to eighty-four pages, fifty of them devoted to East-West relations. The outside specialists were present on 8 September 1983 for the first six hours of the two-day seminar.

Margaret Thatcher devotes two and a half pages of her memoirs to the September 1983 Chequers meeting. A reader of those memoirs might be forgiven for concluding that the only participants apart from the Prime Minister were academics, for neither her ministerial colleagues who were present nor the papers prepared by the Foreign Office and the Ministry of Defence get so much as a mention. She does not, for that matter, name the academic participants, but she does say in her memoirs:

> By the time the seminar went ahead I felt that we did have the right people and some first-class papers. The latter covered almost all of the factors we would have to take into account in the years ahead in dealing with the Soviets and their system. We discussed the Soviet economy, its technological inertia and the consequences of that, the impact of religious issues, Soviet military doctrine and expenditure on defence, and the benefits and costs to the Soviet Union of their control over Eastern Europe. . . . Perhaps for me the most useful paper was the one which described and analysed the power structure of the Soviet state, and which put flesh on the bones of what I had already learned in opposition from Robert Conquest.[12]

One of the points made in that paper on the Soviet power structure, of which I was the author, was that a democratizing process could come from within a ruling Communist Party. That had happened in Czechoslovakia in the second half of the 1960s, a movement that culminated in the Prague Spring of 1968. I suggested that it would be carrying a historical and cultural determinism too far to say that such a development could never take place in the Soviet Union. Probably a main reason, however, why Thatcher alluded to my paper as "the most useful" was because I drew her attention for the first time to Mikhail Gorbachev as a likely future, reform-minded Soviet leader. In that paper, written in advance of the seminar, I had described him as "the best-educated member of the Politburo and probably the most open-minded," adding: "He might well be the most hopeful choice from the point of view both of Soviet citizens and the outside world." Gorbachev's name did not appear in the long Foreign Office submission.

Thatcher underlined, in her pre-seminar reading of it, a number of points in my paper (as she did with all the other papers), but she did not underline what I had written about Gorbachev. The name did not mean anything to her at that point. All eight paper givers were, however, asked to speak for ten minutes each, either making different points or elaborating on a few of those already put in writing. We did this two at a time, and each session was followed by discussion, mainly in the form of questions from the government side of the table, with the Prime Minister very much the principal interrogator. I took the chance to expand on what I had said about Gorbachev as the best hope for reform, following which Thatcher turned to Sir Geoffrey Howe and said: "Should we not invite Mr Gorbachev to Britain?" Howe murmured his agreement.[13]

The invitation to Gorbachev did not follow immediately. The most important decision of principle to result from the 1983 seminar was a change to engagement with the Soviet Union and Eastern Europe. The academics spoke unanimously in favor of that when Thatcher sought their recommendations on policy. Our view was "the more contacts the better, and at all levels—from dissidents to general secretaries." Significantly, that advice was fully in tune with opinion in the Foreign Office, but given Thatcher's view of the FCO, it was important that she hear it from specialists she had invited to take part in the Chequers seminar. Just two months later in New Delhi, Thatcher told Commonwealth leaders during an informal conversation about the Soviet Union that "it is only through contact" that "we can hope to be able to influence others."[14] As a result of the Chequers seminar, it was resolved that the Foreign Secretary should visit all the East European countries and that the Prime Minister should visit Hungary in the first instance. Hungary at that time was the most relaxed of the Communist regimes of east-central Europe.

An invitation could not have been sent to Gorbachev right away, for Andropov was still alive, Konstantin Chernenko was number two in the Soviet Communist Party, and Andrei Gromyko was still, of course, Foreign Minister. If Gorbachev had been singled out for an invitation at this stage, it would probably have done him more harm than good, and it is very unlikely that he would have been given permission to come to Britain. In fact, in the post-seminar deliberations within the government, it was decided that Andropov should be invited to visit London. However, Andropov was already too ill to go anywhere. It was after his death, with Chernenko installed as Soviet leader, that the opportunity arose to invite Gorbachev. He had become second secretary of the Communist Party, and one of the formal duties of the second secretary was to chair the largely ceremonial Foreign Affairs Committee of the Supreme Soviet, the moribund and powerless Soviet legislature. That gave Downing Street and the Foreign Office a convenient way of inviting Gorbachev, through an invitation issued by the chair of the Foreign Affairs Committee of the House of Commons (Sir Anthony Kershaw). A letter in his name (but drafted in the Foreign Office) went to Moscow in June 1984, and Geoffrey Howe told the British Ambassador, Sir Iain Sutherland, that he should "make clear that if Gorbachev comes he will be received at the highest political level (i.e. by the Prime Minister), and have meetings with senior members of the government at which a wide range of questions could be discussed." He added that Gorbachev should be informed that the invitation "reflects the desire of the British government to pursue a broad dialogue with the Soviet Union."[15]

Gorbachev's December 1984 visit to Britain—three months before Chernenko died and Gorbachev succeeded him as Soviet General Secretary—was highly significant, for it was the beginning of an important political relationship with Thatcher. Gorbachev impressed British politicians, the mass media, and the public. He smiled a lot, as did his attractive wife, Raisa, who accompanied him. In his meetings with the Prime Minister and with other ministers, he argued well without resort to dogma and gave the impression of having an open mind. With Chernenko still Soviet leader and Gromyko still Foreign Minister, Gorbachev had to keep an eye on how his performance would be evaluated back home and thus had to maneuver within the limits of existing Soviet policies. When the Soviet Ambassador, Viktor Popov, came with his wife to dinner at St. Antony's College, Oxford, in February 1985—a time when Chernenko still had a month to live—he said in a private conversation I had with him that this had been "a visit by the right man at the right time" and that it had been "successful and useful in many different ways." The ambassador's wife added that one of the reasons the visit had been successful was that the Gorbachevs "did not look like people from Madame Tussauds."[16] That many of Gorbachev's senior colleagues did look like waxworks was the easily understood unspoken sentiment.

On the night before Gorbachev's arrival, I was one of four academics—the others were Alec Nove, Michael Kaser, and Lawrence Freedman—who, together with one businessman, Norman Wooding, were invited to 10 Downing Street to brief the Prime Minister. The others were invited to speak about economic, defense, and foreign policy, and British business interests. I was asked to speak specifically about Gorbachev. (By this time both Thatcher's Private Secretary and her Foreign Policy Adviser were different people from those involved with the Chequers seminar in September 1983. I assume, therefore, that I owed my invitation to Thatcher's recollection of my written and oral observations on Gorbachev.) While everything was being done in advance to make Gorbachev's visit a success, that crucially depended on how Thatcher evaluated him when they finally met. In fact, she was able famously, and in all honesty, to declare at the end of his visit: "I like Mr Gorbachev. We can do business together." At a Chequers seminar in February 1987, in which I participated, Mrs. Thatcher remarked that Gorbachev was "the only Communist leader I can have a good argument with." They did argue a lot, but with mutual respect.

The significance of the rapport they established was the greater because of Thatcher's impeccable anti-communist credentials and because she was the foreign leader whose opinion carried the most weight in Washington. As Gorbachev's 1984 visit came to an end, she flew to the United States and had a meeting with Reagan and his senior officials at Camp David. George Shultz noted in his memoirs that the Prime Minister spoke enthusiastically about Gorbachev.[17] The declassified transcript of the Camp David discussions bears that out. Thatcher remained a hard-liner on arms control issues and very attached to British nuclear weapons, but she was impressed by the fact that Gorbachev could argue freely and flexibly. In her meeting with Reagan, Shultz, George H. W. Bush, and National Security Adviser McFarlane on 22 December 1984 at Camp David, she contrasted Gorbachev favorably with Gromyko, saying that Gorbachev "was much less constrained, more charming, open to discussion and debate, and did not stick to prepared notes."[18]

Thatcher did not have long to wait for another meeting with Gorbachev. Chernenko died on the evening of 10 March 1985, and by the afternoon of 11 March, in the fastest leadership succession in Soviet history, Gorbachev had been chosen to be the country's new leader. Thatcher attended Chernenko's funeral and had an animated conversation with Gorbachev. It had been scheduled to last for fifteen minutes, for there were many foreign heads of government in Moscow, all of them eager to become acquainted with the new and comparatively young General Secretary of the Soviet Communist Party. In fact, the Thatcher-Gorbachev meeting lasted for almost an hour. Geoffrey Howe was present throughout, and he recalled in his memoirs that not everyone in the Foreign Office, when they read the note of the meeting, was happy about the bonhomie. (The FCO contained a variety of views on how to deal with the Soviet Union.) He cites one official as saying that "the PM seems to go uncharacteristically weak at the knees when she talks to the personable Mr Gorbachev." Howe comments: "He need not have worried. Certainly the two leaders were attracted to each other, relished each other's company. But neither Margaret nor Mikhail ever completely lowered their guard."[19]

It was in the light of this and, especially, subsequent meetings between Gorbachev and Thatcher that Sir Percy Cradock, who in early 1984 had succeeded Sir Anthony Parsons as the Foreign Policy Adviser in 10 Downing Street, developed his dyspeptic view of the Gorbachev-Thatcher relationship. Cradock wrote:

> Mrs Thatcher came close to claiming that she had discovered, even invented Gorbachev; her meetings and debates with him were deliberately high profile and added to her, and Britain's, international standing. More seriously, she acted as a conduit from Gorbachev to Reagan, selling him to Washington as a man to do business with, and operating as an agent of influence in both directions.[20]

Neither Cradock nor anyone else, though, has succeeded in explaining why harm rather than good was done by Margaret Thatcher in developing from the outset a strong and increasingly warm relationship with Gorbachev. Her meetings with him did not lead her to abandon any of her views about the injustices and inefficiencies characteristic of communist systems or to modify her emotional attachment to British nuclear weapons, which Gorbachev (and not only Gorbachev) found rather extreme.

THE YEAR 1987 WAS ESPECIALLY IMPORTANT both for putting political reform firmly on the agenda in the Soviet Union and for Thatcher's developing perceptions of what was occurring in Moscow. She had accepted an invitation to go on a high-profile official visit to the Soviet Union in March of that year. Again she held a seminar in advance of it—in February 1987. I was among those who took part. This time there was quite a lot of disagreement among the outside participants, who included the historians Robert Conquest and Sir Michael Howard and the American political scientist Seweryn Bialer. Charles Powell wrote a report of the meeting that tilted the findings very much in the direction of those who were skeptical about the possibility of any fundamental change in the Soviet system. Among the meeting's conclusions, on this account, were that "nothing dramatic or far-reaching" could be expected from Soviet reform and that the Soviet system "might at best evolve in 20 years time into something resembling Yugoslavia today."[21] That was not the view of a number of participants in the seminar, and certainly not my own view (as can easily be verified from the articles I published at the time). Powell did, however, acknowledge that the discussion "revealed a difference between those, principally the experts on the Soviet Union, who were impressed by the scope and energy of Gorbachev's reforms; and those, principally non-specialists, who were not convinced that real change would be either possible or allowed and were sceptical of Gorbachev's motives. To simplify: between enthusiasts and sceptics."

Before long, however, the overall skepticism of the report did not matter. Thatcher had heard contrasting arguments about what was happening in the Soviet Union and had read a lot of articles on the subject. She had also carefully read Gorbachev's speeches. In addition, she had been briefed by the former KGB agent Oleg Gordievsky, who by this time had been helped to defect from the Soviet Union and was living in Britain. In general, the Prime Minister prepared herself very well for her encounters with Soviet politicians and journalists. Her visit was a triumphal success, and it would be fair to say that she returned to Britain in the camp of the enthusiasts. She had become one of those who thought that really important change was taking place in the Soviet Union and that there was a prospect of far-reaching reform. She remained much more doubtful that there would be correspondingly serious change in Soviet foreign and defense policy. In Moscow, Thatcher was accorded a live interview on Soviet television. It made a huge impact on a vast Soviet TV audience ("practically the whole nation," according to the newspaper *Izvestiya*). She was questioned by three Soviet journalists, and they were no match for someone who had done her homework so thoroughly and who was well used to hostile interviews and the adversarial Prime Minister's Questions in the House of Commons.

When they interrogated her about nuclear deterrence, it turned out that she was far better briefed "not only on the issues, but also on the size and capacity of the Soviet nuclear arsenal. She wiped the floor with them."[22]

Many of the Russians I met in those years expressed their delight with Thatcher's performance. Others were annoyed that the home team had been so decisively routed. Thatcher herself later wrote: "The interview was allowed to go out uncut from Soviet television, which I afterwards regarded as proof that my confidence in Mr Gorbachev's basic integrity was not misplaced."[23] Thatcher's visit not only enhanced her standing internationally, it was also quite helpful to Gorbachev. He told the Politburo that he was impressed by her knowledge of what was going on in the Soviet Union and that his conversations with her had helped him see how Soviet policy appeared in western Europe. It prompted him to set up an Institute of Europe in Moscow, a counterpart to the Institute of the United States and Canada, which already existed.[24] Thatcher met former Soviet dissidents, including Andrei Sakharov, who had been brought back from provincial exile and was now playing a part in Soviet public life. She was far from uncritical of Soviet policy, especially foreign and military policy, but made clear her admiration for Gorbachev's reformist course. Thatcher in her memoirs observes: "The welcome I had received—both the warm affection from the Russian crowds, and the respect of the Soviet authorities in long hours of negotiations—suggested that something fundamental was happening under the surface." It had been "quite simply, the most fascinating and most important foreign visit I had made."[25]

Thatcher had another, much briefer meeting with Gorbachev at the end of 1987 when he made a stopover at the RAF Brize Norton air base on his way to Washington for a summit meeting with President Reagan. The transcript of that conversation—made by Gorbachev's aide, Anatoly Chernyaev—shows that it was a remarkably frank encounter. Gorbachev told her that there was no unanimity of views "even in our Politburo," and Thatcher assured him that the same was true of the British Cabinet. Gorbachev volunteered the judgment that "up to the present we have not been able to cross the threshold beyond the Stalinist system of administrative government." Previous attempts at change had been half measures, but now something completely different was being undertaken. The two leaders, as usual, argued about nuclear weapons, but finished on an amicable note, with Thatcher reiterating an invitation to Gorbachev to make an official visit to Britain, which he said he would certainly take up.[26] Gorbachev duly came to Britain on an official visit in April 1989, and Thatcher made two further official trips to the Soviet Union while she was still Prime Minister—in September 1989 and June 1990.

There is a popular myth that change was brought about in the Soviet Union, and the Cold War ended, as a result of Reagan's military buildup and anti-communist rhetoric. That is a great oversimplification of Reagan's policy toward the Soviet Union and of his desire to be remembered as a peacemaker, not a warmonger. It is also a *dangerous* misunderstanding, for often lessons are drawn about policy today on the assumption that military pressure produced—and produces—desired results. In fact, it was far from obvious what the most privileged sections of the Soviet elite had to gain from radical reform or from the asymmetrical arms reductions to which Gorbachev agreed. Certainly, the constituent parts of the Soviet military-industrial complex were very much against these measures. Alexander Yakovlev, who from 1988 supervised international affairs within the Central Committee, and Foreign Minister Eduard Shevardnadze came under increasing domestic attack for pursuing such a policy. Gorbachev was the real target of the critics, but until quite late in the day, the power and authority of the General Secretaryship of the Communist Party made it harder for his opponents to mount a direct attack on him. We should remember that the balance of material and military resources was much more strongly in favor of the United States and against the Soviet Union when Stalin subjugated the countries of east-central Europe to Soviet-style rule in the years immediately after the Second World War. By the 1980s, in contrast, the United States and the Soviet Union each had the means to wipe the other off the face of the earth. American military pressure is a totally inadequate explanation of the policies Gorbachev pursued.

MRS. THATCHER, IN THE MID-1980S especially, played a significant part in getting East-West dialogue going in a serious way by becoming the first major Western politician to appreciate that Mikhail Gorbachev was a very different Soviet leader from any of his predecessors. Her role in persuading Ronald Reagan of that view was particularly important during the period of almost a year between her first meeting with Gorbachev and Reagan's first encounter with the new Soviet leader, in November 1985. While Thatcher was able briefly to act once again as a go-between in the first half of 1989—in this case between Gorbachev and President George H. W. Bush—her role in Cold War diplomacy had passed its peak. At all stages, the U.S.-Soviet relationship was by far the most decisive. In the later phases of ending the Cold War, the German Chancellor, Helmut Kohl, was much more important than Margaret Thatcher. The issue of German unification was eventually settled in bilateral discussions between Kohl and Gorbachev, with support for the Germans coming from Washington. Thatcher, in contrast, but along with President Mitterrand of France, regarded German unity with ill-disguised disapproval. She was much slower than was Gorbachev to accept that German unification was going to take place sooner rather than later and to make a virtue of it. Thatcher's blind spot about a Germany that was a world away from the Germany of her youth in the Second World War diminished her credibility both in Europe and in the United States.

Nevertheless, the fact that such a formidable politician as Margaret Thatcher recognized in the mid-1980s that profound change might be occurring in the Soviet Union and that she was prepared to argue in the capitals of Europe as well as in Washington that Gorbachev deserved support must be counted on the positive side of the ledger when a full tally is made of her Prime Ministership. Engaging with a radically reforming Soviet leader (as Thatcher did, as Reagan did, and as Bush, too, eventually did), rather than persisting with an aggressive stance, was decisively important in bringing the Cold War to a peaceful end and in facilitating the dismantling of communist systems with a minimum of bloodshed.

Paradoxically, Thatcher's position evolved beyond that of the institutionally cautious British Foreign Office. Yet no less paradoxically, Thatcher's conversion to the need for engagement with the countries of communist Europe brought her closer to an underlying position of the Foreign Office and further apart from the outlook of those political allies from outside government who had influenced her when she was leader of the opposition and during her earliest years as Prime Minister. She fought the Cold War with all her might. Yet she parted company with the views of the irredeemable Cold Warriors, who had been among her greatest admirers, when they remained too blinkered to see fundamental change in the communist world—in the Soviet Union first and foremost—even when it was happening before their eyes. Mrs. Thatcher was not so foolish. It is of some historical significance that she was clear-sighted enough to recognize, certainly by 1987, that serious reform was underway in the Soviet Union. And it should be much more than a footnote in the history of the ending of the Cold War that she formed a political and, later, even personal friendship with a politician in the Kremlin (of all places) whom she came to regard as a fellow reformer.

Fall Semester 2010

1. Percy Cradock, *In Pursuit of British Interests: Reflections on Foreign Policy under Margaret Thatcher and John Major* (London, 1997), p. 24.

2. Rodric Braithwaite, *Across the Moscow River: The World Turned Upside Down* (New Haven, 2002), p. 51.

3. Brian Crozier, *The Gorbachev Phenomenon* (London, 1990), p. 244.

4. George Urban, *Diplomacy and Disillusion at the Court of Margaret Thatcher: An Insider's View* (London, 1996), p. 4.

5. Cradock, *In Pursuit of British Interests*, p. 100.

6. Ibid., pp. 100–1.

7. Rodric Braithwaite, "Gorbachev and Thatcher: Witness Remarks," *Journal of European Integration History*, 16, 1 (2010), p. 38.

8. Geoffrey Howe, *Conflict of Loyalty* (London, 1994), p. 350.

9. Francis Pym, *The Politics of Consent* (London, 1984), p. ix.

10. For a much fuller account of this seminar, see Archie Brown, "The Change to Engagement in Britain's Cold War Policy: The Origins of the Thatcher-Gorbachev Relationship," *Journal of Cold War Studies*, 10, 3 (Summer 2009), pp. 3–47.

11. Margaret Thatcher, *The Downing Street Years* (London, 1993), p. 451.

12. Ibid.

13. I first wrote about this—and about a meeting to brief Margaret Thatcher on Gorbachev on the eve of his first visit to Britain a little over a year later—in an article in the *Times Literary Supplement* ("The Leader of the Prologue"), 30 Aug. 1991, pp. 5–6. It was reprinted in Ferdinand Mount, ed., *Communism* (London, 1992), pp. 293–300.

14. Quoted in Howe, *Conflict of Loyalty*, p. 350.

15. Howe to British Embassy, Moscow, telegram no. 536, 14 June 1984, Foreign Office Papers, ESB/020/7.

16. I made a note of the conversation later that same evening—1 Feb. 1985.

17. George P. Shultz, *Turmoil and Triumph: My Years as Secretary of State* (New York, 1993), p. 509.

18. Thatcher-Reagan meeting at Camp David of 22 Dec. 1984; transcript from Reagan Library Archive, available at http://www.margaretthatcher.org/archive.

19. Howe, *Conflict of Loyalty*, p. 430.

20. Cradock, *In Pursuit of British Interests*, p. 201.

21. Cabinet Office Papers A 2162 (Revise), Report by Charles Powell, 01.03.1987, "Seminar on the Soviet Union."

22. Braithwaite, "Gorbachev and Thatcher," p. 36.

23. Thatcher, *Downing Street Years,* p. 483.

24. Anatoly Chernyaev, *My Six Years with Gorbachev* (University Park, Penn., 2000), pp. 104–6.

25. Thatcher, *Downing Street Years,* p. 485.

26. Chernyaev's eighteen-page transcript of the Brize Norton conversation is in the Gorbachev Foundation Archives in Moscow. See "Zapis' besedy M.S. Gorbacheva s prem'er ministrom Velikobritanii M. Tetcher, 7 dekabrya 1987 goda."

19

Invictus

DAN JACOBSON

Out of the night that covers me,
Black as the Pit from pole to pole,
I thank whatever gods may be,
For my unconquerable soul.

Stirring words: no question. And all the more so if one thinks of the man who wrote them: W. E. Henley, the Victorian poet, editor, and man of letters. As a schoolboy, he had suffered the amputation of a leg after it had been attacked by a tubercular infection, and he was subsequently confined to protracted spells of enforced inactivity. In later years, he worked successfully for various newspapers, chiefly in Edinburgh and London. It was in Edinburgh that he became a close friend of Robert Louis Stevenson, who used him (admiringly) as his model for the buccaneering, one-legged Long John Silver of *Treasure Island,* and who collaborated with him in writing four plays. In later years the two men fell out bitterly, and the friendship between them was never resumed. As an editor, Henley also helped promote some of Rudyard Kipling's early work. But the only one of Henley's own writings that has survived the attrition of the years is the poem "Invictus" (i.e., "unconquered"); the rest have fallen by the wayside.[1]

It was to the poem "Invictus" that the veteran journalist John Carlin turned for the title of his book about the 1995 Rugby World Cup, staged in Cape Town.[2] That event became, in effect, a celebration of the triumph of Nelson Mandela, the leader of the African National

Congress, over those who had confined him, along with many of his
leading colleagues, to imprisonment on Robben Island, just off the
coast from Cape Town. The island was and remains a bleak, wind-
tormented place, used by the original Dutch settlers of the Cape for
a variety of disagreeable purposes: it has served in turn as a leper
colony, a lunatic asylum, and finally as a place of punishment for
those like Mandela who had forcibly resisted the roles assigned to
them by the Afrikaner nationalist government. (It is now, in effect,
a place of pilgrimage for visitors, with the highlight of each tour
being a visit to the tiny cell in which Mandela was confined every
night for something like twenty years.) The previous government
had ruled over the country from 1948 to 1990 with what some of its
followers proudly proclaimed to be "a fist of iron"; but in the end, it
finally collapsed under its own weight, largely because of the continuing resistance of the black masses to laws that were designed to
frustrate and humiliate them at almost every turn—not to speak of
the conviction of many South African whites that their government
was leading them toward nothing but self-destruction. The ever-
growing hostility of powers such as Britain, the Netherlands, and
the United States toward the regime also helped greatly to disabuse
some of the government's supporters of the idea that the Western
world, engaged as it was in those days with the struggle against the
Soviet Union, would be bound in the end to oblige them by coming
to their rescue.

BECAUSE THE GAME OF RUGBY IS PLAYED so rarely in the United
States, it may at first sight seem surprising that Clint Eastwood, the
Hollywood actor and moviemaker, seized on the dramatic possibilities of a rugby tournament that had been staged in South Africa
more than ten years before. His interest was roused initially by a
suggestion from his friend and fellow actor Morgan Freeman, who
had visited South Africa well after Mandela's release from jail and
had been captivated by Carlin's book about Mandela and the tournament as a whole. In the upshot, Eastwood's judgment in the matter cannot be faulted; nor that of Carlin; nor that of Mandela himself, who wholeheartedly threw himself into the entire venture. The
concatenation of forces that enabled Mandela to come out of his
cell and take over the reins of government were to make themselves
felt in South Africa and beyond more rapidly than anyone would
have thought possible beforehand.

English rugby and American football are both played with an
oval ball and involve running, kicking, tackling, and scrumming
(or scrimmaging), with the aim of winning territory and scoring by

crossing the opposing team's try line (British) or goal line (American). No sooner had the game been invented—by the boys in the posh fee-paying school of Rugby in Warwickshire, England, in the mid-nineteenth century—than it crossed the Atlantic and began a new life in the United States. Thereafter, the rules under which the games were played in the two countries began to diverge, though the kinship between them is still apparent. Today the American version is played almost exclusively within the United States and its dependencies, while the British code is followed in countries ranging from New Zealand to Argentina, and from Ireland to Romania. One thing certain about the sport, however, in whatever form it is played, is that it has never appealed to sissies.

THE GAME WAS BROUGHT TO SOUTH AFRICA by the British, who arrived at the Cape of Good Hope (as it was then called) during the Napoleonic Wars and who immediately grasped the advantages of seizing for their empire this strategically significant corner of the world. Dutch settlers had taken control of the Cape some two centuries earlier after pushing aside a much feebler attempt by the Portuguese to establish their own right to the territory. Needless to say, none of these interlopers gave any consideration to the wishes of the indigenous inhabitants of the territory, the Bushmen and Hottentots (Khoikhoi). Nor were they to be daunted later by the more formidable tribes (Xhosas, Zulus, and others) occupying territories farther to the east and north. With the Cape safely in their hands, the British naturally brought into the area some of their own habits and institutions, among them the games of cricket and soccer initially, and eventually rugby too. That game in particular, rather than the two others mentioned above, soon became the possession and indeed the passion of many of the Afrikaners, or Boers (as the local Dutch had begun to call themselves), despite their resentment at having been displaced as masters of the land by the British.

To look back at the settlers' takeover of the territories stretching away to the north is to marvel at their belief that people like themselves would always be able to rule in perpetuity over the indigenous population. Yet that was indeed the expectation by the whites of both kinds as they continually went farther and farther north, conquering whatever territories they came upon. Because the colonizers were literate and in possession of firearms, they could hardly doubt that they would always be able to crush whatever resistance the native inhabitants might offer. Indeed, though outright wars for possession of land soon broke out between the two white groups, nothing would shake their belief on that point. In 1910, the two white groups finally resolved their differences, after a fashion, and jointly called into existence a brand-new entity to which they gave the name of the Union of South Africa. The subordinate status of blacks within this arrangement was taken for granted, as was the agreement that only English and Afrikaans would be recognized as the country's official languages. By then, to put it brusquely, the Afrikaners found themselves in control of most of the country's arable land; the immense deposits of gold, diamonds, coal, platinum, and other valuable minerals hidden under its bleak landscapes had effectively fallen into the hands of the English-speaking community.

To make their position even more secure than it already was, successive governments (whether led by Britons or Boers) proceeded to institute systems of control and registration that compelled the black majority on the land to live in a state of virtual helotry—a condition that the wholly Afrikaner-dominated parliament, which, once it came to power shortly after the end of the Second World War, did its best to make impregnable. So-called reserves were marked off in which the rural blacks could live and raise their crops—always, of course, under strict supervision by their traditional elders, who, in turn, were supervised by white officers set directly over the lot. For the rest, the duties of the urbanized blacks were clearly prescribed: they would toil for exceedingly low wages in the mines, farms, factories, and households owned by their white masters. They had to live at a distance from the city centers in so-called separate areas and carry passes that permitted them to work in the white neighborhoods without fear of arrest. At the end of each day, they would return to their slum-like "compounds" and "locations"—with the exception, of course, of those who worked as servants in the houses of their white masters. That they would have no choice in this arrangement was taken for granted; indeed, in those heady days even the Cape coloreds (people of mixed race) were forcibly deprived of the very limited voting rights they had previously possessed.

That, pretty much, was how things would stand—indefinitely, according to the fantastical theories busily being elaborated day after day by the country's rulers. But just as the Afrikaners were eventually to "outbreed" the speakers of English, many of whom were skeptical of the half-mad schemes of grand apartheid (a term invented by members of the Afrikaner nationalist government when referring to their own policies), so too the blacks stubbornly continued to "outbreed" the whites. (This notwithstanding the more and more elaborate restrictions that were constantly being elaborated in order to "keep them in their place"—a phrase much in use then.) One might argue (in quasi-Marxist fashion) that the force that ultimately undid these schemes was the startling growth of the country's economy. As the years went by, it became increasingly obvious to all but the most pigheaded members of the white ruling class that their attempts to confine blacks to the roles of servants, miners, unskilled laborers, and nannies were becoming increasingly inadequate to the advanced industrialized state that South Africa had become. The truth was that without the active cooperation and educational advancement of the country's black communities, everything the whites themselves valued most about their country—the wealth it generated, its military power, its standing in the world, its hospitals and universities and game reserves and much else beside—would fall into ruin. And for that prospect, only the most obdurate "bitter-enders" among them had any appetite at all.

IN THE MEANTIME, THE WORLD AT LARGE was undergoing convulsions of its own—among them, events that observers in South Africa might well have thought remote from their affairs. Chief among these was the fact that in the latter half of the twentieth century, the seemingly immovable Soviet Union was clearly tottering toward its own demise. That this series of events would, within a few years, radically affect political (and sporting) developments in southern Africa would probably have seemed like a bad dream to most white South Africans. Since its inception early in the twentieth century, the multiracial South African Communist Party had been execrated and hounded by the police and other organs of the state; nevertheless, by the end of the Second World War it had managed to establish a significant degree of control over the most organized and determined elements of black opposition. (And of small but effective groups of radical whites too.) As it happened, this state of affairs was eagerly exploited by the Afrikaner nationalist government, precisely in order to keep the anxiety level of its own followers at a fever pitch. Indeed, the Cold War in Europe and elsewhere had provided the South African government with a kind of laissez-passer that enabled it to present itself to the major Western powers as a valuable adjunct in their larger struggles with the Soviet bloc. Yet with the collapse of communism in Europe, both the communist Left and the Afrikaner nationalist Right in South Africa suddenly found themselves bereft. Neither could look anywhere but into themselves for help in what had weirdly become a predicament they shared—no matter how hard both factions struggled to conceal this fact from their followers.

At bottom, the policy of apartheid ("separateness") had always been based on a conviction among most whites—regardless of whether they spoke English or Afrikaans—that virtually all contact between themselves and their black employees had to come under the sign of the master-servant relationship, and that any alteration to this state of affairs would, in effect, amount to a form of racial and political pollution. (Of course, such attitudes were not—and still are not—peculiar to South Africa alone.) Yet as continuing black resistance to apartheid provoked ever-harsher responses from the authorities, and as the nature of the apartheid state itself became increasingly apparent to more and more people abroad, the government's belief in the indefeasible rightness of their cause—as evidenced by the wealth so many of them had long enjoyed and the value of their contribution to Western civilization as a whole—began to crumble. They spluttered and complained about their plight to anyone who would listen to them, yet they could not evade the fact that the nations they most admired were precisely those that were finally turning against them. And they hated it. Especially since they knew, too, that what was now being done to them was precisely what they themselves had done for three centuries and more to their fellow inhabitants of the subcontinent.

During this phase, the country's relations with Great Britain suffered especially, while the people of the Netherlands, the original begetters of the Afrikaner nation, showed no more sympathy to them than did anyone else. Thousands of white and black refugees who had left South Africa to escape apartheid and all its works naturally led the field in whipping up hostility to the government they had fled from; and so did churchmen of all denominations, academics, trade unionists, students in search of a cause, homeless ex-communists, and waifs and strays of many other kinds. Political emissaries sent from South Africa to counter these activities were greeted with hostile demonstrators wherever they went; universities and learned bodies severed their relations with their coevals in South African institutions. Even hardheaded financial speculators and would-be investors shrank from public declarations of support for a country that, in the language of the press in South Africa itself, had become "the skunk of the nations." Admittedly, major purchasers abroad had no wish to boycott the gold or chrome or diamonds or wool that came from the south; nevertheless, the campaigns against the skunk grew louder and louder as the years passed. So did the demands for the release of Nelson Mandela, whose name had by now become as famous, worldwide, as that of any movie star or successful race car driver.

No less damaging to the morale of white South Africa as a whole was the ever-increasing tally of overseas sporting bodies that declined invitations to send representative teams to the subcontinent and that refused to permit visitors from South Africa to play in their own tournaments. Strange though it may seem to say so, that particular form of boycott wounded white South Africans quite as much as any other, since excellence in sports of all kinds had always been one of the arenas in which their countrymen excelled.

THE TURNAROUND BY THE GOVERNMENT from the policies it had vigorously fostered for so long was a slow process, but the more enlightened politicians within the government eventually began to realize that as a prisoner at home and a talisman abroad, Nelson Mandela had become much more a threat to them in jail than he might be if he were released. In fact, some years before his formal release, the authorities had offered him his liberty, provided he agreed to desist from promoting anti-government activities of any kind. To this invitation, he answered, crushingly, "Only free men can negotiate. A prisoner cannot enter into contracts." So he was left to spend yet more time breaking stones on Robben Island. In all, he spent twenty-seven years in confinement; nevertheless, toward the end of that period, the conditions under which he was detained were slowly ameliorated. He was eventually transferred from Robben Island to the mainland. Governmental officials visited him in the more comfortable quarters he had been given, and later took to inviting him to visit them in their offices. Having made it clear from the outset that he would always stand his ground, he also made it clear to all his visitors that he had no interest in taking revenge on the people who had made themselves his jailers for much of his life. The dignity with which he carried himself throughout was in itself enough to bring his visitors to realize that in him they had met an interlocutor who was wilier and more indomitable than themselves, and more generous to them than they had ever been to him.

In fact, the good fortune that South Africa enjoyed in having a black leader so sensitive to the needs of all his fellow countrymen, of whatever race, seems in retrospect to have been little short of miraculous. Ideas that had once appeared unthinkable suddenly became irresistible. Many steps forward and back on both sides had to be taken before Mandela was set free, and some blood was shed in the process; yet once it was done, and once the country had held its first elections in which all adult men and women of all colors were qualified to vote, the country understood that this time there would be no going back. The elections passed off in a more peaceful fashion than anyone would have dared to imagine beforehand. Mandela's opponents were routed. How could they not have been,

given the numbers of disenfranchised who had never before enjoyed the privilege of exercising their vote—not to speak of the success Mandela had already had in proving to his opponents that he
was far from the devil his jailers had painted him to be? His touch
in dealing with his fearful and half-incredulous white public—not
least in wholeheartedly "adopting" the South African rugby team
as his own when the time finally came—was just one instance of his
gift for reconciliation.

SIXTEEN NATIONS SENT REPRESENTATIVE teams to take part in the
tournament. It was the first time in the history of the Cup that all
the games were played in one country alone. Among them, surprisingly perhaps, was a team from the United States, as well as others
from Asia and Oceania, let alone countries like New Zealand and
Great Britain, which had for years meekly bowed their heads to the
insistence of previous South African governments that no players
of color should ever appear on the field to play against an all-white
team. Under the tutelage of Mandela, the former skunk of the nations had become host to the world: a sensation wholly new to everyone who lived there and relished by the country at large to a degree
that no one could have imagined beforehand. At the very end of
the tournament, victory over the New Zealanders (the Kiwis, as they
called themselves) set the seal on the Springboks' triumph. Mandela, dressed in the new South African colors and wearing on his
cap the same number as that borne by Francois Pienaar, the captain
of the team, had watched the game throughout. It was to Pienaar
that Mandela handed the trophy, and it was a greatly moved Pienaar
who, in his turn, held it up to the spectators in the arena and to the
many millions more who were watching on television in South Africa and abroad.

UNLIKE LEADERS OF MANY OTHER newly decolonized states in Africa
and elsewhere, Mandela did not cling to power. After a mere half
dozen years in office as President of South Africa, he chose to retire.
Clearly, he felt old and tired and judged that he had done as much
as he possibly could for his country. In the first years of his retirement, he traveled abroad widely; thereafter, much less readily. Wherever he went, honors of all kinds were showered on him (many hundreds of them, literally) by dignitaries including George W. Bush,
Margaret Thatcher, and the Queen of England, and organizations
such as the Federation of International Football Players. He wrote
an autobiography entitled *Long Walk to Freedom* (1995), which sold

in large numbers, and engaged only rarely in political comment of any kind.

Yes, the tributes paid to Mandela in *Invictus* are discomfiting at moments (but of how many better or worse movies is that not true?); Morgan Freeman, who plays Mandela, is too often confined to uttering deep, wise sentiments for the benefit of the audience at large; there are many bumps in the script's evocation of white South African ways of dealing with strangers (especially when a stranger has suddenly been transformed from a dangerous enemy to a world hero); there is a surplus of shots showing thirty heavyweight rugby players smashing into one another with terrible groans . . . and so on and so forth. All that said, there is much in the film that has to be admired. The views of the country's grand vistas and city centers, not to speak of its slums, are compelling; Morgan Freeman's adoption of Mandela's walk, of his turns of the head and manner of enunciating his words, are beguilingly accurate; Matt Damon's performance as Francois Pienaar, the Afrikaner captain of the South African team, whose loyalty Mandela woos and wins long before the outcome of the final game, is outstanding. Over the years, I have heard many actors from outside South Africa attempt to speak English with an Afrikaans accent, and almost all of them have been a source of embarrassment. Yet Damon carries it all off beautifully, effortlessly. It is hard not to share the pride and relief he displays when the victor's cup is put in his hands.

A HAPPY ENDING, THEN? On the rugby field that day, and in the movie supposedly representing it, and in Carlin's book, yes indeed.

And in real life, subsequently?

No doubt South Africa is less a madhouse today than it was under the old regime, when it was hard at times not to think of it, in its lowest reaches, as a kind of inept, bastard cross between Hitler's Reich and Stalin's USSR. Without doubt, too, some parts of the country have prospered greatly since Francois Pienaar hoisted to the sky the World Cup his team had just won. Yet since then, ongoing scourges have continued to torment the land, the two worst of them being widespread violent crime and AIDS. South Africa now holds not only the Rugby World Cup bestowed on in it 1995, but also, unhappily, the world record for the highest incidence of AIDS (5.7 million people in 2007). Nothing less.

Happy endings are always to be celebrated. How can we do otherwise, knowing that they never endure?

Fall Semester 2010

1.   Invictus

> Out of the night that covers me,
> Black as the Pit from pole to pole,
> I thank whatever gods may be
> For my unconquerable soul.
>
> In the fell clutch of circumstance
> I have not winced nor cried aloud.
> Under the bludgeonings of chance,
> My head is bloody but unbowed.
>
> Beyond this place of wrath and tears
> Looms but the Horror of the Shade,
> And yet the menace of the years
> Finds, and shall find, me unafraid.
>
> It matters not how strait the gate,
> How charged with punishment the scroll.
> I am the master of my fate:
> I am the captain of my soul.

William Ernest Henley

In a note on the poem in his book, John Carlin remarks simply that it "gave heart to Nelson Mandela during his long prison years."

2. John Carlin, *Invictus: Nelson Mandela and the Game That Made a Nation* (New York, 2009); originally published with the title *Playing the Enemy* (2008).

20

The Grand Illusion

GEOFFREY WHEATCROFT

In 1998, the first American president born after the Second World War entertained the first British Prime Minister who had been. And yet memories of those great days hung heavy over the banquet at the White House. Giving the toast, Tony Blair recalled another dinner, in England during the war, when the host was Winston Churchill and the guest was Harry Hopkins, President Roosevelt's personal emissary. As he spoke about Anglo-American friendship, Hopkins quoted Ruth's beautiful words, "Whither thou goest, I will go; and where thou lodgest, I will lodge: thy people shall be my people, and thy God my God." At that, Blair reminded his audience, Hopkins paused before he added, "even to the end"—and "Churchill wept." Hearing that story, Bill Clinton also wept.[1]

This episode is ripe with implications, and illusions, and dangers, and Churchill is at the heart of the story. In his own words, he was "an English-speaking union" in himself, the son of an American mother, and a frequent visitor to America from the age of twenty. He coined—or sometimes borrowed and polished—many famous phrases, from "blood, toil, tears, and sweat" to "an iron curtain". That last was made famous by Churchill in March 1946, speaking in Fulton, Missouri, but in that speech he also spoke about the continuing need for "a special relationship between the British Commonwealth and Empire and the United States."[2]

As Sir Michael Howard has said, this phrase is always associated with him, and adds that not only was this "special relationship" very much the creation of Churchill, but if the notion "survives at all in the United States it does so mainly because of his memory."[3] Howard said that twenty-five years ago. To say that there have been developments since then would be an understatement. As we historians say, stuff happens—and how. Over that quarter century, the world has changed dramatically and in quite unforeseen ways. And nothing has been more fascinating in this period than the Anglo-American relationship. In fact, it is this period that may be seen to have finally demonstrated that the "special relationship" was the great illusion of post-war British history.

Not that everyone had always been enthusiastic about Churchill's concept. Dean Acheson was scornful of the "stupidity" of the expression "special relationship" and tried to suppress its use at the State Department when he was President Truman's secretary of state (1949–53). All of a half century later, when Sir Christopher Meyer was British Ambassador in Washington (1997–2003), he forbade embassy staff from writing or even uttering the words. And quite apart from being a misleading notion, it was one that could be sustained only by a large rewriting—or ignorance—of history.[4]

Although Americans rarely use the phrase, one exception is Senator John McCain. Two years before he ran for president, he visited England, where he was cheered at the Conservative conference and interviewed by the *Spectator*. "The special relationship between our two countries will endure throughout the twenty-first century," he told that magazine. "I say that with total confidence because it's lasted for 200 years."[5] He may have said so with total confidence, but not with a complete grasp of fact.

McCain's "two hundred years" would take us back to the first years of the nineteenth century, or to an event whose bicentenary falls next year. What was special about the relationship in 1812 was that the two countries were at war. When he sits in the Senate, McCain might recall that brave British redcoats burned the Capitol—a deed with which I daresay some Americans might sympathize at present—and when he sings "The Star-Spangled Banner," can he have forgotten that it was a British rocket's red glare?

Thirty-six years earlier, the American republic had begun life with a rebellion against the British Crown, led by such men as Thomas Jefferson, who said of England that he would happily "lend [his] hand to sink the whole island in the ocean," and Benjamin Franklin, who rejoiced that every other nation "wishes to see Britain humbled, having all in their time been offended by her insolence."[6] While in Paris, Franklin invited Edward Gibbon to dine, and replied to Gibbon's curt refusal to meet someone from a hostile country by genially regretting a lost opportunity "to furnish materials to so excellent a writer for the Decline and Fall of the British Empire."[7]

Over the hundred years that followed the 1812 war, the two countries nearly went to war at least three more times, before, during, and after the Civil War. In 1844, James Polk won the Presidency on an aggressively expansionist platform, claiming what is now the Canadian province of British Columbia. The crisis passed as the United States turned south, acquired Texas, and embarked on a war with Mexico instead, but for a time the challenge had been serious enough for Sir Robert Peel to warn Parliament of the imminent danger of an American war.

It was at that very time that the phrase "manifest destiny" was born, and plenty of prominent Americans believed from early days that their destiny was to absorb all of North America, certainly above the Rio Grande. A claim on Canada became the stock-in-trade of patriotic demagogues, and a substantial part of the British army was stationed in Canada for many years to guard against this threat. During the Civil War, a series of events pushed Washington close to armed conflict with London again, and the war left wounds between the United States and England that were not soon healed. Even when they were, as over the CSS *Alabama* dispute, the tone was one becoming familiar: angry American resentment against calm British conciliation.

So it was in 1895, when once more the two came close to war over a trivial, not to say baffling, border dispute between Venezuela and British Guiana: President Cleveland rattled his saber, while Lord Salisbury spoke the soft words. As much to the point, it was recorded at the time of the crisis that whereas the English were horrified by the prospect of such a war, in America a war with England would be the most popular of wars. This reciprocal incomprehension was personified by Joseph Chamberlain, the radical politician who became a Liberal Unionist and then an imperialist.

His own special relationship followed the early deaths of his first two wives, both after giving birth to sons. He was sent to Washington by Salisbury to settle an American-Canadian dispute over fisheries, and met his third wife, Mary Endicott, the daughter of Cleveland's secretary of the army. It was thus that as well as two British Prime Ministers in the past century who had American mothers, a Foreign Secretary and a Prime Minister, the half brothers Austen and Neville Chamberlain, had an American stepmother. And it was Joe Chamberlain who said: "I refuse to think or speak of the United States as a foreign nation."

Not all Americans shared Jefferson's contempt for England, or the bitter hatred of Irish exiles, although plenty did. But then, not many Americans reciprocated Chamberlain's sentiments: they did think and speak of England as a foreign nation. That included President Woodrow Wilson. He viewed all Europeans as aboriginal savages who needed to be brought to the light of redemption by his hand, the English not least. When the European war began, in 1914, Wilson worried privately that he might have to enter it—against the British. He compared himself with James Madison, the one Princeton man who had preceded him at the White House, who was in office when the 1812 war began. The occasion for that war was a British naval blockade, which was again in force a hundred years later, to great American indignation. Indeed, it was reckoned in late 1914 that if forced to enter the war, more Americans would have wanted to fight against England than for it.

After the Great War, Churchill lamented that the United States had not entered it earlier and averted so much needless bloodshed, but this displayed, not for the last time on his part, a failure to understand American domestic politics. When Wilson ran for reelection in 1916, he said that he wouldn't enter the war, and there is no reason to doubt that he meant it. Even when the United States did join the war, it withdrew once more soon afterward. For two decades, America stood apart from the world, and Anglo-American relations were, as David Reynolds observes, "cool and distant."[8] America's "betrayal" of the League of Nations was only the first in a series of U.S. actions—over war debts, naval rivalry, the 1931–2 Manchurian crisis, and the Depression—that convinced British leaders that the United States could not be relied on. That last was the very phrase used by Neville Chamberlain in 1937—"It is always best & safest to count on nothing from the Americans"—and even Churchill expressed private exasperation.[9] By the outbreak of the next war, relations between the two were about as distant as possible between two ostensibly friendly powers.

Even before he became Prime Minister in May 1940, Churchill had begun to correspond with President Roosevelt, and for the next five years, in a Churchillian phrase, he wooed the President as a lover woos his mistress. And yet the more one studies the story, and the more one reads the correspondence between the two, the more one feels that the object of Churchill's fond attentions was curiously unresponsive. Churchill nevertheless persisted in speaking long before Pearl Harbor as though the United States were already an ally, thus setting the tone for later Prime Ministers.

Only last year, on his first visit to Washington as Prime Minister, David Cameron said meekly that Great Britain was a junior partner of the United States, as it had been "a junior partner in 1940." British tabloids delighted in finding old Desert Rats and RAF pilots to remind Cameron bluntly that in 1940 the United States wasn't a partner at all, while General Sir Patrick Cordingley snorted, "If Winston Churchill were alive today he would be dismayed."[10] And yet even that wasn't as extraordinary as something Tony Blair had said nine years earlier.

After 11 September 2001, he very rightly expressed the sympathy and moral support of the British government and people for the Americans in their ordeal, but he didn't leave it there. Visiting a stricken New York, Blair said, "My father's generation went through the Blitz . . . There was one country and one people which stood by us at that time. That country was America and those people were the American people."[11]

Hearing those words at the time, it occurred to me that Blair couldn't share my affection for Una Mae Carlisle. Some of that beguiling African American singer's recordings are memorable because of the Lester Young solos, but "Blitzkrieg Baby" is memorable for its lyrics:

> Blitzkrieg baby, you can't bomb me
> 'Cause I'm pleadin' neutrality
> Got my gun, now can't you see
> Blitzkrieg baby, you can't bomb me.

That was an American hit song in May 1941. By then the bombing of London—the Blitz—and other cities had raged for many months while the United States remained conspicuously, not to say profitably, neutral.

In 1941, few Americans would have wanted to fight against England or see her defeated, but nor did many wish to enter the war. In 1940, Roosevelt, like Wilson before him, had campaigned for reelection on a promise of peace. Speaking in Boston on 30 October, only days before the election, he was unambiguous: "I have said this before, but I shall say it again and again and again: Your boys are not going to be sent into any foreign wars." Thirteen months later, the United States did enter the war, but involuntarily, when Japan bombed Pearl Harbor and Hitler declared war on the United States (and not the other way around, be it remembered).

Churchill immediately proposed himself for a visit to Washington, and despite a response from Roosevelt that fell a long way short of a pressing invitation, he set off in a battleship with a large entourage. Addressing Congress, he made a pleasing little joke about his parentage before returning to his theme that the two nations ought to be eternal allies: "If we had kept together after the last war, if we had taken common measures for our safety, this renewal of the curse need never have fallen upon us."[12]

For the next few years there was much rhetoric about the two nations as one, some harmless—the Irving Berlin song "My British Buddy" isn't sung nowadays much more than "Blitzkrieg Baby"—though some controversial. When General George Patton opened an Anglo-American service club in London by saying that such clubs were invaluable "because undoubtedly it is the destiny of the English and American peoples to rule the world, and the more we see of each other the better," he caused another of the storms that punctuated his career.[13] But behind the public embrace there were many private differences between the allies. And although the Americans and the British were fighting against the same enemy, they were by no means fighting for the same thing.

Less than a year after the defeat of Germany, and his own electoral defeat, Churchill spoke in Fulton, but other events were already casting a different light on his "special relationship." He gave another speech six months later, in Zurich, and a very fine one. "There can be no revival of Europe without a spiritually great France and a spiritually great Germany. The structure of the United States of Europe will be such as to make the material strength of a single State less important."[14] But then look again at Churchill's speech in Fulton.

There was already a natural grouping in the Western Hemisphere, he said, and now an embryonic one in Europe, while "we British have our own Commonwealth of Nations." But did we? Did that phrase have any political meaning—and did the "special relationship" either? At the time, those two questions were posed in sharp form. A month after Churchill's visit to Zurich, and just in time for the midterm elections, President Truman made what the British considered an inflammatory and reckless demand for the admission of more Jews to what was still British Mandatory Palestine. Since the landslide Labour victory in 1945, the Prime Minister had been C. R. Attlee, Churchill's wartime deputy. He now lost patience with Truman, angrily rebuking the President for not having consulted the Prime Minister "of the country which has the actual responsibility for the government of Palestine in order that he might acquaint you with the actual situation and probable results of your action."[15]

In August 1947, India became independent, which is to say, the old Raj was partitioned into two new states. And in November, the General Assembly of the fledgling United Nations debated the partition of Palestine. That had been accepted by the Zionists, who were ready to take part of the territory as a Jewish state, faute de mieux and as a bird in the hand, but it was resolutely rejected by the Palestinians and all other Arabs. The British abstained while hoping that the General Assembly would not vote in favor of partition by the necessary two-thirds majority.

But Washington supported the Zionists and used all its considerable powers of suasion to make others vote in favor. The Latin American republics obediently voted for partition—and so did Australia, Canada, New Zealand, and South Africa, following Washington rather than London. On the other side, newborn India and Pakistan joined a group of thirteen states voting against partition, nine of them Muslim. This should have made two things clear. The "British Commonwealth" now had no political or military meaning. And "special" or otherwise, any relationship the United States had with Great Britain would take second place to other American interests, not least domestic political concerns.

When NATO was founded in 1949, its members were committed to mutual defense for "*the security of the North Atlantic area,*" which I emphasize. As became clear over the years, London and Washington were far from constant companions outside that area. In 1956, President Eisenhower conspicuously (and rightly) did not support the British in their Suez enterprise, while ten years later Harold Wilson politely (and rightly) declined to send British troops to Vietnam. In between, and in the wake of the Suez fiasco, came Harold Macmillan. Like Churchill, he was half-American, and he had, moreover, a family connection with President Kennedy. Macmillan had married Lady Dorothy Cavendish (albeit not quite a marriage made in heaven), whereas Kathleen Kennedy, the sister of John, had married Lady Dorothy's nephew, William, Marquess of Hartington, who was killed in action only weeks after their brief honeymoon in 1944.

The lesson Macmillan took from Suez was that he should stay close to Washington. By contrast, Charles de Gaulle, who came to power also in the lingering aftermath of Suez, decided that the Americans could not be trusted and that he must follow his own course. But then he had done that already during the Second World War, incurring the bitter hatred of President Roosevelt. Writing in 1960, Eden looked back to those days, but was also thinking of more recent events. Although at the time de Gaulle's conduct had seemed "contumacious, especially to our American ally, perhaps we should have learnt from it": "Some of the faults of later years might have been avoided if we had shown more of the same spirit."[16]

It was Macmillan who had coined another phrase. While he was Churchill's wartime proconsul in the Mediterranean, Macmillan had said of the Americans that the English were "Greeks to their Romans." The Americans were a "great big, vulgar, bustling people," as he condescendingly put it, who had to be guided as the Roman emperors had once been by learned advisers.[17] It was unfortunate for the comparison that those sophisticated Greek mentors in Rome were, in fact, slaves, but in any case, this "Greek" idea was really a kind of personal as well as national vanity. The truth was that the "Roman" Americans had no need to be guided or mentored by anyone, and certainly no wish to be.

If anyone should have known that, it was Macmillan. He had been well placed to see how deep wartime tensions between the two nations often were. And again when he was Prime Minister, there were sharp Anglo-American differences over defense. And then something even more telling occurred in late 1962: the Cuban missile crisis took the two superpowers closer to war than ever before or since. At its most acute point, U.S. Air Force Boeings armed with hydrogen bombs were flying along the Arctic coast of Russia at the stage of readiness one level below war. The crisis was eventually defused with a little old-fashioned backstairs wheeling and dealing. And yet throughout this drama, Washington barely bothered to keep the British government informed, let alone ask those wise Greeks for any advice.

One man President Kennedy did consult was Dean Acheson, now a Washington grey eminence. Only weeks after the Cuban crisis, he gave a keynote address at West Point. If not quite a shot heard round the would, Acheson's speech contained words that crossed the Atlantic like a tsunami:

> Great Britain has lost an empire and not yet found a role. The attempt to play a separate power role that is, a role apart from Europe, a role based on the "special relationship" with the US, a role based on being head of a "Commonwealth" which has no political structure or unity . . . —this role is about played out.[18]

It is hard to recapture—or understand—the intense anguish those words caused in London. What he said might strike us as no more than a statement of the obvious, but the horrified British reaction showed how much a sacred talisman that relationship had become.

Not that all Englishmen, or even all Tories, shared Macmillan's delusion. His minister responsible for the first, abortive attempt to enter what was then the Common Market, and has since evolved into the European Union, was Edward Heath. By 1964, Labour was in power under Wilson, of whom his sometime colleague Roy Jenkins said that he wanted to play head prefect to President Johnson's headmaster, even if not to the point of joining the Vietnam War. And by 1965, Heath was Conservative leader. Two years later, as leader of the opposition, he gave a most revealing and neglected series of lectures at Harvard, in which he spoke skeptically about "the so-called special relationship."[19] And although his Prime Ministership (1970–4) could not be called a success, it was notable for his detachment from Washington and for his decisive step of joining the European Economic Community.

In 1975, Heath was ousted as Tory leader by Margaret Thatcher, who became Prime Minister in 1979. Over the next decade, she spoke warmly of the United States, of President Reagan once he reached the White House, and of the Anglo-American relationship. But once again, rhetoric disguised reality, especially outside that North Atlantic area. When Mrs. Thatcher decided in 1982 to remove the Argentine invaders by force from the Falklands, the initial response from Washington was equivocal at best, with some members of the Reagan administration, such as Jeane Kirkpatrick, counseling neutrality, on the ground that the ruling Argentine junta was a useful American ally.

The following year, Thatcher was outraged by the American invasion of Grenada, a British territory of sorts, of which action she had been given no warning. And in the Middle East, she and Reagan were by no means what the Germans call one heart and one soul. Both her admirers and her detractors might be surprised by the robust private dressing-down she gave George Shultz, the Secretary of State, when she visited Washington in early 1986. She wanted to know whether the Israelis were ever going to relinquish the West Bank, she said that there would never be a lasting peace until justice was done for the Palestinians, and she warned Shultz that this wouldn't happen as long as the United States offered Israel unconditional support.

Less than seven years after Thatcher's deposition by her party, Blair became Prime Minister. Before 1997, he had shown rather little interest in foreign affairs, but in office he developed a new international vision. For him, that meant an intense attachment to the United States, as his words that evening in 1998 in the White House made clear: "Whither thou goest . . . even to the end." What no one then could ever have guessed was what "the end" would mean. Blair adroitly transferred his loyalty to the new administration when

President George W. Bush was inaugurated in January 2001, and a bust of Churchill was presented to Bush on behalf of the British people. The president prominently installed it in the White House, and following the 11 September attack, he regularly invoked Churchill's name as the long-gestated plan to invade Iraq came to fruition.

Alongside was his faithful ally Tony Blair. Shortly after 11 September, Bush greeted him with the words, "Thank you for coming, friend," when Blair addressed Congress like Churchill before him. The Prime Minister promised his complete support, with no "implausible and impractical advice from the touchline . . . We will stay with you to the last."[20] As good as his word, Blair backed the invasion of Iraq all along, which is to say that he committed himself to war well before he told Parliament or the British people. British participation in the war was his purely personal achievement, done in face of the skepticism of the electorate, the Foreign Office, most Labour MPs, if they had expressed themselves honestly, and some of Blair's closest colleagues. By early 2003, the Prime Minister's political difficulties were clear even in Washington, and Bush gave Blair an opportunity to stand aside. But he told Bush once more, "I'm with you and I'm going to be with you." Even to the end.

Almost all the justifications advanced for the invasion at the time have been falsified in the event, and the angry debate over the war since has turned on Downing Street's presentation—or misrepresentation—of evidence of weapons of mass destruction, as well as the dubious legality of the war. But Blair did hold one belief with passionate sincerity: it was his duty to support the American administration at all times. Only by displaying complete loyalty could he expect to influence them.

He said this to the Cabinet a year before the invasion. Robin Cook was Blair's first Foreign Secretary until he was demoted, perhaps because of doubts about his absolute reliability, doubts that were in a way confirmed when Cook became the only significant person to resign from Blair's government in protest of the Iraq War. In March 2002, Cook recorded Blair telling the Cabinet, "We must steer close to America. If we don't we will lose our influence to shape what they do."[21] At the same time, he told a trusted journalist that his mission was to embrace Bush so tightly as to "keep the United States in the international system."

Here was "Greeks and Romans" writ new: the Americans needed Blair to keep them in line and to shape their actions. But this was not only more national and personal vanity, it was sheer fantasy. There was never the smallest likelihood that the Bush administration would allow Blair to shape its actions or keep it in the international system, and nor did it: it is now a matter of historical record that he had no such influence at all.

AT THIS POINT, I MIGHT ADDRESS the possible charge that the foregoing account of Anglo-American relations is in some sense "anti-American." There is a simple answer to that. The United States is a sovereign country. That is the point of the Fourth of July. The United States follows its own objectives and instincts, which may or may not be wise and virtuous, and which may or may not coincide with those of other countries, the United Kingdom among them.

At the heart of Macmillan's "Greeks and Romans" was a misconception that Charles Williams, his recent biographer, puts his finger on. Like other Prime Ministers before and since, Macmillan persuaded himself that there was some mystical bond between the two countries, quite failing to see that "the United States, like all great powers, would in the end follow—without necessarily much regard for others—what it perceived from time to time to be its own interests."[22] If he did nothing else, Blair demonstrated this truth more clearly than ever before.

One of the few English journalists—or politicians—to grasp fully what was happening, and its implications, was the late Hugo Young. The year before his untimely death from cancer saw a remarkable swan song, and in the very last column he wrote, in September 2003, he said that "the great overarching fact about the war that Blair will never admit but cannot convincingly deny" was that "he was committed to war months before he said he was." As a result, "we have ceased to be a sovereign nation."[23] Iraq was the apotheosis of the special relationship—and its nemesis.

Even then, it wasn't Iraq that ended Blair's Prime Ministership, but another conflict, one in the Holy Land. One of the ways he sold the war to his reluctant followers was by promising that it would lead to a renewal of the Israeli-Palestinian peace process, as it is forlornly known. Not only was there no such renewal, but Blair was grossly humiliated as well. In April 2004, he went to Washington, but he had been preceded by another Prime Minister, and he found that Ariel Sharon and George Bush had cut a deal. Both men needed something the other could provide. Ahead of his reelection campaign in the autumn, Bush wanted the endorsement of the Israeli leader, and Sharon, having finally decided to withdraw from Gaza, wanted something to sugar the pill and comfort his more intransigent supporters. Bush provided this in the form of an assurance that whatever the outcome, there would be no "right of return" for Palestinian refugees and no going back to the borders before the 1967 war.

Any rights and wrongs of this are for our purposes irrelevant. What matters is that the deal the two cut was a complete repudiation of existing British policy. And yet all Blair could limply say about this fait accompli was that it offered hope for progress.

Resentment had long been simmering in the highest quarters, but it was the events of that April that provoked an unprecedented protest from fifty-two retired ambassadors. The Iraq War had been bad enough, they wrote, but now the international community had been confronted by Sharon and Bush with new policies "which are one-sided and illegal and which will cost yet more Israeli and Palestinian blood."[24]

Two years later came another decisive event, the Israeli war in Lebanon. With little more than one British voter in five supporting the Israeli action, and almost all the Cabinet longing to join the worldwide demand for a cease-fire, Blair would not budge from the American and Israeli line. This led to an internal party revolt that Blair could placate only by saying that he would leave within a year.

And it also provoked a still more ferocious outburst. Sir Rodric Braithwaite had retired after forty years in the Foreign Office, ending as ambassador to Russia and then Chairman of the Joint Intelligence Committee. He has since written two excellent books, on the 1941 battle of Moscow, and *Afgantsy,* on the ill-fated Russian campaign in Afghanistan thirty years ago.[25] For all the discretion for which "the Office" was famous, he exploded with long-suppressed anger in the decorous pages of the *Financial Times:*

> Mr Blair's prime responsibility is to defend the interests of his own country. This he has signally failed to do. Stiff in opinions, but often in the wrong, he has manipulated public opinion, sent our soldiers into distant lands for ill-conceived purposes, misused the intelligence agencies to serve his ends and reduced the Foreign Office to a demoralised cipher because it keeps reminding him of inconvenient facts . . . Mr Blair has done more damage to British interests in the Middle East than Anthony Eden . . . Blair's total identification with the White House has destroyed his influence in Washington, Europe and the Middle East itself: who bothers with the monkey if he can go straight to the organ-grinder?[26]

Seven years before, Blair had been acclaimed by one American admirer as "the leader of the free world," and only two years earlier a book had been published called *Tony Blair: The Making of a World Leader.*[27] Now he seemed much less a world leader than what a Beirut newspaper called him, "Washington's international gofer." And Alan Cowell, the perceptive *New York Times* correspondent, added that "if the Lebanon conflict said anything about what some Britons like to call their special relationship with America, it seemed to be this: in this Middle East war, the only special relationship bound the United States to Israel, not Britain."[28]

In June 2007, Blair departed, with a valedictory tribute from President Bush. Making his unlikely debut as a contributor to the *Sun*, Rupert Murdoch's tabloid, he praised his friend Tony Blair with the words, "I've heard he's been called Bush's poodle. He's bigger than that."[29] Blair left not only Downing Street but Parliament and the country on the same day, having said in his last Commons speech that he was going to head a peace mission in Jerusalem, where his "absolute priority" would be to "prepare the ground for a negotiated settlement."[30]

Days later, Aaron David Miller, a former State Department official who had advised six secretaries of state, said he hoped that Blair didn't see himself as any sort of lead negotiator, since "I know that's not the role that either the President or the Secretary of State wants for him."[31] And to confirm this with greater bluntness, a State Department spokesman, Tom Casey, said that Blair's role would be merely to cajole the Palestinians, adding, "but my understanding is there's certainly no envisioning that this individual would be a negotiator between the Israelis and Palestinians."[32] From "Thank you for coming, friend" to "this individual"!

Since then we have heard one witness after another at the Chilcot inquiry on Iraq saying the same thing as Braithwaite. Blair had no discernible influence in Washington, all the less so because he had given an unconditional commitment in the first place. "We could have achieved more by playing a tougher role," Sir Christopher Meyer said. Blair could have told Bush he would not commit British troops "unless we have palpable progress on the peace process." And in the unkindest cut of all, Meyer added, "I think Margaret Thatcher would have . . . insisted on a coherent political and diplomatic strategy."[33] So would Churchill.

MAYBE AMERICANS TOO HAVE BECOME skeptical about this so-called special relationship. President Barack Obama has felt constrained to utter or mutter the phrase when greeting Prime Ministers, but they say that actions speak louder than words. One of the first things the President did after his inauguration was to have the bust of Churchill removed from the White House and replaced with one of Abraham Lincoln.

Spring Semester 2011

1. John Kampfner, *Blair's Wars* (London, 2003), p. 89.

2. Winston Churchill, in *Blood, Toil, Tears and Sweat: The Speeches of Winston Churchill*, ed. David Cannadine (Boston, 1989), p. 301.

3. Sir Michel Howard, "Afterword: The 'Special Relationship,'" in Wm. Roger Louis and Hedley Bull, eds., *The "Special Relationship": Anglo-American Relations since 1945* (Oxford, 1986), p. 387.

4. Christopher Meyer, *DC Confidential: The Controversial Memoirs of Britain's Ambassador to the U.S. at the Time of 9/11 and the Iraq War* (London, 2005), p. 56.

5. John McCain, interview by Matthew D'Ancona, "John McCain on David Cameron," *Spectator*, 27 Sept. 2006.

6. Thomas Jefferson to John Randolph, 25 Aug. 1775, in Thomas Jefferson, *Writings* (New York, 1984), p. 750; Benjamin Franklin and Silas Deane to the Committee of Secret Correspondence, 12 Mar. 1777, in Jared Sparks, ed., *The Diplomatic Correspondence of the American Revolution*, 2 vols. (Boston, 1829), I, 281.

7. Quoted in Piers Brendon, *The Decline and Fall of the British Empire, 1781–1997* (London, 2007), p. 8.

8. David Reynolds, "The Wartime Anglo-American Alliance," in Louis and Bull, *The "Special Relationship,"* p. 21.

9. Neville Chamberlain to Hilda Chamberlain, 17 Dec. 1937, in *The Neville Chamberlain Diary Letters, Volume Four: The Downing Street Years, 1934–1940*, ed. Robert Self (Aldershot, 2005), p. 294.

10. Quoted in Tim Shipman, "Cameron's Historic Blunder: Fury as PM Says We Were 'Junior Partner' to Americans in 1940," *Daily Mail*, 22 July 2010.

11. Tony Blair, *A Journey: My Political Life* (London, 2010), p. 353.

12. Churchill, in *Blood, Toil, Tears and Sweat*, p. 233.

13. Quoted in Dwight Macdonald, "My Favorite General," *Politics* (May 1944).

14. Churchill, in *Blood, Toil, Tears and Sweat*, pp. 312–13.

15. Quoted in Norman Rose, *"A Senseless, Squalid War": Voices from Palestine, 1945–48* (London, 2009), p. 127.

16. Anthony Eden, *The Reckoning: The Memoirs of Anthony Eden, Earl of Avon* (Boston, 1965), p. 250.

17. Charles Williams, *Harold Macmillan* (London, 2009), p. 128.

18. Quoted in Douglas Brinkley, "Dean Acheson and the 'Special Relationship': The West Point Speech of December 1962," *Historical Journal*, 33, 3 (Sept. 1990), p. 601.

19. Edward Heath, *Old World, New Horizons: Britain, Europe, and the Atlantic Alliance* (Cambridge, Mass., 1970), p. 63.

20. Richard W. Stevenson, "Bush at His Side, Blair Is Resolute in War's Defense," *New York Times*, 18 July 2003.

21. Robin Cook, *The Point of Departure* (London, 2003), p. 116.

22. Williams, *Harold Macmillan*, p. 476.

23. Hugo Young, "Under Blair, Britain Has Ceased to Be a Sovereign State," *Guardian*, 16 Sept. 2003.

24. Matthew Tempest, "Diplomats Attack Blair's Israel Policy," *Guardian*, 26 Apr. 2004.

25. Rodric Braithwaite, *Afgantsy: The Russians in Afghanistan, 1979–1989* (London, 2011).

26. Rodric Braithwaite, "Mr. Blair Should Recognize His Errors and Go," *Financial Times*, 2 Aug. 2006.

27. Philip Stephens, *Tony Blair: The Making of a World Leader* (New York, 2004).

28. Alan Cowell, "Letter from Britain: The Latest Crises Do Little for Blair's Political Standing," *New York Times,* 15 Aug. 2006.

29. Rebekah Wade, "Blair Ain't My Poodle Says Bush," *Sun,* 27 June 2007.

30. *Parliamentary Debates (Hansard),* June 27, 2007.

31. David Blair, "Blair Won't Have Power to Mediate on Peace," *Telegraph,* 30 June 2007.

32. Quoted in Geoffrey Wheatcroft, "The Church in England: Downright Un-American," *New York Times,* 25 Nov. 2007.

33. Christopher Meyer, "The Transatlantic Relationship," *The Iraq Inquiry,* 26 Nov. 2009.

British Studies at
the University of Texas, 1975–2011

Fall Semester 1975

Paul Scott (Novelist, London), 'The *Raj Quartet*'

Ian Donaldson (Australian National University), 'Humanistic Studies in Australia'

Fritz Fellner (Salzburg University), 'Britain and the Origins of the First World War'

Roger Louis (History), 'Churchill, Roosevelt, and the Future of Dependent Peoples during the Second World War'

Michael Holroyd (Biographer, Dublin), 'Two Biographies: Lytton Strachey and Augustus John'

Max Beloff (Buckingham College), 'Imperial Sunset'

Robin Winks (Yale University), 'British Empire-Commonwealth Studies'

Warren Roberts (HRHRC) and David Farmer (HRHRC), 'The D. H. Lawrence Editorial Project'

Harvey C. Webster (University of Louisville), 'C. P. Snow as Novelist and Philosopher'

Anthony Kirk-Greene (Oxford University), 'The Origins and Aftermath of the Nigerian Civil War'

Spring Semester 1976

Joseph Jones (English), 'World English'

William S. Livingston (Government), 'The British Legacy in Contemporary Indian Politics'

John Higley (Sociology), 'The Recent Political Crisis in Australia'

Round Table Discussion, 'Reassessments of Evelyn Waugh': Elspeth Rostow (Dean, General and Comparative Studies), Standish Meacham (History), and Alain Blayac (University of Paris)

Jo Grimond (former Leader of the Liberal Party), 'Liberal Democracy in Britain'

Round Table Discussion, 'The Impact of Hitler on British Politics': Gaines Post (History), Malcolm Macdonald (Government), and Roger Louis (History)

Round Table Discussion, 'Kipling and India': Robert Hardgrave (Government), Gail Minault (History), and Chihiro Hosoya (University of Tokyo)

Kenneth Kirkwood (Oxford University), 'The Future of Southern Africa'

C. P. Snow, 'Elite Education in England'

Hans-Peter Schwarz (Cologne University), 'The Impact of Britain on German Politics and Society since the Second World War'

B. K. Nehru (Indian High Commissioner, London), 'The Political Crisis in India'

Round Table Discussion, 'Declassification of Secret Documents: The British and American Experiences Compared': Robert A. Divine (History), Harry J. Middleton (LBJ Library), and Roger Louis (History)

Fall Semester 1976

John Farrell (English), 'Revolution and Tragedy in Victorian England'

Anthony Honoré (Oxford University), 'British Attitudes to Legal Regulation of Sex'

Alan Hill (English), 'Wordsworth and America'

Ian Nish (London School of Economics), 'Anglo-American Naval Rivalry and the End of the Anglo-Japanese Alliance'

Norman Sherry (University of Lancaster), 'Joseph Conrad and the British Empire'

Peter Edwards (Australian National University), 'Australia through American Eyes: The Second World War and the Rise of Australia as a Regional Power'

Round Table Discussion, 'Britain and the Future of Europe': David Edwards (Government), Steven Baker (Government), Malcolm Macdonald (Government), William S. Livingston (Government), and Roger Louis (History)

Michael Hurst (Oxford University), 'The British Empire in Historical Perspective: The Case of Joseph Chamberlain'

Ronald Grierson (English Banker and former Public Official), 'The Evolution of the British Economy since 1945'

Marian Kent (University of New South Wales), 'British Oil Policy between the World Wars'

Constance Babington-Smith (Cambridge University), 'The World of Rose Macaulay'

Round Table Discussion, 'Adam Smith after 200 Years': William Todd (History), Walt Rostow (History and Economics), and James McKie (Dean, Social and Behavioral Sciences)

Spring Semester 1977

Carin Green (Novelist) and Elspeth Rostow (American Studies), 'The Achievement of Virginia Woolf'

Samuel H. Beer (Professor of Government, Harvard University), 'Reflections on British Politics'

David Fieldhouse (Oxford University), 'Decolonization and the Multinational Corporations'

Gordon Craig (Stanford University), 'England and Europe on the Eve of the Second World War'

John Lehmann (British Publisher and Writer), 'Publishing under the Bombs— The Hogarth Press during World War II'

Round Table Discussion, 'The Author, His Editor, and Publisher': Philip Jones (University of Texas Press), William S. Livingston (Government), Michael

Mewshaw (English), David Farmer (HRC), Roger Louis (History), and William Todd (History),

Dick Taverne (former Member of Parliament), 'The Mood of Britain: Misplaced Gloom or Blind Complacency?'

Round Table Discussion, 'The Origins of World War II in the Pacific': James B. Crowley (Yale University), Lloyd C. Gardner (Rutgers University), Akira Iriye (University of Chicago), and Roger Louis (History)

Rosemary Murray (Cambridge University), 'Higher Education in England'

Burke Judd (Zoology) and Robert Wagner (Zoology), 'Sir Cyril Burt and the Controversy over the Heritability of IQ'

Round Table Discussion, 'The Wartime Reputations of Churchill and Roosevelt: Overrated or Underrated?': Alessandra Lippucci (Government), Roger Louis (History), William S. Livingston (Government), and Walt Rostow (Economics)

Fall Semester 1977

Donald L. Weismann (Art and Art History), 'British Art in the Nineteenth Century: Turner and Constable—Precursors of French Impressionism'

Standish Meacham (History), 'Social Reform in England'

Joseph Jones, 'Recent Commonwealth Literature'

Lewis Hoffacker (former US Ambassador), 'The Katanga Crisis: British and Other Connections'

Round Table Discussion, 'The Copyright Law of 1976': James M. Treece (Law), Roger Louis (History), Warren Roberts, and Bill Todd (History)

Round Table Discussion, 'Freedom at Midnight: A Reassessment of Britain and the Partition of India Thirty Years After': Charles Heimsath (Visiting Professor of Indian History), Bob Hardgrave (Government), Thomasson Jannuzi, (Center for Asian Studies), C. P. Andrade (Comparative Studies), and William S. Livingston (Government),

Lord Fraser of Kilmorack (Conservative Party Organization), 'The Tory Tradition of British Politics'

Bernth Lindfors (English), 'Charles Dickens and the Hottentots and Zulus'

Albert Hourani (Oxford University), 'The Myth of T. E. Lawrence'

Mark Kinkead-Weekes (University of Kent) and Mara Kalnins (British Writer), 'D. H. Lawrence: Censorship and the Expression of Ideas'

J. D. B. Miller (Australian National University), 'The Collapse of the British Empire'

Round Table Discussion, 'The Best and Worst Books of 1977': Peter Green (Classics), Robert King (Dean, Social and Behavioral Sciences), William S. Livingston (Government), Bob Hardgrave (Government), Roger Louis (History), and Warren Roberts (HRHRC)

Spring Semester 1978

Round Table Discussion, 'British Decadence in the Interwar Years': Peter Green (Classics), Malcolm Macdonald (Government), and Robert Crunden (American Studies),

Round Table Discussion, R. Emmet Tyrrell's *Social Democracy's Failure in Britain*: Terry Quist (UT Undergraduate), Steve Baker (Government), and Roger Louis (History),

Stephen Koss (Columbia University), 'The British Press: Press Lords, Politicians, and Principles'

John House (Oxford University), 'The Rhodesian Crisis'
T. S. Dorsch (Durham University), 'Oxford in the 1930s'
Stephen Spender (English Poet and Writer), 'Britain and the Spanish Civil War'
Okot p'Bitek (Ugandan Poet), 'Idi Amin's Uganda'
David C. Goss (Australian Consul General), 'Wombats and Wivveroos'
Leon Epstein (University of Wisconsin), 'Britain and the Suez Crisis of 1956'
David Schoonover (Library Science), 'British and American Expatriates in Paris in the 1920s'
Peter Stansky (Stanford University), 'George Orwell and the Spanish Civil War'
Alexander Parker (Spanish and Portuguese), 'Reflections on the Spanish Civil War'
Norman Sherry (Lancaster University), 'Graham Greene and Latin America'
Martin Blumenson (Department of the Army), 'The Ultra Secret'

Fall Semester 1978

W. H. Morris-Jones (University of London), 'Power and Inequality in Southeast Asia'
Round Table Discussion, 'The British and the Shaping of the American Critical Mind: Edmund Wilson's *Letters on Literature and Politics*': Hartley Grattan (History), Gilbert Chase (American Studies), Bob Crunden (American Studies), and Roger Louis (History),
James Roach (Government), 'The Indian Emergency and its Aftermath'
Bill Todd (History), 'The Lives of Samuel Johnson'
Lord Hatch (British Labour Politician), 'The Labour Party and Africa'
John Kirkpatrick (HRHRC), 'Max Beerbohm'
Brian Levack (History), 'Witchcraft in England and Scotland'
M. R. Masani (Indian Writer), 'Gandhi and Gandhism'
A. W. Coates (Economics), 'The Professionalization of the British Civil Service'
John Clive (Harvard University), 'Great Historians of the Nineteenth Century'
Geoffrey Best (University of Sussex), 'Flight Path to Dresden: British Strategic Bombing in the Second World War'
Kurth Sprague (English), 'T. H. White's *Once and Future King*'
Gilbert Chase (American Studies), 'The British Musical Invasion of America'

Spring Semester 1979

Round Table Discussion, 'P. N. Furbanks's Biography of E. M. Forster': Peter Green (Classics), Alessandra Lippucci (Government), and Elspeth Rostow (LBJ School)
Round Table Discussion, 'E. M. Forster and India': Roger Louis (History), Bob Hardgrave (Government), Gail Minault (Professor of History), Peter Gran (History), and Bob King (Dean of Liberal Arts)
Paul M. Kennedy (University of East Anglia), 'The Contradiction between British Strategic Policy and Economic Policy in the Twentieth Century'
Richard Rive (Visiting Fulbright Research Fellow from South Africa), 'Olive Schreiner and the South African Nation'
Charles P. Kindleberger (Massachusetts Institute of Technology), 'Lord Zuckerman and the Second World War'
John Press (English Poet), 'English Poets and Postwar Society'
Richard Ellmann (Oxford University), 'Writing a Biography of Joyce'
Michael Finlayson (Scottish Dramatist), 'Contemporary British Theater'

Lawrence Stone (Institute for Advanced Study, Princeton), 'Family, Sex, and Marriage in England'

C. P. Snow, 'Reflections on the Two Cultures'

Theodore Zeldin (Oxford University), 'Are the British More or Less European than the French?'

David Edwards (Government), 'How United the Kingdom: Greater or Lesser Britain?'

Michael Holroyd (British Biographer), 'George Bernard Shaw'

John Wickman (Eisenhower Library), 'Eisenhower and the British'

Fall Semester 1979

Robert Palter (Philosophy), 'Reflections on British Philosophers: Locke, Hume, and the Utilitarians'

Alfred Gollin (University of California, Santa Barbara), 'Political Biography as Political History: Garvin, Milner, and Balfour'

Edward Steinhart (History), 'The Consequences of British Rule in Uganda'

Paul Sturges (Loughborough University, UK), and Dolores Donnelly (Toronto University), 'History of the National Library of Canada'

Sir Michael Tippett (British Composer), 'Moving into Aquarius'

Steven Baker (Government), 'Britain and United Nations Emergency Operations'

Maria Okila Dias (University of São Paulo), 'Intellectual Roots of Informal Imperialism: Britain and Brazil'

Alexander Parker (Spanish and Portuguese), 'Reflections on *Brideshead Revisited*'

Barry C. Higman (University of the West Indies), 'West Indian Emigrés and the British Empire'

Gaines Post (History), 'Britain and the Outbreak of the Second World War'

Karen Gould (Art and Art History), 'Medieval Manuscript Fragments and English Seventeenth-Century Collections: New Perspectives from *Fragmenta Manuscripta*'

Round Table Discussion of Jeanne MacKenzie's *Dickens: A Life:* John Farrell (English), Eric Poole (HRHRC) and James Bieri (English):

Joseph O. Baylen (Georgia State University), 'British Journalism in the Late Victorian and Edwardian Eras'

Peter T. Flawn (President, University of Texas), 'An Appreciation of Charles Dickens'

Spring Semester 1980

Annette Weiner (Anthropology), 'Anthropologists in New Guinea: British Interpretations and Cultural Relativism'

Bernard Richards (Oxford University), 'Conservation in the Nineteenth Century'

Thomas McGann (History), 'Britain and Argentina: An Informal Dominion?'

Mohammad Ali Jazayery (Center for Middle Eastern Studies), 'The Persian Tradition in English Literature'

C. Hartley Grattan (History) 'Twentieth-Century British Novels and the American Critical Mind'

Katherine Whitehorn (London *Observer*), 'An Insider's View of the *Observer*'

Guy Lytle (History), 'The Oxford University Press's *History of Oxford*'

C. P. Snow, 'Reflections on *The Masters*'

Harvey Webster, '*The Masters* and the Two Cultures'

Brian Blakeley (Texas Tech University), 'Women and the British Empire'

Stephen Koss (Columbia University), 'Asquith, Balfour, Milner, and the First World War'

Tony Smith (Tufts University), 'The Expansion of England: New Ideas on Controversial Themes in British Imperialism'

Stanley Ross (History), 'Britain and the Mexican Revolution'

Rowland Smith (Dalhousie University), 'The British Intellectual Left and the War, 1939–1945'

Richard Ellmann (Oxford University), 'Oscar Wilde: A Reconsideration and Problems of the Literary Biographer'

James Bill (Government), 'The United States, Britain, and the Iranian Crisis of 1953'

Fall Semester 1980

Decherd Turner (HRHRC), 'The First 1000 Days'

Roger Louis (History), 'Britain and Egypt after the Second World War'

Alistair Horne (Woodrow Wilson Center), 'Britain and the Fall of France'

Round Table Discussion, 'Literary Fraud: H. R. Trevor-Roper and the Hermit of Peking': Edward Rhodes (History), Peter Green (Classics), William Todd (History), and Roger Louis (History),

Mark Kinkead-Weekes (Kent University), 'D. H. Lawrence's *Rainbow:* Its Sense of History'

Sir John Crawford (Australian National University), 'Hartley Grattan: In Memoriam'

John Stubbs (University of Waterloo), 'The Tory View of Politics and Journalism in the Interwar Years'

Donald L. Weismann (Art and Art History), 'British Art in the Nineteenth Century'

Fran Hill (Government), 'The Legacy of British Colonialism in Tanzania'

R. W. B. Lewis (Yale University), 'What's Wrong with the Teaching of English?'

Charlene Gerry (British Publisher), 'The Revival of Fine Printing in Britain'

Peter Gran (History), 'The Islamic Response to British Capitalism'

Tina Poole (HRHRC) 'Gilbert and Sullivan's Christmas'

Spring Semester 1981

Bernard N. Darbyshire (Visiting Professor of Government and Economics), 'North Sea Oil and the British Future'

Christopher Hill (Oxford University), 'The English Civil War'

Elizabeth Heine (UT San Antonio), and Roger Louis (History), 'A Reassessment of Leonard Woolf'

Bernard Richards (Oxford University), 'D. H. Lawrence and Painting'

Miguel Gonzalez-Gerth (Spanish and Portuguese), 'Poetry Once Removed: The Resonance of English as a Second Language'

John Putnam Chalmers (HRHRC), 'English Bookbinding from Caedmon to Le Carré'

Peter Coltman (Architecture), 'The Cultural Landscapes of Britain: 2,000 Years of Blood, Sweat, Toil & Tears to Wrest a Living from this Bloody Mud'

Thomas H. Law (former Regent, University of Texas), 'The Gold Coins of the English Sovereigns'

Round Table Discussion, 'Canadian-American Economic Relations': Sidney Weintraub (LBJ School), James W. McKie (Economics), and Mary Williams (Canadian Consulate, Dallas)

Amedée Turner (European Parliament), 'Integrating Britain into the European Community'

Muriel C. Bradbrook (Cambridge University), 'Two Poets: Kathleen Raine and Seamus Heaney'

Ronald Sampson (Industrial Development Department, Aberdeen), 'Scotland—Somewhat of a British Texas?'

Fall Semester 1981

Jerome Bump (English), 'From Texas to England: The Ancestry of Our Victorian Architecture'

Lord Fraser of Kilmorack, 'Leadership Styles of Tory Prime Ministers since the Second World War'

William Carr (University of Sheffield), 'A British Interpretation of American, German, and Japanese Foreign Policy 1936–1941'

Iqbal Narain (Rajasthan University, Jaipur), 'The Ups and Downs of Indian Academic Life'

Don Etherington (HRHRC), 'The Florence Flood, 1966: The British Effort—or: Up to our Necks in Mud and Books'

E. V. K. Fitzgerald (Visiting Professor of Economics), 'The British University: Crisis, Confusion, and Stagnation'

Robert Crunden (American Studies), 'A Joshua for Historians: Mordecai Richter and Canadian Cultural Identity'

Bernth Lindfors (English), 'The Hottentot Venus and Other African Attractions in Nineteenth-Century England'

Chris Brookeman (London Polytechnic), 'The British Arts and Society'

Nicholas Pickwood (Freelance Book Conservator), 'The Libraries of the National Trust'

Kurth Sprague (English), 'John Steinbeck, Chase Horton, and the Matter of Britain'

Martin J. Wiener (Rice University), 'Cultural Values and Socio-Economic Behavior in Britain'

Werner Habicht (University of Würzburg), 'Shakespeare in Nineteenth-Century Germany'

Spring Semester 1982

Stevie Bezencenet (London College of Printing), 'Contemporary Photography in Britain'

Jane Marcus (English), 'Shakespeare's Sister, Beethoven's Brother: Dame Ethel Smyth and Virginia Woolf'

Wilson Harris (English) and Raja Rao (Philosophy), 'The Quest for Form: Britain and Commonwealth Perspectives'

Al Crosby (American Studies), 'The British Empire as a Product of Continental Drift'

Lord St. Brides (Visiting Scholar), 'The White House and Whitehall: Washington and Westminster'

Elizabeth Fernea (English and Middle East Studies), 'British Colonial Literature of the Middle East'

Maurice Evans (Actor and Producer), 'My Early Years in the Theater'

Joan Bassin (Kansas City Art Institute), 'Art and Industry in Nineteenth-Century England'

Eugene N. Borza (Pennsylvania State University), 'Sentimental British Philhelle-nism: Images of Greece'

Ralph Willett (University of Hull), 'The Style and Structure of British Television News'

Roger Louis (History), 'Britain and the Creation of the State of Israel'

Peter Russell (Oxford University), 'A British Historian Looks at Portuguese Histo-riography of the Fifteenth Century'

Rory Coker (Physics), 'Frauds, Hoaxes and Blunders in Science—a British Tradition?'

Ellen DuBois (State University of New York, Buffalo), 'Anglo-American Perspec-tives on the Suffragette Movement'

Donald G. Davis, Jr. (Library Science), 'Great Expectations—and a Few Illusions: Reflections on an Exchange Teaching Year in England'

Anthony Rota (Bertram Rota Ltd.), 'The Changing World of the Bookdealer'

Eisig Silberschlag (Visiting Professor of Judaic Studies), 'The Bible as the Most Popular Book in English'

Fall Semester 1982

Woodruff Smith (UT San Antonio), 'British Overseas Expansion'

The Rt. Hon. George Thomas (Speaker of the House of Commons), 'Parliamen-tary Democracy'

Nigel Nicolson (English Historian and Biographer), 'The English Country House as an Historical Document'

Lord St. Brides (Visiting Scholar), 'A Late Leaf of Laurel for Evelyn Waugh'

Lt. Col. Jack McNamara, USMC (Ret.), 'The Libel of Evelyn Waugh by the *Daily Express*'

James Wimsatt (English), 'Chaucer and Medieval French Manuscripts'

Christopher Whelan (Visiting Professor, UT Law School), 'Recent Developments in British Labour Law'

Brian Wearing (University of Canterbury, Christchurch), 'New Zealand: In the Pacific, but of It?'

Robert Hardgrave (Government), 'The United States and India'

James McBath (University of Southern California), 'The Evolution of *Hansard*'

Paul Fromm (University of Toronto), 'Canadian–United States Relations: Two Solitudes'

John Velz (English), 'When in Disgrace: Ganzel's Attempt to Exculpate John Payne Collier'

Roger Louis (History), 'British Origins of the Iranian Revolution'

Spring Semester 1983

Sir Ellis Waterhouse (Oxford University), 'A Comparison of British and French Painting in the Late Eighteenth Century'

E. J. L. Ride (Australian Consul General), 'Australia's Place in the World and Her Relationship with the United States'

Edward Bell (Royal Botanic Gardens, Kew), 'Kew Gardens in World History'

The Very Rev. Oliver Fiennes (Dean of Lincoln), 'The Care and Feeding of Magna Carta'

C. V. Narasimhan (former Under-Secretary of the United Nations), 'Last Days of the British Raj: A Civil Servant's View'

Warren G. Osmond, 'Sir Frederic Eggleston and the Development of Pacific Consciousness'

Richard Ellmann (Oxford University), 'Henry James among the Aesthetes'

Janet Caulkins (University of Wisconsin–Madison), 'The Poor Reputation of Cornish Knights in Medieval Literature'

Werner Habicht (University of Würzburg), 'Shakespeare and the Third Reich'

Gillian Peele (Oxford University), 'The Changing British Party System'

John Farrell (English), 'Scarlet Ribbons: Memories of Youth and Childhood in Victorian Authors'

Peter Russell (Oxford University), 'A Not So Bashful Stranger: *Don Quixote* in England, 1612–1781'

Sir Zelman Cowen (Oxford University), 'Contemporary Problems in Medicine, Law, and Ethics'

Dennis V. Lindley (Visiting Professor of Mathematics), 'Scientific Thinking in an Unscientific World'

Martin Blumenson (Department of the Army), 'General Mark Clark and the British in the Italian Campaign of World War II'

Fall Semester 1983

Anthony King (University of Essex), 'Margaret Thatcher and the Future of British Politics'

Alistair Gillespie (Canadian Minister of Energy, Mines, and Resources), 'Canadian-British Relations: Best and Worst'

Charles A. Owen, Jr. (University of Connecticut), 'The Pre-1400 Manuscripts of the *Canterbury Tales*'

Major-General (Ret.) Richard Clutterbuck (University of Exeter), 'Terrorism in Malaya'

Wayne A. Wiegand (University of Kentucky), 'British Propaganda in American Public Libraries during World War I'

Stuart Macintyre (Australian National University, Canberra), 'Australian Trade Unionism between the Wars'

Ram Joshi (Visiting Professor of History), 'Is Gandhi Relevant Today?'

Sir Denis Wright (former British Ambassador to Iran), 'Britain and the Iranian Revolution'

Andrew Horn (University of Lesotho), 'Theater and Politics in South Africa'

Philip Davies (University of Manchester), 'British Reaction to American Politics: Overt Rejection, Covert Assimilation'

H. K. Singh (Embassy of India), 'United States-Indian Relations'

Round Table Discussion, 'Two Cheers for Mountbatten: A Reassessment of Lord and Lady Mountbatten and the Partition of India': Roger Louis (History), Ram Joshi (Visiting Professor of History), and J. S. Mehta (LBJ School)

Spring Semester 1984

M. S. Venkataramani (Jawaharlal Nehru University), 'Winston Churchill and Indian Freedom'

Sir John Thompson (British Ambassador to the United Nations), 'The Falklands and Grenada in the United Nations'

Robert Farrell (Cornell University), 'Medieval Archaeology'

Allon White (University of Sussex), 'The Fiction of Early Modernism'

Round Table Discussion, 'Orwell's *Nineteen Eighty-Four*': Peter Green (Classics), Roger Louis (History), Miguel Gonzalez-Gerth (Spanish and Portuguese), Standish Meacham (History), and Sid Monas (Slavic Languages and History)

Uriel Dann (University of Tel Aviv), 'Hanover and Britain in the Time of George II'

José Ferrater-Mora (Bryn Mawr College), 'A. M. Turing and his "Universal Turing Machine"'

Rüdiger Ahrens (University of Würzburg), 'Teaching Shakespeare in German Universities'

Michael Brock (Oxford University), 'H. H. Asquith and Venetia Stanley'

Herbert Spiro (Free University of Berlin), 'What Makes the British and Americans Different from Everybody Else: The Adversary Process of the Common Law'

Nigel Bowles (University of Edinburgh), 'Reflections on Recent Developments in British Politics'

Harold Perkin (Rice University), 'The Evolution of Citizenship in Modern Britain'

Christopher Heywood (Sheffield University), '*Jane Eyre* and *Wuthering Heights*'

Dave Powers (Kennedy Library), 'JFK's Trip to Ireland, 1963'

R. W. Coats (Visiting Professor of Economics), 'John Maynard Keynes: The Man and the Economist'

David Evans (Astronomy), 'Astronomy as a British Cultural Export'

Fall Semester 1984

John Henry Faulk, 'Reflections on My Sojourns in the British Middle East'

Lord Fraser of Kilmorack, 'The Thatcher Years—and Beyond'

Michael Phillips (University of Edinburgh), 'William Blake and the Rise of the Hot Air Balloon'

Erik Stocker (HRHRC), 'A Bibliographical Detective Story: Reconstructing James Joyce's Library'

Amedée Turner (European Parliament), 'Recent Developments in the European Parliament'

Michael Hurst (Oxford University), 'Scholars versus Journalists on the English Social Classes'

Charles Alan Wright (Law), 'Reflections on Cambridge'

J. M. Winter (Cambridge University), 'Fear of Decline in Population in Britain after World War I'

Henk Wesseling (University of Leiden), 'Dutch Colonialism and the Impact on British Imperialism'

Celia Morris Eckhardt (Biographer and author of *Fannie Wright*), 'Frances Wright and *England as the Civilizer*'

Sir Oliver Wright (British Ambassador to the United States), 'British Foreign Policy—1984'

Leonard Thompson (Yale University), 'Political Mythology and the Racial Order in South Africa'

Flora Nwapa (Nigerian Novelist), 'Women in Civilian and Military Rule in Nigeria'

Richard Rose (University of Strathclyde), 'The Capacity of the Presidency in Comparative Perspective'

Spring Semester 1985

Bernard Hickey (University of Venice), 'Australian Literary Culture: Short Stories, Novels, and "Literary Journalism"'

Kenneth Hafertepe (American Studies), 'The British Foundations of the Smithsonian Castle: The Gothic Revival in Britain and America'

Rajeev Dhavan (Visiting Professor, LBJ School and Center for Asian Studies), 'Race Relations in England: Trapped Minorities and their Future'

Sir John Thompson (British Ambassador to the United Nations), 'British Techniques of Statecraft'

Philip Bobbitt (Law), 'Britain, the United States, and Reduction in Strategic Arms'

David Bevington (Drama Critic and Theater Historian), 'Maimed Rites: Interrupted Ceremony in *Hamlet*'

Standish Meacham (History), 'The Impact of the New Left History on British and American Historiography'

Iris Murdoch (Novelist and Philosopher), and John O. Bayley (Oxford University), 'Themes in English Literature and Philosophy'

John P. Chalmers (HRHRC), 'Malory Illustrated'

Thomas Metcalf (University of California, Berkeley), 'The Architecture of Empire: The British Raj in India'

Robert H. Wilson (English), 'Malory and His Readers'

Lord St. Brides, '*A Passage to India:* Better Film than Novel?'

Derek Pearsall (York University), 'Fire, Flood, and Slaughter: The Tribulations of the Medieval City of York'

E. S. Atieno Odhiambo (University of Nairobi), 'Britain and Kenya: The Mau Mau, the "Colonial State," and Dependency'

Francis Robinson (University of London), 'Indian Muslim Religious Leadership and Colonial Rule'

Charles B. MacDonald (U.S. Army), 'The British in the Battle of the Bulge'

Brian Levack (History), 'The Battle of Bosworth Field'

Kurth Sprague (English), 'The Mirrors of Malory'

Fall Semester 1985

A. P. Thornton (University of Toronto), 'Whatever Happened to the British Commonwealth?'

Michael Garibaldi Hall (History), and Elizabeth Hall (LBJ School), 'Views of Pakistan'

Ronald Steel (Visiting Professor of History), 'Walter Lippmann and the British'

Douglas H. M. Branion (Canadian Consul General), 'Political Controversy and Economic Development in Canada'

Decherd Turner and Dave Oliphant (HRHRC), 'The History of the Publications of the HRHRC'

Robert Fernea (Anthropology), 'The Controversy over Sex and Orientalism: Charles Doughty's *Arabia Deserta*'

Desley Deacon (Government), 'Her Brilliant Career: The Context of Nineteenth-Century Australian Feminism'

John Lamphear (History), 'The British Colonial "Pacification" of Kenya: A View from the Other Side'

Kingsley de Silva (University of Peradeniya, Sri Lanka), 'British Colonialism and Sri Lankan Independence'

Thomas Hatfield (Continuing Education), 'Colorado on the Cam, 1986: From "Ultra" to Archaeology, from Mr. Micawber to Mrs. Thatcher'

Carol Hanbery MacKay (English), 'The Dickens Theater'

Round Table Discussion, 'The Art of Biography: Philip Ziegler's *Mountbatten*': Ronald Brown, Jo Anne Christian, Roger Louis (History), Harry Middleton (LBJ Library), and Ronald Steel

Spring Semester 1986

Round Table Discussion, '*Out of Africa:* The Book, the Biography, and the Movie': B. J. Fernea (English and Middle Eastern Studies), Bernth Lindfors (English), and Roger Louis (History)

Robert Litwak (Woodrow Wilson Center), 'The Great Game: Russian, British, and American Strategies in Asia'

Gillian Adams Barnes (English), and Jane Manaster (Geography), 'Humphrey Carpenter's *Secret Gardens* and the Golden Age of Children's Literature'

Laurie Hergenhan (University of Queensland), 'A Yankee in Australia: The Literary and Historical Adventures of C. Hartley Grattan'

Brian Matthews (Flinders University, Adelaide), 'Australian Utopianism of the 1880s'

Richard Langhorne (Cambridge University), 'Apostles and Spies: The Generation of Treason at Cambridge between the Wars'

Ronald Robinson (Oxford University), 'The Decline and Fall of the British Empire'

William Rodgers (Social Democratic Party), 'Britain's New Three-Party System: A Permanent or Passing Phenomenon?'

John Coetzee (University of Cape Town), 'The Farm Novel in South Africa'

Ayesha Jalal, (Cambridge University), 'Jinnah and the Partition of India'

Andrew Blane (City College of New York), 'Amnesty International: From a British to an International Movement'

Anthony Rota (Antiquarian Bookseller and Publisher), 'London Pride: 1986'

Elspeth Rostow (LBJ School), 'The Withering Away of Whose State? Colonel Qaddafi's? Reflections on Nationalism at Home and Abroad, in Britain and in the Middle East'

Ray Daum (HRHRC), 'Broadway—Piccadilly!'

Fall Semester 1986

Round Table Discussion: Dean Robert King and Members of the '"Unrequired Reading List" Committee—The British Component'

Paul Sturges (Loughborough University, UK), 'Popular Libraries in Eighteenth-Century Britain'

Ian Bickerton (University of Missouri), 'Eisenhower's Middle East Policy and the End of the British Empire'

Marc Ferro (Visiting Professor of History), 'Churchill and Pétain'

David Fitzpatrick (Visiting Professor of History, Queen's University, Ontario), 'Religion and Politics in Ireland'

Adam Watson (University of Virginia), 'Our Man in Havana—or: Britain, Cuba, and the Caribbean'

Norman Rose (Hebrew University), 'Chaim Weizmann, the British, and the Creation of the State of Israel'

Elaine Thompson (American University), 'Legislatures in Canberra and Washington'

Roger Louis (History), 'Suez Thirty Years After'

Antonia Gransden (University of Nottingham), 'The Writing of Chronicles in Medieval England'

Hilary Spurling (British Biographer and Critic), 'Paul Scott's *Raj Quartet:* The Novelist as Historian'

J. D. B. Miller (Australian National University), 'A Special and Puzzling Relationship: Australia and the United States'

Janet Meisel (History), 'The Domesday Book'

Spring Semester 1987

Round Table Discussion, 'Contemporary Perspectives on Evolution': Miguel Gonzalez-Gerth (Spanish and Portuguese), Robert Fernea (Anthropology), Joe Horn (Psychology), Bruce Hunt (History), and Delbert Thiessen (Psychology)

Alistair Campbell-Dick (Strategic Technology), 'Scottish Nationalism'

Anthony Mockler (British Freelance Historian and Biographer), 'Graham Greene: The Interweaving of His Life and Fiction'

Michael Crowder (Visiting Professor of African History, Amherst College), 'The Legacy of British Colonialism in Africa'

Carin Green (Classics), 'Lovers and Defectors: Autobiography and *The Perfect Spy*'

Lord St. Brides, 'The Modern British Monarchy'

Victor Szebehely (Aerospace Engineering), 'Sir Isaac Newton'

Patrick McCaughey (National Gallery of Victoria, Melbourne), 'The Persistence of Landscape in Australian Art'

Adolf Wood (*Times Literary Supplement*), 'An Informal History of the *TLS*'

Nissan Oren (Hebrew University), 'Churchill, Truman, and Stalin: The End of the Second World War'

Sir Michael Howard (Oxford University), 'Britain and the First World War'

Sir John Graham (former British Ambassador to NATO), 'NATO: British Origins, American Security, and the Future Outlook'

Daniel Mosser (Virginia Polytechnic Institute and State University), 'The Chaucer Cardigan Manuscript'

Sir Raymond Carr (Oxford University), 'British Intellectuals and the Spanish Civil War'

Michael Wilding (University of Sydney), 'The Fatal Shore? The Convict Period in Australian Literature'

Fall Semester 1987

Round Table Discussion, 'Anthony Burgess: The Autobiography': Peter Green (Classics), Winfred Lehmann (Linguistics), Roger Louis (History), and Paul Woodruff (Philosophy)

Robert Crunden (History and American Studies), 'Ezra Pound in London'

Carol MacKay (English), and John Henry Faulk (Austin), 'J. Frank Dobie and Thackeray's Great-Granddaughter: Another Side of *A Texan in England*'

Sarvepalli Gopal (Jawaharlal Nehru University and Oxford University), 'Nehru and the British'

Robert D. King (Dean of Liberal Arts), 'T. S. Eliot'

Lord Blake (Visiting Professor of English History and Literature), 'Disraeli: Problems of the Biographer'

Alain Blayac (University of Montpellier), 'Art as Revelation: Gerard Manley Hopkins's Poetry and James Joyce's *Portrait of the Artist*'

Mary Bull (Oxford University), 'Margery Perham and Africa'

R. J. Moore (Flinders University, Adelaide), 'Paul Scott: The Novelist as Historian, and the *Raj Quartet* as History'

Ian Willison (British Library), 'New Trends in Humanities Research: The *History of the Book in Britain* Project'

The Duke of Norfolk, 'The Lion and the Unicorn: Ceremonial and the Crown'

Hans Mark (Chancellor, UT System), 'The Royal Society, the Royal Observatory, and the Development of Modern Research Laboratories'

Henry Dietz (Government), 'Sherlock Holmes: A Centennial Celebration'

Spring Semester 1988

Lord Jenkins (Oxford University), 'Changing Patterns of British Government from Asquith via Baldwin and Attlee to Mrs. Thatcher'

Lord Thomas (author of *The Spanish Civil War* and *Cuba, or the Pursuit of Freedom)*, 'Britain, Spain, and Latin America'

Round Table Discussion, 'Chinua Achebe: The Man and His Works': Barbara Harlow (English), Bernth Lindfors (English), Wahneema Lubiano (English), and Robert Wren (University of Houston)

Charles Townshend (Keele University, UK), 'Britain, Ireland, and Palestine, 1918–1947'

Richard Morse (Woodrow Wilson Center), 'T. S. Eliot and Latin America'

Chinua Achebe (Nigerian Novelist), 'Anthills of the Savannah'

Tapan Raychaudhuri (Oxford University), 'The English in Bengali Eyes in the Nineteenth Century'

Lord Chitnis (Rowntree Trust and the British Refugee Council), 'British Perceptions of U.S. Policy in Central America'

Kurth Sprague (English), 'Constance White: Sex, Womanhood, and Marriage in British India'

George McGhee (former US Ambassador to Turkey and Germany), 'The Turning Point in the Cold War: Britain, the United States, and Turkey's Entry into NATO'

Robert Palter (Trinity College), 'New Light on Newton's Natural Philosophy'

J. Kenneth McDonald (CIA), 'The Decline of British Naval Power, 1918–1922'

Yvonne Cripps (Visiting Professor of Law), '"Peter and the Boys Who Cry Wolf": *Spycatcher*'

Emmanuel Ngara (University of Zimbabwe), 'African Poetry: Nationalism and Cultural Domination'

Kate Frost (English), 'Frat Rats of the Invisible College: The Wizard Earl of Northumberland and His Pre-Rosicrucian Pals'

B. Ramesh Babu (Visiting Professor of Government), 'American Foreign Policy: An Indian Dissent'

Sir Antony Ackland (British Ambassador to the United States), 'From Dubai to Madrid: Adventures in the British Foreign Service'

In the Spring Semester 1988, British Studies helped sponsor four lectures by Sir Brian Urquhart (former Under-Secretary of the United Nations) under the general title 'World Order in the Era of Decolonization.'

Fall Semester 1988

Round Table Discussion on Richard Ellman's *Oscar Wilde:* Peter Green (Classics), Diana Hobby (Rice University), Roger Louis (History), and Elspeth Rostow (American Studies),

Hugh Cecil (University of Leeds), 'The British First World War Novel of Experience'

Alan Knight (History), 'Britain and the Mexican Revolution'

Prosser Gifford (Former Deputy Director, Woodrow Wilson Center, Washington, DC), and Robert Frykenberg (University of Wisconsin–Madison), 'Stability in Post-Colonial British Africa: The Indian Perspective'

Joseph Dobrinski (Université Paul-Valéry), 'The Symbolism of the Artist Theme in *Lord Jim*'

Martin Stannard (University of Leicester), 'Evelyn Waugh and North America'

Lawrence Cranberg (Fellow, American Physical Society), 'The Engels-Marx Relationship and the Origins of Marxism'

N. G. L. Hammond (Bristol University), 'The British Military Mission to Greece, 1943–1944'

Barbara Harlow (English), 'A Legacy of the British Era in Egypt: Women, Writing, and Political Detention'

Sidney Monas (Slavic Languages and History), 'Thanks for the Mummery: *Finnegans Wake,* Rabelais, Bakhtin, and Verbal Carnival'

Robert Bowie (Central Intelligence Agency), 'Britain's Decision to Join the European Community'

Shirley Williams (Social Democratic Party), 'Labour Weakness and Tory Strength—or, The Strange Death of Labour England'

Bernard Richards (Oxford University), 'Ruskin's View of Turner'

John R. Clarke (Art History), 'Australian Art of the 1960s'

Round Table Discussion on Paul Kennedy's *The Rise and Fall of the Great Powers:* Alessandra Lipucci (Government), Roger Louis (History), Jagat Mehta (LBJ School), Sidney Monas (Slavic Languages and History), and Walt Rostow (Economics and History)

Spring Semester 1989

Brian Levack (History), 'The English Bill of Rights, 1689'

Hilary Spurling (Critic and Biographer), 'Paul Scott as Novelist: His Sense of History and the British Era in India'

Larry Carver (Humanities Program), 'Lord Rochester: The Profane Wit and the Restoration's Major Minor Poet'

Atieno Odhiambo (Rice University), 'Re-Interpreting Mau Mau'

Trevor Hartley (London School of Economics), 'The British Constitution and the European Community'

Archie Brown (Oxford University), 'Political Leadership in Britain, the Soviet Union, and the United States'

Lord Blake (Editor, *Dictionary of National Biography*), 'Churchill as Historian'

Weirui Hou (Shanghai University), 'British Literature in China'

Norman Daniel (British Council), 'Britain and the Iraqi Revolution of 1958'

Alistair Horne (Oxford University), 'The Writing of the Biography of Harold Macmillan'

M. R. D. Foot (Editor, *Gladstone Diaries*), 'The Open and Secret War, 1939–1945'

Ian Willison (former Head of the Rare Books Division, British Library), 'Editorial Theory and Practice in The History of the Book'

Neville Meaney (University of Sydney), 'The "Yellow Peril": Invasion, Scare Novels, and Australian Political Culture'

Round Table Discussion on *The Satanic Verses:* Kurth Sprague (American Studies), Peter Green (Classics), Robert A. Fernea (Anthropology), Roger Louis (History), and Gail Minault (History and Asian Studies)

Kate Frost (English), 'John Donne, Sunspots, and the British Empire'

Lee Patterson (Duke University), 'Chaucerian Commerce'

Edmund Weiner and John Simpson (Editors of the new *OED*), 'Return to the Web of Words'

Ray Daum (HRHRC), 'Noel Coward and Cole Porter'

William B. Todd (History), 'Edmund Burke on the French Revolution'

Fall Semester 1989

D. Cameron Watt (London School of Economics), 'Britain and the Origins of the Second World War: Personalities and Politics of Appeasement'

Gary Freeman (Government), 'On the Awfulness of the English: The View from Comparative Studies'

Hans Mark (Chancellor, UT System), 'British Naval Tactics in the Second World War: The Japanese Lessons'

T. B. Millar (Menzies Centre for Australian Studies, London), 'Australia, Britain, and the United States in Historical Perspective'

Dudley Fishburn (Member of Parliament and former Editor of *The Economist*), '*The Economist*'

Lord Franks (former Ambassador in Washington), 'The "Special Relationship"'

Herbert L. Jacobson (Drama Critic and friend of Orson Welles), 'Three Score Years of Transatlantic Acting and Staging of Shakespeare'

Roy Macleod (University of Sydney) 'The "Practical Man": Myth and Metaphor in Anglo-Australian Science'

David Murray (Open University), 'Hong Kong: The Historical Context for the Transfer of Power'

Susan Napier (UT Assistant Professor of Japanese Language and Literature), 'Japanese Intellectuals Discover the British'

Dr. Karan Singh (Ambassador of India to the United States), 'Four Decades of Indian Democracy'

Paul Woodruff (Philosophy), 'George Grote and the Radical Tradition in British Scholarship'

Herbert J. Spiro (Government), 'Britain, the United States, and the Future of Germany'

Robert Lowe (*Austin American-Statesman*), '"God Rest You Merry, Gentlemen": The Curious British Cult of Sherry'

Spring Semester 1990

Thomas F. Staley (HRHRC), 'Harry Ransom, the Humanities Research Center, and the Development of Twentieth-Century Literary Research Collections'

Thomas Cable (English), 'The Rise and Decline of the English Language'

D. J. Wenden (Oxford University), 'Sir Alexander Korda and the British Film Industry'

Roger Owen (Oxford University), 'Reflections on the First Ten Years of Thatcherism'

Robert Hardgrave (Government), 'Celebrating Calcutta: The Solvyns Portraits'

Donatus Nwoga (University of Nigeria, Nsukka), 'The Intellectual Legacy of British Decolonization in Africa'

Francis Sitwell (Etonian, Seaman, and Literary Executor), 'Edith Sitwell: A Reappraisal'

Robert Vitalis (Government), 'The "New Deal" in Egypt: Britain, the United States, and the Egyptian Economy during World War II'

James Coote (Architecture), 'Prince Charles and Architecture'

Harry Eckstein (University of California, Irvine), 'British Politics and the National Health Service'

Alfred David (Indiana University), 'Chaucer and King Arthur'

Ola Rotimi (African Playwright and Theater Director), 'African Literature and the British Tongue'

Derek Brewer (Cambridge University), 'An Anthropological Study of Literature'

Neil MacCormick (University of Edinburgh), 'Stands Scotland Where She Should?'

Janice Rossen (Senior Research Fellow, HRHRC), 'Toads and Melancholy: The Poetry of Philip Larkin'

Ronald Robinson (Oxford University), 'The Decolonization of British Imperialism'

Fall Semester 1990

Round Table Discussion on 'The Crisis in the Persian Gulf': Hafez Farmayan (History), Robert Fernea (Anthropology), Roger Louis (History), and Robert Stookey (Center for Middle Eastern Studies)

John Velz (English), 'Shakespeare and Some Surrogates: An Account of the Anti-Stratfordian Heresy'

Michael H. Codd (Department of the Prime Minister and Cabinet, Government of Australia), 'The Future of the Commonwealth: An Australian View'

John Dawick (Massey University, New Zealand), 'The Perils of Paula: Young Women and Older Men in Pinero's Plays'

Gloria Fromm (University of Illinios, Chicago), 'New Windows on Modernism: The Letters of Dorothy Richardson'

David Braybrooke (Government), 'The Canadian Constitutional Crisis'

Sidney Monas (Slavic Languages and History), 'Paul Fussell and World War II'

James Fishkin (Government), 'Thought Experiments in Recent Oxford Philosophy'

Joseph Hamburger (Yale University), 'How Liberal Was John Stuart Mill?'

Richard W. Clement (University of Kansas), 'Thomas James and the Bodleian Library: The Foundations of Scholarship'

Michael Yeats (Former Chairman of the Irish Senate and only son of the poet William Butler Yeats), 'Ireland and Europe'

Round Table Discussion on 'William H. McNeill's *Arnold J. Toynbee: A Life*': Standish Meacham (Dean, Liberal Arts), Peter Green (Classics), Roger Louis (History), and Sidney Monas (Slavic Languages and History)

Jeffrey Meyers (Biographer and Professor of English, University of Colorado), 'Conrad and Jane Anderson'

Alan Frost (La Trobe University, Melbourne), 'The Explorations of Captain Cook'

Sarvepalli Gopal (Jawaharlal Nehru University), 'The First Ten Years of Indian Independence'

Round Table Discussion on 'The Best and Worst Books of 1990': Alessandra Lippucci (Government), Roger Louis (History), Tom Staley (HRHRC), Steve Weinberg (Physics), and Paul Woodruff (Philosophy)

Spring Semester 1991

David Hollway (Prime Minister's Office, Government of Australia), 'Australia and the Gulf Crisis'

Diane Kunz (Yale University), 'British Post-War Sterling Crises'

Miguel Gonzalez-Gerth (Spanish Literature and the HRHRC), 'T. E. Lawrence, Richard Aldington, and the Death of Heroes'

Robert Twombly (English), 'Religious Encounters with the Flesh in English Literature'

Alan Ryan (Princeton University), 'Bertrand Russell's Politics'

Hugh Kenner (Johns Hopkins University), 'The State of English Poetry'

Patricia Burnham (American Studies), 'Anglo-American Art and the Struggle for Artistic Independence'

Round Table Discussion on 'The Churchill Tradition': Lord Blake (former Provost of Queen's College, Oxford), Lord Jenkins (Chancellor, Oxford University), Field Marshal Lord Carver (former Chief of the Defence Staff), Sir Michael Howard (former Regius Professor, Oxford, present Lovett Professor of Military and Naval History, Yale University), with a concluding comment by Winston S. Churchill, M.P.

Woodruff Smith (UT San Antonio), 'Why Do the British Put Sugar in Their Tea?'

Peter Firchow (University of Minnesota), 'Aldous Huxley: The Poet as Centaur'

Irene Gendzier (Boston University), 'British and American Middle Eastern Policies in the 1950s: Lebanon and Kuwait; Reflections on Past Experience and the Post-War Crisis in the Gulf'

John Train (*Harvard* Magazine and *Wall Street Journal*), 'Remarkable Catchwords in the City of London and on Wall Street'

Adam Sisman (Independent Writer, London), 'A. J. P. Taylor'

Roger Louis (History), 'The Young Winston'

Adrian Mitchell (Melbourne University), 'Claiming a Voice: Recent Non-Fiction Writing in Australia'

Bruce Hevly (University of Washington), 'Stretching Things Out versus Letting Them Slide: The Natural Philosophy of Ice in Edinburgh and Cambridge in the Nineteenth Century'

Henry Dietz (Government), 'Foibles and Follies in Sherlock's Great Game: Some Excesses of Holmesian Research'

Summer 1991

Roger Louis (History), and Ronald Robinson (Oxford University), 'Harold Macmillan and the Dissolution of the British Empire'

Robert Treu (University of Wisconsin–Lacrosse), 'D. H. Lawrence and Graham Greene in Mexico'

Thomas Pinney (Pomona College), 'Kipling, India, and Imperialism'

Ronald Heiferman (Quinnipiac College), 'The Odd Couple: Winston Churchill and Chiang Kai-shek'

John Harty (Alice Lloyd College, Kentucky), 'The Movie and the Book: J. G. Ballard's *Empire of the Sun*'

A. B. Assensoh (Southern University, Baton Rouge), 'Nkrumah'

Victoria Carchidi (Emory and Henry College), 'Lawrence of Arabia on a Camel, Thank God!'

James Gump (University of California, San Diego), 'The Zulu and the Sioux: The British and American Comparative Experience with the "Noble Savage"'

Fall Semester 1991

Round Table Discussion on Noel Annan's *Our Age:* Peter Green (Classics), Robert D. King (Dean, Liberal Arts), Roger Louis (History), and Thomas F. Staley (HRHRC)

Christopher Heywood (Okayama University), 'Slavery, Imagination, and the Brontës'

Harold L. Smith (University of Houston, Victoria), 'Winston Churchill and Women'

Krystyna Kujawinska-Courtney (University of Lodz), 'Shakespeare and Poland'

Ewell E. Murphy, Jr. (Baker Botts, Houston), 'Cecil Rhodes and the Rhodes Scholarships'

I. N. Kimambo (University of Dar es Salaam), 'The District Officer in Tanganyika'

Hans Mark (Chancellor, UT System), 'The Pax Britannica and the Inevitable Comparison: Is There a Pax Americana? Conclusions from the Gulf War'

Richard Clutterbuck (Major-General, British Army, Ret.), 'British and American Hostages in the Middle East: Negotiating with Terrorists'

Elizabeth Hedrick (English), 'Samuel Johnson and Linguistic Propriety'

The Hon. Denis McLean (New Zealand Ambassador to the United States), 'Australia and New Zealand: The Nuisance of Nationalism'

Elizabeth Richmond (English), 'Submitting a Trifle for a Degree: Dramatic Productions at Oxford and Cambridge in the Age of Shakespeare'

Kenneth Warren, M.D. (Director for Science, Maxwell Macmillan), 'Tropical Medicine: A British Invention'

Adolf Wood (*Times Literary Supplement*), 'The Golden Age of the *Times Literary Supplement*'

Eugene Walter (Poet and Novelist), 'Unofficial Poetry: Literary London in the 1940s and 1950s'

Sidney Monas (Slavic Languages and History), 'Images of Britain in the Poetry of World War II'

St. Stephen's Madrigal Choir, 'Celebrating an English Christmas'

Spring Semester 1992

Jeremy Treglown (Critic and Author), 'Wartime Censorship and the Novel'

Toyin Falola (History), 'Nigerian Independence, 1960'

Donald S. Lamm (W.W. Norton and Company), 'Publishing English History in America'

Colin Franklin (Publisher and Historian of the Book), 'The Pleasures of Eighteenth-Century Shakespeare'

Thomas F. Staley (HRHRC), '*Fin de Siècle* Joyce: A Perspective on One Hundred Years'

Sarvepalli Gopal (Jawaharlal Nehru University), '"Drinking Tea with Treason": Halifax and Gandhi'

Michael Winship (English), 'The History of the Book: Britain's Foreign Trade in Books in the Nineteenth Century'

Richard Lariviere (Sanskrit and Asian Studies), 'British Law and Lawyers in India'
Round Table Discussion on A. S. Byatt's *Possession:* Janice Rossen (Visiting Scholar, HRHRC), John P. Farrell (English), and Roger Louis (History)
William H. McNeill (University of Chicago), 'Arnold Toynbee's Vision of World History'
Derek Brewer (Cambridge University), 'The Interpretation of Fairy Tales: The Implications for English Literature, Anthropology, and History'
David Bradshaw (Oxford University), 'Aldous Huxley: Eugenics and the Rational State'
Steven Weinberg (Physics), 'The British Style in Physics'
Sir David Williams (Cambridge University), 'Northern Ireland'

Summer 1992

R. A. C. Parker (Oxford University), 'Neville Chamberlain and Appeasement'
Adrian Wooldridge (Oxford University and *The Economist*), 'Reforming British Education: How It Happened and What America Can Learn'
Chris Wrigley (Nottingham University), 'A. J. P. Taylor: An English Radical and Modern Europe'

Fall Semester 1992

Round Table Discussion on E. M. Forster's *Howards End:* The Movie and the Book, Robert D. King (Linguistics), Roger Louis (History), Alessandra Lippucci (Government), and Thomas F. Staley (HRHRC)
Lord Skidelsky (Warwick University), 'Keynes and the Origins of the "Special Relationship"'
Sir Samuel Falle (former British Ambassador), 'Britain and the Middle East in the 1950s'
Ian MacKillop (University of Sheffield), 'We Were That Cambridge: F. R. Leavis and *Scrutiny*'
Walter Dean Burnham (Government), 'The 1992 British Elections: Four-or-Five-More Tory Years?'
Don Graham (English), 'Modern Australian Literature and the Image of America'
Richard Woolcott (former Secretary of the Australian Department of Foreign Affairs), 'Australia and the Question of Cooperation or Contention in the Pacific'
Ian Willison (1992 Wiggins Lecturer, American Antiquarian Society), 'The History of the Book in Twentieth-Century Britain and America'
Iain Sproat, (Member of Parliament), 'P. G. Wodehouse and the War'
Standish Meacham (History), 'The Crystal Palace'
Field Marshal Lord Carver (former Chief of the British Defence Staff), 'Wavell: A Reassessment'
Lesley Hall (Wellcome Institute for the History of Medicine, London), 'For Fear of Frightening the Horses: Sexology in Britain since William Acton'
Michael Fry (University of Southern California), 'Britain, the United Nations, and the Lebanon Crisis of 1958'
Brian Holden Reid (King's College, London), 'J. F. C. Fuller and the Revolution in British Military Thought'

Neil Parsons (University of London), '"Clicko," or Franz Taaibosch: A Bushman Entertainer in Britain, Jamaica, and the United States *c.* 1919–40'

John Hargreaves (Aberdeen University), 'God's Advocate: Lewis Namier and the History of Modern Europe'

Round Table Discussion on Robert Harris's *Fatherland:* Henry Dietz (Government), Robert D. King (Linguistics), Roger Louis (History), and Walter Wetzels (Germanic Languages)

Kevin Tierney (University of California), 'Robert Graves: An Outsider Looking In, or An Insider Who Escaped?'

Spring Semester 1993

Round Table Discussion on 'The Trollope Mystique': Janice Rossen (author of *Philip Larkin* and *The University in Modern Fiction*), Louise Weinberg (Law School), and Paul Woodruff (Plan II Honors Program and Philosophy)

Bruce Hunt (History), 'To Rule the Waves: Cable Telegraphy and British Physics in the Nineteenth Century'

Martin Wiener (Rice University), 'The Unloved State: Contemporary Political Attitudes in the Writing of Modern British History'

Elizabeth Dunn (HRHRC), 'Ralph Waldo Emerson and Ireland'

Jason Thompson (Western Kentucky University), 'Edward William Lane's "Description of Egypt"'

Sir Michael Howard (Yale University), 'Strategic Deception in the Second World War'

Gordon A. Craig (Stanford University), 'Churchill'

Round Table Discussion on the Indian Mathematician Ramanujan: Robert D. King (Linguistics), James W. Vick (Mathematics), and Steven Weinberg (Physics)

Martha Merritt (Government), 'From Commonwealth to Commonwealth, and from Vauxhall to *Vokzal:* Russian Borrowing from Britain'

Sidney Monas (Slavic Languages and History), 'James Joyce and Russia'

Peter Marshall (King's College, London), 'Imperial Britain and the Question of National Identity'

Michael Wheeler (Lancaster University), 'Ruskin and Gladstone'

Anthony Low (Cambridge University), 'Britain and India in the Early 1930s: The British, American, French, and Dutch Empires Compared'

Summer 1993

Alexander Pettit (University of North Texas), 'Lord Bolingbroke's *Remarks on the History of England*'

Rose Marie Burwell (Northern Illinois University), 'The British Novel and Ernest Hemingway'

Richard Patteson (Mississippi State University), 'New Writing in the West Indies'

Richard Greene (Memorial University, Newfoundland), 'The Moral Authority of Edith Sitwell'

Fall Semester 1993

Round Table Discussion on 'The British and the Shaping of the American Critical Mind—Edmund Wilson, Part II': Roger Louis (History), Elspeth Rostow (American Studies), Tom Staley (HRHRC), and Robert Crunden (History and American Studies)

Roseanne Camacho (University of Rhode Island), 'Evelyn Scott: Towards an Intellectual Biography'

Christopher Heywood (Okayama University), 'The Brontës and Slavery'

Peter Gay (Yale University), 'The Cultivation of Hatred in England'

Linda Ferreira-Buckley (English) 'England's First English Department: Rhetoric and More Rhetoric'

Janice Rossen (HRHRC), 'British University Novels'

Ian Hancock (O Yanko Le Redzosko) (Linguistics and English), 'The Gypsy Image in British Literature'

James Davies (University College of Swansea), 'Dylan Thomas'

Jeremy Lewis (London Writer and Editor), 'Who Cares about Cyril Connolly?'

Sam Jamot Brown (British Studies) and Robert D. King (Linguistics), 'Scott and the Antarctic'

Martin Trump (University of South Africa), 'Nadine Gordimer's Social and Political Vision'

Richard Clogg (University of London), 'Britain and the Origins of the Greek Civil War'

Herbert J. Spiro (United States Ambassador, Ret.), 'The Warburgs: Anglo-American and German-Jewish Bankers'

Colin Franklin (Publisher and Antiquarian Bookseller), 'Lord Chesterfield: Stylist, Connoisseur of Manners, and Specialist in Worldly Advice'

Jeffrey Segall (Charles University, Prague), 'The Making of James Joyce's Reputation'

Rhodri Jeffreys-Jones (University of Edinburgh), 'The Myth of the Iron Lady: Margaret Thatcher and World Stateswomen'

John Rumrich (English), 'Milton and Science: Gravity and the Fall'

J. D. Alsop (McMaster University), 'British Propaganda, Espionage, and Political Intrigue'

Round Table Discussion on 'The Best and the Worst Books of 1993': David Edwards (Government), Creekmore Fath (Liberal Arts Foundation), Betty Sue Flowers (English), and Sidney Monas (Slavic Languages and History)

Spring Semester 1994

Thomas F. Staley (HRHRC), 'John Rodker: Poet and Publisher of Modernism'

Martha Fehsenfeld, and Lois More Overbeck (Emory University), 'The Correspondence of Samuel Beckett'

M. R. D. Foot (Historian and Editor), 'Lessons of War on War: The Influence of 1914–1918 on 1939–1945'

Round Table Discussion on 'Requiem for Canada?' David Braybrooke (Government), Walter Dean Burnham (Government), and Robert Crunden (American Studies)

Ross Terrill (Harvard University), 'Australia and Asia in Historical Perspective'

Sir Samuel Falle (British Ambassador and High Commissioner), 'The Morning after Independence: The Legacy of the British Empire'

Deborah Lavin (University of Durham), 'Lionel Curtis: Prophet of the British Empire'

Robin W. Doughty (Geography), 'Eucalyptus: And Not a Koala in Sight'

Al Crosby (American Studies and History), 'Captain Cook and the Biological Impact on the Hawaiian Islands'

Gillian Adams (Editor, *Children's Literature Association Quarterly*), 'Beatrix Potter and Her Recent Critics'

Lord Amery, 'Churchill's Legacy'

Christa Jansohn (University of Bonn), and Peter Green (Classics), '*Lady Chatterley's Lover*'

R. A. C. Parker (Oxford University), 'Neville Chamberlain and the Coming of the Second World War'

John Velz (English), 'King Lear in Iowa: Jane Smiley's *A Thousand Acres*'

Jan Schall (University of Florida), 'British Spirit Photography'

Daniel Woolf (Dalhousie University), 'The Revolution in Historical Consciousness in England'

Fall Semester 1994

Kenneth O. Morgan (University of Wales), 'Welsh Nationalism'

Round Table Discussion on Michael Shelden's *Graham Greene: The Man Within:* Peter Green (Classics), Roger Louis (History), and Thomas F. Staley (HRHRC)

Robert D. King (Linguistics), 'The Secret War, 1939–1945'

Brian Boyd (University of Auckland), 'The Evolution of Shakespearean Dramatic Structure'

Lord Weatherill (former Speaker of the House of Commons), 'Thirty Years in Parliament'

Hans Mark (Aerospace Engineering), 'Churchill's Scientists'

Steven Weinberg (Physics), 'The Test of War: British Strengths and Weaknesses in World War II'

Dennis Welland (University of East Anglia), 'Wilfred Owen and the Poetry of War'

Alan Frost (La Trobe University), 'The *Bounty* Mutiny and the British Romantic Poets'

W. O. S. Sutherland (English), 'Sir Walter Scott'

Hazel Rowley (Deakin University, Melbourne), 'Christina Stead's "Other Country"'

Herman Bakvis (Dalhousie University), 'The Future of Democracy in Canada and Australia'

Peter Stansky (Stanford University), 'George Orwell and the Writing of *Nineteen Eighty-Four*'

Henry Dietz (Government), 'Sherlock Homes and Jack the Ripper'

James Coote (Architecture), 'Techniques of Illusion in British Architecture'

Round Table Discussion on 'The Best and Worst Books of 1994': Dean Burnham (Government), Alessandra Lippucci (Government), Roger Louis (History), Sidney Monas (Slavic Languages and History), and Janice Rossen (HRHRC)

Spring Semester 1995

Elizabeth Butler Cullingford (English), 'Anti-Colonial Metaphors in Contemporary Irish Literature'

Thomas M. Hatfield (Continuing Education), 'British and American Deception of the Germans in Normandy'

Gary P. Freeman (Government), 'The Politics of Race and Immigration in Britain'

Donald G. Davis, Jr. (Library and Information Science), 'The Printed Word in Sunday Schools in Nineteenth-Century England and the United States'

Brian Bremen (English), "Healing Words: The Literature of Medicine and the Medicine of Literature'

Frances Karttunen (Linguistic Research Center), and Alfred W. Crosby (American Studies and History), 'British Imperialism and Creole Languages'

Paul Lovejoy (York University, Canada), 'British Rule in Africa: A Reassessment of Nineteenth-Century Colonialism'

Carol MacKay (English), 'Creative Negativity in the Life and Work of Elizabeth Robins'

John Brokaw (Theatre and Dance), 'The Changing Stage in London, 1790–1832'

Linda Colley (Yale University), 'The Frontier in British History'

Iwan Morus (University of California, San Diego), 'Manufacturing Nature: Science, Technology, and Victorian Consumer Culture'

Brian Parker (University of Toronto), 'Jacobean Law: The Dueling Code and "A Faire Quarrel" (1617)'

Kate Frost (English), '"Jack Donne the Rake": Fooling around in the 1590s'

Mark Kinkead-Weekes (University of Kent), 'Beyond Gossip: D. H. Lawrence's Writing Life'

Summer 1995

S. P. Rosenbaum (University of Toronto), 'Leonard and Virginia Woolf at the Hogarth Press'

Maria X. Wells (HRHRC), 'A Delicate Balance: Trieste, 1945'

Kevin Tierney (University of California, Berkeley), 'Personae in Twentieth Century British Autobiography'

Fall Semester 1995

Brian Levack (History), 'Witchcraft, Possession, and the Law in Jacobean England'

Janice Rossen (HRHRC), 'The Home Front: Anglo-American Women Novelists and World War II'

Dorothy Driver (University of Cape Town), 'Olive Schreiner's Novel *From Man to Man*'

Philip Ziegler (London), 'Mountbatten Revisited'

Joanna Hitchcock (Director, University of Texas Press), 'British and American University Presses'

Samuel H. Beer (Harvard University), 'The Rise and Fall of Party Government in Britain and the United States, 1945–1995'

Richard Broinowski (Australian Ambassador to Mexico and Central America), 'Australia and Latin America'

John Grigg (London), 'Myths about the Approach to Indian Independence'

Round Table Discussion on *Measuring the Mind* (Adrian Wooldridge) and *The Bell Curve* (Richard J. Herrnstein and Charles Murray): David Edwards (Government), Sheldon Ekland-Olson (Dean of Liberal Arts), Joseph Horn (Psychology), and Robert D. King (Linguistics)

Paul Addison (University of Edinburgh), 'British Politics in the Second World War'

John Sibley Butler (Sociology), 'Emigrants of the British Empire'

Round Table Discussion on the Movie *Carrington*: Peter Green (Classics), Robin Kilson (History), Roger Louis (History), Sidney Monas (Slavic Languages and History), and Elizabeth Richmond-Garza (English)

Spring Semester 1996

Kevin Kenny (History), 'Making Sense of the Molly Maguires'

Brigadier Michael Harbottle (British Army), 'British and American Security in the Post-Cold War'

Carol MacKay (English), 'The Singular Double Vision of Photographer Julia Margaret Cameron'

John Ramsden (University of London), '"That Will Depend on Who Writes the History": Winston Churchill as His Own Historian'

Jack P. Greene (Johns Hopkins University), 'The *British* Revolution in America'

Walter D. Wetzels (German), 'The Ideological Fallout in Germany of Two British Expeditions to Test Einstein's General Theory of Relativity'

Thomas Pinney (Pomona College), 'In Praise of Kipling'

Michael Charlesworth (Art History), 'The English Landscape Garden'

Stephen Gray (South African Novelist), 'The Dilemma of Colonial Writers with Dual Identities'

Jeremy Black (University of Durham), 'Could the British Have Won the War of American Independence?'

Dagmar Hamilton (LBJ School), 'Justice William O. Douglas and British Colonialism'

Gordon Peacock and Laura Worthen (Theatre and Dance), 'Not Always a Green and Pleasant Land: Tom Stoppard's *Arcadia*'

Bernard Crick (University of London), 'Orwell and the Business of Biography'

Geoffrey Hartman (Yale University), 'The Sympathy Paradox: Poetry, Feeling, and Modern Cultural Morality'

Dave Oliphant (HRHRC), 'Jazz and Its British Acolytes'

R. W. B. Lewis (Yale University), 'Henry James: The Victorian Scene'

Alan Spencer (Ford Motor Company), 'Balliol, Big Business, and Mad Cows'

Peter Quinn: A Discussion of His Novel, *Banished Children of Eve*

Summer 1996

Martin Stannard (Leicester University), 'Biography and Textual Criticism'

Diane Kunz (Yale University), 'British Withdrawal East of Suez'

John Cell (Duke University), 'Who Ran the British Empire?'

Mark Jacobsen (U.S. Marine Corps Command and Staff College), 'The North-West Frontier'

Theodore Vestal (Oklahoma State University), 'Britain and Ethiopia'

Warren F. Kimball (Rutgers University), 'A Victorian Tory: Churchill, the Americans, and Self-Determination'

Louise B. Williams (Lehman College, City University of New York), 'British Modernism and Fascism'

Fall Semester 1996

Elizabeth Richmond-Garza (English and Comparative Literature), 'The New Gothic: Decadents for the 1990s'

Robin Kilson (History), 'The Politics of Captivity: The British State and Prisoners of War in World War I'

Sir Brian Fall (Oxford University), 'What Does Britain Expect from the European Community, the United States, and the Commonwealth?'

Roger Louis (History), 'Harold Macmillan and the Middle East Crisis of 1958'

Ian Willison (Editor, *The Cambridge History of the Book in Britain*), 'The History of the Book and the Cultural and Literary History of the English-Speaking World'

Walter L. Arnstein (University of Illinois), 'Queen Victoria's Other Island'

Noel Annan (London), '*Our Age* Revisited'

Michael Cohen (Bar-Ilan University, Tel Aviv), 'The Middle East and the Cold War: Britain, the United States, and the Soviet Union'

Reba Soffer (California State University, Northridge), 'Catholicism in England: Was it Possible to Be a Good Catholic, a Good Englishman, and a Good Historian?'
Wilson Harris (Poet and Novelist), 'The Mystery of Consciousness: Cross-Cultural Influences in the Caribbean, Britain, and the United States'
H. S. Barlow (Singapore), 'British Malaya in the late Nineteenth Century'
Donald G. Davis, Jr. (Library and Information Science), 'British Destruction of Chinese Books in the Peking Siege of 1900'
Round Table Discussion on the Film *Michael Collins:* Elizabeth Cullingford (English), Kevin Kenny (History), Robin Kilson (History), and Roger Louis (History)
A. G. Hopkins (Cambridge University), 'From Africa to Empire'
Austin Chapter of the Society for the Preservation and Encouragement of Barber Shop Quartet Singing in America

Spring Semester 1997

Round Table Discussion on 'T. S. Eliot and Anti-Semitism': Robert D. King (Jewish Studies), Sidney Monas (Slavic Languages and History), and Thomas F. Staley (HRHRC)
Phillip Herring (University of Wisconsin–Madison), 'Djuna Barnes and T. S. Eliot: The Story of a Friendship'
Bryan Roberts (Sociology), 'British Sociology and British Society'
Andrew Roberts (London), 'The Captains and the Kings Depart: Lord Salisbury's Skeptical Imperialism'
Colin Franklin (London), 'In a Golden Age of Publishing, 1950–1970'
Susan Pedersen (Harvard University), 'Virginia Woolf, Eleanor Rathbone, and the Problem of Appeasement'
Andrew Seaman (Saint Mary's University, Halifax, Nova Scotia), 'Thomas Raddall: A Novelist's View of Nova Scotia during the American Revolution'
Gordon Peacock (Theatre and Dance), 'Noel Coward: A Master Playwright, a Talented Actor, a Novelist and Diarist: Or a Peter Pan for the Twentieth Century?'
Roland Oliver (University of London), 'The Battle for African History, 1947–1966'
Alistair Horne (Oxford University), 'Harold Macmillan's Fading Reputation'
Richard Begam (University of Wisconsin–Madison), 'Samuel Beckett and the Debate on Humanism'
Christopher Waters (Williams College), 'Delinquents, Perverts, and the State: Psychiatry and the Homosexual Desire in the 1930s'
Sami Zubaida (University of London), 'Ernest Gellner and Islam'
Walter Dean Burnham (Government), 'Britain Votes: The 1997 General Election and Its Implications'

Fall Semester 1997

Judith Brown (Oxford University), 'Gandhi: A Victorian Gentleman'
Thomas Cable (English), 'Hearing and Revising the History of the English Language'
Round Table Discussion on 'The Death of Princess Diana': Judith Brown (Oxford), David Edwards (Government), Elizabeth Richmond-Garza (English), Anne Baade (British Studies), Alessandra Lippucci (Government), and Kevin Kenny (History)
David Hunter (Music Librarian, Fine Arts Library), 'Handel and His Patrons'

Anne Kane (Sociology), 'The Current Situation in Ireland'

James S. Fishkin (Government), 'Power and the People: The Televised Deliberative Poll in the 1997 British General Election'

Howard D. Weinbrot (University of Wisconsin–Madison), 'Jacobitism in Eighteenth-Century Britain'

J. C. Baldwin, M.D. (Houston), 'The Abdication of King Edward VIII'

Kenneth E. Carpenter (Harvard University), 'Library Revolutions Past and Present'

Akira Iriye (Harvard University), 'Britain, Japan, and the International Order after World War I'

Anthony Hobson (London), 'Reminiscences of British Authors and the Collecting of Contemporary Manuscripts'

David Killingray (University of London), 'The British in the West Indies'

Alan Knight (Oxford University), 'British Imperialism in Latin America'

Round Table Discussion on King Lear in Iowa: The Movie '*A Thousand Acres*': Linda Ferreira-Buckley (English), Elizabeth Richmond-Garza (English), Helena Woodard (English), and John Velz (English)

Timothy Lovelace (Music) and the Talisman Trio

Spring Semester 1998

Richard Ollard (Biographer and Publisher), 'A. L. Rowse: Epitome of the Twentieth Century'

Round Table Discussion of Arundhati Roy's *The God of Small Things:* Phillip Herring (HRHRC), Brian Trinque (Economics), Kamala Visweswaran (Anthropology), and Robert Hardgrave (Government)

Jonathan Schneer (Georgia Institute of Technology), 'London in 1900: The Imperial Metropolis'

Trevor Burnard (University of Canterbury, New Zealand), 'Rioting in Goatish Embraces: Marriage and the Failure of White Settlement in British Jamaica'

Felipe Fernández-Armesto (Oxford University), 'British Traditions in Comparative Perspective'

Michael Mann (University of California, Los Angeles), 'The Broader Significance of Labour's Landslide Victory of 1997'

Dane Kennedy (University of Nebraska), 'White Settlers in Colonial Kenya and Rhodesia'

Round Table Discussion on 'Noel Annan, Keynes, and Bloomsbury': Jamie Galbraith (LBJ School), Elspeth Rostow (LBJ School), and Walt Rostow (Economics and History)

Lisa Moore (English), 'British Studies—Lesbian Studies: A Dangerous Intimacy?'

James Gibbs (University of the West of England), 'Wole Soyinka: The Making of a Playwright'

Marilyn Butler (Oxford University), 'About the House: Jane Austen's Anthropological Eye'

R. J. Q. Adams (Texas A&M University), 'Britain and Ireland, 1912–1922'

John M. Carroll (Asian Studies), 'Nationalism and Identity in pre-1949 Hong Kong'

Round Table Discussion on the Irish Referendum: Anne Kane (Sociology), Kevin Kenny (History), Roger Louis (History), and Jennifer O'Conner (History)

Fall Semester 1998

Louise Hodgden Thompson (Government), 'Origins of the First World War: The Anglo-German Naval Armaments Race'

John P. Farrell (English), 'Thomas Hardy in Love'

Carol MacKay (English), 'The Multiple Conversions of Annie Besant'

Roy Foster (Oxford University), 'Yeats and Politics, 1898–1921'

Robert Olwell (History), 'British Magic Kingdoms: Imagination, Speculation, and Empire in Florida'

Sara H. Sohmer (Texas Christian University), 'The British in the South Seas: Exploitation and Trusteeship in Fiji'

Helena Woodard (English), 'Politics of Race in the Eighteenth Century: Pope and the Humanism of the Enlightenment'

D. A. Smith (Grinnell College), 'Impeachment? Parliamentary Government in Britain and France in the Nineteenth Century'

Round Table Discussion on the Irish Insurrection of 1798: Robert Olwell (History), Lisa Moore (English), and Kevin Kenny (History)

Robert D. King (Jewish Studies), 'The Accomplishments of Raja Rao: The Triumph of the English Language in India'

Donald G. Davis, Jr. (Library and Information Science and History), 'Religion and Empire'

A. D. Roberts (University of London), 'The Awkward Squad: African Students in American Universities before 1940'

Chaganti Vijayasree (Osmania University, Hyderabad), 'The Empire and Victorian Poetry'

Martha Deatherage (Music), 'Christmas Celebration: Vauxhall Gardens'

Spring Semester 1999

Round Table Discussion on *Regeneration,* Pat Barker's Trilogy on the First World War: Betty Sue Flowers (English), Roger Louis (History), and Paul Woodruff (Humanities)

Alistair Campbell-Dick (Cybertime Corporation), 'The Immortal Memory of Robert Burns'

Hugh Macrae Richmond (University of California, Berkeley), 'Why Rebuild Shakespeare's Globe Theatre?'

Ralph Austen (University of Chicago), 'Britain and the Global Economy: A Post-Colonial Perspective'

Jerome Meckier (University of Kentucky), 'Aldous Huxley's American Experience'

Peter Marsh (Syracuse University), 'Joseph Chamberlain as an Entrepreneur in Politics: Writing the Life of a Businessman Turned Statesman'

Roger Adelson (Arizona State University), 'Winston Churchill and the Middle East'

Margot Finn (Emory University), 'Law, Debt, and Empire: The Calcutta Court of Conscience'

Fred M. Leventhal (Boston University), 'The Projection of Britain in America before the Second World War'

Larry Siedentop (Oxford University), 'Reassessing the Life of Isaiah Berlin'

Ross Terrill (Harvard University), 'R. H. Tawney's Vision of Fellowship'

Juliet Fleming (Cambridge University), 'The Ladies' Shakespeare'

Elizabeth Fernea (English and Middle Eastern Studies), 'The Victorian Lady Abroad: In Egypt with Sophia Poole and in Texas with Mrs. E. M. Houstoun'

Richard Schoch (University of London), 'The Respectable and the Vulgar: British Theater in the Mid-Nineteenth Century'

Ferdinand Mount (Editor, *TLS*), 'Politics and the *Times Literary Supplement*'

Fall Semester 1999

Round Table Discussion on the Boer War, 1899–1902: Barbara Harlow (English), John Lamphear (History), and Roger Louis (History)

Sharon Arnoult (Southwest Texas State University), 'Charles I: His Life after Death'

Kenneth O. Morgan (Oxford University), 'Lloyd George, Keir Hardie, and the Importance of the "Pro-Boers"'

Richard Cleary (Architecture), 'Walking the Walk to Talk the Talk: The Promenade in Eighteenth-Century France and England'

Keith Kyle (Journalist and Historian), 'From Suez to Kenya as Journalist and as Historian'

Malcolm Hacksley (National English Literary Museum, Grahamstown, South Africa), 'Planting a Museum, Cultivating a Literature'

Ben Pimlott (University of London), 'The Art of Writing Political Biography'

Geraldine Heng (English), 'Cannibalism, the First Crusade, and the Genesis of Medieval Romance'

A. P. Martinich (Philosophy), 'Thomas Hobbes: Lifelong and Enduring Controversies'

Round Table Discussion on Lyndall Gordon, *T. S. Eliot: An Imperfect Life:* Brian Bremen (English), Thomas Cable (English), Elizabeth Richmond-Garza (Comparative Literature), and Thomas F. Staley (HRHRC)

Shula Marks (University of London), 'Smuts, Race, and the Boer War'

Round Table Discussion on the Library of the British Museum: William B. Todd (English), Irene Owens (Library and

Information Science), and Don Davis (Library and Information Science and Department of History).

Henry Dietz (Government), *'The Hound of the Baskervilles'*

Spring Semester 2000

Susan Napier (Asian Studies), 'The Cultural Phenomenon of the Harry Potter Fantasy Novels'

Round Table Discussion on *Dutch: A Memoir of Ronald Reagan:* A Chapter in the 'Special Relationship?': Roger Louis (History), Harry Middleton (LBJ Library), and Elspeth Rostow (LBJ School)

Norman Rose (Hebrew University, Jerusalem), 'Harold Nicolson: A Curious and Colorful Life'

Charlotte Canning (Theatre and Dance), 'Feminists Perform Their Past'

John Ripley (McGill University), 'The Sound of Sociology: H. B. Tree's *Merchant of Venice*'

Sergei Horuji (Russian Academy of Sciences), 'James Joyce in Russia'

Janice Rossen (Biographer and Independent Scholar), 'Philip Toynbee'

Max Egremont (Novelist and Biographer), 'Siegfried Sassoon's War'

Paul Taylor (London School of Economics and Political Science), 'Britain and Europe'

Lord Selborne (Royal Geographical Society), 'The Royal Geographical Society: Exploration since 1830'

Craig MacKenzie (Rand Afrikaans University, Johannesburg), 'The Mythology of the Boer War: Herman Charles Bosman and the Challenge to Afrikaner Romanticism'

Peter Catterall (Institute of Contemporary British History, London), 'Reform of the House of Lords'

Bernard Porter (University of Newcastle), 'Pompous and Circumstantial: Sir Edward Elgar and the British Empire'

Craufurd D. Goodwin (Duke University), 'Roger Fry and the Debate on "Myth" in the Bloomsbury Group'

Jamie Belich (University of Auckland), 'Neo-Britains? The "West" in Nineteenth-Century Australia, New Zealand, and America'

Round Table Discussion on Norman Davies, *The Isles:* Sharon Arnoult (Midwestern State University, Wichita Falls), Raymond Douglas (Colgate University), Walter Johnson (Northwestern Oklahoma State University), David Leaver (Raymond Walters College, Cincinnati), and John Cell (Duke University)

Fall Semester 2000

Round Table discussion on Paul Scott, the Raj Quartet, and the Beginning of British Studies at UT—Peter Green (Classics), Robert Hardgrave (Government and Asian Studies), and Roger Louis (History)

Suman Gupta (Open University), 'T. S. Eliot as Publisher'

Jeffrey Cox (University of Iowa), 'Going Native: Missionaries in India'

Kevin Kenny (Boston College), 'Irish Nationalism: The American Dimension'

Joseph Kestner (University of Tulsa), 'Victorian Battle Art'

James E. Cronin (Boston College), 'From Old to New Labour: Politics and Society in the Forging of the "Third" Way'

Gerald Moore (Mellon Visiting Research Fellow, HRHRC), 'When Caliban Crossed the Atlantic'

Richard Howard (Shakespearean Actor, London), '"Health and Long Life to You": A Program of Irish Poetry and Prose Presented by an Englishman, with Anecdotes'

Stephen Foster (Northern Illinois University), 'Prognosis Guarded: The Probable Decolonization of the British Era in American History'

Frank Prochaska (University of London), 'Of Crowned and Uncrowned Republics: George V and the Socialists'

Robert H. Abzug (History and American Studies), 'Britain, South Africa, and the American Civil Rights Movement'

Paula Bartley (Visiting Research Fellow, HRHRC), 'Emmeline Pankhurst'

Thomas Jesus Garza (Slavic Languages), 'A British Vampire's Christmas'

Spring Semester 2001

Betty Sue Flowers (UT Distinguished Teaching Professor), 'From Robert Browning to James Bond'

Larry Carver (English), 'Feliks Topolski at the Ransom Center'

Oscar Brockett (Theatre and Dance), 'Lilian Baylis and England's National Theatres'

Linda Levy Peck (George Washington University), 'Luxury and War'

R. James Coote (Architecture), 'Architectural Revival in Britain'

Adam Roberts (Oxford University), 'Britain and the Creation of the United Nations'

Mark Southern (Germanic Studies), 'Words over Swords: Language and Tradition in Celtic Civilization'

Round Table discussion on Ben Rogers, *A Life of A. J. Ayer:* David Braybrooke (Government and Philosophy), Al Martinich (History and Philosophy), David Sosa (Philosophy), and Paul Woodruff (Plan II and Philosophy)

Bartholomew Sparrow (Government), 'British and American Expansion: The Political Foundations'

Jose Harris (Oxford University), 'Writing History during the Second World War'

Charles Loft (Westminster College), 'Off the Rails? The Historic Junctions in Britain's Railway Problem'

Dan Jacobson (University of London), 'David Irving and Holocaust Denial'—Special Lecture

Dan Jacobson (University of London), 'Self-Redemption in the Victorian Novel'

George S. Christian (British Studies), 'The Comic Basis of the Victorian Novel'

Paul Taylor (London *Independent*), 'Rediscovering a Master Dramatist: J. B. Priestley'

Fall Semester 2001

Round Table Discussion on Ray Monk's Biography of Bertrand Russell, *The Ghost of Madness*—Al Martinich (History and Philosophy), David Sosa (Philosophy and British Studies), and Paul Woodruff (Plan II and Philosophy)

Alex Danchev (Keele University), 'The Alanbrooke Diaries'

Robert M. Worcester (LSE and Market Opinion Research International), 'Britain and the European Union'

Martha Ann Selby (Asian Studies), 'The Cultural Legacy of British Clubs: Manners, Memory, and Identity among the New Club-Wallahs in Madras'

Roger Owen (Harvard University), 'Lord Cromer and Wilfrid Blunt in Egypt'

James Loehlin (English), 'A Midsummer Night's Dream'

Jeffrey Meyers (Biographer), 'Somerset Maugham'

Elspeth Rostow (LBJ School), 'From American Studies to British Studies—And Beyond'

Nicholas Westcott (British Embassy), 'The Groundnut Scheme: Socialist Imperialism at Work in Africa'

Round Table Discussion on 'The Anglo-American Special Relationship': Gary Freeman (Government), Roger Louis (History), Elspeth Rostow (American Studies), and Michael Stoff (History)

Christopher Heywood (Sheffield University), 'The Brontës: A Personal History of Discovery and Interpretation'

James Bolger (New Zealand Ambassador and former Prime Minister), 'Whither New Zealand? Constitutional, Political, and International Quandaries'

R. J. Q. Adams (Texas A&M), 'Arthur James Balfour and Andrew Bonar Law: A Study in Contrasts'

Ferdinand Mount (Editor, *Times Literary Supplement*), 'British Culture since the Eighteenth Century: An Open Society?'

James Loehlin (English), 'A Child's Christmas in Wales'

Spring Semester 2002

Round Table Discussion on Adam Sisman, *Boswell's Presumptuous Task:* Samuel Baker (English), Linda Ferreira-Buckley (English), Julie Hardwick (History), and Helena Woodward (English)

A. G. Hopkins (History), 'Globalization: The British Case'

Susan Napier (Asian Studies), 'J. R. R. Tolkein and *The Lord of the Rings:* Fantasy as Retreat or Fantasy as Engagement?'

Wilfrid Prest (Adelaide University), 'South Australia's Paradise of Dissent'

Tom Palaima (Classics), 'Terence Rattigan's *Browning Version*'

Alan H. Nelson (University of California, Berkeley), 'Thoughts on Elizabethan Authorship'

Penelope Lively (London), 'Changing Perceptions of British and English Identity'

Hans Mark (Aerospace Engineering), 'The Falklands War'

David Butler (Oxford University), 'Psephology—or, the Study of British Elections'

Robert L. Hardgrave (Government), 'From West Texas to South India and British Studies'

Geoffrey Wheatcroft (London), 'The Englishness of English Sport'

Eileen Cleere (Southwestern University), 'Dirty Pictures: John Ruskin and the Victorian Sanitation of Fine Art'

Jamie Belich (Auckland University), 'A Comparison of Empire Cities: New York and London, Chicago and Melbourne'

Churchill Conference—Geoffrey Best (Oxford University), Sir Michael Howard (Oxford University), Warren Kimball (Rutgers University), Philip Ziegler (London), Roger Louis (History)

Catherine Maxwell (University of London), 'Swinburne's Poetry and Criticism'

Round Table Discussion on Churchill and the Churchill Conference: Rodrigo Gutierrez (History), Adrian Howkins (History), Heidi Juel (English), David McCoy (Government), Joe Moser (English), Jeff Rutherford (History), William S. Livingston (UT Senior Vice President), and Roger Louis (History)

Fall Semester 2002

James K. Galbraith (LBJ School of Public Affairs), 'The Enduring Importance of John Maynard Keynes'

Michael Green (University of Natal), 'Agatha Christie in South Africa'

Sumit Ganguly (Asian Studies), 'Kashmir: Origins and Consequences of Conflict'

Margaret MacMillan (University of Toronto), 'At the Height of His Power: Lloyd George in 1919'

Douglas Bruster (English), 'Why We Fight: *Much Ado About Nothing* and the West'

John Darwin (Oxford University), 'The Decline and Rise of the British Empire: John Gallagher as an Historian of Imperialism'

Kevin Kenny (Boston College), 'The Irish in the British Empire'

David Wallace (University of Pennsylvania), 'A Chaucerian's Tale of Surinam'

Peter Bowler (Queen's University, Belfast), 'Scientists and the Popularization of Science in Early Twentieth-Century Britain'

Bernardine Evaristo (London), 'A Feisty, Funky Girl in Roman England'

Frank Moorhouse (Australia), 'Dark Places and Grand Days'

David Cannadine (University of London), 'C. P. Snow and the Two Cultures'

Round Table Discussion on 'Edmund S. Morgan's Biography of Benjamin Franklin'—Carolyn Eastman (History), Bruce Hunt (History), Roger Louis (History), Alan Tully (History)

Mark Lawrence (History), 'The Strange Silence of Cold War England: Britain and the Vietnam War'

Tom Cable (English), 'The Pleasures of Remembering Poetry'

Spring Semester 2003

Round Table Discussion on 'W. G. Sebald—*Rings of Saturn*': Brigitte Bauer (French and Italian), Sidney Monas (History and Slavic Languages), Elizabeth Richmond-Garza (English and Comparative Literature), Walter Wetzels (Germanic Studies)

Diana Davis (Geography), 'Brutes, Beasts, and Empire: A Comparative Study of the British and French Experience'

Colin Franklin (Publisher), 'Rosalind Franklin—Variously Described as "The Dark Lady of DNA" and "The Sylvia Plath of Molecular Biology"'

Sidney Monas (History and Slavic Languages), 'A Life of Irish Literature and Russian Poetry, Soviet Politics and International History'

Neville Hoad (English), 'Oscar Wilde in America'

Selina Hastings (London), 'Rosamond Lehman: Eternal Exile'

Bernard Wasserstein (Glasgow University), 'The British in Palestine: Reconsiderations'

Anne Chisholm (London), 'Frances Partridge: Last of the Bloomsberries'

Philip Morgan (Johns Hopkins University), 'The Black Experience and the British Empire'

Jeremy duQuesnay Adams (Southern Methodist University), 'Joan of Arc and the English'

Didier Lancien (University of Toulouse), 'Churchill and de Gaulle'

Avi Shlaim (Oxford University), 'The Balfour Declaration and Its Consequences'

Martin J. Wiener (Rice University), 'Murder and the Modern British Historian'

Winthrop Wetherbee (Cornell University), 'The Jewish Impact on Medieval Literature: Chaucer, Boccaccio, and Dante'

Philippa Levine (University of Southern California), 'Sex and the British Empire'

Summer 2003

Donald G. Davis, Jr. (History and the School of Information), 'Life without British Studies Is Like . . .'

Kurth Sprague (English and American Studies), 'Literature, Horses, and Scandal at UT'

David Evans (Astronomy), 'An Astronomer's Life in South Africa and Texas'

Tom Hatfield (Continuing Education), 'Not Long Enough! Half a Century at UT'

Fall Semester 2003

Richard Oram (HRHRC), 'Evelyn Waugh: Collector and Annotator'

Round Table Discussion on 'Booker Prize Winner James Kelman: Adapting a Glasgow Novel for the Texas Stage': James Kelman (Glasgow), Mia Carter (English), Kirk Lynn, and Dikran Utidjian

Simon Green (All Souls College, Oxford University), 'The Strange Death of Puritan England, 1914–1945'

Elizabeth Richmond-Garza (English and Comparative Literature), '*Measure for Measure*'

Lewis Hoffacker (U.S. Ambassador), 'From the Congo to British Studies'

A. P. Thornton (University of Toronto), 'Wars Remembered, Revisited, and Reinvented'

Deryck Schreuder (University of Western Australia), 'The Burden of the British Past in Australia'

Robert Mettlen (Finance), 'From Birmingham to British Studies'

Paul Schroeder (University of Illinois), 'The Pax Britannica and the Pax Americana: Empire, Hegemony, and the International System'

Ferdinand Mount (London), 'A Time to Dance: Anthony Powell's *Dance to the Music of Time* and the Twentieth Century in Britain'

Brian Bond (University of London), '*Oh! What a Lovely War:* History and Popular Myth in Late-Twentieth Century Britain'

Wendy Frith (Bradford College, England), 'The Speckled Monster: Lady Mary Wortley Montagu and the Battle against Smallpox'

Harry Middleton (LBJ Library), 'The Road to the White House'

Jeremy Lewis (London), 'Tobias Smollett'

Christian Smith (Austin, Texas), 'Christmas Readings'

Spring Semester 2004

Round Table Discussion on 'The Pleasures of Reading Thackeray': Carol Mackay (English), Judith Fisher (Trinity University), George Christian (British Studies)

Thomas F. Staley (HRHRC), '"Corso e Recorso:" A Journey through Academe'

Patrick O'Brien (London School of Economics), 'The Pax Britannica, American Hegemony, and the International Order, 1793–2004'

Michael Wheeler (former Director of Chawton House Library), 'England Drawn and Quartered: Cultural Crisis in the Mid-Nineteenth Century'

Walter Wetzels (Germanic Studies), 'Growing Up in Nazi Germany, and later American Adventures'

Kathleen Wilson (State University of New York, Stony Brook), 'The Colonial State and Governance in the Eighteenth Century'

Elizabeth Fernea (English and Middle Eastern Studies), 'Encounters with Imperialism'

Chris Dunton (National University of Lesotho), 'Newspapers and Colonial Rule in Africa'

Miguel Gonzalez-Gerth (Spanish and Portuguese), 'Crossing Geographical and Cultural Borders—and Finally Arriving at British Studies'

Peter Stansky (Stanford University), 'Bloomsbury in Ceylon'

Round Table Discussion on *The Crimson Petal and the White:* John Farrell (English), Betty Sue Flowers (LBJ Library), Roger Louis (History), Paul Neimann (English)

Ann Curthoys (Australian National University), 'The Australian History Wars'

Martha Ann Selby (Asian Studies), 'Against the Grain: On Finding My Voice in India'

Steven Isenberg (UT Visiting Professor of Humanities), 'A Life in Our Times'

Summer 2004

Carol Mackay (English), 'My Own Velvet Revolution'

Erez Manela (Harvard University), 'The "Wilsonian Moment" in India and the Crisis of Empire in 1919'

Scott Lucas (Birmingham University), '"A Bright Shining Mecca": British Culture and Political Warfare in the Cold War and Beyond'

Monica Belmonte (U.S. Department of State), 'Before Things Fell Apart: The British Design for the Nigerian State'

Dan Jacobson (London), 'Philip Larkin's "Elements"'

Bernard Porter (University of Newcastle), '"Oo Let 'Em In? Asylum Seekers and Terrorists in Britain, 1850–1914'

Fall Semester 2004

Richard Drayton (Cambridge University), 'Anglo-American "Liberal" Imperialism, British Guiana, 1953–64, and the World Since September 11'

David Washbrook (Oxford University), 'Living on the Edge: Anxiety and Identity in "British" Calcutta, 1780–1930'

Joanna Hitchcock (University of Texas Press), 'An Accidental Publisher'

Alan Friedman (English), '*A Midsummer Night's Dream*'

Antony Best (London School of Economics), 'British Intellectuals and East Asia in the Inter-war Years'

John Farrell (English), 'Beating a Path from Brooklyn to Austin'

Christopher Middleton (Liberal Arts), 'Relevant to England—A Reading of Poems'

Gail Minault (History and Asian Studies), 'Growing Up Bilingual and Other (Mis)adventures in Negotiating Cultures'

Roger Louis (History), 'Escape from Oklahoma'

John Trimble (English), 'Writing with Style'

Niall Ferguson (Harvard University), 'Origins of the First World War'

James Hopkins (Southern Methodist University), 'George Orwell and the Spanish Civil War: The Case of Nikos Kazantzakis'

James Currey (London), 'Africa Writes Back: Publishing the African Writers Series at Heinemann'

Sidney Monas (History and Slavic Languages), 'A Jew's Christmas'

Geoffrey Wheatcroft (London), '"In the Advance Guard": Evelyn Waugh's Reputation'

Spring Semester 2005

Katharine Whitehorn (London), 'It Didn't *All* Start in the Sixties'

Gertrude Himmelfarb (Graduate School, City University of New York),' The Whig Interpretation of History'

Kurt Heinzelman (English and HRHRC), 'Lord Byron and the Invention of Celebrity'

Brian Levack (History), 'Jesuits, Lawyers, and Witches'

Richard Cleary (Architecture), 'When Taste Mattered: W. J. Battle and the Architecture of the Forty Acres'

Edward I. Steinhart (Texas Tech University), 'White Hunters in British East Africa, 1895–1914'

Don Graham (English), 'The Drover's Wife: An Australian Archetype'

A. C. H. Smith, (London) 'Literary Friendship: The 40-Year Story of Tom Stoppard, B. S. Johnson, and Zulfikar Ghose'

Paul Woodruff (Philosophy and Plan II), 'A Case of Anglophilia—And Partial Recovery: Being an Account of My Life, with Special Attention to the Influence of England upon My Education'

Toyin Falola (History), 'Footprints of the Ancestors'

Robert Abzug (History) 'Confessions of an Intellectual Omnivore: The Consequences on Scholarship and Career'

Deirdre McMahon (Mary Immaculate College, University of Limerick), 'Ireland and the Empire-Commonwealth, 1918–1972'

James Coote (Architecture), 'Building with Wit: Sir Edwin Lutyens and British Architecture'

Jay Clayton (Vanderbilt University), 'The Dickens Tape: Lost and Found Sound before Recording'

Christopher Ricks (Oxford University), 'The Force of Poetry: Shakespeare and Beckett'

Summer 2005

Blair Worden (Oxford University), 'Poetry and History of the English Renaissance'

Robert Bruce Osborn (British Studies), 'The Four Lives of Robert Osborn'

Alessandra Lippucci (Government), 'Perseverance Furthers: A Self-Consuming Artifact'

William H. Cunningham (former President of the University of Texas), 'Money, Power, Politics, and Ambition'

David V. Edwards (Government), 'Friendly Persuasion in the Academy'

Elizabeth Richmond-Garza (English), 'A Punk Rocker with Eight Languages'

Richard Lariviere (Liberal Arts), 'Confessions of a Sanskritist Dean'

Fall Semester 2005

Celebration of 30th Anniversary and Publication of *Yet More Adventures with Britannia*

Robert D. King (Jewish Studies), 'T.S. Eliot Reconsidered'

Round Table Discussion on 'The London Bombings': James Galbraith (LBJ School), Elizabeth Cullingford (English), Clement Henry (Government), Roger Louis (History)

Dolora Chapelle Wojciehowski (English), 'The Erotic Uncanny in Shakespeare's *Twelfth Night*'

Karl Hagstrom Miller (History), 'Playing Pensativa: History and Music in Counterpoint'

James D. Garrison (English), 'Translating Gray's *Elegy*'

Miguel Gonzalez-Gerth (Spanish and Portuguese), 'Another Look at Orwell: The Origins of *1984*'

Round Table Discussion on 'The Imperial Closet: Gordon of Khartoum, Hector McDonald of the Boer War, and Roger Casement of Ireland': Barbara Harlow (English), Neville Hoad (English), John Thomas (HRHRC)

Guy Ortolano (Washington University in St. Louis), 'From *The Two Cultures* to *Breaking Ranks:* C.P. Snow and the Interpretation of the 1960s'

Catherine Robson (University of California, Davis), 'Poetry and Memorialization'

Round Table Discussion on 'Britain and the Jewish Century': Lauren Apter (History), Robert D. King (Jewish Studies),

Sidney Monas (History and Slavic Languages)

Hans Mark (Aerospace Engineering), 'Churchill, the Anglo-Persian Oil Company, and the Origins of the Energy Crisis: From the Early 20th Century to the Present'

Randall Woods (University of Arkansas), 'LBJ and the British'

Spring Semester 2006

Richard Gray (London), 'Movie Palaces of Britain'

Samuel Baker (English), 'The Lake Poets and the War in the Mediterranean Sea'

Thomas F. Staley (HRHRC), 'Graham Greene and Evelyn Waugh'

Gary Stringer (Texas A&M), 'Love's Long Labors Coming to Fruition: The John Donne Variorum Donne'

Caroline Elkins (Harvard University), 'From Malaya to Kenya: British Colonial Violence and the End of Empire'

Grigory Kaganov (St. Petersburg), 'London in the Mouth of the Neva'

Graham Greene (London), 'A Life in Publishing'

John Davis (Oxford University), 'Evans-Pritchard: Nonetheless A Great Englishman'

Barry Gough (Wilfrid Laurier University), 'Arthur Marder and the Battles over the History of the Royal Navy'

Ivan Kreilkamp (Indiana University), '"Bags of Meat": Pet-Keeping and the Justice to Animals in Thomas Hardy'

James Wilson (History), 'Historical Memory and the Mau Mau Uprising in Colonial Kenya'

Anne Deighton (Oxford University), 'Britain after the Second World War: Losing an Empire and Finding a Place in a World of Superpowers'

Steve Isenberg (Liberal Arts), 'Auden, Forster, Larkin, and Empson'

Harriet Ritvo (MIT), 'Animals on the Edge'

Peter Quinn (New York), 'Eugenics and the Hour of the Cat'

Dan Jacobson (London), 'Kipling and South Africa'

Fall Semester 2006

Michael Charlesworth (Art and Art History) and Kurt Heinzelman (English), 'Tony Harrison's "v."'

Peter Stanley (Australian War Memorial), 'All Imaginable Excuses: Australian Deserters and the Fall of Singapore'

Selina Hastings (London), 'Somerset Maugham and "Englishness"'

James W. Vick (Mathematics), 'A Golden Century of English Mathematics'

John O. Voll (Georgetown University), 'Defining the Middle East and the Clash of Civilizations'

James Loehlin (English), 'The Afterlife of Hamlet'

Daniel Topolski (London), 'The Life and Art of Feliks Topolski'

John Darwin (Oxford University), 'The British Empire and the British World'

David Cannadine (University of London), 'Andrew Mellon and Plutocracy Across the Atlantic'

John Lonsdale (Cambridge University), 'White Settlers and Black Mau Mau in Kenya'

Kate Gartner Frost (English), 'So What's Been Done about John Donne Lately?'

John Summers (Harvard University), 'The Power Elite: C. Wright Mills and the British'

Marrack Goulding (Oxford University), 'Has it been a Success? Britain in the United Nations'

Priya Satia (Stanford University), 'The Defence of Inhumanity: British Military and Cultural Power in the Middle East'

Don Graham (English), 'Burnt Orange Britannia: A Missing Contributor!'

Spring Semester 2007

Bernard Porter (Newcastle University), 'Empire and British Culture'

Paul Sullivan (Liberal Arts Honors Program), 'The Headmaster's Shakespeare: John Garrett and British Education'

Round Table Discussion on 'The Queen': Elizabeth Cullingford (English), Karen King (American Studies), Roger Louis (History), Bryan Roberts (Sociology)

Martin Francis (University of Cincinnati), 'Cecil Beaton's Romantic Toryism and the Symbolism of Wartime Britain'

Susan Crane (Columbia University), 'Animal Feelings and Feelings for Animals in Chaucer'
Michael Charlesworth (Art History), 'The Earl of Strafford and Wentworth Castle'
Adam Sisman (London), 'Wordsworth and Coleridge'
Jenny Mann (Cornell University), 'Shakespeare's English Rhetoric: Mingling Heroes and Hobgoblins in *A Midsummer Night's Dream*'
David Atkinson (Member of Parliament), 'Britain and World Peace in the 21st Century'
Bertram Wyatt-Brown (University of Florida), 'T. E. Lawrence, Reputation, and Honor's Decline'
Roger Louis (History), 'All Souls and Oxford in 1956: Reassessing the Meaning of the Suez Crisis'
Indivar Kamtekar (Jawaharlal Nehru University), 'India and Britain during the Second World War'
Cassandra Pybus (University of Sydney), 'William Wilberforce and the Emancipation of Slaves'
Stephen Howe (University of Bristol), 'Empire in the 21st Century English Imagination'
Geoffrey Wheatcroft (London), 'The Myth of Malicious Partition: The Cases of Ireland, India, and Palestine'
Charles Rossman (English), 'D. H. Lawrence and the "Spirit" of Mexico'
Kenneth O. Morgan (House of Lords), 'Lloyd George, the French, and the Germans'

Fall Semester 2007

R. J. Q. Adams (Texas A&M), 'A. J. Balfour's Achievement and Legacy'
Robin Doughty (Geography), 'Saving Coleridge's Endangered Albatross'
Caroline Williams (University of Texas), 'A Victorian Orientalist: John Frederick Lewis and the Artist's Discovery of Cairo'
Susan Pedersen (Columbia University), 'The Story of Frances Stevenson and David Lloyd George'
Eric S. Mallin (English), 'Macbeth and the Simple Truth'
Mark Oaten, M.P., 'How "Special" Is the Special Relationship?'
Dan Birkholz (English), 'Playboys of the West of England: Medieval Cosmopolitanism and Familial Love'
Jeremy Lewis (London), 'The Secret History of Penguin Books'
Matthew Jones (Nottingham University), 'Britain and the End of Empire in South East Asia in the Era of the Vietnam War'
Martin Wiener (Rice University), '"Who knows the Empire whom only the Empire knows?": Reconnecting British and Empire History'
Book Launch: *Penultimate Adventures with Britannia* (Follett's Intellectual Property)
Hermione Lee and Christopher Ricks (Oxford), 'The Elusive Brian Moore: His Stature in Modern Literature'
Gabriel Gorodetsky (Tel Aviv University), 'The Challenge to Churchill's Wartime Leadership by Sir Stafford Cripps (the "Red Squire")'
Helena Woodard (English), 'Black and White Christmas: The Deep South in the Eighteenth Century'

Spring Semester 2008

Round Table Discussion on Tim Jeal's new biography, *Stanley: The Impossible Life of Africa's Greatest Explorer,* Diana Davis (Geography), A. G. Hopkins (History), Roger Louis (History)

Elizabeth Richmond-Garza (English and Comparative Literature), 'New Year's Eve 1900: Oscar Wilde and the Masquerade of Victorian Culture'

Robert Hardgrave (Government), 'The Search for Balthazar Solvyns and an Indian Past: The Anatomy of a Research Project'

Lucy Chester (University of Colorado), 'Zionists, Indian Nationalism, and British Schizophrenia in Palestine'

Michael Brenner (University of Pittsburgh), 'Strategic and Cultural Triangulation: Britain, the United States, and Europe'

Roger Morgan (European University, Florence), 'The British "Establishment" and the Chatham House Version of World Affairs'

Jason Parker (Texas A&M), 'Wilson's Curse: Self-Determination, the Cold War, and the Challenge of Modernity in the "Third World"'

Stephen Foster (Northern Illinois University), 'The American Colonies and the Atlantic World'

A. G. Hopkins (History), 'Comparing British and American "Empires"'

James Turner (Notre Dame University), 'The Emergence of Academic Disciplines'

Dror Wahrman (Indiana University), 'Invisible Hands in the Eighteenth Century'

Narendra Singh Sarila (Prince of Sarila), 'Mountbatten and the Partition of India'

Pillarisetti Sudhir (American Historical Association), 'The Retreat of the Raj: Radicals and Reactionaries in Britain'

Keith Francis (Baylor University), 'What Did Darwin Mean in *On the Origin of Species*? An Englishman and a Frenchman Debate Evolution'

Fall Semester 2008

'Ted and Sylvia'—Round Table Discussion, (UT English), Judith Kroll, Kurt Heinzelman, Betty Sue Flowers, Tom Cable

Roby Barrett (Middle East Institute), 'The Question of Intervention in Iraq, 1958–59

John Kerr (San Antonio), 'Cardigan Bay'

Sue Onslow (London School of Economics), 'Julian Amery: A Nineteenth-Century Relic in a Twentieth-Century World?'

John Rumrich (English), 'Reconciliation in *The Winter's Tale:* The Literary Friendship of Robert Greene and William Shakespeare'

Richard Jenkyns (Oxford), 'Conan Doyle: An Assessment beyond Sherlock Holmes'

Theresa Kelley (University of Wisconsin), 'Romantic British Culture and Botany in India'

Sir Adam Roberts (Oxford), 'After the Cold War'

Geoffrey Wheatcroft (London), 'Churchill and the Jews'

Sir Brian Harrison (Oxford), 'Prelude to the Sixties'

Eric Kaufmann (London School of Economics), 'The Orange Order in Northern Ireland'

Robert McMahon (Ohio State University), 'Dean Acheson: The Creation of a New World Order and the Problem of the British'

Mark Metzler (History), 'Eye of the Storm: London's Place in the First Great Depression, 1872–96'

James Loehlin (English), Christmas Party at the New Campus Club, reading passages from Charles Dickens, *A Christmas Carol*

Spring Semester 2009

Margaret MacMillan (Oxford University), 'The Jewel in the Crown'

Bernard Wasserstein (University of Chicago), 'Glasgow in the 1950s'

Dominic Sandbrook (London), 'The Swinging Sixties in Britain'

Karl Meyer and Shareen Brysac (New York Times and CBS), 'Inventing Iran, Inventing Iraq: The British and Americans in the Middle East'

Albert Lewis (R. L. Moore Project), 'The Bertrand Russell Collection: The One That Got Away from the HRC'

Sir David Cannadine (Institute of Historical Research, London), 'Colonial Independence'; Linda Colley (CBE, Princeton University), 'Philip Francis and the Challenge to the British Empire'

George Scott Christian (English and History), 'Origins of Scottish Nationalism: The Trial of Thomas Muir'

Discussion led by Brian Levack and Roger Louis (History), 'Trevor-Roper and Scotland'

Warren Kimball (Rutgers University), 'Churchill, Roosevelt, and Ireland'

Ferdinand Mount (London) and R. J. Q. Adams (Texas A&M), 'A. J. Balfour and his Critics'

Dan Jacobson (London), Betty Sue Flowers (LBJ Library), and Tom Staley (HRHRC), Tribute to Betty Sue Flowers—'Hardy and Eliot'

John Darwin (Nuffield College, Oxford), 'Britain's Global Empire'

Saul Dubow (Sussex University), 'Sir Keith Hancock and the Question of Race'

Weslie Janeway (Cambridge), 'Darwin's Cookbook'

Julian Barnes, Barbara Harlow, Miguel Gonzalez-Gerth, 'Such, Such Was Eric Blair'

Cassandra Pybus (Visiting Fellow, UT Institute of Historical Studies), 'If you were regular black . . . ': Slavery, Miscegenation, and Racial Anxiety in Britain'

Fall Semester 2009

Peter Green (Classics), 'The Devil in Kingsley Amis'

John Farrell (English), 'Forgiving Emily Brontë'

Samuel Baker (English), 'Wedgwood Gothic'

Louise Weinberg (Law), 'Gilbert and Sullivan: The Curios Persistence of Savoyards'

Elizabeth Richmond-Garza (English), 'Love in a Time of Terror: King Lear and the Potential for Consolation'

John Rumrich (English), 'John Milton and the Embodied Word'

Round Table Discussion on Effective Teaching: Tom Cable (English), David Leal (Government), Lisa Moore (English), Bob Woodberry (Sociology)

James M. Vaughn (History and British Studies), 'The Decline and Fall of Whig Imperialism, 1756–1783'

Round Table Discussion on Bloomsbury: Betty Sue Flowers (English), Roger Louis (History), Lisa Moore (English), David Sosa (Philosophy)

Sir Harold Evans, 'Murder Most Foul'

Peter Cain (Sheffield Hallam University), 'The Radical Critique of Colonialism'

John Gooch (Leeds University), 'Pyrrhic Victory? England and the Great War'

Maya Jasanoff (Harvard University), 'The British Side of the American Revolution'

Maeve Cooney (British Studies), Christmas Party at the Littlefield Home, reading O. Henry's 'The Gift of the Magi'

Spring Semester 2010

Thomas Jesus Garza (UT Language Center), 'The British Vampire's Slavic Roots'

Marilyn Young (New York University), 'The British and Vietnam'

Daniel Howe (University of California at Los Angeles), 'What Hath God Wrought'

Roberta Rubenstein (American University), 'Virginia Woolf and the Russians'

Samuel R. Williamson (University of the South at Sewanee), 'The Possibility of Civil War over Ireland in 1914'

Steve Pincus (Yale), 'The First Modern Revolution: Reappraising the Glorious Events of 1688'

Selina Hastings (London), 'Somerset Maugham: A Life Under Cover'

Eugene Rogan (Oxford), 'Modern History through Arab Eyes'

T. M. Devine (University of Edinburgh), 'Did Slavery Make Scotland Great?'

Phillip Herring (University of Wisconsin–Madison), 'A Journey through James Joyce's *Ulysses*'

Alison Bashford (Harvard), 'Australia and the World Population Problem, 1918–1954'

Berny Sèbe (Birmingham University), 'French and British Colonial Heroes in Africa'

J. L. Berry (Austin, Texas), 'The Post-Twilight of the British Empire on the Zambian Copper Belt'

Bernard Porter (University of Newcastle), 'The Myth of Goths and Vandals in British Architecture'

Fall Semester 2010

Jonathan Schneer (Georgia Institute of Technology), 'The Balfour Declaration'

Larry Carver (Liberal Arts Honors Program), 'Reacting to the Past: How I Came to Love Teaching Edmund Burke'

Thomas Pinney (Pomona College), 'Kipling and America'

Donna Kornhaber (English), 'Accident and Artistry in *The Third Man*'

Doug Bruster (English), 'Rating *A Midsummer Night's Dream*'

Peter Stansky (Stanford University), 'Julian Bell: From Bloomsbury to Spain'

Crawford Young (University of Wisconsin, Madison), 'The British Empire and Comparative Decolonization'

Jeffrey Cox (University of Iowa), 'From the Kingdom of God to the Third World'

Roberta Rubenstein (American University), 'Approaching the Golden Anniversary: Dorris Lessing's *The Golden Notebook*'

Kenneth O. Morgan (House of Lords), 'Aneurin Bevan: Pragmatist and Prophet of the Old Left'

Robert Vitalis (University of Pennsylvania), 'From the Persian Gulf to the Gulf of Mexico: What We Know About BP'

James Curran (Sydney University), 'The Great Age of Confusion: Australia in the Wake of Empire'

Archie Brown (St Antony's College, Oxford), 'Margaret Thatcher and the End of the Cold War'

Phyllis Lassner (Northwestern University), 'The End of Empire in the Middle East and the Literary Imagination'

Spring Semester 2011

Tillman Nechtman (Skidmore College), 'Nabobs: Empire and the Politics of National Identity in Eighteenth-Century Britain'

Brian Levak (History), 'Demonic Possession in Early Modern Britain'

David Kornhaber (English), 'George Bernard Shaw: Modernist'

Lisa L. Moore (English), 'Sister Arts: The Erotics of Lesbian Landscape'

Bartholomew Sparrow (Government), 'Brent Scowcroft, Mrs. Thatcher, and National Security'

Philip Bobbitt (Law School and LBJ School), 'The Special Relationship'

Deborah Harkness (UCLA), 'Fiction and the Archives: The Art and Craft of the Historian'

Peter Clarke (Trinity Hall, Cambridge), 'The English-Speaking Peoples'

A. G. Hopkins (History), 'The United States, 1783–1861: Britain's Honorary Dominion?'

Reba Soffer (California State University at Northridge), 'Intellectual History, Life, and Fiction'

Joanna Lewis (London School of Economics), 'Harold Macmillan and the Wind of Change'

Andrew Lycett (London), 'Arthur Conan Doyle and Rudyard Kipling'

Geoffrey Wheatcroft (London), 'The Grand Illusion: Britain and the United States'

Priscilla Roberts (University of Hong Kong), 'Henry James and the Erosion of British Power'

John Higley (Government), 'Degeneration of Ruling Elites? Recent American and British Elites'